AGING—ITS CHEMISTRY

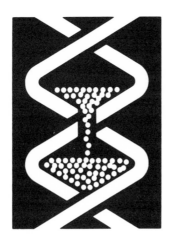

Arnold O. Beckman, Founder and Chairman of the Board,
Beckman Instruments, Inc.

Arnold O. Beckman Conference in Clinical Chemistry
(3rd: 1979: Colorado Springs)

AGING—ITS CHEMISTRY

Proceedings of the Third Arnold O. Beckman
Conference in Clinical Chemistry

Edited by
Albert A. Dietz

Executive Editor
Virginia S. Marcum

The American Association for Clinical Chemistry

1725 K Street, N.W.
Washington, DC 20006

2110 Cloverdale, Box 5218
Winston-Salem, NC 27103

Other books published by the American Association for Clinical Chemistry:
  The Clinical Biochemistry of Cancer. Proceedings of the Second Arnold
    O. Beckman Conference in Clinical Chemistry
  Clinician and Chemist: The Relation of the Laboratory to the Physician.
    Proceedings of the First Arnold O. Beckman Conference in Clinical
    Chemistry
  Clinical Immunochemistry: Chemical and Cellular Bases and Applications
    in Disease
  Second International Symposium on Clinical Enzymology
  A National Understanding for the Development of Reference Materials and
    Methods for Clinical Chemistry. Proceedings of a Conference

Library of Congress Cataloging in Publication Data:

Arnold O. Beckman Conference in Clinical Chemistry, 3d,
    Colorado Springs, 1979.
    Aging—Its Chemistry.

    Includes bibliographical references and index.
    1. Aging—Congresses.   2.   Biological chemistry—
Congresses.   I.   Dietz, Albert Arnold Clarence,
1910–   II.   American Association for Clinical
Chemistry.   III.   Title.
QP86.A76   1979   612'.67   80–65825
ISBN 0–915274–10–8

To George F. Grannis (1926–1980): As he was devoted to clinical chemistry, so we dedicate this volume to his memory.

Contents

ix

Foreword

The unceasing and accelerating generation of new knowledge related to the body creates a continuing need for ever-better communications among research scientists, clinical laboratory scientists, physicians, and others concerned with health and disease. The need is nurtured by the seemingly insatiable demand of the public for better and broader health services. Any serious effort to meet these demands must envisage synergistic utilization of information and skills from many disciplines, not only chemistry and medicine but also biology in its broadest aspects, computer science, statistics, economics, and especially politics. How can the capabilities in these widely different fields be brought together in a coordinated, enlightened manner to work on the problems of health and disease?

One approach, taken by the American Association for Clinical Chemistry, is the holding of a series of annual conferences, each focused on a specific, carefully selected topic. The invited speakers are persons of recognized stature in their respective fields. The size of the audience is deliberately restricted, and the program is structured in a manner that encourages active participation by all, through questions and answers, arguments, and debates over issues raised and points of view presented by the speakers.

The first Arnold O. Beckman Conference, held in 1977, was devoted to The Relationship between Clinical Chemists and Physicians. A candid and mutually beneficial exchange of views resulted. The second Conference, held in 1978, was on The Clinical Chemistry of Cancer; although I was unable to be present and thereby form a first-hand personal opinion, all evidence indicates that the Conference was an outstanding success. The third Conference, held in October 1979, dealt with the subject of The Clinical Chemistry of Aging, and was similarly successful. The upcoming fourth Conference will focus on Nutrition.

Cancer and cardiovascular ailments are widely recognized as the top killers of our time. Aging should not be overlooked, however, for unless one takes the path of early demise, most of us will likely succumb to the cumulative depredations of the aging process. For most people, aging unquestionably is an unwelcome phenomenon, at least from mid-life on. Tremendous efforts are spent in attempts, often of dubious efficacy, to delay the aging process. Huge sums of money are spent on cosmetics and cosmetic surgery in the hope that aging may be concealed from the external world. Vanity aside, one cannot escape an increasing awareness of the impact of aging upon one's life as the years roll by.

Aging obviously involves the body's chemistry, both as cause and effect. As one result of the highly successful conquest of infectious diseases, the population of elderly persons is steadily increasing. It is timely and important, in the interest of improved diagnosis and therapy of ailments of the elderly, that the role of chemistry in aging be examined in some detail. That was the purpose of the third Conference. The papers presented at the Conference, together with ensuing dialogue, are published in this book and present many expert insights into significant relationships between the body's chemistry and the biological phenomenon of aging.

It is a pleasure to commend highly Dr. Albert A. Dietz and his associates in the American Association for Clinical Chemistry for their splendid performance in staging the Conference and in compiling the presentations for publication. This book provides a valuable and useful record of the Proceedings and makes it conveniently possible for any interested person to benefit from the Conference.

Arnold O. Beckman

January, 1980

Prologue

Interest in gerontology and geriatric medicine has increased greatly in the last decade. Even so, there is a great lag in the application of science to the problems of the elderly. Unfortunately, the development of our knowledge of the clinical chemistry in problems of aging is behind that of the progress in geriatric medicine. It is the purpose of this conference to briefly review our knowledge of what happens in aging, to show how little is known, and, most importantly, to learn what the science of clinical chemistry can do to improve knowledge that will lead to the improvement of the quality of life for the elderly.

As with so many things, general interest and interest in research are related to the appropriations of Congress. Seventeen years ago, Congress established the National Institute of Child Health and Development. Thereafter activity in pediatric research expanded. Problems in aging were allocated to this same institute, where for FY 1975 aging research received less than 10% of the funding of the Institute—about $15 million. In May 1974, the National Institute on Aging was signed into existence by President Nixon, but it was not until May of 1976 that Dr. Robert N. Butler officially became Director and the Institute became active. The FY 1977 budget was only $26 million, at a time when the United States was pouring $9 billion into nursing homes for the aged. Interest in gerontology and geriatrics is on the increase, and it may not be long before these topics receive the attention they need. Various government agencies, including the Veterans Administration, are putting a premium on research on aging. For FY 1980, the Congressional allocation for the National Institute on Aging is $70 million, about 2% of the NIH budget. That Congress feels the need for research on aging is indicated by the 24% increase above the funds requested by the Institute, a greater percentage increase than for any of the other allocations for research for FY 1980.

One hundred years ago, when Bismarck set 65 as a retirement age, few lived to retire. Since then, the number of people reaching that age has increased. By 1900, 4% of the population was 65 or older. This proportion now stands at 11%, and early in next century it will pass 20%. At present, one-third of all medical costs are for this 11%, and by the end of the century, at current rates of increase, one-half of all medical costs will be incurred by the elderly.

Before 1965, less than a dozen medical schools offered courses in aging. This year, virtually all of the 120 schools are offering some type of program in geriatrics. The first chair in geriatric medicine was founded two years ago at Cornell University School of Medicine in New York City. No doubt more are on their way.

As the average age of our populace increases, the problems of the elderly take on greater importance, and the need for more research on aging increases. The prospects are now dim that the average life span can be extended beyond that programmed for four score and four years, life expectancy in the absence of disease. The basic goal of the National Institute of Aging is to improve the quality of life. We need to work toward making it possible for all individuals to utilize the full potential inherent in their genes. Aging is a function of life, and there is nothing we can do to eliminate the function; however, the natural course life takes can be altered.

Clinical chemistry will play a large role in guiding physicians in increasing the quality of life for their patients. Many of the necessary methods are now available to clinical chemists, but their adjustment to and use for interpretation of problems of aging lag behind the general knowledge of geriatrics. For example, reference values, used to diagnose disease and assess health, are usually given for and based on persons between the ages of 20 and 40. In this age group, the interindividual variances are relatively small. In the group younger than 20, the variance is much greater if the postnatal and pubertal periods are included. By adjusting for these latter two periods and accounting for variation in sex, the degree of variance in values for the young approaches that of the 20- to 40-year-old group. In the elderly, the variances are also large; however, we have not yet learned to take into account the factors that give this large variance. Therein lies a challenge for the future development in clinical chemistry.

For this conference we have sought to learn the reference values needed to assess the health of the elderly and have discussed the additional information needed for improved diagnosis and treatment. In the first section, we look at the physiological changes that occur with aging, and review the theories that attempt to explain the changes. Data on age-related changes are presented next, and techniques for studying the changes in humans are discussed. Degenerative changes accompanying aging are described in the third section. The basic research techniques used to study the causes of aging are evaluated in the fourth section. The final section is devoted to the practical application of clinical chemistry to the understanding of problems in providing health care to the elderly. Throughout the volume are many suggestions upon which future research can be based. It is hoped that readers will assimilate the information and build on it in their laboratories.

* * *

The efforts of many enter into the preparation of a volume such as this. We are indebted to the work and enthusiasm of the members of the committee planning the symposium, including: Drs. Edward W. Bermes, Jr., George F. Grannis, Joseph Meites, and Samuel Natelson. The expertise of Drs. Grannis and Meites in aging research was of special help. Dr. Grannis was to help in the editing of the volume, but his early demise prevented this. The valuable suggestions of Drs. Samuel Goldstein and W. H. Chris Walker are also appreciated.

I am grateful to the Veterans Administration for the time and the encouragement for the planning of the symposium and the editing of this volume. Thanks are due Miss Tina Lubrano for her help in the preparation of this volume.

The Association and I are especially indebted to the generous support of Dr. Arnold O. Beckman. His contribution and his interest and enthusiasm were instrumental in the success of the symposium and in making it possible to relay the information for the enlightenment of others.

Albert A. Dietz

Conference Participants

(1, speakers; 2, co-authors; 3, session moderators)

Richard C. Adelman, Ph.D.[1]
Director, Institute on Aging
Temple University
Philadelphia, PA 19140

A. Douglas Bender, Ph.D.[1]
Vice President, R&D Operations
Smith Kline & French Laboratories
Philadelphia, PA 19101

Edward W. Bermes, Jr., Ph.D.[3]
Director, Clinical Laboratories
McGaw Hospital
Loyola University of Chicago
Stritch School of Medicine
Maywood, IL 60153

D. Paul Blattler, Ph.D.[1]
Bio Statistics Institute
881 Oakway Road
Eugene, OR 97401

John W. Chamberlain, M.Sc.[2]
Graduate Student
Department of Medical
  Biophysics
Ontario Cancer Institute
Toronto, Ontario, Canada M4X
  1K9

Albert A. Dietz, Ph.D.[3]
Principal Scientist, Research
  Service
VA Hospital
Hines, IL 60141
Professor of Biochemistry
Loyola University of Chicago
Stritch School of Medicine
Maywood, IL 60153

Lêda S. Felicio, Ph.D.[1]
Postdoctoral Fellow
Gerontology Research Institute
Ethel Percy Andrus Gerontology
  Center
University of Southern Califor-
  nia
Los Angeles, CA 90007

John M. Fidler, Ph.D.[2]
Department of Immunopathol-
  ogy
Scripps Clinic and Research
  Foundation
La Jolla, CA 92037

Caleb E. Finch, Ph.D.[2]
Professor, Molecular Biology
  and Gerontology
Ethel Percy Andrus Gerontology
  Center

University of Southern California
Los Angeles, CA 90007

Dale Gillibrand[2]
Upjohn—Laboratory Procedures
Woodland Hills, CA

Ralph Goldman, M.D.[1]
Assistant Chief Medical Director
  for Extended Care
Department of Medicine and
  Surgery
Veterans Administration
Washington, DC 20420

Samuel Goldstein, M.D.[1]
Professor of Medicine and Asso-
  ciate in Biochemistry
McMaster University
Hamilton, Ontario, Canada L8S
  4J9

Gilbert S. Gordan, M.D., Ph.D.[1]
School of Medicine
University of California
San Francisco, CA 94143

George F. Grannis, Ph.D.[1]†
Professor of Pathology
The Ohio State University
Columbus, OH 43210

Darshan Grewal[2]
Department of Chemistry
Holy Cross Hospital
Mission Hills, CA

Robert L. Habig, Ph.D.[3]
Hospital Laboratories

Duke University Medical Center
Durham, NC 27710

Calvin B. Harley, Ph.D.[2]
Graduate Student
Department of Biochemistry
McMaster University
Hamilton, Ontario, Canada L8S
  4J9

Ronald W. Hart, Ph.D.[1]
Professor, Department of Ra-
  diology
Director CBERG
University Hospitals
The Ohio State University
Columbus, OH 43210

Leonard Hayflick, Ph.D.[1]
Bruce Lyon Memorial Research
  Laboratory
Children's Hospital Medical
  Center
Oakland, CA 94609

William P. Hazzard, M.D.[1]
Professor of Medicine
Chief, Division of Gerontology
  and Geriatric Medicine
University of Washington
  School of Medicine
Harborview Medical Center
Seattle, WA 98105

Malcolm Hodkinson, M.A.,
  D.M., F.R.C.P.[1]
Professor of Geriatric Medicine
Royal Postgraduate Medical
  School
Hammersmith Hospital
London, W12 OHS, England

Rachmiel Levine, M.D.[1]
Deputy Director for Research
City of Hope National Medical
  Center
Duarte, CA 91010

Leopold Liss, M.D.[1]
Division of Neuropathology
The Ohio State University
Columbus, OH 43210

Andrea Manni, M.D.[2]
Department of Medicine
Case Western Reserve University
School of Medicine
Cleveland, OH 44106

Joseph Meites, Ph.D.[1]
Professor of Physiology
Michigan State University
East Lansing, MI 48824

Edward L. Morgan, Ph.D.[2]
Department of Immunopathology
Scripps Clinic and Research
  Foundation
La Jolla, CA 92037

Samuel Natelson, Ph.D.[3]
Ft. Sanders Presbyterian Hospital
Knoxville, TN 37916

James F. Nelson, Ph.D.[1]
Postdoctoral Fellow
Gerontology Research Institute
Ethel Percy Andrus Gerontology
  Center

University of Southern California
Los Angeles, CA 90007

Olof H. Pearson, M.D.[1]
University Hospitals of Cleveland
Cleveland, OH 44106

Jeffrey W. Pollard, Ph.D.[2]
Postdoctoral Fellow
Department of Medical
  Biophysics
Ontario Cancer Institute
Toronto, Ontario, Canada M4X
  1K9

Paul E. Segall, Ph.D.[2]
Postgraduate Research Physiologist
Department of Physiology–
  Anatomy
University of California
Berkeley, CA 94720

Nathan W. Shock, Ph.D.[1]
Scientist Emeritus
National Institute on Aging
Gerontology Research Center
Baltimore City Hospitals
Baltimore, MD 21224

Clifford P. Stanners, Ph.D.[2]
Professor of Medical Biophysics
Ontario Cancer Institute
Toronto, Ontario, Canada M4X
  1K9

Ralph E. Stephens[2]
College of Pharmacy

xix

The Ohio State University
Columbus, OH 43210

Henry A. Stevens, Ph.D.[2]
Department of Psychology and
  Psychiatry
University of British Columbia
Vancouver, British Columbia,
  Canada

Bernard L. Strehler, Ph.D.[1]
Professor of Biology
Molecular Biology
University of Southern Califor-
  nia
Los Angeles, CA 90007

William M. Thurlbeck, M.D.[1]
Professor and Head, Department
  of Pathology
The University of Manitoba
Health Sciences Centre
Winnipeg, Manitoba, Canada
  R3E 0Z3

Paola S. Timiras, M.D., Ph.D.[1]
Professor of Physiology
Chairman, Department of Phy-
  siology–Anatomy
University of California
Berkeley, CA 94720

Cynthia Vaughan, R.N., M.A.[2]
Medical Writer
Formerly, Clinical Coordinator
  of Nursing

New York University Medical
  Center
New York, NY 10003

Richard F. Walker[2]
NIH Postdoctoral Fellow
Department of Physiology–
  Anatomy
University of California
Berkeley, CA 94720

William H. C. Walker, Ph.D.[3]
Department of Pathology
McMaster University Medical
  Center
Hamilton, Ontario, Canada L8S
  4J9

William O. Weigle, Ph.D.[1]
Department of Immunopathol-
  ogy
Scripps Clinic and Research
  Foundation
La Jolla, CA 92037

David R. Weir, M.D.[1]
Associate Professor of Medicine,
  Emeritus
School of Medicine
Case Western Reserve Univer-
  sity
Cleveland, OH 44106
La Jolla, CA 92037

Roman J. Wojtyk, M.Sc.[2]
Graduate Student
Department of Medicine
McMaster University
Hamilton, Ontario, Canada L8S
  4J9

Attendees

*Linda Acomb
University of Texas
Houston, TX

Frank D. Amsbaugh
Fremont Medical Laboratory
Fremont, CA

Robert L. Arends, Ph.D
Columbia Hospital
Milwaukee, WI

Robert H. Barnes, M.D.
Phoenix, AZ

Arnold O. Beckman, Ph.D.
Beckman Instruments, Inc.
Irvine, CA

Paige K. Besch, Ph.D.
Baylor College of Medicine
Houston, TX

Harold Broenstein, M.D.
Mount Zion Hospital
San Francisco, CA

Pauline Bruno, D.N.Sc.
University of Washington
Seattle, WA

William J. Campbell, Ph.D.
AACC
Washington, DC

Wendell T. Caraway, Ph.D.
Flint, MI

William H. Card, M.D.
Madison, WI

Susan Coiner, Ph.D.
Southwest Missouri State University
Springfield, MO

Larry H. Coleman, Ph.D.
CRL Biosciences Research Laboratory
St. Paul, MN

Clarence D. Cone, Jr., Ph.D.
Veterans Administration
Yorktown, VA

Gene F. Conway, M.D.
Georgetown, OH

Ann Copeland, Ph.D.
Tacoma, WA

---

* Beckman Fellows.

Arlene Crowe, Ph.D.
Hotel Dieu Hospital
Kingston, Ontario, Canada

Roy L. Donnerberg, M.D.
Columbus, OH

Russell Eilers, M.D.
Bio-Science Enterprises
Van Nuys, CA

Lawrence Z. Feigenbaum, M.D.
Mount Zion Hospital
San Francisco, CA

Linda Felver
Intercollegiate Center for Nursing Education
Spokane, WA

P. V. Fennessey, Ph.D.
University of Colorado
Denver, CO

Douglas G. Finner
Holly Hill, FL

Edward E. Fisher, M.D.
Pocatello, ID

Craig C. Foreback, Ph.D.
Henry Ford Hospital
Detroit, MI

Albert Forlano, Ph.D.
El Dorado, TX

Donald T. Forman, Ph.D.
North Carolina Memorial Hospital
Chapel Hill, NC

Alfred Free, Ph.D.
Ames Research Laboratory
Elkhart, IN

Herbert A. Fritsche, Ph.D.
M.D. Anderson Hospital
Houston, TX

Gerald E. Gallwas
Beckman Instruments
Fullerton, CA

Philip J. Garry, Ph.D.
University of New Mexico
Albuquerque, NM

Leo E. Gaudette, Ph.D.
Tabershaw Occupational Medicine
Rockville, MD

Helen Gigliotti, Ph.D.
California State University
Fresno, CA

Eric Goldapple
Montreal, Quebec, Canada

Adrian Hainline, Jr., Ph.D.
Center for Disease Control
Atlanta, GA

W. Knowlton Hall, Ph.D.
Augusta, GA

David Harris, M.D.
Hays, KS

Jean Hatton
St. Mary's Hospital
Streator, IL

Roger B. Hickler, M.D.
University of Massachusetts
  Medical Center
Worcester, MA

Philip Hooper, M.D.
Albuquerque, NM

*Norman Huang, Ph.D.
Baylor College of Medicine
Houston, TX

Herbert W. Huntsinger
Oakville, CA

George Ingels, M.D.
Norman, OK

Nancy E. Johnson, Ph.D.
Madison, WI

Anthea Kelly, M.D.
CHU of Sherbrooke
Sherbrooke, Quebec, Canada

Douglas Kimball, Ph.D.
Laboratory of Clinical Medicine
Sioux Falls, SD

Vincent Ko, M.D.
Northbrook, IL

Diana Koin, M.D.
St. Luke's Hospital
Denver, CO

Anthony Koller, Ph.D.
Michael Reese Medical Center
Chicago, IL

Charles Knouse, D.O.
Ohio University College of Os-
  teopathic Medicine
Athens, OH

Vivien Lahiri, M.S.
Medical Oncology Center
Bakersfield, CA

John D. Lodmell, Ph.D.
Saginaw, MI

Virginia Marcum
Clinical Chemistry
Winston-Salem, NC

T. R. Marcus
Baycrest Hospital
Toronto, Ontario, Canada

K. Lorne Massey, M.D.
University Hospital
Saskatoon, Saskatchewan,
  Canada

Jonathan R. Matias
Orentreich Medical Group
New York, NY

C. R. McEwen, Ph.D.
Beckman Instruments, Inc.
Palo Alto, CA

Monty H. McLean
Beckman Instruments, Inc.
Fullerton, CA

Z. D. Meachum, Jr., Ph.D.
LSU Medical Center Hospital
Shreveport, LA

Samuel Meites, Ph.D.
Childrens Hospital
Columbus, OH

Marc Micozzi, M.D.
Applied Chemical
Morristown, NJ

Kathleen Newell, Ph.D.
Kansas State University
Manhattan, KS

George E. Nichoalds, Ph.D.
University of Tennessee
Memphis, TN

Hipolito V. Nino, Ph.D.
Beckman Instruments, Inc.
Fullerton, CA

Kent Opheim, Ph.D.
Children's Orthopedic Hospital
Seattle, WA

Vasudeva N. Paniker, Ph.D.
Nogales, AR

Alan Peterson, M.D.
University Hospital
Seattle, WA

Elmer M. Plein, Ph.D.
University of Washington
Seattle, WA

Joy B. Plein, Ph.D.
University of Washington
Seattle, WA

Allen Pusch, M.D.
LaGrange Park, IL

Max Rafelson, Ph.D.
Rush–Presbyterian–St. Luke's
    Medical Center
Chicago, IL

*Lakshmi Ramanathan, Ph.D.
Mount Sinai Hospital
New York, NY

Jack T. Ratner, M.D.
Maimonides Hospital
Montreal, Quebec, Canada

Kathleen Sargent, Ph.D.
Carney Hospital
Boston, MA

Carol Sassmanshausen
Austin, TX

Kenneth S. Schneider, M.D.
Duke University Medical Center
Durham, NC

J. Schouten, M.D.
Slotervaart Hospital
Amsterdam, Netherlands

Reuben Schucher, Ph.D.
Montreal, Quebec, Canada

Frank A. Sedor, Ph.D.
Duke University Medical Center
Durham, NC

George Sharpe, M.D.
Kensington, MD

Jerry Simmons, M.D.
Laboratory Services
Ann Arbor, MI

Ken Slickers, Ph.D.
Medical College of Ohio
Toledo, OH

Libia Socarra, M.D.
VA Medical Center
Chillicothe, OH

Donald D. Soules, Ph.D.
Oakwood Hospital Laboratory
Dearborn, MI

David Steenblock, D.O.
Wholistic Medical Service
El Toro, CA

J. Robert Swanson, Ph.D.
University of Oregon
Portland, OR

Michael Thompson
Colorado Springs, CO

*Dennis Todd, Ph.D.
Ohio State University
Columbus, OH

*Russell Tracy, Ph.D.
Mayo Clinic
Rochester, MN

A. van den Ende, Ph.D.
Amsterdam, Holland

R. G. A. van Wayjen
Amsterdam, Holland

H. King Wade, III, M.D.
Denver, CO

Lorna Williamson, Ph.D.
Swedish Hospital
Seattle, WA

A Legend

Wei Po-Yang is credited with the first chemistry experiment on immortality. He found a chemical for everlasting life and went with his disciples and dog to a mountaintop to drink his brew. He and his dog drank up and promptly fell dead. One disciple followed suit and also died. The others gave up and left to arrange for burials. But, on returning, they found the Master, dog, and disciple had disappeared, having found immortality and leaving the rest behind to die a more traditional death. The secret was lost.

Will someone rediscover the secret?

I

NORMAL AGING AND SENESCENCE

An overview of the physiological changes which occur as individuals age, and a review of some of the theories proposed to explain aging—Albert A. Dietz, Moderator

How old would you be if you didn't know how old you was?
SATCHEL PAIGE

Physiological and Chronological Age

Nathan W. Shock

The fact that older individuals are apt to perform many tasks less effectively than younger subjects has been recognized for a long time. Many of these changes in performance seem to progress with the passage of time. However, only relatively recently have systematic quantitative observations been made on normal human subjects to characterize in quantitative terms the age differences in specific physiological and psychological functions so that average patterns of change can be described for specific functions and performances. In all of these studies gerontology has followed the pattern used in the study of growth and development of children; that is, chronological age (time after birth) has been used to order events. Aging or the passage of time is not in itself a cause of the events (differences in performance) that we call aging—it is only a grid for recording the passage of time within which events occur. As a system, however, chronological time has certain advantages: (a) it is traditional and readily understood; (b) it is expressed in recognizable units (years, months, etc.); and (c) it can be determined with a high degree of accuracy in societies in which birth certificates are kept.

On the other hand, both common observations and data from controlled studies indicate that a wide range of performance scores for a given task may occur among individuals of the same chronological age. In short, chronological age alone is often a poor predictor of test performance. Some individuals are judged to be "prematurely" old, whereas others are judged exceptionally "well-preserved." These judgments of discrepancies between measured or observed performance capabilities and the presumed "normal" performance for a given chronological age have led to the presumption that a more reliable index of performance could be de-

3

veloped around the idea of "physiological" or "functional" age.

The idea that the use of some index of physiological age could serve as a more appropriate criterion for retirement than chronological age has had great appeal. For example, the European Bureau of the World Health Organization, at a seminar in Kiev in 1963, recommended that methods be developed for the determination of biological age (1) to provide a more rational basis for dealing with retirement and employment of older workers. In 1970 who sponsored a detailed report on the assessment of biological age in man, which summarized much of the data available at that time on age differences in physiological functions and made recommendations about possible approaches to the development of an index of biological age (2). Pressures for the development of an index of functional age that could serve to determine the time of retirement have also come from unions and from workers who wish to continue to work beyond any specific chronological age such as 65 years. Similarly, recent legislative changes, which have removed the requirement for mandatory retirement at age 65 years (in all but a few occupations), have stimulated cries from management for the development of tests to objectively and reliably identify workers who could be retired on the basis of general physical and mental performance. Ideally, a single score, based on an appropriate combination of scores in a number of specific tests, would serve as an index of an individual's physiological or functional age. As will be indicated, however, the development of a single index of physiological or functional age is extremely improbable. Human behavior is much too complex to expect such a simple solution.

In this paper I shall review the current state of knowledge about age differences in some physiological and psychological functions, examine the assumptions involved in developing an index of physiological age, review the attempts that have been made to develop such an index, and relate what we know about aging to the requirements for an index of physiological age.

Age Differences in Physiological Function

A number of studies have related the performance of specific organ systems to chronological age in normal human subjects. Although some physiological functions, such as glucose concen-

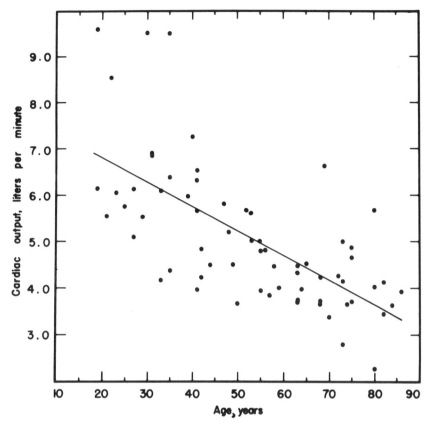

Fig. 1. Resting cardiac output (L/min) in normal men, aged 20 to 87 years

Source: 4

trations in fasting subjects, blood pH, and blood osmolality, do not change systematically with age, most functions show progressive decrements with advancing age (3). Although the regression average on age is statistically significant for most functions, the variation among subjects is large; thus, a linear regression on age over the span of 30 to 90 years gives as good a representation of age trends as any other.

Figure 1 illustrates age differences in resting cardiac output determined by the dye-dilution technique in normal men aged 20–87 years (4). The age regression of approximately 1% decrease per decade is statistically significant. However, at any chronological age, the range of individual values is large. Note in Figure 1

5

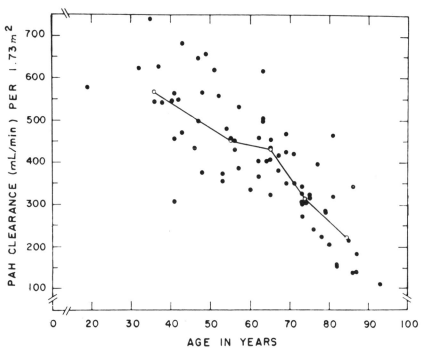

Fig. 2. Renal plasma flow (mL/min per 1.73 m²) in normal men aged 20 to 93 years, measured by clearance of p-aminohippurate (PAH)

Source: 5

that some 70-year-olds have resting cardiac outputs as good as the average for subjects at least 20 years their junior.

Figure 2 shows values for resting renal plasma flow determined by the clearance of p-aminohippurate in 96 normal men aged 20–93 years (5). The linear regression on age is statistically significant, but individual variability at any chronological age is great. Other physiological function tests (vital capacity, forced expiratory volume at 1.0 s, maximum breathing capacity, increase in blood pressure, auditory and visual acuity, muscle strength, cardiovascular and metabolic response to standardized exercise, glucose tolerance, reaction time, and nerve conduction velocity) show significant correlations (range, −0.88 to 0.24) and linear regressions on age (6). In all, 43 different tests were identified with correlations with age that exceeded 0.25 (without regard to sign). In most studies the number of subjects tested at each decade has been relatively small, and because of the high variance of results it has

6

not been possible to demonstrate statistically that a nonlinear regression gives a better fit to the data than a linear regression.

In fact, when kidney function was tested by measuring the 24-h creatinine clearance in 548 normal men aged 17 to 96 years, the regression on age, when calculated for each decade, increased progressively with age after age 60, as shown in Figure 3 (7). As more subjects are examined, perhaps other nonlinear age regressions will be identified. Preliminary results indicate the possibility that hemoglobin content of the blood, blood cholesterol, grip strength, maximum work rate, visual memory, and reaction time may not show linear regressions over the entire age span (8).

Physiological Age

The broad span of test values shown by subjects of the same chronological age has led to the concept that individuals have some general underlying "rate of aging" that does not necessarily correspond to their chronological ages. The 70-year-old subject whose cardiac output is as good as that of the average 60-year-old is assumed to be physiologically younger than his 70-year-old peers. The basic question is whether this assumption is true or not. If the assumption is true, an individual with test values that are better than the mean for his chronological age group should have a greater probability of living for the next 10 or 20 years than individuals with values worse than the average.

As Figure 4 shows, the average changes over time in the performances of different organ systems proceed at different rates (9). Thus nerve conduction velocity diminishes on the average by only about 10% between the ages of 30 and 70 years (Figure 4b), in contrast to renal functions, which decrease by 50% over the same age span (Figure 4d). Furthermore, the same individual may show different levels of performance among different organ systems. Thus a 60-year-old subject may have a cardiac output equivalent to the average values for 60-year-olds, but a kidney function equal to the average value for 40-year-olds. These differences in organ performance indicate clearly that each subject must be evaluated on a variety of performances. The critical question is, can scores on a number of different kinds of performances be combined to yield a meaningful single performance score for

7

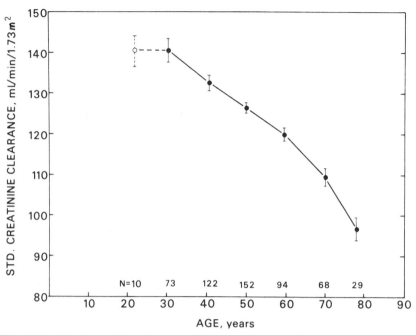

Fig. 3. Standard creatinine clearance (mL/min per 1.73 m²) among normal men aged 20 to 80 years

Vertical bars indicate ± 1 standard error of the mean. Source: 7

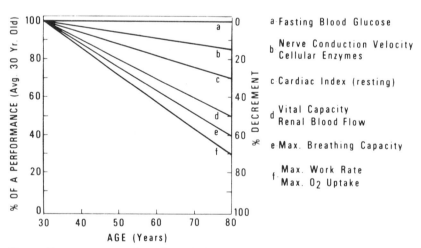

Fig. 4. Decrements in physiological functions in normal men aged 30 to 80 years, expressed as percent of average values for 30-year-olds

Source: 9

8

an individual, or must we be content with making comparisons between rank orders achieved by different subjects in specific tests? That is, must we assign an index of physiological age for each test? Examination of available test data on normal human subjects leads to the conclusion that at present we must examine performance on individual tests. There is no evidence that a general factor of physiological age exists. We are confronted with many "physiological ages," each related to a specific performance.

Percentile Ranks and Standard Scores

It is possible to assign a percentile rank score to an individual, indicating his rank order among other subjects of the same chronological age with respect to specific functions such as kidney function *(7)* and glucose tolerance *(10)*. Figures 5 and 6 illustrate nomograms that have been constructed to facilitate the calculation of percentile ranks for individual subjects. A straight line drawn between the subject's age and his observed creatinine clearance (or glucose tolerance) will intersect the percentile rank scale at his percentile rank. A man at the 50-percentile rank has a creatinine clearance that is the same as the average for his age group (in this case, 70-year-olds). Subjects with high percentile ranks have performances better than the average for their age peers.

Where normative data are available, relative performances of different organ systems can be compared within the same subject because the dimensions of the test have been removed. That is, percentile scores on kidney function and glucose tolerance can be directly compared, whereas creatinine clearance and glucose concentrations cannot.

Assumptions Underlying an Index of Physiological Age

Although the concept of physiological age is simple and straightforward, the derivation of an appropriate index involves a number of assumptions that must be explicitly stated and examined. The first assumption is that there is a common factor of physiological age that is expressed to various degrees among different tests; in other words, that some underlying aging process regulates or even determines the expression of aging among different organs and tissues. If this hypothesis is true, factor analysis

9

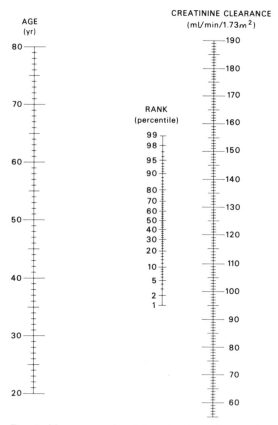

Fig. 5. Nomogram for determination of age-adjusted percentile rank in creatinine clearance of normal men

A straight line connecting the subject's age with his observed creatinine clearance intersects the rank scale at his percentile rank. Source: *7*

of the results of many different tests made on the same group of subjects over the total age span (20 to 90 years) should yield identifiable factors other than age itself. Although several early studies *(11–13)* reported the isolation of a general age factor from groups of tests, subsequent studies on larger populations, for whom a broad spectrum of tests was available, failed to obtain clear-cut evidence for the presence of general aging factors *(8, 14)*. The age factors reported were usually characterized by groups of closely related tests, such as pulmonary function tests. Few

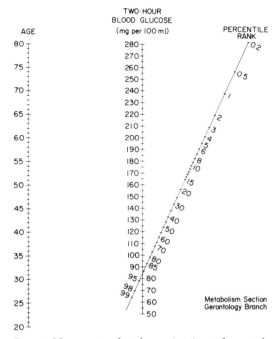

Fig. 6. Nomogram for determination of age-adjusted percentile rank in glucose tolerance of normal men, based on amount of glucose in blood 2 h after oral ingestion of 1.75 g of glucose per kilogram of body weight

A straight line connecting the subject's age with his 2-h blood glucose value intersects the rank scale at his percentile rank. Source: *10*

of the factors loaded significantly on tests that differed very greatly. For example, Costa and McCrae *(14)* factor-analyzed increments (or decrements) in scores for more than 40 variables that occurred in measurements separated by a five-year interval; no general aging factor was found among the 20 factors that were isolated, and they concluded that factor analysis was notably unsuccessful in reducing the dimensions of the data.

Borkan *(8)* conducted a factor analysis of 14 physiological tests administered to 650 normal men (aged 20 to 96 years) in the Baltimore Longitudinal Study of Aging (Table 1). Five factors were isolated that accounted for only 33.8% of the total variance. The first factor had its highest loadings on measures of lung function, maximum work, lean body mass (creatinine excretion and

Table 1. **Tests from the Baltimore Longitudinal Study of Aging Utilized in Factor and Profile Analysis for Physiological Age**

Forced expiratory volume in 1.0 s
Systolic blood pressure
Blood hemoglobin
Serum albumin
Serum globulin
Plasma glucose 2 h after oral ingestion of glucose
Auditory threshold
Visual acuity
Basal oxygen consumption
Cortical bone thickness from hand roentgenogram
Creatinine excretion
Maximum work rate (cranking)
Maximum rate of tapping
Reaction time: auditory—choice

oxygen consumption), and cortical bone thickness; this factor accounted for only 15% of the variance. The other four factors loaded on only one or two tests and cumulatively accounted for only an additional 15% of the total variance. Thus factor analysis failed to indicate the presence of a general "age" factor that might represent physiological age.

When multiple-regression analysis is used to predict physiological age, the regression of each variable on chronological age is assumed to be linear. As pointed out previously, however, this may not be true for the total adult age span. Some functions may show an increased rate of change as age advances (Figure 3). Other variables, for example, blood cholesterol and body weight, pass through a maximum at late middle age, and still others may show no age changes before some critical age. In view of these different patterns of aging, it is clear that no *single* "standard score" for physiological age can be assigned to an individual.

It is sometimes assumed that standard scores based on performances of an individual on different tests can be combined arithmetically to give an overall score. In view of the points made previously (no evidence for a general aging factor, and nonlinear age regressions), this procedure of summing or averaging standard scores is obviously inappropriate.

It is also assumed that individuals with test performances that are poorer than the average for their age peers are physiologically older, and hence should have a greater probability of dying within the next five, 10, or 15 years, than individuals with low scores (scores more like those of younger subjects). This is a question of fact, which requires continued observations over 10 to 15 years on the same subjects. Data from the Baltimore Longitudinal Study of Aging show that this assumption is true for a number of physiological tests; i.e., the average values for calculated physiological age were higher for a group of subjects who died than for the survivors (8, 15). The survivors were physiologically younger or healthier at the time they were tested than were those who died.

Current Studies on an Index of Physiological Age

Most investigators who have attempted to derive an index of physiological age have used a multiple-regression approach. In this technique, weights are assigned to a set of variables so as to maximize the correlation of the resulting linear combination with some criterion variable. Because chronological age is the only criterion available, the analysis seeks the equation that gives the best prediction of chronological age from the scores on individual tests. It is assumed that the mean functional age for any cohort is the chronological age, which is what we mean when we say that a man has the heart of a 40-year-old, even though he is 60. Regression analysis has the advantage that we can calculate the relative weights of tests included in the battery used for determining the calculated chronological age. Analysis of regression coefficients can identify the relative importance of each test in the battery in determining the calculated chronological age.

Table 2 briefly summarizes some of the characteristics of 11 studies that have attempted to derive an index of physiological age. Although various degrees of success in identifying a variable labeled "physiological" or "functional" age were claimed, there was little agreement about which specific tests were most appropriate in identifying physiological age. Table 2 highlights the discrepancies in results reported by different investigators. For example, the number of subjects tested in each study ranged from 1080 to 102; the number of tests evaluated in a single study ranged from 22 to seven. Maximum correlations with chronological age ranged from −0.88 to −0.42. Some of the studies included both

Table 2. Indices of Physiological Age Studies

Authors and year published (ref. no.)	No. of subjects M	No. of subjects F	Age range, yr	Variables Physiol. tests, no.	r with chron. age (range)	Psychol. tests, no.	r with chron. age (range)
Borkan, 1978 (8)	1062	—	18–96	13	−0.69 −0.02	1	0.50 —
Costa and McCrae, 1977 (14)	649	—	25–75	17	−0.42 0.01	—	—
Damon, 1977 (16)	600	—	25–75	10	+0.64 0.11	—	—
Webster and Logie, 1976 (17)	—	1080	21–83	7	−0.58 0.12	—	—
Furukawa et al., 1975 (18)	111	—	21–83	22	−0.88 0.26	—	—
Fozard and Thomas, 1975 (19)	969	—	25–81	5	−0.63 −0.17	7	−0.45 0.17
Heikkinen et al., 1974 (20)	456	—	25–57	6	−0.61 0.30	1	—
Dirken, 1972 (21)	316	—	30–69	13	−0.72 0.12	5	−0.49 0.25
Heron and Chown, 1967 (13)	300	240	24–70	M 8 / F 8	−0.70 −0.15 / −0.70 −0.27	7	−0.63 −0.27 / −0.50 −0.19
Hollingsworth et al., 1965 (22)	169	268	20–70	9	−0.60 −0.23	—	—
Jalavisto, 1965 (12)	—	130	40–93	12	−0.55 0.10	4	−0.55 −0.24
Clark, 1960 (11)	102		20–70	6	−0.67 −0.21	7	−0.49 0.34

physiological and psychological tests in the test battery, whereas others included only physiological tests.

For example, Damon (16) used only anthropometric measurements to derive a regression equation predicting chronological age. Webster and Logie (17) used four physiological tests administered to 1080 women. Furukawa et al. (18) applied a total of 22 physiological tests, including a number of stress tests based on the rate of recovery of heart rate, blood pressure, respiration, and oxygen uptake after standardized exercise. However, inclusion of these stress tests did not improve the accuracy of the prediction of chronological age to any great extent. Fozard and Thomas (19) reported data on both physiological and psychological tests on 969 veterans aged 25 to 81 years. Heikkinen et al. (20) included a mental test (digit symbol test) with five physiological tests to predict chronological age. The Dirken (21) study is of special significance, involving 316 men employed in different manufacturing concerns in the Netherlands.

Hollingsworth et al. (22) derived a regression equation based on observations from nine physiological tests on Japanese subjects in Hiroshima. Clark (11) tested 102 subjects, 10 men and 10 women at each decade from 20 to 70 years of age with both physiological and psychological tests; subjects for this study were respondents to an advertisement in the local newspaper. With the great heterogeneity in tests used and subject population tested, it is easy to understand why there is so little agreement between the results from different studies.

Over 45 different tests were included in the 11 studies. The correlations with chronological age ranged from zero to as high as −0.88 (range of accommodation of the eye). Among the tests, only 13 were included in three or more studies (Table 3), and the correlations of specific tests with chronological age varied considerably from study to study. Thus the correlation between (e.g.) vital capacity and age varied from −0.77 to −0.40 in different studies. The effect of sampling errors—and thus the hazard of drawing conclusions about the measurement of physiological age—is illustrated by the data from Table 3. Almost all of the tests administered showed low correlations with age in some of the populations tested.

Stepwise regression studies showed that the reliability of the estimate of chronological age was greater when based on three

Table 3. **Range of Correlations with Chronological Age for Tests Used in Three or More Studies**

Variable	No. studies	Correlation with chronological age	
		High	Low
Range of accommodation of the eye[a]	3	−0.88	−0.57
Vital capacity	8	−0.77	−0.40
Forced expiratory volume in 1.0 s	6	−0.70	−0.38
Systolic blood pressure	11	0.69	−0.16
Height	4	−0.68	−0.09
Hearing loss (4000 cps)	7	0.66	−0.42
Blood cholesterol[a]	4	0.57	−0.23
Visual acuity	4	−0.57	−0.42
Weight	3	0.55	−0.15
Diastolic blood pressure	5	0.54	−0.10
Reaction time[a]	6	0.52	−0.26
Grip strength	7	−0.52	−0.21
Tapping rate	5	−0.44	−0.18

[a] Regression on age is nonlinear.

or four tests than when based on any single test. However, the inclusion of more than three subtests seldom improved the prediction of chronological age significantly. The tests contributing the most to the calculated chronological age in these studies are vital capacity (or forced expiratory volume), hearing loss at 4000 cycles/s, visual acuity, range of accommodation of the eye, and reaction time. Other tests such as maximum oxygen uptake, kidney blood flow, vibratory sensitivity, reasoning ability, and word-association latency are potentially valuable, but at present have not been administered to a large enough population to judge their usefulness.

Although Dirken (21) has claimed that the calculated functional age scores he derived from regression equations based on 12 tests[1] were regarded as "somewhat applicable" and "very well applicable" in reaching decisions about job placement and retirement by 82 out of 120 respondents from personnel management, there is no evidence that the test battery has received widespread use.

---

[1] The tests were pitch ceiling, visual acuity, positioning, picture recognition, reaction time, choices, concentration (mental), categorizational ability, maximum breath frequency with exercise, maximum systolic blood pressure during work, aerobic work capacity, maximum work load, and functional expiratory volume in 1.0 s.

However, his approach and methods are the best currently available because he recognized the potential error inherent in the multiple-regression technique (i.e., regression to the mean) and introduced appropriate correction factors in his regression equations. He also included responses to stress in the test battery, i.e., respiratory and cardiovascular responses to maximum exercise. The critical test of whether such tests of responses to stress can predict future physiological performances of an individual has not been applied to a broad enough spectrum of subjects to permit a reliable evaluation.

Physiological Age as a Predictor of Performance or Survival

Two studies in which repeated measurements have been made on the same subjects over a period of 10 to 15 years have been analyzed to assess their usefulness in predicting subsequent performance or viability. These studies are the Boston Veterans Administration Study of Normative Aging (14) and the Baltimore Longitudinal Study of Aging (8).

Functional Age

The data bank for the Boston Veterans Administration Study consists of measurements made at five-year intervals on about 2000 apparently normal men, 20 to 75 years old, with respect to about 150 anthropometric, biomedical, psychological, and psychosocial variables. Measurements repeated after intervals of five and 10 years were available on 18 anthropometric and physiological tests on 200 to 660 subjects. Costa and McCrae (14) utilized these observations to test the usefulness of the concept of "functional age."

Functional ages were computed for each subject from a previously derived regression equation to predict chronological age from a series of anthropometric measurements (16). An analysis of variance of the changes that occurred in 10 anthropometric measurements over a five-year period in more than 1400 subjects showed that, although chronological age had a significant effect on several of the variables (grip strength, sitting height), relative functional age had no effect whatsoever. With the large number of subjects involved in the analysis, one could reasonably expect to find a difference if the functionally older subjects were aging more rapidly. On the other hand, the changes in anthropometric measurements that occur in five-year intervals are very small and, although statistically significant, may not be physiologically important.

A more detailed multiple-regression analysis was made to test the relative effectiveness of functional age and chronological age in predicting the change in 20 biomedical variables over five- and 10-year intervals (14). In general, chronological age was as good or better than functional-age indicators in predicting both changes with time and absolute levels of performance.

A factor analysis of scores indicating changes in the variables over a five- or 10-year interval (that is, the amount of change that occurred over the five or 10 years) showed neither a general aging factor nor major subsystems in which consistent rates of change could be found. Costa and McCrae could find no evidence for the utility of functional age (14); in their opinion, the effects of aging must be evaluated in terms of performance on specific tests or tasks.

I emphasize that the negative conclusions about the concept of physiological age are based on the relatively poor ability to predict future performance from test scores of physiological age. There are, however, other situations where the application of these methods may have value in identifying some of the concomitants of variation in physiological age. For example, Webster and Logie (17) compared the physiological ages (calculated from a multiple-regression equation) of smokers and nonsmokers. The physiological age of smokers was greater than that of nonsmokers of the same chronological age. Furukawa et al. (18) found that the calculated physiological age of hypertensives was greater than that of normotensives of the same chronological age; because blood pressure was one of the measurements included in the regressions equation used to calculate physiological age, however, this result has no physiological significance.

Profile Analysis, from the Baltimore Longitudinal Study of Aging

Borkan (8) has taken a somewhat different approach to examining the concept of physiological age. Rather than depend on the multiple-regression approach used in previous studies, Borkan examined profile charts that indicate the rank order of performance, based on standard scores of individual subjects or groups of subjects relative to their chronological-age peers. This approach requires data on a substantial number of subjects at each decade who have been subjected to a wide variety of tests.

Data from the Baltimore Longitudinal Study of Aging include detailed tests and measurements of anthropometric, biochemical, physiological, psychological, and social characteristics of more than 1100 men, aged 17 to 102 years. All subjects are apparently normal community residents who have volunteered to participate in the study; their participation involves a two and one-half day visit to the Gerontology Research Center every 18 to 24 months. Participants in the study are self recruited; that is, subjects are recommended by an associate, friend, or relative already in the study; 86% of the subjects have professional, technical, or managerial occupations, and 90% have had some college education (23). The study was begun in 1958 with about 100 subjects. Because additional subjects have been recruited each year, about 650 subjects are now regular members of the panel, who have been examined, on the average, five times.

From about 200 different tests and observations available for each subject, Borkan selected 32 variables to examine in detail for their suitability in indicating physiological age. After eliminating redundant tests, as well as those that changed relatively little over the adult age span, 24 variables remained. Further analysis reduced the list to 15 apparently independent variables (see Table 1). As previously mentioned, factor analysis of these variables failed to isolate a single general age factor. The first factor isolated explained only 12.3% of the variance, and inclusion of all five factors accounted for only 33% of the variance. This means that, to characterize the age status of an individual, performance on specific tests must be examined.

Borkan utilized a graphic-pattern profile analysis (24) to compare physiological age of different subjects or groups of subjects with contrasting characteristics. According to this technique, a standard z-score was computed for the performance of each subject on each test. The z-score is comparable to a percentile rank score, in that it indicates the extent to which an individual's score deviates from the average value for subjects in a given age decade. The unit of measurement used in this scale is the standard deviation of the distribution of scores of all subjects in the specified

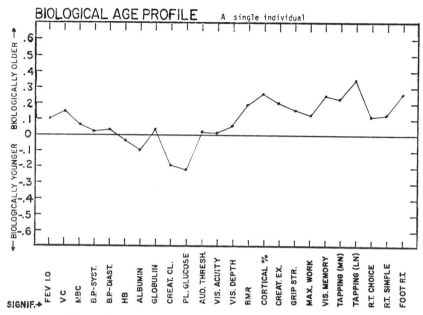

Fig. 7. Physiological age profile of a man who is physiologically "older" than his age peers

Source: 25

age group. The outcome of this procedure was that each person's raw cross-sectional scores on 24 variables were converted into 24 physiological-age scores, all expressed in standard deviation units above or below the mean for the appropriate age group.

Profiles of individuals were constructed by plotting each of the standard tests along the abscissa and standard scores for each test on the ordinate (Figure 7) (25). Profiles for groups of subjects were similarly plotted, with mean standard score values calculated as the group mean. Positive values mean that the individual is physiologically "older" than the average subject of the same chronological age, "old" with respect to a specific test performance.

Follow-up information about death made it possible to test the validity of the physiological-age profiles by comparing the profile average of subjects who died within a five- to 10-year period with the profile of survivors. Presumably, the subjects who died would have been physiologically "older" when they were

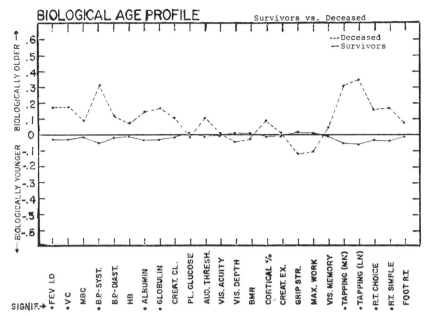

Fig. 8. Average profiles of physiological age for subjects who died within 10 years of testing (- - - -) compared with profiles for survivors (————)

Survivors were significantly "younger" than the deceased on tests marked (●). Source: *25*

tested than the survivors. Indeed, examination of scores for the dead and the survivors showed that standard scores for nine of the 24 variables were significantly higher (greater physiological age) for the group of 166 subjects who died than for the survivors, whereas scores for two of the variables were significantly lower (lower physiological age) (Figure 8) *(25)*. When subjects who reported poor health were compared with subjects who reported good health, those reporting poor health were physiologically "older."

Methods derived for comparing profiles on a quantitative basis *(26)* were not applied to these observations. Nevertheless, visual inspection of profiles indicates that nonsurvivors and individuals who reported poor health status had performed less effectively on several of the tests than had survivors and subjects reporting good health. Whether the survivors are physiologically "younger," or are simply healthier, cannot be said with assurance.

Summary

Although the concept of physiological or functional age has had great appeal in explaining the marked individual differences in performances among subjects of the same chronological age, its usefulness has not been established. Evidence for the existence of a general aging process other than the passage of time (chronological age) is not very convincing. Factor analysis of data from different tests applied to the same subjects has yielded conflicting results. Some studies have identified a general aging factor that can explain as much as 50% of the variance; other studies have found only multiple factors, each of which explains only a small part of the total variance. Hence the effects of aging are best investigated in terms of specific tests and functions.

Predictions of future performance are seldom made, because longitudinal observations over long periods (15 to 20 years) are required to test outcomes. In a few studies data have been collected over 15 to 20 years, and in these studies the probability of surviving for 10 years was shown to be less in a group of subjects whose scores on specific physiological tests were less than the average score achieved by subjects of the same average chronological age.

In view of the lack of clear-cut evidence for the existence of an aging factor that is common to different types of physiological performance but different from chronological age itself, I doubt that any composite score can be derived that will characterize the general "physiological age" of an individual. The effects of age can be determined for specific performances, and the rank order of an individual can be assessed for any performance with respect to his age peers at any given time; however, the predictive values of such scores for future performance of individuals is very low.

References

1. Ries, W., Problems associated with biological age. *Exp. Gerontol.* **9**, 145–149 (1974).
2. Bourlière, F., The assessment of biological age in man. Public Health Papers No. 37, World Health Organization, Geneva, 1970, 67 pp.
3. Shock, N. W., The biological basis of aging. In *Frontiers of Medicine,*

G. M. Meade, Ed., Plenum Press, New York, NY, 1977, pp 167–200.

4. Brandfonbrener, M., Landowne, M. M., and Shock, N. W., Changes in cardiac output with age. *Circulation* **12**, 557–566 (1955).

5. Davies, D. F., and Shock, N. W., Age changes in glomerular filtration rate, effective renal plasma flow and tubular excretory capacity in adult males. *J. Clin. Invest.* **29**, 496–507 (1950).

6. Shock, N. W., Indices of functional age. In *Aging: A Challenge for Science and Social Policy,* Institute de la Vie, Vichy, France, Apr. 24–30, 1977, Oxford University Press, in press.

7. Rowe, J. W., Andres, R., Tobin, J. D., Norris, A. H., and Shock, N. W., The effect of age on creatinine clearance in men: A cross-sectional and longitudinal study. *J. Gerontol.* **31**, 155–163 (1976).

8. Borkan, G. A., The assessment of biological age during adulthood. Ph.D. thesis, University of Michigan, Ann Arbor, MI, 1978, 260 pp.

9. Shock, N. W., Energy metabolism, caloric intake and physical activity in the aging. In *Nutrition in Old Age,* Xth Symposia of the Swedish Nutrition Foundation. L. A. Carlson, Ed., Almqvist & Wiksell, Uppsala, Sweden, 1972, pp 12–23.

10. Andres, R., Aging and carbohydrate metabolism. In *Nutrition in Old Age* (see ref. *9*), pp 24–31.

11. Clark, J. W., The aging dimension; a factorial analysis of individual differences with age on psychological and physiological measurements. *J. Gerontol.* **15**, 183–187 (1960).

12. Jalavisto, E., The role of simple tests measuring speed of performance in the assessment of biological vigor: A factorial study in elderly women. In *Behavior, Aging, and the Nervous System,* A. T. Welford and J. E. Birren, Eds., Charles C Thomas, Springfield, IL, 1965, pp 353–365.

13. Heron, A., and Chown, S., *Age and Function.* Little Brown & Co., Boston, MA, 1967, 182 pp.

14. Costa, P. T., Jr., and McCrae, R. R., Functional age: A conceptual and empirical critique. Paper presented at conference, *"Epidemiology of Aging,"* Bethesda, MD, Mar. 28–29, 1977 (in press—Govt. Printing Office).

15. Shock, N. W., Andres, R., Norris, A. H., and Tobin, J., Patterns of longitudinal changes in renal function. In *Recent Advances in Gerontology, Proc. XI International Congress of Gerontology, Tokyo, Japan, August 20–25, 1978.* Excerpta Medica, Amsterdam, 1979, pp 525–527.

16. Damon, A., Predicting age from body measurements and observations. *Aging Hum. Dev.* **3**, 169–173 (1977).

17. Webster, I. W., and Logie, A. R., A relationship between functional

age and health status in female subjects. *J. Gerontol.* **31**, 546–550 (1976).

18. Furukawa, T., Inoue, M., Kajiya, F., Inada, H., Takasugi, S., Fukui, S., Takeda, H., and Abe, H., Assessment of biological age by multiple regression analysis. *J. Gerontol.* **30**, 422–434 (1975).

19. Fozard, J. L., and Thomas, J. C., Jr., Psychology of aging. In *Modern Perspectives in the Psychiatry of Old Age,* J. G. Howells, Ed., Bruner/Mazel, Inc., New York, NY, 1975, pp 107–169.

20. Heikkinen, R., Kiiskinen, A., Kayhty, B., Rimpela, M., and Vuori, I., Assessment of biological age. *Gerontologia* **20**, 33–43 (1974).

21. Dirken, J. M., Ed., *Functional Age of Industrial Workers.* Wolters-Noordhoff, Groningen, Netherlands, 1972, 251 pp.

22. Hollingsworth, J. W., Hashizume, A., and Jablon, S., Correlations between tests of aging in Hiroshima subjects. An attempt to define "physiologic age." *Yale J. Biol. Med.* **38**, 11–26 (1965).

23. Stone, J. L., and Norris, A. H., Activities and attitudes of participants in the Baltimore Longitudinal Study. *J. Gerontol.* **21**, 575–580 (1966).

24. Garn, S. M., Applications of pattern analysis to anthropometric data. *Ann. N.Y. Acad. Sci.* **63**, 537–552 (1955).

25. Borkan, G. A., and Norris, A. H., Assessment of biological age using a profile of physical parameters. *J. Gerontol.* **35**, 177–184 (1980).

26. Cattell, R. B., Eber, H. W., and Tatusuoka, M., *Handbook for the Sixteen Personality Factor Questionnaire.* Chapter 11. Institute for Personality and Ability Testing, Champaign, IL, 1970, pp 137–160.

A Critique of Theories of Biological Aging

Bernard L. Strehler

In enumerating most of the major theories of aging that have thus far been proposed, I will try to present key evidence bearing on each of these theories and to estimate the probable range of effects the postulated processes contribute to the overall process. Later, I will present as a synopsis a unifying and relatively simple synthesis of the concepts critiqued.

For the purposes of this presentation, I define aging as that complex of changes that, with the passage of time, gradually leads to the death of individual members of highly evolved species, and propose that "true" aging can be distinguished from age-associated changes on the basis of four criteria (1): intrinsicality, universality, progressiveness, and, most importantly, deleteriousness (2). Moreover, I will make two generalizations at the outset: first, *every conceivable kind of deteriorative process* will occur at *some* rate in both aging and non-aging systems; second, aging is *not a necessary consequence of the differentiated or multicellular state.* Its almost universal occurrence among multicellular organisms is probably a by-product of some other advantage carried by the genome of a species, rather than an intrinsic quality of complex systems.

The use of the term critique in the title of a paper carries with it the implication that all theories will shortly be discounted as inadequate—or more likely, that all theories except those of the author will be disposed of at the nearest idea-recycling collection station. Another frequently used tactic is to ignore theories that did not originate with the author of a particular paper. This avoids the embarrassment of pointing out others' intellectual inadequacies and focusses attention where it should be, on the reasonableness and consistency with observation of an author's own favorite assembly of ideas.

In the following paragraphs, I will use a slightly different approach, namely, to state most of the major "theories" of aging (see Outline), summarize briefly the evidence bearing on them, and estimate the range of the probable contribution (listed as % PC) to an explanation of aging that each such process ostensibly makes. The value of such an approach, if properly executed, is that it permits the reader to choose which of the many haystacks available may include the greatest number of needles.

Evolutionary Selection for a Limited Life Span

This concept was first outlined in the late 19th century by Weismann *(3)*, who suggested that aging conferred adaptive value to species that age, by causing the elimination of weak, old individuals and their replacement by young ones. In this form, the argument is circular, in that it sets out to explain what it assumes, as Comfort *(4)* has pointed out. Others have suggested the more reasonable thesis that aging per se has evolutionary value by promoting the turnover of genes and the production of new recombinants. This argument ignores the fact that nearly all species in the wild do not die of old age, but rather of predation or accidents. For the above reasons, except in special cases enumerated elsewhere *(5)*, the probable contribution of this theory toward the explanation of the phenomenon of aging (% PC) is most likely less than 1%.

Post-Reproductive Failure

As suggested by Medawar and others *(6, 7)*, senescence is not directly affected strongly by the force of natural selection because it usually occurs after the peak of the reproductive period. Thus, this lack of selection for longevity may be a major indirect factor in its ubiquity. % PC=10%.

Failure of Coordinating Systems

Neural failure. In higher vertebrates the failure of the central nervous system and the sensory and motor organs interacting with it is certainly a major cause or concommitant of aging. If accidental death is at least partly attributable to failure of the

26

Outline of alternative theories of aging

A. Genetically programmed mechanisms of aging
   1. Evolutionary selection for limited life span
   2. Post-reproductive failure (absence of selection for greater longevity)
   3. Failure of coordinating systems
      a. Neural
      b. Neuroendocrine
      c. Endocrine
      d. Immunoendocrine
      e. Cyto-immune
   4. Pleiotropic side effects of advantageous qualities
      a. Mitotic arrest
      b. Clonal aging
      c. Autoimmunity
      d. Menopause
B. Aging secondary to genetic qualities (entropic increase)
   1. Informational failure
      a. Base substitution, deletion, etc.
      b. Loss of DNA segments: tandem repeats; unique segments
      c. Single strand breaks
      d. Misrepair
      e. Self-amplifying errors: mis-transcription; mis-translation
   2. Structural damage or loss
      a. Enzyme inactivation
      b. "Cross-linkage"
      c. Cell loss
      d. Tissue disorganization
   3. Accumulation of dysfunctional materials
      a. Age-pigments
      b. Amyloid
      c. Viruses and viral products
      d. Inactive receptors
      e. Inactive proteins
      f. Lytic enzymes
      g. Inhibitors
         (1) Mitotic
         (2) Transcriptional
         (3) Translational: general and specific codons
         (4) Other
      h. Autoimmune deposits
      i. Altered connective tissue elements
         (1) Collagen
         (2) Elastin
         (3) Ground substance

central nervous system to anticipate dangers efficiently, then about 5% of deaths at all ages are due its malfunction *(2, 8–10)*. PC=5–25%.

Neuroendocrine aging. Neuroendocrine failure during aging of experimental animals has not, in my opinion, been sufficiently studied to permit a firm conclusion regarding its importance *(11)*. However, it seems likely that this is one of the "weak links" in human physiology during aging. PC=1–50%.

Endocrine aging. This theory has been a center of conjecture since the days of Voronoff *(12)*. There is little doubt that post-menopausal deteriorative changes in bone (osteoporosis) as well as many other afflictions of older humans are influenced by deficiencies in hormonal function, particularly of steroid hormones *(13)*. There is considerable doubt, however, that hormone-supplement therapy among the aged is an unmixed blessing, because of its various side effects. To summarize, the aging of the endocrine system is clearly an important concommitant of overall physiological aging, but it is uncertain whether most of the other declines in physiological function derive in part, at least, from endocrine dysfunction. Among the most clearly established endocrine changes that result in widespread secondary pathology is adult-onset diabetes *(14)*. Effects of pineal, thymal (epithelial), parathyroid, and even thyroid aging (if any) are essentially unstudied, as far as I am aware, except for the last. Nevertheless, the cumulative effect of aging of endocrine systems is probably very substantial and probably contributes more than 25% to the total disabilities from which elderly humans suffer. PC=15–40%.

Immunoendocrine and cytoimmune failure. Decreased responsiveness of the immune system, particularly of thymus-derived cells (T-cells) *(15)*, is characteristic of older laboratory animals and of humans, as reflected in increased susceptibility to infections, increased frequencies of autoimmune diseases *(16)*, and decreased resistance to neoplasia *(17)*. Thus, the aging of this system, including its interaction with humoral factors and changes in the properties of lymphocytes per se, is probably one of the very most important of all systemic-cellular changes that occur during normal human aging. Measured in terms of causes of death (if antibiotics and adequate public health measures are absent), immune failure is probably *the* most important cellular-systemic aspect of the aging process as a whole. Moreover, reinstatement of juvenile immune function is probably the most readily attainable of the various interventions currently contemplated or within reach. PC=20–60%.

Pleiotropic Side Effects of Advantageous Qualities

Mitotic arrest. The arrest of mitosis in certain kinds of cells (neurons and muscle, for example) during the later stages of development is necessary for normal maturation of vertebrates such as humans *(18)*. However this cessation of mitosis is mediated, it provides for both an optimum body size, as first emphasized by Bidder *(19)*, and the establishment of semipermanent connectivities within the brain. These synapses, properly facilitated through experience, provide a means through which past experience can be engrammed within the structure of the cortex and permit the brain to carry out its key predictive functions *(20)*. Because many of the most striking changes that occur during aging are observable in these post-mitotic cells and because at least one component of this class of cell (its DNA) is not replenished during the lifetime of an individual, I believe that a very large fraction of age-dependent functional decrements is the *indirect* result of this arrest of cell division. In a sense, mitotic arrest may be considered as the cause of many other decrements in function discussed earlier (e.g., neural dysfunction) and in the following paragraphs. Thus, as much as 95% of total decreases in physiological performance with age may well be ascribable to those cellular/molecular events that program particular groups of cells to stop dividing at specific stages of development. PC=50–95%.

Clonal aging. The important discovery that even cells that can be induced to divide in vivo possess a limited number of potential doublings under culture conditions *(21)* not only provides an analogy to similar processes that occur in protozoa such as paramecia *(22)*, but also represents an experimental system in which events that lead to mitotic arrest may be studied in vitro under controlled conditions. It is not of crucial importance whether any particular cell type actually exhausts its division potential during a normal lifetime or whether recent findings of growth-factor dependence of the doubling of vascular endothelial cells are exceptions to the kind of clonal aging termed the Hayflick phenomenon *(23)*.

29

What is important, in my view, is that WI-38 and similar cell types provide highly reproducible systems for the study of the control of cell division in normal diploid cells. On the basis of the relatively poor correlation between donor age and doubling potential (24), it seems unlikely that clonal aging of this type is a major contributor to the debilities of old age. PC=1–10%.

Autoimmunity. The incidence of certain autoimmune diseases increases with age, and perhaps every aged person possesses antibodies to one or another tissue. In my unexpert opinion, however, the contribution made by side effects or aberrations of the body's ability to tolerate or not tolerate self is probably small compared with the major decrements in health ascribable to other kinds of immune failure (16, 25). PC=5–20%.

Menopause. The female menopause probably serves several useful functions evolutionarily. Firstly, it makes it more likely that the mother upon whom a young human generally depends will be alive until the child reaches adulthood; secondly, cessation of ovulation in early mid-life probably serves to reduce the burden of aneuploidy, which increases so dramatically during the third to fifth decade of life—e.g., trisomy-21 (26). Whatever the mechanism underlying the initiation of menopause eventually turns out to be (and for that matter, the mechanism responsible for the high rate of follicular atresia throughout early life and adulthood), it seems very likely that side effects of the menopause contribute substantially to many debilities that afflict older women, particularly osteoporosis and perhaps hormone-dependent mammary tumors. PC=5–15%.

Informational Failure

In the sense that all dysfunction reflects a kind of failure of components of a system to interact (communicate) efficiently, many of the specific theories summarized above (and subsequently) may also be considered as failures in informational systems. However, the very basic kinds of informational transactions mediated by DNA, RNA, and the protein-synthesizing and -modifying systems of cells clearly fall into a special category, both because we understand many of the intimate details of how genetic information is copied, transcribed, and translated, and because this knowledge permits the design of experiments to test specific hypotheses of aging at the level of genetic informational systems. Informational malfunctions also occur in the central nervous system, as emphasized earlier, but the mechanisms involved are undoubtedly considerably different from those that operate at the molecular level of organization. In the next group of paragraphs, various potential or established kinds of molecular informational failure are discussed briefly.

Damage to primary DNA structure. The simplest kind of damage to DNA is hydrolysis of covalent bonds. Depurination, for example, which to my knowledge has not been studied as a function of age, would result in a local loss of DNA-encoded information, unless a suitable repair system exists. Similarly, base substitutions or deamination of cytosine or of adenine would change the meaning of altered "sense" strands. Fortunately, less than one-fourth of such deaminations would result in a total loss of the function specified by a given gene (because human cells are at least diploid, and only a change in the "sense" strand could have an effect on what is coded for, and then only if the altered sequence codes for an amino acid different from the normal one). Additions or deletions during replication *(27)* of one or more nucleotides would yield genes coding for "nonsense" products. In my opinion, the above kinds of mutations, inducible by chemical mutagens or high-energy radiation, are *not* major factors in the deterioration of function during aging. This tentative conclusion is based on the fact that the amount of mutagen required to shorten life greatly exceeds that required to produce a whole lifetime's dosage of detectable mutations, i.e., "point mutations" or chromosomal aberrations *(28, 29)*. PC=1–20%.

Loss of tandem repeats. However, another class of "mutations," the excision or inactivation of tandemly duplicated portions of the genome, may eventually turn out to be extremely central to the aging process, at least in higher mammals. The number of copies of genes that code for ribosomal RNA (rRNA) or for rDNA, as measured through annealing experiments, decreases markedly in non-dividing cell types, and the rate of this decrease is proportionally greater in short-lived species *(30–33)*. Because rRNA is required for every kind of protein synthesis, its loss or the loss of other "general-purpose genes" present in multiple copies could well decrease the maximum rate of synthesis, in response to a major challenge. The rate of rRNA synthesis is reportedly slower in older tissues *(34, 35)*, but this could well be due to limiting factors other than the dosage of rDNA. It is my opinion, I hope not too biased, that a very major part of the decline in maximum work rate that accompanies aging is the indirect result of loss of rDNA, which is in turn the delayed indirect result of the previous arrest of cell division *(36)*. PC=30–40%.

Loss of unique DNA segments. Some evidence exists that unique sequences of nucleotides that are "reverse repeats" are exchanged during embryogenesis of sea urchins *(37)*. This phenomenon opens up the possibility that such regions may be susceptible to excision or to "nonsense"-producing inversions through crossing-over in somatic cells *(38)*. No tests of this possibility as a function of age have been carried out. PC=1–30%.

Single-stranded breaks. On the basis of increases in transcribability of in situ-denatured DNA as a function of age, Makinodan and Price *(39)* have inferred that the number of single-stranded scissions in rodent brains increases with age. PC=1–20%.

Misrepair. Much of the damage to DNA that occurs because of endogenous mutagens, exposure to ultraviolet light, etc. is repaired by an elaborate system of repair enzymes, many of which are specific for particular kinds of damage. Because the efficiency of repair of ultraviolet-induced damage is a direct function of the life span of a species, as first shown by Hart and Setlow *(40)*, either failure to repair damage to DNA or "misrepair" could well lead to the inactivation or even excision of key genes or genes in multiple, tandemly duplicated copies. For example, the presence of an efficient enzyme that repairs single-stranded breaks before a second break (necessary for crossing-over? see reference *41*) occurs, will reduce the frequency of crossing-over, the frequency of exchange between homologous chromosomes (it is not known whether the kind of crossing-over that occurs between sister chromatids during mitosis of somatic cells also occurs in post-mitotic cells), and the excision of episomes of tandemly duplicated genes. Because of the direct correlation between efficiency of DNA repair and life span, faulty repair of damage to DNA would appear to be a major contender for certain kinds of damage that could lead to senescence (e.g., rDNA cistron loss). PC=10–50%.

Self-amplifying errors. The error theory of Medvedev and Orgel

(42–44) implies that errors in either the transcription or translation of genetic information may in some instances be self-amplifying, leading to the catchy concept of an "error catastrophe." Because the contribution of such errors to dysfunction depends upon the rate of turnover of faulty components compared with the rates of synthesis of functional ones, Orgel has, perhaps prematurely, proposed that the error theory is erroneous. Evidence derived from the studies of Popp et al. *(45)* and others on the frequency of isoleucine substitution in human hemoglobin beta-chains (isoleucine does not normally occur in this protein) indicates no significant increase in this amino acid as a function of donor age (in a limited number of cases), whereas the amount of this amino acid in beta-chains derived from irradiated Marshall Islanders is substantially increased. This evidence suggests that, at least in dividing cell lines, error frequency in both transcription and translation does not increase with age but can be significantly increased by mutagens. Further study is probably required to decide whether this theory is relevant to the aging process. PC=1–5%.

Structural Damage or Loss

Age changes in tissues and cells *(2)* may take three different forms: *(a)* loss or damage to functional elements, *(b)* changes in arrangement of functional elements, and *(c)* accumulation of nonfunctional entities. Each of these kinds of processes may themselves take a variety of forms, and much of the literature on aging consists of documentation of one kind of change or another. The following paragraphs outline the main lines of evidence bearing on each.

Enzyme inactivation. Until 1970, when the Gershons *(46–48)* reported that certain enzymes derived from old tissues had a lower activity per unit of "enzyme" protein, no evidence existed for changes in the properties of specific enzymes during aging. Since then, several enzymes have been shown to exhibit this property *(49);* others remain unchanged *(50).* The origins of these alterations are at present undefined, but obvious changes such as deamidination, changes in SH-groups, and denaturation seem not to be responsible. In some instances there apparently are alterations in tertiary structure. Other possible sources of these alterations include racemization, perhaps deamidination in some cases, and "partial" denaturation. The changes that have been studied do not appear to be random in nature, because the denaturation kinetics appear to follow the sum of two first-order inactivations that have differing rate constants. This kind of change may turn out to be a very important proximal cause of cellular dysfunction. A possible explanation of the process is that protein turnover is generally slower in older organisms, thereby permitting the slow accumulation of greater and greater fractions of inactive substances (2).

Cross-linkage. The concept that functional molecules may become inactivated through the formation of cross-linkages has received considerable attention. The best-documented instances, however, are the cross-linkages that occur during the maturation of connective tissues such as collagen and elastin (51–54). In these cases, the cross-linking moeities appear to be aldehyde groups (primarily derived from lysine), which form Schiff bases that are reduced to form secondary amines (e.g., lysinonorleucine) or aldol condensates with hydroxylysine. Subtle cross-linkages in membrane subunits may well be responsible for some of the changes with age in surface receptors. Antioxidants in some cases seem to retard the aging process, but it is uncertain whether the effects are due to anorexic side effects of these additives (55,56). To the degree that the age pigments that accumulate in post-mitotic tissues represent the results of cross-linkage [perhaps involving the reactive intermediate, malonyl dialdehyde (57)] and impair cellular function, cross-linkage may be a very substantial contributor to the debilities of advanced age. PC=10–60%.

Cell loss and tissue disorganization. In such key systems as the central nervous system, cell loss, particularly in layer 4 of the cortex (58) and from the Purkinje cell layer of the cerebellum (59), is substantial—up to 20% of these cells are lost in a century. It is very difficult to evaluate the effect of this amount of loss on function, primarily because the brain possesses considerable redundancy, both in structure and in the storage of memory engrams. The effects of rearrangements of cells within tissues are even more difficult to evaluate than simple cell loss. Taken together, cell loss and tissue disorganization may well account for 30% or more of the dysfunctions of advanced age. PC=10–45%.

34

Accumulation of Dysfunctional Materials

This general category probably accounts for a considerable fraction of functional loss with age. Some of the items included in this list also appear in the previous category because the disappearance of a functional element may also be accompanied by the accumulation of its inactivated form. Dysfunctional materials can be subdivided into two major subcategories: those that simply displace functional materials, and those that have a definite negative, destructive, or inhibitory effect. Probably both kinds of accumulative injury are part of the aging process.

Age pigments. The so-called lipofuscin (brown-lipid) age pigments—first described in detail by German pathologists near the turn of the century (60) and first noted in neurons by Purkinje (61)—are among the most conspicuous of the changes that can be observed microscopically in aging tissues, particularly in postmitotic tissues (62). In human myocardium, they occupy as much as 12% of the intracellular volume at advanced ages, and they may occupy as much as 80% of the cell volume of aged human pyramidal cells (63) or cells of the dentate gyrus (64). They are characterized by an affinity for lipid-soluble dyes, a bright fluorescence under ultraviolet light, and essential insolubility in both organic and inorganic solvents (65–67). In general, they are believed to be the insoluble residues of proteins that have become cross-linked, perhaps through reactions of amino groups with such endogenously produced cross-linkers as malonyl dialdehyde (68). The latter substance is not only produced spontaneously during the auto-oxidation of unsaturated lipids, but is also a by-product of the formation of prostaglandins and thromboxanes from the epoxides of arachidonic acid (69). Because of the multiple reactions this double aldehyde can undergo, insoluble polymers of it, less proteins, are formed through aldol condensations and probably through other kinds of reactions such as acetal and Schiff-base formation. Like its homolog, glutaraldehyde, it is a good fixative. Despite the considerable volume age pigments may occupy, there is no absolute consensus regarding the degree to which their accumulation impairs cellular function. It has been argued that age pigments are harmless because they are present in large amounts in certain brain stem nuclei whose cells seem to remain intact and functional into advanced age *(70);* conversely, such conditions as Batten's disease (juvenile amaurotic idiocy, a recessive human mutation) lead both to cell death and to early death of the victim of the disease from neural malfunction, starting with blindness and ending in the loss of purely vegetative functions *(71)*. I am inclined to the view that the accumulation of large amounts of lipofuscin is probably harmful, if only because it occupies such a high percentage of cellular volume and because it evidently displaces functional structures such as polysomes in aged neural tissues *(35)*. PC=20–50%.

Amyloid accumulation. Amyloid, at least one form of which is derived from deposits of incomplete antibodies (light chains), accumulates extracellularly in tissues of older animals, particularly in animals suffering from wasting diseases *(72)*. Some strains of laboratory rodents have enormous deposits of amyloid in many of their key tissues. It is difficult to imagine that this substance is without harmful effect, in light of the space it occupies and the probable impediment it constitutes to the free ingress and egress of nutrients and waste products. However, some older individuals are relatively free (completely free?) of this substance, so it probably is better considered as a by-product of a particular pathology than as a mark of aging per se. In the absence of other pathologies, the contribution amyloid makes to "normal aging" is therefore probably quite negligible. PC=1–20%.

Viruses and viral products. Viral-inclusion bodies have been noted in many different kinds of aged animals; for example, semi-crystalline intranuclear deposits of viruses have been reported in Drosophila *(73)*. Perhaps more germane to the aging of humans is the deterioration induced by "slow viruses" (e.g., Jakob–Creutzfeldt syndrome and kuru) *(74)*. Perhaps such a devastating disease as senile dementia (Alzheimer's disease) *(10, 75)* is also due to a viral infection that has a relatively long incubation period before producing detectable lesions. Similarly, viruses analogous to SV-40 *(76)*, capable of transforming normal cells into the oncogenic state, may be particularly important in the increased incidence of specific kinds of neoplasms, once the immune defenses of the body are decreased as a result of aging. At our present state of knowledge, even more subtle viruses, which slowly drain the working reserve of the system, may be not only important but also universally present in higher forms of life *(77)*. PC=20–40%.

Lytic enzymes. Because some lipofuscin granules contain some of the enzymes found in lysosomes, deDuve *(78)* has postulated that the accumulation of these hydrolytic enzymes in older tissues is a major cause of cell death and dysfunction in advanced age. This hypothesis is difficult to evaluate because it is uncertain whether the association of lytic enzymes with age pigments is a transitory stage in the development of some kinds of lipofuscin. Because isolated lipofuscin granules are not enriched in their complement of lysosomal enzymes *(79)*, I am inclined to discount the importance of these substances as vectors of normal aging; however, the issue is by no means resolved. PC=5–10%.

Mitotic inhibitors. As emphasized earlier, a possible key vector in setting the stage for later aging is the production, at specific times during development, of substances that arrest one or another key step in the mitotic process. Because the chemistry of some such substances—perhaps the so-called chalones *(80, 81)*—is still poorly defined, it is difficult to determine what continuing role, if any, they play in the aging process. Nevertheless, mitotic inhibitors that lead to the arrest of mitosis of neurons, muscles, and other key non-replenishing cell types are probably very central to aging. Their delayed effects may account indirectly for many of the overall decrements in function that define aging. PC=40–90%.

Transcriptional inhibitors. It has not yet been established whether inhibitors analogous to the repressors that control operon expression in prokaryotes play a major role in the onset of senescence. We know that the variety of polymerases present in aging tissues decreases, at least in aging plant tissues *(82–84)*, but modulation of repression through the selective inhibition of specific groups of RNA polymerases has not been established as a general phenomenon. PC=5–90%.

Inhibitors of translation and other inhibitors of cell function. One means through which differential gene expression might be modulated is through the selective activation and repression of ability to translate genetic messages *(85–88)*. Such inhibitors fall logically into two categories: substances that inhibit synthesis generally (e.g., anti-initiation or elongation factors) and substances that inhibit the translation of specific code words or groups of code words. The latter concept is set forth as the "codon restriction theory of development and aging" *(88);* although substantial evidence is consistent with the hypothesis that different cell types possess selective abilities to decode different messages by virtue of the groups of transfer RNA's that they are able to aminoacylate *(2),* the evidence is by no means conclusive that this is a major factor in the regulation of gene expression and repression. Old plant tissues contain substances that selectively inhibit the amino-acylation of certain isoaccepting species of tRNA *(89).* Of even greater interest is the fact that different groups of code words are used in specifying messages characteristic of different cell types. Evidence bearing on this thesis is discussed elsewhere in detail *(90).* I am too close to the subject to venture a quantitative estimate of its importance to the aging process. Further studies are needed to test the hypothesis critically, particularly studies like those reported by Stacey and Allfrey *(91),* in which it was demonstrated that microinjected messages that specify duck globin are translatable by only a restricted fraction of embryonic duck or chick cells, but are readily translated by all injected HeLa cells. PC=1–100%.

Altered connective-tissue elements. The contribution of cross-linkage of collagen and perhaps of elastin to aging has been discussed previously. Except for solar elastosis and the instance of changes in basement membrane collagen, most of the changes reported seem to be adaptive rather than deleterious maturational alterations. On the other hand, the deposition of collagen by vascular smooth muscle after injury, as well as its infiltration by calcium salts, is an obvious accompaniment of aging in most humans. Other species, contrariwise, normally show little vascular pathology, even though they obviously age. PC=5–40%.

Synopsis

The numerous theories of aging summarized and discussed above are not in most cases alternatives to each other; rather, they represent an interrelated group of mechanisms that may be synthesized into a non-contradictory general theory containing the following elements.

- Aging results from the selective switching off of certain groups of genes during development or later life.
- Key among such repressed genes are those that arrest the further division of certain important cell types such as neurons, muscles, certain endocrine cells, and perhaps immunocytes. Although the sites of such inhibitory functions are not yet identified, selective translational abilities may be a major factor in the "stage-setting" phase of the ontogeny of senescence.
- After attainment of maturity, many different kinds of disorganizing events, particularly those that affect some kinds of DNA (e.g., rDNA), begin to be expressed. Genetic damage is accompanied by the accumulation of various inactive substances and by decreased resistance to environmental and endogenous pathogenic agents.
- In some key tissues not only do cells become less able to carry out work at the same rate as was possible at earlier ages, but also a certain fraction of them succumb to internal or external insults.
- Nearly all of the mechanisms discussed above probably contribute to the gradual decline in function that characterizes aging, but some of them (e.g., age-pigment accumulation, rDNA loss, rRNA depletion, accumulation of inactive enzymes, deceleration of protein synthesis, inactivation of receptor sites on membranes, and various kinds of cross-linkage) are probably of greater importance than others.

In summary, the solution to the puzzle of aging depends on the assignment of relative weights to the various potential processes involved. The tentative contributions (PC values) I have listed are, at best, only gross approximations, and key processes yet to be discovered probably also make major contributions. The next decades will, I hope, permit a more complete understanding of the process—a result that will almost inevitably flow from the rapid increase in fundamental molecular/cellular knowledge and from the involvement of increasing numbers of highly talented individuals in aging research during the coming years and decades. When the outlines of the process are more fully understood, we can more propitiously make projections regarding the degree to which the process can be ameliorated for present and future generations of our species.

Supported in part by NASA Grant 7367 and by gifts from Mrs. B. Hubbard and Mrs. J. Barnett.

References

1. Strehler, B. L., Origin and comparison of the effects of time and high-energy radiations on living systems. *Q. Rev. Biol.* **34**, 117–142 (1959).
2. Strehler, B. L., *Time, Cells and Aging*, 2nd ed., Academic Press, New York, NY, 1977.
3. Weismann, A., *Essays upon Heredity and Kindred Biological Problems*, Oxford University Press (Clarendon), London and New York, 1891.
4. Comfort, A., *The Biology of Senescence*, 3rd ed., Elsevier, New York, NY, 1956, p 11.
5. Strehler, B. L., Environmental factors in aging and mortality. *Environ. Res.* **1**, 46 (1967).
6. Williams, G. C., Pleiotropy, natural selection and the evolution of senescence. *Evolution* **11**, 398 (1957).
7. Medawar, P. B., *An Unsolved Problem in Biology*, Lewis, London, 1951.
8. Birren, J. E., and Schaie, K. W., Eds., *Handbook of the Psychology of Aging*, Van Nostrand, New York, NY, 1977.
9. Strehler, B. L., Genetic and neural aspects of redundancy and aging. In *Vth European Symposium on Basic Research in Gerontology*, U. J. Schmidt, Ed., Perimed, Erlangen, F.R.G., 1977, pp 36–61.
10. Terry, R., and Gershon, S., *Neurobiology of Aging*, Raven Press, New York, NY, 1976.
11. Finch, C. E., and Hayflick, L., Eds., *Handbook of the Biology of Aging*, Van Nostrand, New York, NY, 1977.
12. Voronoff, S., *The Conquest of Life*, New York, NY, 1928.
13. Engle, E. T., and Pincus, G., *Hormones and the Aging Process*, Academic Press, New York, NY, 1956.
14. Andres, R., Diabetes and aging. *Hosp. Prac.* **2**, 63–69 (1967).
15. Kay, M., and Makinodan, T., Immunobiology of aging: Evaluation of current status. *Clin. Immunol. Immunopathol.* **6**, 394–413 (1976).
16. Walford, L., *The Immunologic Theory of Aging*, Williams and Wilkins, Baltimore, MD, 1969.
17. Teller, M. N., Age changes and immune resistance to cancer. In *Advances in Gerontological Research*, Academic Press, New York, NY, 1972, pp 25–41.
18. Cowdry, E. V., Ageing of individual cells. In *Problems of Ageing: Biological and Medical Aspects*, E. V. Cowdry, Ed., Williams and Wilkins, Baltimore, MD, 1942, pp 626–658.
19. Bidder, G. P., The mortality of plaice. *Nature (London)* **15**, 495 (1925).

20. Strehler, B. L., Molecular and systemic aspects of brain aging: Psychobiology of informational redundancy. In ref. *10*, pp 281–311.
21. Hayflick, L., The limited in vitro lifetime of human diploid cell strains. *Exp. Cell. Res.* **37**, 614–636 (1965).
22. Woodruff, L. L., Eleven thousand generations of paramecium. *Q. Rev. Biol.* **1**, 436–438 (1926).
23. Johnson, L. K., *Abs. Geront. Soc.* (1979), in press.
24. Martin, G. M., Sprague, C. A., and Epstein, C. J., Replicative lifespan of cultivated human cells: Effects of donors' age, tissue, and genotype. *Lab. Invest.* **23**, 86–92 (1970).
25. Meredith, P. J., and Walford, R. L., Autoimmunity, histocompatibility, and aging. *Mech. Ageing Dev.* **9**, 61–77 (1979).
26. Penrose, L. S., Mongolian idiocy (mongolism) and maternal age. *Ann. N.Y. Acad. Sci.* **57**, 494–502 (1954).
27. Muzyczka, N., Poland, R. L., and Bessman, M. J., Studies on the biochemical basis of spontaneus mutation. *J. Biol. Chem.* **247**, 7116 (1969).
28. Curtis, H. J., Biological mechanisms underlying the aging process. *Science* **141**, 686–694 (1963).
29. Curtis, H. J., and Crowley, C., Chromosome aberrations in liver cells in relation to the somatic theory of aging. *Radiat. Res.* **19**, 337–344 (1963).
30. Johnson, R., and Strehler, B. L., Loss of genes coding for ribosomal RNA in aging brain cells. *Nature (London)* **240**, 412–414 (1972).
31. Johnson, R., Chrisp, C., and Strehler, B. L., Selective loss of ribosomal RNA genes during the aging of post-mitotic tissues. *Mech. Ageing Dev.* **1**, 183–198 (1972).
32. Strehler, B. L., Chang, M. P., and Johnson, L. K., Loss of hybridizable rDNA from postmitotic tissues during aging. I. Age-dependent loss in human myocardium. *Mech. Ageing Dev.* **11**, 371 (1979).
33. Strehler, B. L., and Chang, M. P., Loss of hybridizable rDNA from postmitotic tissues during aging: II. Age-dependent loss in human cerebral cortex—hippocampal and somatosensory comparison. *Mech. Ageing Dev.* **11**, 379 (1979).
34. Andrew, W., *Cellular Changes with Age,* Charles C Thomas, Springfield, IL, 1952.
35. Mann, D. M. A., and Yates, P. O., Lipoprotein pigments—their relationship to aging in the human nervous system. I. The lipofuscin content of nerve cells. II. The melanin content of pigmented nerve cells. *Brain* **97**, 481–488 and 489–498 (1964).
36. Strehler, B. L., Elements of a unified theory of aging: Integration of alternative models. In *Alternstheorien,* D. Platt, Ed., Schattauer, Stuttgart, F.R.G., 1976, pp 5–36.

37. Dickinson, G. D., and Baker, R. F., Evidence for translocation of DNA sequences during sea urchin embryogenesis. *Proc. Natl. Acad. Sci. USA* **75,** 5627–5630 (1978).

38. Tice, R., Chaillet, M., and Schneider, E. L., Evidence derived from sister chromatid exchanges of restricted rejoining of chromatid subunits. *Nature (London)* **256,** 642–644 (1975).

39. Price, G. B., Modak, S. P., and Makinodan, T., Age-associated changes in the DNA of mouse tissue. *Science* **171,** 917–920 (1971).

40. Hart, R. W., and Setlow, R. V., Correlation between DNA excision repair and lifespan in a number of mammalian species. *Proc. Natl. Acad. Sci. USA* **71,** 2169–2173 (1974).

41. Watson, J. D., *Molecular Biology of the Gene,* 3rd ed., Benjamin, Menlo Park, NJ, 1976.

42. Medvedev, Sh. A., *Aktual. Vopr. Sovr. Biol.* **51,** 299 (1961).

43. Orgel, L. E., The maintenance of the accuracy of protein synthesis and its relevance to ageing. *Proc. Natl. Acad. Sci. USA* **49,** 517–521 (1963).

44. Orgel, L. E., The maintenance of the accuracy of protein synthesis and its relevance to ageing: A correction. *Proc. Natl. Acad. Sci. USA* **67,** 1426–1429 (1970).

45. Popp, R. A., Bailiff, E. G., Hirsch, G. P., and Conrad, R. A., Errors in human hemoglobin as a function of age. *Interdiscp. Top. Gerontol.* **9,** 209–218 (1976).

46. Gershon, H., and Gershon, D., Detection of inactive enzyme molecules in ageing organisms. *Nature* **227,** 1214–1217 (1970).

47. Gershon, H., and Gershon, D., Altered enzyme molecules in senescent organisms: Mouse muscle aldolase. *Mech. Ageing Dev.* **2,** 33–41 (1973).

48. Reiss, U., and Rothstein, M., Age-related changes in isocitric lyase from the free living nematode, *Turbatrix aceti. J. Biol. Chem.* **250,** 826–830 (1975).

49. Rothstein, M., Aging and the alteration of enzymes. *Mech. Ageing Dev.* **4,** 325–338 (1975).

50. Steinhagen-Thiessen, E., and Hilz, H., The age-dependent decrease in creatine kinase and aldolase activities in human striated muscle is not caused by an accumulation of faulty proteins. *Mech. Ageing Dev.* **5,** 447–457 (1976).

51. Verzar, F., and Huber, K., Thermic contraction of single tendon fibers from animals of different ages after treatment with formaldehyde, urethane, glycerol, acetic acid and other substances. *Gerontologia* **2,** 81–103 (1958).

52. Chvapil, M., and Hruza, Z., The influence of aging and undernutri-

tion on chemical contractility and relaxation of collagen fibres in rats. *Gerontologia* **3**, 241–252 (1959).

53. Franzblau, C., Faris, B., and Papaioannou, R., Lysinonorleucine. A new amino acid from the hydrosylates of elastin. *Biochemistry* **8**, 2833–2837 (1969).

54. Gallop, P. M., Blumenfeld, O. O., Henson, E., and Schneider, A. L., Isolation and identification of alpha-amino aldehydes and collagen. *Biochemistry* **7**, 2409–2430 (1968).

55. Harman, D., Prolongation of the normal lifespan and inhibition of spontaneous cancer by antioxidants. *J. Gerontol.* **16**, 247–254 (1961).

56. Comfort, A., Antioxidants and the control of ageing. *Nederl. Tijds. Gerontol.* **2**, 82–87 (1971).

57. Tappel, A., Fletcher, B., and Deamer, D., Effect of antioxidants and nutrients on lipid peroxidation fluorescent products and aging parameters of the mouse. *J. Gerontol.* **28**, 415–424 (1973).

58. Brizzee, K. R., Ordy, J. M., Hansche, J., and Kaack, B., Quantitative assessment of changes in neuron and glia cell packing density and lipofuscin accumulation with age in the cerebral cortex of a nonhuman primate *(Macaca mulatta)*. In ref. *10*, pp 229–244.

59. Ellis, R. S., Norms for structural changes in the human cerebellum from birth to old age. *J. Comp. Neurol.* **32**, 1–34 (1920).

60. Stubel, H., Die Floureszenz tienscher Gewebe in ultraviolottem Licht. *Pflueger's Arch. Gesamte Physiol.* **142**, 1–14 (1911).

61. Purkinje, J. E., Neuste Untersuchungen aus der Nerve- und Hirnanatomie. In *Bericht über die Versammlung deutscher Naturforscher und Aerzte in Prag im Septembeer 1837*. K. Sternberg and J. V. Von Krombholz, Eds., Prag, Hasse, pp 177–180.

62. Strehler, B., Mark, D., Mildvan, A. S., and Gee, M., Rate and magnitude of age pigment accumulation in the human myocardium. *J. Gerontol.* **14**, 430–439 (1959).

63. Reichel, W., Hollander, J., Clark, J. H., and Strehler, B. L., Lipofuscin accumulation as a function of age and distribution in rodent brain. *J. Gerontol.* **23**, 71–78 (1968).

64. Treff, W. M., *Das Involutionsmuster des Nucleus Dentatus Cerebelli Altern*. D. Platt, Ed., Schattauer, Stuttgart, F. R. G., 1974.

65. Hendley, D. D., Mildvan, A. S., Reporter, M. C., and Strehler, B. L., Properties of isolated human cardiac age pigments. I. Preparation and physical properties. *J. Gerontol.* **18**, 144–150 (1963).

66. Hendley, D. D., Mildvan, A. S., Reporter, M. C., and Strehler, B. L., Properties of isolated human cardiac age pigments. II. Chemical and enzymatic properties. *J. Gerontol.* **18**, 250–259 (1963).

67. Bjorkerud, S., Isolated lipofuscin granules: A survey of a new field. *Adv. Gerontol. Res.* **1**, 257–288 (1964).
68. Gedigk, P., and Fischer, R., Uber die Entsehung von Lipopigmente in Muskelfasern unter Untersuchungen beim experimentellen Vitamin E-Mangel der Ratte und an Organen des Menschen. *Virchows Arch. Pathol. Anat. Physiol.* **332**, 431–468 (1959).
69. Samuelsson, B., The role of prostaglandin endoperoxidases and thromboxanes as bioregulators. In Abstracts, *Intra-Science Symposium— New Biochemical Aspects of Prostaglandins and Thromboxanes*, Santa Monica, CA, Dec. 1–3, 1976.
70. Brody, H., An examination of cerebral cortex and brain stem aging. In ref. *10*, pp 177–181.
71. Zeman, W., and Rider, J. A., Eds., *The Dissection of a Degenerative Disease; Proceedings of Four Round-Table Conferences on the Pathogenesis of Batten's Disease.* American Elsevier, New York, NY, 1975.
72. Lesher, S., Grahn, D., and Sallese, A., Amyloidosis in mice exposed to daily gamma irradiation. *J. Natl. Cancer Inst.* **19**, 1119–1131 (1957).
73. Miquel, J., Aging of male *Drosophila melanogaster:* Histological, histochemical and ultrastructural observations. *Adv. Gerontol. Res.* **3**, 39–71 (1971).
74. Gajdusek, D. C., Slow virus infection and activation of latent infections in aging. *Adv. Gerontol. Res.* **4**, 201–219 (1972).
75. Nandy, K., and Sherwin, I., Eds., *The Aging Brain and Senile Dementia,* Plenum Press, New York, NY, 1977.
76. Reddy, V. B., Thimmappaya, R. D., Subramanian, K. N., Zain, S., Pan, J., Ghosh, P. K., Celma, M. L., and Weissman, S. M., The genome of simian virus 40. *Science* **200**, 494–502 (1978).
77. Chase, D. G., and Pico, L., Expression of A- and C-type particles in early mouse embryos. *J. Natl. Cancer Inst.* **51**, 1971–1975 (1973).
78. Novikoff, A. B., Beaufay, H., and DeDuve, C., Electron microscopy of lysome-rich fractions from rat liver. *J. Biophys. Biochem. Cytol.* **179**, Suppl. 2, 84 (1956).
79. Hendley, D. D., and Strehler, B. L., Enzyme activities of lipofuscin age pigments: Comparative histochemical and biochemical studies. *Biochim. Biophys. Acta* **99**, 406–417 (1965).
80. Bullough, W. S., Mitotic control in adult mammalian tissues. *Biol. Rev., Cambridge Philos. Soc.* **50**, 99–127 (1975).
81. Rytomaa, T., and Toivonen, H., Chalones: Concepts and results. *Mech. Ageing Dev.* **9**, 471–480 (1979).
82. Johnson, L. K., Strehler, B. L., and O'Brien, T. J., Developmental transitions between chromatin-bound and soluble RNA polymerase in the soybean hypocotyl. *Biochim. Biophys. Acta* **519**, 428–439 (1978).
83. Johnson, L. K., O'Brien, T. J., and Strehler, B. L., Developmental

restrictions on hormone modulated gene transcription. I. Effects of auxin on template capacity and chromatin-bound RNA polymerase. *Mech. Ageing Dev.* **8,** 113–130 (1978).

84. Johnson, L. K., and Strehler, B. L., Developmental restrictions on transcription: Determinants of the developmental program and their role in aging. *Mech. Ageing Dev.* **9,** 535–552 (1979).

85. Ames, B. N., and Hartman, P. E., The histamine operon. *Cold Spring Harbor Symp. Quant. Biol.* **28,** 349–361 (1963).

86. Stent, G., The operon on its third anniversary. *Science* **144,** 816–821 (1964).

87. Strehler, B. L., Code degeneracy and the aging process: A molecular genetic theory of aging. *7th Int. Congr. Gerontol.,* 1966, pp 177–183.

88. Strehler, B. L., et al., The codon restriction theory of aging and development. *J. Theoret. Biol.* **33,** 429–474 (1971).

89. Bick, M. D., and Strehler, B. L., Leucyl-tRNA synthetase activity in old cotyledons: Evidence on repressor accumulation. *Mech. Ageing Dev.* **1,** 33–42 (1972).

90. Strehler, B. L., Aging research: Current and future. *J. Invest. Dermatol.* **73,** 2–7 (1979).

91. Stacey, D., and Allfrey, V. G., Microinjection studies of duck globin messenger RNA translation in human and avian cells. *Cell* **9,** 725–732 (1976).

Physiological Aging in the Central Nervous System: Perspectives on "Interventive" Gerontology

Paola S. Timiras, Paul E. Segall, and Richard F. Walker

The long-held view that aging is associated with profound pathologic changes in the central nervous system is being gradually replaced by the view that under normal circumstances, e.g., absence of major vascular alterations and diseases, the central nervous system retains much of its structural and functional competence well into advanced age. Thus, neither a loss of neurons (1, 2) nor a failure of regenerative capacity of synapses (3–5) has been consistently demonstrated in old animals. However, changes do occur in the morphology (e.g., accumulation of lipofucsin, loss of Nissl substance, appearance of neurofibrillary tangles, loss of dendrites and dendritic spines) and biochemistry (e.g., alterations in neurotransmitters) of the aging central nervous system, and may be responsible for the accompanying decrements in neurologic function and abnormalities of behavior and mental state (6). Indeed, because of the important regulatory role of the central nervous system on all body systems, even subtle changes in its function, such as those associated with old age, would be sufficient to profoundly alter the integration of the physiologic responses necessary for adaptation and survival. In complex organisms, including humans, changes in the integrative function of the central nervous system, rigorously timed by a "pacemaker," perhaps situated in the brain and depending on neuroendocrine interactions, could be responsible for triggering the physiologic events governing not only growth and maturation, but aging as well.

Both the nervous and endocrine systems are central to the timetable of physiologic events that control birth, growth, puberty, adulthood, and senescence (7, 8). The close interrelation between

46

the central nervous system and endocrines is amply documented and is manifest, for example, in the conversion of neuronal inputs, through the release of neurotransmitters such as monoamines, into secretion of hormones (factors) by the neurosecretory cells of the hypothalamus. The hypothalamic (-releasing or -inhibiting) hormones, in turn, carry the information to the pituitary, which translates it into endocrinologic signals that determine the output of peripheral endocrines. The hormones act on specific receptors in target organs and tissues to regulate differentiation, growth, and metabolism; in the central nervous system, also an important target organ, hormones modify excitability and behavior, and regulate by positive and negative feedback the synthesis and release of hypothalamic and, subsequently, pituitary hormones.

The complexity of the neuroendocrine interrelations makes the study of their possible role in aging extremely difficult. Nevertheless, current advances in our understanding of the nervous system and endocrine pathophysiology and biochemistry (e.g., metabolism and function of brain monoamines; structure, secretion, and function of hypothalamic hormones; hypothalamic and pituitary feedbacks and their sensitivity to hormones; structural properties of hormones; hormone-receptor interactions at the target-cell level) open the way to experimental designs suitable for the exploration of eventual neuroendocrine causes of the aging process. Regardless of whether ongoing and future research will validate such an approach, the hypothesis of a "biologic masterplan" timed by neural and endocrine signals provides a useful framework within which to design experiments—not only to understand the aging process better, but also to find interventions capable of modifying the course of the life span (9).

Our present study is divided into three parts. In the first, consisting of hitherto unpublished observations, the amounts of the major monoamines—norepinephrine, dopamine, and serotonin—are compared in selected brain areas of developing, adult, and aged rats. These data underline the importance of neurotransmitter specificity, interactions, and rhythmicity. In the second part, observed alterations in brain monoamines will be related to the aging of the reproductive function in experiments designed to test the effects of topical (hypothalamic) and systemic administration of monoamine agonists and antagonists on that function. Most of these data have been or are being published elsewhere, and only

47

a summary of major results will be presented here, the reader being referred to the appropriate articles for more detail. In the third part, consisting of both new and previous data, we investigate the effectiveness of dietary and pharmacologic interventions that reduce the amounts of serotonin present and affect its metabolism in modifying development and aging.

Changes in Brain Monoamines with Aging

The experiments in this portion of our study involved 100 female Long–Evans rats killed and studied at prespecified ages: at 55 days, shortly after sexual maturity has been achieved; at four to six months, young and full adulthood, respectively; at 10 to 11 months, the time of onset of aging manifestations (for example, with respect to reproductive function, the time when breeder animals are retired); and at 22 months, an age at which manifestations of senescence are more advanced (10–12). The animals used are from our departmental rat colony, in which optimum conditions of husbandry are maintained and for which extensive physiologic data have been reported (13) and accumulated over the years. The average life span of animals in this colony is 30 months (12). Previously published data concerning the aging of the central nervous system in these animals encompass morphologic studies [e.g., the number of neurons and glial cells (1) and amount of lipofucsin accumulation (14) in the cerebral cortex] and biochemical studies [e.g., amino acid distribution in selected brain areas (15) and cholinergic systems in the brain and spinal cord (7, 16)].

In the current studies, the animals were decapitated, always at the same time of the day (between 1000 and 1200 hours). The selection of the time of death and its constancy are important inasmuch as some of the monoamines, particularly serotonin, undergo a circadian rhythm (17). Immediately upon decapitation, the brain was removed, placed on ice, and rapidly dissected into the following regions: cerebral hemispheres (minus the caudate nucleus), caudate nucleus, cerebellum, mesodiencephalon (minus the hypothalamus), and pons medulla. Tissues were then frozen and stored at −80 °C until assayed for monoamines according to our modification of the methods of Chang (18) and Maickel et al. (19).

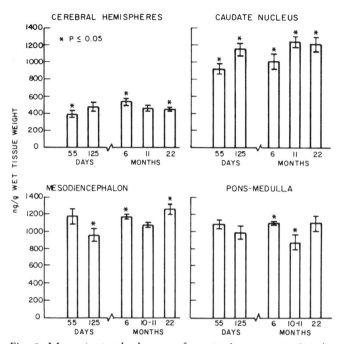

Fig. 1. Mean ± standard error of serotonin concentration (y-axes) in selected regions of the female rat brain at various times from sexual maturity (55 days) to old age (22 months)

n = 10 rats, except at 11 and 22 months, where n = 5 rats per age group. *, Serotonin concentrations significantly different (by t-test) within individual brain region

Despite definite regional differences, serotonin concentrations tend to increase progressively with advancing age (Figure 1). For example, in the caudate nucleus, serotonin increases significantly between 55 and 125 days, and then again between six and 10 to 11 months, at which age it seems to stabilize at a high concentration. Similarly, in the mesodiencephalon, serotonin is more abundant in old than in young adult rats. On the other hand, in the cerebral hemispheres, serotonin concentration, after an initial developmental increase, decreases to relatively low amounts in old animals; in the pons medulla, the concentration remains unchanged during early development but shows significant fluctuations thereafter, with a decrease between six and 10 to 11 months and an increase from then to 22 months.

Norepinephrine concentrations also show marked regional dif-

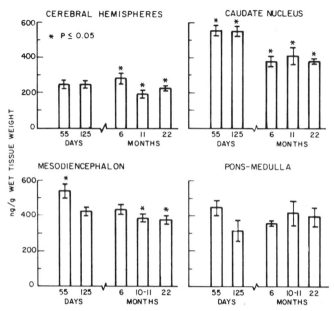

Fig. 2. Mean ± standard error of norepinephrine concentration (*y*-axes) in selected regions of the female rat brain at various times from sexual maturity to old age

Ages, n, and significance as in Fig. 1

ferences but, in general, are greater in the young and the mature rats than in the old animals (Figure 2). This decline with age is particularly well illustrated in the caudate nucleus and the mesodiencephalon and, to a lesser extent, in the cerebral hemispheres. In the pons medulla, changes in norepinephrine concentration with age do occur but are not statistically significant; concentrations in this region appear to be more constant than in the others.

We measured dopamine concentration in the cerebral hemispheres and in the caudate nucleus, where it is highest. Again, regional differences are evident, with more than twice as much dopamine in the caudate as in the cerebral hemispheres (Figure 3). In both regions, however, concentrations are low at 55 days, reach the highest values in adulthood (between four and 10 to 11 months) and markedly decline in the aged rats.

The ratios between serotonin and dopamine or norepinephrine have been calculated in selected brain areas and are presented in Figure 4. The ratio of serotonin to dopamine in the caudate

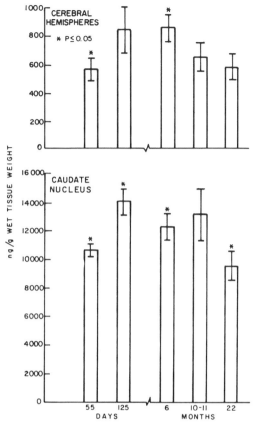

Fig. 3. Mean ± standard error of dopamine concentration (y-axes) in selected regions of the female rat brain at various times from sexual maturity to old age

Ages, n, and significance as in Fig. 1

nucleus shows a consistent and progressive increase with age; in
contrast, the ratio in the cerebral hemispheres remains essentially
unchanged at all ages. On the other hand, the ratio of serotonin
to norepinephrine increases with age in the cerebral hemispheres,
whereas in the mesodiencephalon an increase occurs only at 22
months and is not statistically significant. Similarly, in the pons
medulla (not shown in Figure 4), the ratio between serotonin
and dopamine or norepinephrine remains unchanged at all ages.

As indicated earlier, perhaps more important than the actual

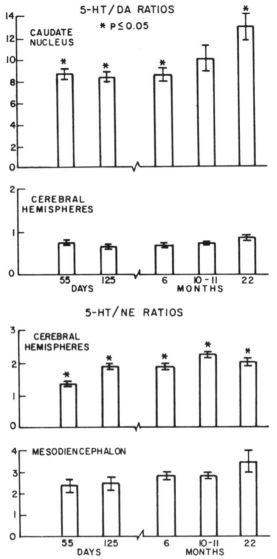

Fig. 4. Ratios of serotonin (5-HT) to dopamine (DA) and norepinephrine (NE) concentrations in selected brain regions at various times from time of sexual maturity (55 days) to old age (22 months) in female rats

Bars, means ± standard error; *, ratios that are significantly different

amounts of the monoamines are their intra- and interregional relations. At a very simplistic level, serotonin may be viewed as an inhibitory neurotransmitter, and dopamine and norepinephrine as essentially excitatory. Thus, the increasing ratio of serotonin to dopamine or norepinephrine with advancing age may be taken as an indication of a growing imbalance between inhibitory and excitatory impulses, with a prevalance of inhibition. However, the ultimate effects of a neurotransmitter depend on the potential it generates at the postsynaptic neuron. Thus, in the caudate nucleus, dopamine increases the postsynaptic inhibitory potential on cholinergic cells and thereby regulates their rate of firing. In conditions such as Parkinson's disease, in which dopamine concentrations are greatly decreased in the caudate nucleus and other extrapyramidal structures, this inhibition is lacking, and an excitatory state emerges. Therefore, with aging, the progressive decrease in dopamine in the caudate nucleus reported here could explain the increasing incidence of parkinsonism in old people. In the caudate nucleus, even though the ratio of serotonin to dopamine increases with age, the ensuing alterations might tend to greater excitability rather than increased inhibition. In the cerebral hemispheres, on the other hand, where these neurotransmitters seem to have their classical role of mediators of inhibitory and excitatory impulses, the increase of the ratio of serotonin to norepinephrine may be more significant functionally than independent changes in either neurotransmitter. Neurotransmitter imbalances may also result from the desynchronization of interregional communications, with the cell body of the specific neurotransmitters being often located away from the axonal terminals where the neurotransmitter is released. Finally, inasmuch as neurotransmitters are also responsive to environmental (internal and external) cues, imbalances in the ratio of one neurotransmitter to another with aging may lead to alterations in rhythmic activities and thereby alter those biologic functions—such as the reproductive function in the female—that depend upon them (see below).

Reproductive Aging Simulated by Altered Brain Monoamines

If monoamines play a role in controlling the major events of the life span, and if such a role is mediated, at least in part, through neuroendocrine signals, then we may postulate that by altering concentrations, metabolism, or rhythmicity of mono-amines, it is possible to modify the timetable of development and aging of one or of several functions. This possibility is particularly evident with respect to the reproductive function. Indeed, aging in the female reproductive system is currently thought to result from functional changes in the activity of monoaminergic neurons of the hypothalamus, an area of the brain strongly implicated in the regulation of many of the biologic rhythms. Catecholamines, primarily norepinephrine, regulate the phasic gonadotropin secretion from the anterior pituitary in young females (20). Thus, it has been suggested that an altered metabolic status of these compounds might represent a primary lesion responsible for the loss of reproductive cycles in aged animals.

However, certain contradictory observations reported by several different laboratories have denied the validity of this hypothesis. In an attempt to clarify this problem, we applied various drugs, including p-chlorophenylalanine (PCPA), diethyldithiocarbamate, and α-methyl-p-tyrosine, capable of blocking serotonin, norepinephrine, or dopamine synthesis or activity topically in the rostral hypothalamus, which contains regulatory neural components of cyclic reproductive function. This regulatory function has been determined primarily by experiments in which lesions of this area abolish reproductive cycles but local stimulation reinstates cycles in previously acyclic rats. In our experiments, the effects of the monoamine blockers on the pituitary–ovarian axis were evaluated in terms of vaginal and ovarian cyclicity and amounts of hormones. Antimetabolites of serotonin induce an anovulatory syndrome in young rats that closely resembles a reproductive dysfunction in old animals (comparable with the human menopause) (21, 22). In contrast, when catecholamine synthesis is inhibited, estrous cyclicity is disrupted, but the reproductive physiology, ovarian morphology, and endocrine profiles of the experimental animals do not resemble comparable parameters in normally aging rats. For example, serotonin-blocked and aging rats show constant vaginal estrus, polyfollicular ovaries without corpora lutea, and increased amounts of serum gonadotropin. In contrast, catecholamine-blocked rats undergo persistent diestrus and have well-developed corpora lutea, and serum amounts of luteinizing hormone (lutropin) are significantly less than those observed after serotonin inhibition or in aged rats (22).

To determine the underlying mechanisms of action of each drug, we examined these pharmacologic effects in greater detail and found that blockage of serotonin synthesis by PCPA prevented the characteristic surge of lutropin (necessary for ovulation) from occurring on proestrus day. Paradoxically, enhancement of serotonin synthesis by systemic administration of the serotonin precursor, 5-hydroxytryptophan, had the same effect. This apparent contradiction was resolved with the observation that both treatments abolished the daily rhythm of serotonin in the hypothalamus. This rhythm may be essential for the regulation of a typical preovulatory surge of lutropin. The importance of serotonin rhythmicity, rather than its actual concentration, is supported by the fact that PCPA and 5-hydroxytryptophan equally abolish the serotonin rhythm and lutropin surge, though actual quantities of the indoleamine are differentially affected by each treatment; these observations suggest that daily changes in hypothalamic serotonin are permissive of or stimulatory to a surge of lutropin *(23)*.

To test the requirement of a stimulatory signal generated by the serotonin circadian rhythm for the phasic secretion of lutropin, we altered photoperiods to modify the dynamics of serotonin metabolism on proestrus. Under standard lighting conditions, hypothalamic serotonin concentrations increase, preceding the "critical period" for initiation of those processes that lead to a surge of lutropin. To modify the timing of these increases, we either reversed the photoperiod, thereby shifting the serotonin rhythm out of its "normal" phase relationship with the lutropin surge, or abolished the serotonin rhythm by exposing the rats to continuous light for two days before proestrus. Both conditions produced atypical lutropin secretion, which was incapable of causing ovulation. We suggest, therefore, that timing or activation cues for preovulatory secretion of lutropin are provided by serotonergic signals associated with the circadian rhythm of hypothalamic serotonin *(23)*. On the basis of similarities in aged rats and rats with PCPA-induced anovulation, we conclude that naturally occurring changes in brain serotonin metabolism can lead to reproductive senescence.

If cyclic reproductive function is dependent upon the integrity of serotonin neural circuitry, then treatments that prevent the development of reproductive cycles or accelerate their failure with advancing age would also depress serotonin rhythms in the brain. To test this hypothesis, we gave testosterone, which "masculinizes" the hypothalamus and lowers its serotonin content, to neonatal female rats in low and high doses. Alternatively, PCPA, which blocks serotonin synthesis, was given to three-day-old female rats. All treatments accelerate the onset of puberty, designated in rats by the time of vaginal opening and correlated with decreased amounts of hypothalamic and pineal gland serotonin during development. Each treatment also shortens the reproductive life span, designated as the period of adulthood during which regular and unambiguous estrous cycles occur. The onset of cyclic instability and the failure of cyclicity are, in all cases, associated with attenuation and ultimate loss of serotonin rhythms in the pineal gland and hypothalamus (24, 25).

Given these observations, we conclude that cyclic female reproductive function requires a viable serotonergic component, which provides signals to stimulate a surge of lutropin and subsequent ovulation, in an appropriate endocrine environment. Disturbances of this serotonergic system(s), experimentally with drugs or naturally over time, produce comparable reproductive dysfunctional syndromes.

Dietary and Pharmacologic Depression of Brain Serotonin: Effects on Growth, Maturation, and Aging

The results presented earlier in this paper and those reported in the literature show an increase in serotonin and in its metabolism in specific brain areas with aging, often associated with a decrease in brain catecholamines (26). The ensuing imbalance between inhibitory and excitatory inputs might alter the synchrony of the signals necessary for controlling the major biologic rhythms, such as those regulating development and aging of the reproductive function. One can thus hypothesize that alterations in neurotransmitter balances by dietary interventions such as feeding the animals a low-tryptophan diet (tryptophan being the precursor of serotonin) or by pharmacologic means such as long-term administration of serotonin inhibitors, like PCPA, might also induce alterations in growth, development, and aging.

To test this hypothesis, we conducted several dietary and pharmacologic studies. In Table 1, the amounts of serotonin in the

56

mesodiencephalon are shown after various treatments: two graded degrees of tryptophan deficiency (as presented in Table 2); chronic parenteral administration of PCPA; and quantitative food restriction. The mesodiencephalon was chosen as representative of a severely affected brain area and one containing a large number of serotonergic cell bodies. As shown in Table 1, serotonin concentrations are markedly decreased except in animals undergoing quantitative food restriction, where the amounts remain unchanged. Whether these changes in brain serotonin are responsible for the alterations in growth, maturation, and aging described under these different experimental conditions remains to be ascertained. Current studies in our laboratory are underway to clarify the role of serotonin.

Historically, the "caloric" restriction of juvenile rodents has been the most effective means of modifying the process of aging in the laboratory. With this technique, the life span of male rats has been increased from 1056 to more than 1800 days of age. Translated into human terms, this age would equal 180 years (27).

In our laboratory, we have explored the impact of a diet deficient in tryptophan on several aspects of growth, development, and aging. Three-week-old animals (age of weaning) were placed on tryptophan-deficient diets for periods ranging from several months to nearly two years and then fed a standard (normal) diet. These rats showed the following responses: a delay in the aging of thermoregulatory homeostasis, as indicated by the youthful response to whole-body immersion in ice water; a delay in the aging of the reproductive system, as shown by giving birth at ages as late as 28 months; a displacement of the first appearance of tumors from 18 to 30 months of age; postponement of senescence of the coat; and an increase in the maximum life span over that of controls (45 vs 41 months) (10, 11). Even when the tryptophan-deficient diet was initiated at three or as late as 13 months of age, some aspects of aging could be retarded (11).

Recent innovations with respect to the tryptophan-deficient diet include modification of the salt concentrations to be more suitable to young animals than in previous studies (10, 11), and the preparation of two diets with graded degrees of tryptophan deficiency (see Table 2), both less severe than in the original diet, which contained approximately 17% of the amount of tryptophan required for optimum growth. With the original, more severely

Table 1. Serotonin Concentration in the Mesodiencephalon of 55-Day-Old Female Rats under Various Treatments[a]

Treatment[b]	Serotonin (mean ± SD), ng/g wet weight
Control (9)	1170 ± 84
T-17% (5)	320 ± 34
Pair-fed 17% (5)	1200 ± 57
T-25% (5)	500 ± 39
T-33% (5)	534 ± 87
PCPA (11)	358 ± 85[c]

[a] Beginning at 21 days of age, control animals were fed Purina Laboratory Chow or a Teklad tryptophan-deficient diet with tryptophan supplemented to produce amounts considered adequate for normal growth and development (T-100%). T-17, 25, and 33% refer to the tryptophan-deficient diet with tryptophan added to produce amounts equal to 17, 25, or 33% of controls' diet. Food was available ad lib. Pair-fed 17% animals were fed an amount (weight) of control diet equal to the weight of T-17% diet consumed. In PCPA-treated animals, 300 mg/kg of body weight was injected subcutaneously every fourth day, also beginning at 21 days of age.
[b] Number in parenthesis is number of animals per group.
[c] Projected from 5-hydroxytryptophan values of 40- and 70-day-old PCPA-treated rats.

Table 2. Content of Tryptophan-Deficient Diets Prepared by Teklad Test Diets (Madison, WI)

Dietary constituents	Tryptophan-deficient diet, 25% of control (TD78464)	Tryptophan-deficient diet, 33% of control (TD78465)	Control: normal (100%) tryptophan (TD78466)
	g/kg		
Casein, hydrolysate, acid (salt-free)	150.0	150.0	150.0
Corn, ground yellow	722.0	721.85	720.5
Torula yeast	8.0	8.0	8.0
L-Methionine	2.0	2.0	2.0
L-Isoleucine	4.0	4.0	4.0
Sucrose	4.0	4.0	4.0
Corn oil	50.0	50.0	50.0
Mineral mix, Jones-Foster (cat. no. 170800)	50.0	50.0	50.0
Vitamin mix, Teklad (cat. no. 40060)	10.0	10.0	10.0
L-Tryptophan	—	0.15	1.5

deficient diet, impairment of growth was associated with neurologic symptoms and relatively high mortality during the period when the animals were fed the experimental diet *(10, 11)*. With the new diets, in which tryptophan content represents 25% and 33% of the required amounts, neurologic signs (tremors, convulsions) are less frequent and severe, and mortality is greatly reduced, even though growth and maturation are significantly altered. Experiments with these diets are still in progress: the long-term effects on persistence of physiologic competence, incidence and severity of pathology, age at onset of senescent changes, and, finally, length of life span remain to be determined.

In parallel with these nutritional studies, we also conducted pharmacologic studies with drugs such as PCPA that can lower the amount of serotonin in the brain. Adding large quantities (7.0 g/kg of diet) of PCPA to the diet of weaning rats for 30 days arrested growth and maturation in a manner similar to that observed in the rats receiving the tryptophan-deficient diet. However, toxicity and mortality were high, and there were side effects, including cataracts *(11)*. When lesser amounts of PCPA were administered parenterally, serotonin concentrations were drastically decreased in most brain areas studied (Table 1); however, growth was not affected, although maturation (as measured by reproductive function) was significantly disturbed *(28)*.

Several investigators have attempted to modify the aging of laboratory rodents by utilizing drugs that alter brain monoamine metabolism, such as L-DOPA *(29, 30)* and lergotrile mesylate *(31–33)*, which counteract the decline in the amount of dopamine in the brain with aging *(34)*. The results of these treatments may be related to the effects of low tryptophan diets, inasmuch as very high amounts of L-DOPA depress brain serotonin metabolism *(35)* and also affect the function of the anterior pituitary *(33)*.

Indeed, in most of the reported nutritional and pharmacologic experiments, neurochemical changes are associated with marked endocrine disturbances. For example, while fed the tryptophan-deficient diet, rats show low concentrations of thyrotropin in plasma *(36)* and pituitary (S. Ooka, unpublished data) as well as low concentrations of thyroxine and triiodothyronine in plasma *(36)*; ovaries are smaller than usual or not developed *(12)*; age-related growth of the adrenals is suppressed; and the pituitary manifests microscopic and ultramicroscopic alterations, particularly in the protein synthetic membrane system *(37)*. Alterations in the peripheral endocrines under these conditions are similar to those usually associated with anterior pituitary insufficiency. In agreement with these observations, various investigators have reported that surgical hypophysectomy in rats can also delay various manifestations of aging *(38–40)*. Because the function of the anterior pituitary is regulated by influences from the central nervous sytem, especially those acting through the hypothalamus, these data further support the hypothesis that alterations in neural signals and neurotransmitter imbalance are important in the etiopathology of aging.

Supported by Grants AG05068 and AG00043 from the National Institute on Aging.

References

1. Brizzee, K. R., Sherwood, N., and Timiras, P. S., A comparison of cell populations at various depth levels in cerebral cortex of young adult and aged Long–Evans rats. *J. Gerontol.* **23**, 289–298 (1968).
2. Diamond, M. C., The aging brain: Some enlightening and optimistic results. *Am. Sci.* **66**, 66–71 (1978).
3. Scheff, S. W., Bernardo, L. S., and Cotman, C. W., Decrease in adrenergic axon sprouting in the senescent rat. *Science* **202**, 775–778 (1978).
4. Landfield, P. W., Waymire, J. C., and Lynch, G., Hippocampal aging and adrenocorticoids: Qualitative correlations. *Science* **202**, 1098–1102 (1978).
5. Cotman, C. W., and Scheff, S. W., Synaptic growth in aged animals. In *Physiology and Cell Biology of Aging (Aging,* **8***)*, A. Cherkin, C. E. Finch, N. Kharasch, T. Makinodan, F. L. Scott, and B. L. Strehler, Eds., Raven Press, New York, NY, 1979, pp 109–120.
6. Timiras, P. S., and Bignami, A., Pathophysiology of the aging brain. In *Special Review of Experimental Aging Research. Progress in Biology,* M. F. Elias, B. E. Eleftheriou, and P. K. Elias, Eds., EAR, Inc., Bar Harbor, MA, 1976, pp 351–378.
7. Timiras, P. S., *Developmental Physiology and Aging,* Macmillan, New York, NY, 1972, pp 502–526.
8. Walker, R. F., Segall, P. E., and Timiras, P. S., Neuroendocrinology of aging. In *The Aging Nervous System,* G. J. Maletta and F. J. Pirozzolo, Eds., Praeger Publishers, New York, NY, 1979, pp 89–109.
9. Timiras, P. S., Biological perspectives on aging: In search of a masterplan. *Am. Sci.* **66**, 605–613 (1978).

10. Segall, P. E., and Timiras, P. S., Age-related changes in thermoregulatory capacity of tryptophan-deficient rats. *Fed. Proc.* **34,** 83–85 (1975).
11. Segall, P. E., and Timiras, P. S., Pathophysiologic findings after chronic tryptophan deficiency in rats: A model for delayed growth and aging. *Mech. Ageing Dev.* **5,** 109–124 (1976).
12. Segall, P. E., Modification of aging by restriction of dietary tryptophan. Ph.D. thesis, University of California, Berkeley, CA.
13. Long, J. A., and Evans, H. M., *The Oestrus Cycle in the Rat and Its Associated Phenomena,* University of California Press, Berkeley, CA, 1922, pp 1–148.
14. Brizzee, K. R., Cancilla, P. A., Sherwood, N., and Timiras, P. S., The amount and distribution of pigments in neurons and glia of the cerebral cortex. *J. Gerontol.* **24,** 127–135 (1969).
15. Timiras, P. S., Hudson, D. B., and Oklund, S., Changes in central nervous system free amino acids with development and aging. In *Neurobiological Aspects of Maturation and Aging (Progress in Brain Research,* **40**), D. H. Ford, Ed., Elsevier, Amsterdam, 1973, pp 267–275.
16. Valcana, T., and Timiras, P. S., Choline acetyltransferase activity in various brain areas of aging rats. *Proceedings, 8th International Congress of Gerontology (Abstracts),* Washington, DC, 1969, p 24.
17. Quay, W. B., Differences in circadian rhythms in 5-hydroxytryptamine according to brain region. *Am. J. Physiol.* **215,** 1448–1453 (1968).
18. Chang, C. C., A sensitive method for spectrophotofluorometric assay of catecholamines. *Int. J. Neuropharmacol.* **3,** 643–649 (1964).
19. Maickel, R. P., Cox, R. H., Jr., Saillant, J., and Miller, F. P., A method for the determination of serotonin and norepinephrine in discrete brain areas of rat brain. *Neuropharmacology* **7,** 274–281 (1968).
20. Sawyer, C. H., Some recent developments in brain–pituitary–ovarian physiology. First Jeoffrey Harris Memorial Lecture. *Neuroendocrinology* **17,** 97–124 (1975).
21. Eisenberg, E., and Walker, R. F., Physiological aspects of menopause: Clinical and experimental studies. In *Hormones in Development and Aging,* A. Vernadakis and P. S. Timiras, Eds., Spectrum Publications, New York, NY (in press).
22. Walker, R. F., Cooper, R. L., and Timiras, P. S., Constant estrus: Role of rostral hypothalamic monoamines in development of reproductive dysfunction in aging rats. *Endocrinology* (in press).
23. Walker, R. F., and Timiras, P. S., Serotonin circadian rhythm: A daily signal associated with lutropin release in the female rat. (Submitted for publication.)
24. Walker, R. F., and Timiras, P. S., Sexual maturation in rats treated neonatally with antiaminergic drugs. *Fed. Proc.* **38,** 1108 (1979).
25. Walker, R. F., and Timiras, P. S., Serotonin in development of cyclic

reproductive function. In *Serotonin: Current Aspects of Neurochemistry and Function*, B. Haber, Ed., Plenum Press, New York, NY, in press.

26. Simpkins, J. W., Mueller, G. P., Huang, H. H., and Meites, J., Evidence for depressed catecholamine and enhanced serotonin metabolism in aging male rats: Possible relation to gonadotropin secretion. *Endocrinology* **100**, 1672–1678 (1977).

27. Ross, M. H., Nutritional regulation of longevity. In *The Biology of Aging*, J. A. Behnke, C. E. Finch, and G. B. Moment, Eds., Plenum Press, New York, NY, 1978, pp 173–189.

28. Hudson, D. B., Potter, C. A., and Timiras, P. S., Effects of chronic serotonin suppression on sexual development and distribution of brain monoamines in the rat. *Pharmacologist* **21**, 241 (1979).

29. Cotzias, G. C., Miller, S. T., Nicholson, A. R., Jr., Matson, W. H., and Tang, L. C., Prolongation of the lifespan in mice adapted to large amounts of L-DOPA. *Proc. Natl. Acad. Sci. USA* **71**, 2466–2469 (1974).

30. Cotzias, G. C., Miller, S. T., Tang, L. C., Papavasiliou, P. S., and Wang, Y. Y., Levodopa, fertility and longevity. *Science* **196**, 549–551 (1977).

31. Clemens, J. A., and Bennett, D. R., Do aging changes in the preoptic area contribute to loss of cyclic endocrine function? *J. Gerontol.* **32**, 19–24 (1977).

32. Clemens, J. A., and Fuller, R. W., Chemical manipulation of some aspects of aging. In *Pharmacological Intervention in the Aging Process* (*Adv. Exp. Med. Biol.* **97**), J. Roberts, R. C. Adelman, and V. Cristofalo, Eds., Plenum Press, New York, NY, 1977, pp 187–206.

33. Clemens, J. A., Fuller, R. W., and Owen, N. V., Some neuroendocrine aspects of aging. In *Parkinson's Disease II* (*Adv. Exp. Med. Biol.* **133**), C. E. Finch, D. E. Potter, and A. D. Kenny, Eds., Plenum Press, New York, NY, 1978, pp 77–100.

34. Finch, C. E., Age-related changes in brain catecholamines: A synopsis of findings in C57BL/6J mice and other rodent models. In *Parkinson's Disease II* (see ref. *33*), pp 15–39.

35. Algeri, S., and Cerletti, C., Effects of L-DOPA administration on the serotonergic system in rat brain: Correlation between levels of L-DOPA accumulated in the brain and depletion of serotonin and tryptophan. *Eur. J. Pharmacol.* **27**, 191–197 (1974).

36. Ooka, H., Segall, P. E., and Timiras, P. S., Neural and endocrine development after chronic tryptophan deficiency in rats: II. Pituitary-thyroid axis. *Mech. Ageing Dev.* **7**, 19–24 (1978).

37. Segall, P. E., Ooka, H., Rose, K., and Timiras, P. S., Neural and endocrine development after chronic tryptophan deficiency in rats:

I. Brain monoamine and pituitary responses. *Mech. Ageing Dev.* **7,** 1–17 (1978).

38. Denckla, W. D., Role of the pituitary and thyroid glands in the decline of minimal O_2 consumption with age. *J. Clin. Invest.* **53,** 572–581 (1974).

39. Everitt, A. V., and Ficarra, M. A., Effects of hypophysectomy on the aging of skeletal muscle in rat hind leg. *11th International Congress of Gerontology (Abstracts for Sectional Sessions),* Tokyo Sci. Med. Publ. Inc., Tokyo, 1978, p 43.

40. Bolla, R., Nuclear RNA synthesis in hypophysectomized rats. *9th Annual National Meeting, American Aging Association (Abstracts),* Washington, DC, 1979, p 9.

Ovarian Hormones and the Etiology of Reproductive Aging in Mice

James F. Nelson, Lêda S. Felicio, and Caleb E. Finch

The loss of fertility is an early event of aging, occurring during midlife in many short- and long-lived female mammals *(1)*. In humans, reproductive decline begins in the fourth decade of life, as indicated by increased spontaneous abortions and birth defects *(2, 3)*; these changes precede the average age of menopause, 50 years *(4)*, by more than a decade. In rats and mice, decreased fertility is usually apparent by eight to 10 months of age, well before the complete cessation of ovulatory cycles *(1, 5)*. Thus, the relative chronology and some major manifestations of reproductive decline are similar in short- and long-lived mammals, indicating the value of animal models for studying loss of reproductive capacity in females.

In this paper we have focused on determining the factor(s) responsible for reproductive decline in rodents. Much of the discussion is based on published and unpublished studies from our laboratory involving the C57BL/6J mouse. Whereas the study of reproductive aging is often restricted to individuals near or in a post-reproductive state, our emphasis is on the earliest changes in reproductive function and their endocrine correlates. This approach is based on the assumption that alterations in endocrine and neural factors during the initial, rather than the final, phase of aging are more likely to lead to correct conclusions about causality and less likely to be secondary to disease states or a prolonged dysfunctional condition.

Early Age-Related Changes in Fertility

Decreased litter size characterizes the onset of reproductive decline in rats *(6)*, hamsters *(7)*, and mice *(8, 9)*. Studies in our labora-

64

tory indicate that the average litter size (live pups) of 11- to 12-month-old C57BL/6J mice is only one-half that of 3- to 7-month-old mice *(9)*. Fetal resorptions, visible after day 11 of pregnancy, are doubled in older mothers and account for about 75% of this loss; implantation losses account for the remainder *(10)*. Average gestation length is prolonged by two days at this age and is inversely correlated with litter size *(9)*. However, prolonged gestation appears to be a consequence, rather than a cause, of reduced litter size, because the average litter size at birth is no less than the

Table 1. Frequency Distributions in Aging C57BL/6J Mice of Viable Fetuses Prior to Parturition and of Live Pups at Birth[a]

	Viable fetuses[b]		Live pups[c]	
No. per litter	No. of litters	% of all litters	No. of litters	% of all litters
1–2	8	19.5	8	25.8
3–4	13	31.7	10	32.3
5–6	12	29.3	9	29.0
7–8	6	14.6	3	9.7
9–10	2	4.9	1	3.2
Mean no. per litter	4.50		4.68	
(SEM)	(0.34)		(0.70)	

[a] Retired breeders, 11 to 12 months old.
[b] Forty-one litters checked at days 17, 18, and 19 of gestation.
[c] Thirty-one litters checked at days 20, 21, and 22 of gestation (at birth).
Source: *10*, and our own unpublished data.

mean number of viable fetuses seen just before parturition (Table 1).

The incidence of fetal resorptions increases significantly in 11- to 12-month-old mothers on day 13 of pregnancy, and remains stable thereafter; similarly, the proportion of mice with all sites resorbing increases markedly and becomes maximum at day 13 *(10)*. The absence of an increase in resorptions after this day suggests that the placental–ovarian–uterine interactions necessary for maintenance and development of viable embryos during the latter half of pregnancy are unimpaired, and that events on or before day 13 are responsible for the high incidence of resorbed fetuses.

Hormonal Correlates of Reduced Fertility

Pregnancy failure is attributable to a finite number of possibilities: impaired ovulation and fertilization, fetal abnormalities, altered hormonal support, or uterine refractoriness to hormonal stimulation. There appears to be little impairment in ovulation or fertilization during the initial stage of reproductive decline. Ovulation and fertilization rates, as determined by the number of ruptured follicles and preimplantation embryos, do not decline significantly in C57BL/6J mice until 12 to 14 months of age *(8, 11)*, well after the onset of decreased fertility. The incidence of fetal aneuploidy increases significantly during aging *(3)*, but its incidence in 11-month-old C57BL/6J mice is only 8% *(12)*, and thus probably does not account for the 50% decrease in litter size at this age. Although studies of uterine responsiveness to hormonal stimulation are not exhaustive, there appears to be no gross impairment in uterotropic responses to estradiol *(13)*. The uterine decidual-cell response, induced by exogenous hormone treatment and trauma, is impaired in 10-month-old C57BL/6J mice *(14)*, but no comparable impairment in decidual formation is observed during actual pregnancy *(10)*. Thus, the decidual response to implanting blastocysts is unimpaired at an age when its experimental induction is markedly diminished. Whatever the uterine refractoriness to environmental stimuli, it is apparent only under experimental conditions, and there is no evidence that it plays a role in the initial loss of fertility.

We have thus focused on the possibility that altered concentrations of ovarian hormones in plasma are involved in the initial decline in reproductive capacity, and have found substantial deficits and dyssynchronies in steroid concentrations during pregnancy. In older mice, progesterone is 10–40% lower during the first six days of pregnancy than in young mice (Figure 1). No major age differences in plasma estrogens are found during this phase of pregnancy (Figure 2) *(15)*. The greatest decrease in plasma progesterone occurs on day 4. Experiments indicate this day is crucial in terms of adequate hormonal support for implantation success and maintenance of viable embryos. For example, treatment of young rats with antiserum to progesterone on days 3 and 4 of gestation delays implantation and increases fetal resorptions *(16)*. Supplemental progesterone administered to ovariectomized preg-

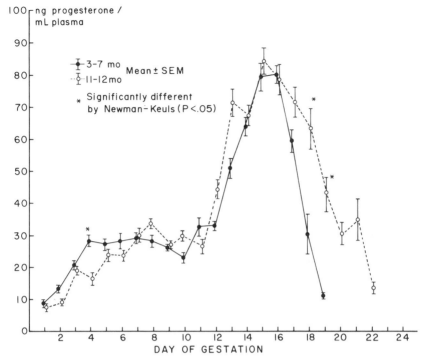

Fig. 1. Plasma progesterone during pregnancy in C57BL/6J mice

Data from Holinka et al. *(10)*

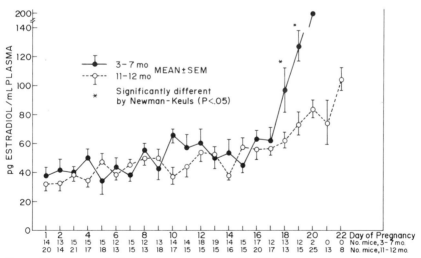

Fig. 2. Plasma estradiol during pregnancy in C57BL/6J mice

Data from Holinka et al. *(15)*

nant rats *(17)* or to hypophysectomized pregnant mice *(18)* is sufficient to maintain pregnancy and prevent fetal resorptions.

After the sixth day of pregnancy, plasma concentrations of progesterone and estrogen are indistinguishable between young and older mice until the onset of the characteristic pre-parturitional changes in steroid hormone concentrations (Figures 1 and 2). The pre-parturitional decrease in progesterone, and corresponding increase in estrogen are significantly delayed in older mothers *(9)*. Because experimental prevention of the decrease in plasma progesterone delays parturition and increases stillbirths in young rats *(19, 20)*, the delay in the decline of progesterone in older mothers could account for prolonged gestation and, consequently, decreased litter size. However, the delayed hormonal changes are more likely the consequence, rather than the cause, of decreased litter size, because the average litter size in older mice is not significantly lower than the number of pre-parturitional viable fetuses (Table 1).

These studies on the onset of reproductive decline suggest that reduced litter size, prolonged gestation, and delayed pre-parturitional hormone changes are all primarily consequences of a reduction in the number of viable fetuses. Fewer fetuses per litter is in turn due principally to increased resorptions and secondarily to fewer implantations. Because fetal resorptions and implantation failure can be induced by experimentally lowering progesterone concentrations during early pregnancy *(16)*, the pre-implantation decrease in plasma progesterone may play a major initiatory role in the subsequent events that culminate in decreased fertility.

Early Age-Related Changes in Estrous Cyclicity

Regular estrous cycles cease in most rats and mice by 20 months of age. However, the onset of irregularities in the estrous cycle occurs much earlier *(5, 21, 22)*. In a longitudinal study designed to identify the nature and variability in time of onset of these irregularities, we observed some mice with lengthened cycles as early as nine months of age (Figure 3) and a steady decline in cycle frequency for the entire population, beginning around 11 months of age (Figure 4). The initial decrease in cycle frequency

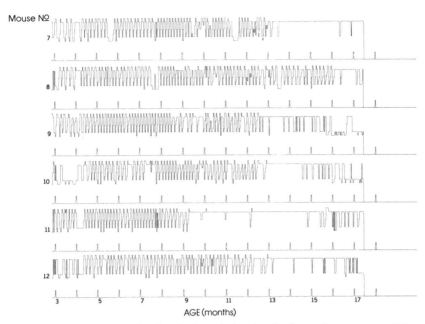

Fig. 3. Representation of individual variation in the loss of estrous cyclicity during aging in C57BL/6J mice

An estrous cycle is represented by the interval between two peaks. Peaks represent fully cornified smears, troughs represent fully leukocytic smears

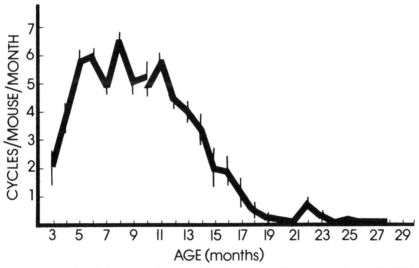

Fig. 4. Age-related change in the monthly frequency of estrous cycles in C57BL/6J mice as determined by vaginal smears

is associated with a one-day increase in the average cycle length. This prolongation is accounted for by a shift in the modal cycle frequency from four to five days, and by a significant increase in the frequency of cycles of six days and longer (Figure 5).

Prolongation of estrous cycles coincides with the initial phase of decreased fertility in our colony. In rats, lengthened estrous cycles induced by experimentally delaying ovulation for 24 to 48 h increases the incidence of aneuploid embryos and fetal deaths several-fold *(23, 24)*. Similarly, aging rats with prolonged cycles have a higher incidence of pre- and post-implantation abnormali-

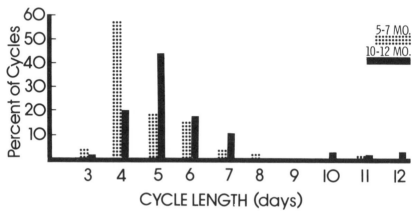

Fig. 5. Frequency distribution of the length of the estrous cycle in female C57BL/ 6J mice five to seven and 10 to 12 months old

ties than age-matched rats with four- to five-day cycles *(25)*. Although we cannot therefore infer that age-related lengthening of the estrous cycle leads to decreased fertility by delaying ovulation, these observations strengthen the possibility that early changes in estrous cyclicity may be an initial event leading to decreased fertility in C57BL/6J mice.

A Hormonal Correlate of Prolonged Estrous Cycles

The length of the estrous cycle is governed by a complex interplay of gonadal, hypothalamic, and pituitary hormones *(26)*. Ovulation, the functional endpoint of the estrous cycle, is triggered by a surge of luteinizing hormone (LH; lutropin[1]), which is secreted from the anterior pituitary gland on the afternoon of proestrus. Although peak concentrations of estradiol at proestrus are unimpaired in 10- to 11-month-old C57BL/6J mice, after proestrus, plasma estradiol decreases significantly more in old than in young mice (Figure 6). The subsequent pre-ovulatory increase in estradiol appears to be delayed in older mice by approximately one day, which closely parallels the increase in the length of the

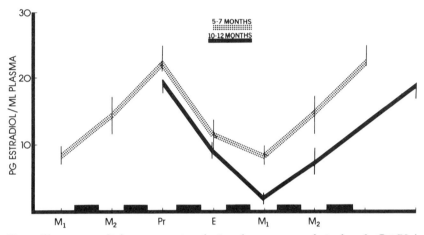

Fig. 6. Plasma estradiol concentration during the estrous cycle in female C57BL/6J mice five to seven and 10 to 12 months old

estrous cycle at this age. The possible significance of this delay is indicated by studies showing that administration of antiserum to estradiol on the morning of proestrus blocks the surge of LH and prolongs the estrous cycle (27).

No comparable alteration in estradiol concentrations has been observed during the estrous cycle in 11-month-old rats (28), but these animals were reported still to be cycling regularly. In humans, however, significant decreases in plasma estradiol concentrations are associated with the irregular menstrual cycles that characterize the pre-menopausal period (29).

---

[1] Luteinizing hormone is the term used by the American Endocrine Society, and is preferred by the authors; lutropin is the corresponding term recommended by the IUPAC-IUB Commission on Biological Nomenclature.—*Ed.*

Ovarian vs Extra-Ovarian Regulation of Initial Reproductive Decline

Although much effort has been directed toward identifying the anatomical site(s) responsible for cessation of cyclicity and fertility, the evidence remains inconclusive. Ovarian failure was once widely held to be the cause of infertility, because of the knowledge of the steady depletion of ovarian oocytes during development and aging *(21, 30)*. Although oocyte loss ultimately sets an upper limit on the duration of fertility, it cannot account for the initial decline. Fertility in mice, rats, and hamsters begins to decline several months before any decrease in ovulatory rate occurs *(31)*; moreover, no qualitative changes (e.g., abnormal ova) have been observed during the initial phase of decline, although their incidence increases in the advanced stage of reproductive failure in mice *(11)*. The strongest evidence against qualitative changes in ova as a major factor in the initial loss of fertility are studies of heterochronic ova transfer. These studies have shown that in mice the age of the host rather than the donor is the primary determinant of pregnancy success *(32)*. In the hamster, ova transfer studies implicate the age of the ovum as well as the host environment *(33)*.

Although changes in ovulatory rate or quality appear to be exonerated in the C57BL/6J mouse, evidence now suggests that the other principal function of the ovary, hormonal secretion, is impaired during the initial decline in fertility and estrous cyclicity. Studies in our laboratory have demonstrated marked alterations in plasma concentrations of ovarian steroids during the estrous cycle and pregnancy in aging mice *(9, 10;* Nelson, Felicio, and Finch, unpublished data). Whether these changes are primarily ovarian in origin remains to be determined. However, studies in the rat indicate that ovarian Δ^5-3β-hydroxy-steroid dehydrogenase (EC 1.1.1.145), a key enzyme in steroidogenesis that may be relatively independent of pituitary gonadotropins *(34, 35)*, begins a steady age-related decline at six months *(36)*. Although these studies suggest that ovarian steroidogenesis may be impaired at an early age, age-related changes in vitro or as a result of experimental manipulation may, of course, proceed at a different rate than in vivo. The decidual-cell response, for example, was markedly impaired when induced artificially at an age when no deficit is apparent under the natural stimulus of pregnancy *(14)*.

Although central mechanisms governing gonadotropin secretion are impaired in senescent, acyclic rats *(37–39)*, there is little evidence that hypothalamic or pituitary malfunction contributes to the initial decline of reproductive function. In middle-aged rats and mice still showing regular cycles, the pre-ovulatory rise in LH is both attenuated and slightly delayed (*40;* Flurkey, Gee, and Finch, unpublished data). This alteration may reflect either intrinsic changes in the hypothalamus and pituitary or an alteration in the ovarian signal (estradiol) that triggers the surge of LH. A recent report also indicates that the induction of an LH surge by exogenous ovarian steroid treatment is impaired in irregularly cycling rats, suggesting altered responsiveness of hypothalamic–pituitary mechanisms at the onset of reproductive decline *(39)*. However, this impairment could reflect a change, similar to the exogenously induced decidual-cell response, that is detectable only under experimental conditions and that has no bearing on the etiology of initial reproductive decline. The results of experiments on middle-aged rodents are intriguing, but further work is needed to determine whether intrinsic changes in the hypothalamus or pituitary contribute to the initial decline of reproductive function.

Our efforts to determine whether a central impairment occurs during the initial phase of reproductive aging have been directed toward the intracellular mechanism of steroid action in the hypothalamus and pituitary. The initial step in steroid action is believed to be the binding of the steroid to a cytoplasmic receptor, which then translocates to the nucleus and initiates alterations in gene activity. The ensuing alterations in protein synthesis lead to the characteristic tissue responses to the steroid *(41, 42)*. During aging, decreased concentrations of cytoplasmic receptors have been found in numerous *(43–45)* but not all *(46, 47)* tissues. In some cases these alterations are correlated with altered biochemical responses to the hormones *(43)*. Although our studies of the cytoplasmic estradiol receptor in the hypothalamus and pituitary reveal no alteration of total binding capacity at the onset of reproductive decline, the possibility remains that some defect exists in the intracellular mechanism of action.

In an attempt to identify such an impairment, we measured the concentration of unoccupied cytoplasmic receptor during the estrous cycle, as an index of its extent of translocation. The pre-ovulatory increase in plasma estradiol leads to an increased occupation of cytoplasmic estradiol-receptor sites, which rapidly translocate to the nucleus (48). After proestrus, as estradiol concentrations decrease, unoccupied cytoplasmic receptors are replenished. The occupation of receptors is unimpaired at proestrus, but during the pre-ovulatory period, when the plasma estradiol increase is delayed in older mice, there is a corresponding delay in the onset of increased occupation of receptor sites (Figure 7). Thus there appears to be no impairment in the initial intracellular step of estradiol action in the hypothalamus and pituitary that is independent of the age-related change in plasma estradiol. However, this delay in receptor occupation provides a possible molecular mechanism whereby the prolongation of the estrous cycle is mediated.

An Ovarian Contribution to the Ultimate Failure of Hypothalamic–Pituitary Regulation of Estrous Cyclicity

Although a hypothalamic–pituitary role in the initial decline of reproductive capacity has not been demonstrated, its role in the post-cyclic rodent is established. We and others (49, 50) have demonstrated that transplantation of young ovaries into senescent, acyclic mice and rats is ineffective in re-initiating cyclic function, as determined by the vaginal smear (Table 2). However, following the lead of a study in the rat by Aschheim (49), we have found that removal of the ovaries from mice at the age of onset of estrous cyclicity, followed by ovarian grafts at an age when cyclicity cannot be restored in intact mice, results in a significant restoration of cyclicity (Table 2). Recently, long-term ovariectomy in rats has been reported to restore the ability of exogenous steroid treatment to induce a pre-ovulatory-type LH surge (51), which cannot be induced in intact, acyclic age-matched rats (38, 39). Administration of estradiol to young rats accelerates the onset of acyclicity and is associated with neuronal degeneration in the hypothalamic arcuate nucleus (52), a key regulatory center for gonadotropin secretion (53). These observations indicate that the continued action during adult life of some ovarian factor, presumably estradiol, gradually alters hypothalamic or pituitary mecha-

74

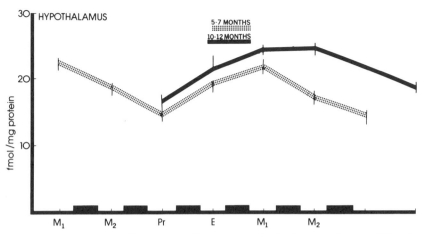

Fig. 7. Unoccupied cytoplasmic estradiol receptors in the hypothalamus of female C57BL/6J mice five to seven and 10 to 12 months old

Table 2. **Analysis of Ovarian Transplant Studies in Female C57BL/6J mice**

				Mean (SEM)	
Age, months			*Mice*	*Cycle length of*	*Duration of cycling after*
Host	*Ovarian donor*	*No. mice*	*with ≥ 2 cycles*[a]	*responders, days*	*transplantation,*[b] *months*
5–6	5	10	100%	5.3 (0.65)	5.5 (1.2)
26	5	8	25%	8.0 (2.6)	2.4 (0.6)
26[c]	5	9	100%	6.6 (2.4)	3.0 (1.2)

[a] Cycles were defined as a sequence of smears: proestrus followed by estrus or metestrus (cornified epithelial cells) and then diestrus (leukocytes), followed again by proestrus.

[b] The period of time during which cycles were observed. The termination of cycling was defined by the time after which no further cycles occurred for 10 days.

[c] Long-term ovariectomized mice, ovariectomized at two months of age and given ovarian transplants at 26 months of age.

nism or both, and thereby impairs the control of cyclic gonadotropin release.

The influence of gonadal steroids during perinatal development on the duration of estrous cyclicity in adulthood is a well-known phenomenon. Exogenous estradiol or testosterone, administered in physiological doses during the first 10 days of life, prevents the development of estrous cyclicity and ovulation after puberty in the female rat *(54)*. At lower doses, androgens administered

75

during this so-called critical period permit the appearance of cyclicity but foreshorten its duration according to dosage *(55, 56)*. The finding that the age of onset of acyclicity is advanced in direct proportion to the dose of androgen raises the possibility that endogenous steroids in neonatal rodents may set an upper limit on the duration of cyclicity. Recent studies, showing that the proximity of female to male fetuses affects adult female reproductive parameters *(57)*, indicate that physiological variation of endogenous hormones during the perinatal period can produce significant variability in adult reproductive function. Thus, we hypothesize that the variable onset of cyclic irregularity and the variable age of cyclic cessation reflects interanimal variation in the low but detectable concentrations of endogenous gonadal steroids in female rodents *(58)* during neonatal life.

Taken together, these results suggest that endogenous ovarian hormones play a role both during perinatal development and adulthood in regulating at least one component of reproductive aging: loss of estrous cyclicity. Whether the ovarian hormones act upon the same central mechanisms during aging as during development should provide a subject of much fruitful study.

Conclusions

Early alterations in the circulatory patterns of estradiol and progesterone coincide with the onset of lengthened estrous cycles and reduced fertility in C57BL/6J mice. That these altered patterns contribute to the altered physiological functions observed is consistent with experimental work indicating causality.

Continued exposure to endogenous ovarian hormones during adulthood ultimately renders rodents incapable of responding to the ovarian hormonal stimuli necessary for estrous cyclicity. These findings extend to the adult an "organizing" influence of gonadal steroids on the brain, heretofore limited to the perinatal period.

These results support the view that hormones mediate age-related changes in physiological function in two distinct ways. First, they act acutely, through altered patterns of secretion or clearance, to bring about impaired function. Secondly, hormones act chronically during adulthood, altering mechanisms involved in maintaining normal function.

This research was supported by grants from the N.I.H. (AG 00117, AG 00446) and the Eli Lilly Research Foundation. We are indebted to Mr. Leonard C. Brown for careful preparation of the manuscript. This paper is contribution No. 43 from the Neurobiology Laboratory, University of Southern California.

References

1. Talbert, G., Aging of the female reproductive system. In *Handbook of the Biology of Aging*, C. E. Finch and L. Hayflick, Eds., Van Nostrand, New York, NY, 1977, pp 318–356.

2. Book, J. A., Fraccaro, M., Hagert, C. G., and Lindsten, J., Congenital malformations in children of mothers aged 42 and over. *Nature* **181**, 1545–1546 (1958).

3. Kram, D., and Schneider, E. L., An effect of reproductive aging: Increased risk of genetically abnormal offspring. In *The Aging Reproductive System*, **4**, *Aging*, E. L. Schneider, Ed., Raven Press, New York, NY, 1978, pp 237–270.

4. Frommer, D. J., Changing age of the menopause. *Br. Med. J.* ii, 349–351 (1964).

5. Thung, P. J., Boot, L. M., and Mühlbock, O., Senile changes in the oestrous cycle and in ovarian structure in some inbred strains of mice. *Acta Endocrinol.* **23**, 8–32 (1956).

6. Ingram, D. L., Mandl, A. M., and Zuckerman, S., The influence of age on litter-size. *J. Endocrinol.* **17**, 280–285 (1958).

7. Connors, T. J., Thorpe, L. W., and Soderwall, A. L., An analysis of preimplantation embryonic death in senescent golden hamsters. *Biol. Reprod.* **6**, 131–135 (1972).

8. Harman, S. M., and Talbert, G. B., The effect of maternal age on ovulation, corpora lutea of pregnancy, and implantation failure in mice. *J. Reprod. Fertil.* **23**, 33–39 (1970).

9. Holinka, C. F., Tseng, Y.-C., and Finch, C. E., Prolonged gestation, elevated preparturitional progesterone, and reproductive aging in C57BL/6J mice. *Biol. Reprod.* **19**, 807–816 (1978).

10. Holinka, C. F., Tseng, Y.-C., and Finch, C. E., Reproductive aging in C57BL/6J mice: Plasma progesterone, viable embryos and resorption frequency throughout pregnancy. *Biol. Reprod.* **20**, 1201–1211 (1979).

11. Parkening, T. A., Lau, I.-F., Saksena, S. K., and Chang, M.-C., Circulating plasma levels of pregnenolone, progesterone, estrogen, luteinizing hormone, and follicle stimulating hormone in young and aged C57BL/6J mice during various stages of pregnancy. *J. Gerontol.* **33**, 191–196 (1978).

12. Fabricant, J. D., and Schneider, E. L., Studies of the genetic and immunologic components of the maternal age effect. *Dev. Biol.* **66,** 337–343 (1978).
13. Holinka, C. F., Hetland, M. D., and Finch, C. E., The response to a single dose of estradiol in the uterus of ovariectomized C57BL/6J mice during aging. *Biol. Reprod.* **17,** 262–264 (1977).
14. Holinka, C. F., and Finch, C. E., Age-related changes in the decidual response of the C57BL/6J mouse uterus. *Biol. Reprod.* **16,** 385–393 (1977).
15. Holinka, C. F., Tseng, Y.-C., and Finch, C. E., Impaired preparturitional rise of plasma estradiol in aging C57BL/6J mice. *Biol. Reprod.* **21,** 1009–1013 (1979).
16. Raziano, J., Ferin, M., and Vande Wiele, R. L., Effects of antibodies to estradiol-17beta and to progesterone on nidation and pregnancy in rats. *Endocrinology* **90,** 1133–1138 (1973).
17. Dickman, Z., and Hart, J. R., Significance of daily administration of progesterone and estrogen for the maintenance of pregnancy in the ovariectomized rat. *Endocrinology* **90,** 1667–1669 (1972).
18. Choudary, J. B., and Greenwald, G. S., Ovarian activity in the intact or hypophysectomized pregnant mouse. *Anat. Rec.* **163,** 359–372 (1969).
19. Walker, S. M., and Matthews, J. I., Some reactions of the rat to treatment with progesterone and estrone in late pregnancy. *Proc. Soc. Exp. Med.* **71,** 320–322 (1949).
20. Moore, H. C., Intra-uterine foetal death during prolonged pregnancy in rats receiving progesterone: The effect of ovariectomy and oestrogens. *J. Obst. Gynaecol. Br. Commonw.* **70,** 151–153 (1963).
21. Aschheim, P., Aging in the hypothalamic–hypophyseal–ovarian axis in the rat. In *Hypothalamus, Pituitary, and Aging,* A. V. Everitt and J. A. Burgess, Eds., C. C Thomas, Springfield, IL, 1976, pp 376–418.
22. Nelson, J. F., Felicio, L. S., Sims, C., and Finch, C. E., Age-related changes in the estrus cycle of the C57BL/6J mouse. *Gerontol. Soc. Program and Abstracts,* 30th Ann. Meeting, San Francisco, CA, 1977 p 103.
23. Butcher, R. L., and Fugo, N. W., Overripeness and the mammalian ova. II. Delayed ovulation and chromosome anomalies. *Fertil. Steril.* **18,** 297–304 (1967).
24. Butcher, R. L., Blue, J. D., and Fugo, N. W., Overripeness and the mammalian ova. III. Fetal development at midgestation and at term. *Fertil. Steril.* **20,** 223–231 (1969).
25. Fugo, N. W., and Butcher, R. L., Effects of prolonged estrous cycles on reproduction in aged rats. *Fertil. Steril.* **22,** 98–101 (1971).
26. Schwartz, N. B., Dierschke, D. J., McCormack, C. E., and Waltz,

P. W., Feedback regulation of reproductive cycles in rats, sheep, monkeys and humans, with particular attention to computer modeling. In *Frontiers in Reproduction and Fertility Control*, R. O. Greep and M. A. Koblinsky, Eds., MIT Press, Cambridge, MA, 1977, pp 55–89.

27. Ferin, M., Tempone, A., Zimmering, P. E., and Vande Wiele, R. L., Effect of antibodies to 17 beta-estradiol and progesterone on the estrous cycle of the rat. *Endocrinology* **85**, 1070–1078 (1969).

28. Lu, K. H., Chang, R. J., and Klebzik, G. S., Daily patterns of ovarian and pituitary hormone secretion in old female rats just prior to the onset of estrous cycle irregularity and during chronic anovulation. *The Endocrine Society 61st Annual Meeting*, Anaheim, CA, 1979, p 106.

29. Sherman, B. M., West, J. H., and Korenman, S. G., The menopausal transition: Analysis of LH, FSH, estradiol and progesterone concentrations during menstrual cycles of older women. *J. Clin. Endocrinol. Metab.* **42**, 629–636 (1976).

30. Jones, E. C., and Krohn, P. L., The relationships between age, numbers of oocytes and fertility in virgin and multiparous mice. *J. Endocrinol.* **21**, 469–475 (1961).

31. Talbert, G. B., Effect of aging of the ovaries and female gametes on reproductive capacity. In *The Aging Reproductive System*, **4**, *Aging* (see ref. *3*), pp 59–84.

32. Talbert, G. B., and Krohn, P. L., Effect of maternal age on viability of ova and uterine support of pregnancy in mice. *J. Reprod. Fertil.* **11**, 399–406 (1966).

33. Blaha, G. C., Egg transfer between old and young mammals. In *Aging Gametes*, R. J. Blandau, Ed., S. Karger, Basel, 1975, pp 219–230.

34. Ruben, B. L., Comparisons of the dehydroisoandrosterone Δ^5-3β-hydroxysteroid dehydrogenase and the Δ^5-pregnenolone Δ^5-3β-hydroxysteroid dehydrogenase activity of ovaries of control, hemiovariectomized, gonadotrophin-treated and "androgen-sterilized" young rats. *Endocrinology* **83**, 626–628 (1968).

35. Turolla, E., Gaetani, M., Baldratti, G., and Aguggini, G., Histochemistry of ovarian 20α-hydroxysteroid dehydrogenase in mature hypophysectomized rats. *Experientia* **24**, 345–347 (1968).

36. Leathem, J. H., and Shapiro, B. H., Aging and ovarian Δ^5-3β-hydroxysteroid dehydrogenase in rats. *Proc. Soc. Exp. Biol. Med.* **148**, 793–794 (1975).

37. Gosden, R. G., and Bancroft, L., Pituitary function in reproductively senescent female rats. *Exp. Gerontol.* **11**, 157–160 (1976).

38. Peluso, J. J., Steger, R. W., and Hafez, E. S. E., Regulation of LH secretion in aged female rats. *Biol. Reprod.* **16**, 212–215 (1977).

39. Meites, J., Huang, H. H., and Simpkins, J. W., Recent studies on neuroendocrine control of reproductive senescence in rats. In *The Aging Reproductive System*, **4**, *Aging* (see ref. *3*), pp 213–235.
40. Van Der Schoot, P., Changing pro-oestrous surges of luteinizing hormone in ageing 5-day cyclic rats. *J. Endocrinol.* **69**, 287–288 (1976).
41. King, R. J. B., and Mainwaring, W. I. P., *Steroid–Cell Interactions*. University Park Press, Baltimore, MD, 1974, 440 pp.
42. McEwen, B. S., Luine, V. N., Plapinger, L., and DeKloet, E. R., Putative estrogen and glucocorticoid receptors in limbic brain. *J. Steroid. Biochem.* **6**, 971–977 (1975).
43. Roth, G. S., Hormone receptor changes during adulthood and senescence: Significance for aging research. *Fed. Proc.* **38**, 1910–1914 (1979).
44. Shain, S. A., and Axelrod, L. R., Reduced high affinity 5α-dihydrotestosterone receptor capacity in the ventral prostate of aging rat. *Steroids* **21**, 801–812 (1973).
45. Holinka, C. F., Nelson, J. F., and Finch, C. E., Effect of estrogen treatment on estradiol binding capacity in uteri of aged rats. *Gerontologist* **15**, 30 (1975).
46. Nelson, J. F., Holinka, C. F., Latham, K. R., Allen, J. K., and Finch, C. E., Corticosterone binding in cytosols from brain regions of mature and senescent male C57BL/6J mice. *Brain Res.* **115**, 345–351 (1976).
47. Latham, K., and Finch, C. E., Hepatic glucocorticoid binders in mature and senescent C57BL/6J male mice. *Endocrinology* **98**, 1434–1443 (1976).
48. Ginsburg, M., MacLusky, N. J., Morris, I. D., and Thomas, P. J., Physiological variation in abundance of oestrogen high-affinity sites in hypothalamus, pituitary and uterus of rat. *J. Endocrinol* **64**, 443–449 (1975).
49. Aschheim, P., Résultats fournis par la greffe hétérochrone des ovaires dans l'étude de la régulation hypothalamo–hypophyso–ovarienne de la ratte sénile. *Gerontologia* **10**, 65–75 (1964).
50. Zeilmaker, G. H., Effects of prolonged feeding of an ovulation inhibitor (Lyndiol) on ageing of the hypothalamic–ovarian axis and pituitary gland tumorigenesis in rats. *J. Endocrinol.* **43**, xxi–xxii (1969).
51. Elias, K. A., Huffman, L. J., and Blake, C. A., Age of ovariectomy affects subsequent plasma LH responses in old age rats. *The Endocrine Society 61st Annual Meeting*, Anaheim, CA, 1979, p 106.
52. Brawer, J. R., Naftolin, F., Martin, J., and Sonnenschein, C., Effects of a single injection of estradiol valerate on the hypothalamic arcuate nucleus and on reproductive function in the female rat. *Endocrinology* **103**, 501–512 (1978).

53. Gorski, R. A., Localization and sexual differentiation of the nervous structures which regulate ovulation. *J. Reprod. Fertil. (Suppl. 1)* 67–88 (1966).

54. Gorski, R. A., Gonadal hormones and the perinatal development of neuroendocrine function. In *Frontiers in Neuroendocrinology*, L. Martini and W. F. Ganong, Eds., Oxford University Press, New York, NY, 1971, pp 237–290.

55. Swanson, H. E., and van der Werff ten Bosch, J. J., The "early-androgen" syndrome: Its development and the response to hemi-spaying. *Acta Endocrinol.* 45, 1–12 (1964).

56. Sheridan, P. J., Zarrow, M. X., and Denenberg, V. H., Androgenization of the neonatal female rat with very low doses of androgen. *J. Endocrinol.* 57, 33–45 (1973).

57. Vom Saal, F. S., and Bronson, F. H., In utero proximity of female mouse fetuses to males: Effect on reproductive performance during later life. *Biol. Reprod.* 19, 842–853 (1978).

58. Dohler, K. D., and Wuttke, W., Changes with age in levels of serum gonadotropins, prolactin, and gonadal steroids in pre-pubertal male and female rats. *Endocrinology* 97, 898–907 (1975).

Decline in Reproductive Function with Age in Humans and Rats

Joseph Meites

The fundamental neuroendocrine and endocrine mechanisms regulating reproductive functions in mammalian species are essentially similar, although some prominent differences exist. Thus the luteinizing-hormone-releasing factor (LHRH) of the hypothalamus is the same decapeptide in all mammalian species examined, and releases both the luteinizing hormone (LH) and follicle-stimulating hormone (FSH) from the pituitary gland.[1] In female mammals, FSH and LH act on the ovaries to induce follicular growth, ovulation, and formation of the corpus luteum. In males, FSH and LH act on the testes to promote spermatogenesis and testosterone secretion. During the estrous and menstrual cycles, the positive feedback by estrogen is responsible for the preovulatory surge of LH and FSH, which produces ovulation. The negative feedback by estrogen and progesterone on gonadotropin secretion, usually seen during the luteal phase of the cycle, is similar among mammalian species. Castration removes the inhibitory influence of the gonadal steroids and increases the LH and FSH secretion. Nonprimate species do not menstruate, and primate species lack the behavioral phenomenon of "heat."

Interactions among the hypothalamus, pituitary, and ovaries normally occur during the estrous and menstrual cycles, as follows. During the follucular phase, the follicles develop and secrete estrogen under the combined stimulation of FSH and LH. Before ovulation, estrogen secretion increases, which acts via hypothalamic LHRH to produce a surge of LH and FSH release. Ovulation and

---

[1] These are the terms used by The Endocrine Society. The corresponding recommendations of the IUPAC-IUB Commission on Biological Nomenclature are as follows: luliberin (LHRH), lutropin (LH), and follitropin (FSH).—*Ed.*

formation of the corpus luteum are induced mainly by the increase in LH, which acts synergistically with FSH.

During the luteal phase, progesterone secretion by the corpus luteum is promoted in primates mainly by LH, but in rats and several other rodent species principally by prolactin. Estrogen also is secreted by the ovaries during the luteal phase, and this, combined with the predominant progesterone, feeds back negatively on the hypothalamus to restrain any further surge of LH and FSH secretion. If fertilization fails to occur, the corpus luteum degenerates and secretion of progesterone and estrogen decreases, resulting in renewal of the cycle (also menstruation in primates).

A decline in reproductive functions with aging appears to be characteristic of all mammalian species studied. I will compare some of the changes in the reproductive system (hypothalamus, pituitary, gonads, and reproductive tract) of aging rats and human subjects of both sexes. The rat and other laboratory animals have some obvious advantages over humans for studies on aging of the reproductive system. For example, rats have a maximum life span of two and one-half to three years under good laboratory conditions, and can be maintained in a controlled environment. Female rats begin to show estrous cycles when they are 35 to 50 days old, cycle regularly every four or five days, and usually cease to cycle by 10 to 15 months of age. By contrast, human females come to puberty when 11 to 13 years old and cease to undergo menstrual cycles between 40 and 50 years of age. Male rats come into puberty at about 50 to 60 days of age, and human males at about 13 to 15 years. Both male rats and men show a more gradual decline in reproductive functions than women, and some spermatogenesis and testosterone production may continue into old age.

Women

For two to three years before menopause (cessation of menstrual cycles), the cycles tend to become irregular and there is an increase in the number of anovulatory cycles. The ovaries may form cystic follicles, and there is inadequate development and often early involution of the corpus luteum, leading to shortening of the cycle. There also may be a shortened follicular phase. Both estrogen and progesterone secretion decline, and the ovaries show a

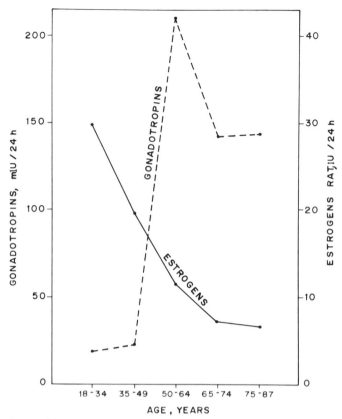

Fig. 1. Urinary estrogens and gonadotropins in aging women

Source: Timiras (22)

diminished capacity to respond to gonadotropic stimulation. The decrease in secretion of gonadal steroids leads to an increase in release of gonadotropins, as much as 15-fold in FSH and about threefold in LH (Figure 1). The total number of ova in the ovaries at the onset of menopause may number about 10 000, compared with about 600 000 at birth. An increased percentage of these ova appear to be faulty as women approach the menopause, which results in an increased incidence of abnormal offspring (Down's syndrome, etc.).

In postmenopausal women, the ovaries become fibrotic and lose their follicles, and few or no ovulations occur. Secretion of ovarian estrogen is very low, and secretion of gonadotropins remains high.

84

There is evidence that gonadotropin secretion in the postmenopausal period remains high for about 15 years, and then declines, but still is above premenopausal values. With the decrease in estrogen secretion, the reproductive tract undergoes retrogressive changes. The uterus and fallopian tubes undergo a marked decrease in size and weight. The uterine mucosa becomes thin, atrophic, and nonsecretory, and there is a decrease in myometrial thickness. The vagina shows a narrowing of the opening and a shrinkage of the mucosa (1, 2).

Whereas estradiol is the primary estrogen produced by women during the reproductive years, estrone is the main estrogen found in the postmenopausal period. Estrone comes mainly from the conversion of androstenedione in fat deposits and perhaps also in the blood and liver (1). The total amount of estrogen secreted in the postmenopausal period is far below that of the reproductive years. The ability of the hypothalamo-pituitary system of menopausal or postmenopausal women to respond to stimuli that normally elicit release of LH and FSH has not been adequately tested in women, but the marked increase in these hormones indicates that this system remains functional, although perhaps at a different level than during the reproductive years.

A decrease in brain catecholamines has been reported in old humans (3), and catecholamines, particularly norepinephrine in the hypothalamus, have been shown to be stimulatory for gonadotropin release (4). L-DOPA, the precursor of the catecholamines, reportedly reinitiated menstrual bleeding in some postmenopausal women (5), but whether this produced follicular growth or ovulation was not determined. The pituitary of postmenopausal women remains responsive to LHRH, but the degree of responsiveness has not been adequately studied (1).

Dilman (6) has postulated that the climacteric state is due primarily to diminished hypothalamic sensitivity to estrogen. However, most of the available evidence indicates that the major cause for the loss of menstrual cycles lies in ovarian failure and not in the inability of the hypothalamo-pituitary system to function adequately.

Female Rats

Some of my coworkers and I have described previously (7, 8) some of the salient features exhibited by aging female rats as they approach and reach the end of their reproductive life. As rats age, they ovulate fewer eggs and have smaller litters. Female rats between 10 and 15 months of life first show irregularities in their cycles (characterized by lengthening of the cycle from four or five days to six, seven, or more days) with prolonged periods of estrous or diestrous. This is followed by a constant-estrous syndrome, with many well-developed and some cystic follicles, no corpora lutea, and estrogen secretion similar to that of the cycling rat. This constant-estrous syndrome may last for many months, and appears in the majority of aging female rats. It is usually followed by prolonged pseudopregnancies of irregular length, lasting 10 to 30 days or more, with many corpora lutea in the ovaries actively secreting high amounts of progesterone; the prolonged pseudopregnancies are interspersed with ovulations. In the oldest rats, two to three years old, the ovaries become atrophic and the uterus appears infantile. Anestrous rats secrete very little estrogen or progesterone, and usually have pituitary tumors that secrete large amounts of prolactin, but almost no gonadotropins.

Secretion of LH, FSH, and ovarian steroids by old rats in constant estrous or pseudopregnancy differs from that in young cycling rats, mainly because there is no surge of these hormones such as occurs during the normal preovulatory period (9). In old anestrous rats, amounts of serum LH, FSH, and ovarian hormones are much lower than in young rats. In all old female rats, prolactin secretion is higher than in young cycling rats, and is associated with an increased incidence of mammary and pituitary tumors. In response to stimuli that normally release LH and FSH, the hypothalamo-pituitary systems of old rats definitely show a decreased capacity to release these hormones. Thus castration results in a much smaller increase in LH and FSH release in old, non-cycling rats than in young, cycling rats. Gonadotropin release in response to the positive feedback action by estrogen and progesterone also is greatly decreased in old ovariectomized rats, which indicates that retrogressive changes have occurred in the function of the hypothalamo-pituitary system.

We have demonstrated a decrease in hypothalamic turnover of catecholamines and an increase in serotonin turnover in old female and male rats, compared with young mature rats of both sexes (10). This is believed to be important, because catecholamines, particularly norepinephrine, stimulate gonadotropin release, whereas serotonin usually inhibits it *(4)*. Treatments that increase brain catecholamines, such as administration of L-DOPA or iproniazid, frequently produce ovulation and reinitiation of estrous cycles in old, constant-estrous rats *(10)*. Direct electrical stimulation of the hypothalamus or injection of LHRH, LH, progesterone, or corticotropin also induces ovulation or cycling in old female rats (Figure 2).

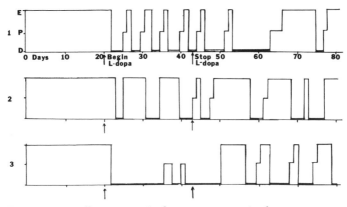

Fig. 2. L-DOPA effects on vaginal smear patterns in three representative constant-estrous rats, showing (1) regular estrous cycles during treatment and irregular cycles after treatment; (2) irregular estrous cycles during treatment and post-treatment; (3) one period of pseudopregnancy during treatment, followed by irregular estrous cycles

E, estrous; P, proestrous; D, diestrous

This demonstrates that the ovaries of old female rats retain their capacity to function, and that the major cause(s) for loss of estrous cycles are due to changes in function of the hypothalamo-pituitary system. Other evidence that the ovaries of old rats retain functional capacity is the observation that, upon their transplantation to young rats whose ovaries have been removed, estrous cycles resume *(11)*. We have even induced some pregnancies in old non-cycling female rats by mating them with young male rats, although the young died *in utero* because of problems encountered in the reproductive tract *(7)*. Thus the ovaries of female rats retain a potential for near-normal function throughout their life span, even though estrous cycles usually cease by about midlife.

Men

The decline in sexual activity in aging men has been well documented, and is associated at least in part with a reduction in testosterone secretion by the testes. Testosterone is known to stimulate growth and function of the reproductive organs (penis, prostate, and seminal vesicles) and, with the gonadotropic hormones, to stimulate spermatogenesis. It also promotes development of the secondary sex characteristics and sex drive. Several authors have reported that in aging men there is a decrease in weight of the testes; atrophic changes in many, but not all, seminiferous tubules; a decrease in spermatogenic activity; and a decrease in Leydig cells, which secrete testosterone (12, 13).

A decline in androgen secretion after about age 50 (Figure 3), has been observed by many investigators, although elderly men display a wide range of hormone concentrations in blood. Associated with the decrease in free testosterone, the biologically active form, is an increase in protein-bound testosterone, which is inactive. A very recent report on a longitudinal study by Harman (unpublished) in healthy, educated, and relatively affluent men has shown no significant decrease in testosterone secretion between the ages of 30 and 80, indicating that the decrease in testosterone secretion reported in earlier studies may not be universal in all men. There is an increase in urinary estrogens in elderly men, resulting in an increased estrogen/testosterone ratio. The source of the estrogen appears to be androstenedione, which is aromatized to estrone by peripheral tissues. Administration of human choriogonadotropin to older men was reported to produce a smaller increase in plasma testosterone than in younger men, but because the older men started with a lower baseline value, the percentage increase was the same in both groups.

An increase in LH and FSH concentrations in blood begins at about 50 years of age in aging men (Figure 4), but is much smaller than in postmenopausal women. The increase in FSH is more prominent than the increase in LH, as in women. The increase in gonadotropin secretion is apparently a consequence of the decrease of testosterone secretion. Several investigators have studied the response of the pituitary to LHRH in aging men, and most have found that the release of LH is less than in younger men (12). The capacity of the hypothalamus to release LHRH in elderly

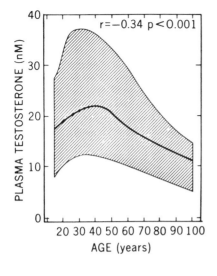

Fig. 3. Total (free and bound) plasma testosterone (nmol/L) in aging men

Solid line, mean; *shaded area,* range of individual values. Source: Baker et al. *(23)*

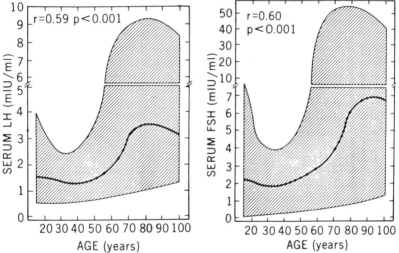

Fig. 4. Serum LH *(left)* and FSH *(right)* concentrations (int. unit/L) in aging men

Solid line, mean; *shaded area,* range. Source: Baker et al. *(23)*

men has not yet been tested, although the increase in LH and FSH suggests that it remains operative. A progressive increase in concentrations of prolactin in serum has also been observed in aging men *(14),* which may be related to the gradual increase in serum estrogen. The increase in prolactin release may contribute to the greater incidence of prostatic tumors in elderly men because prolactin can act synergistically with LH and testosterone to promote growth of this tissue (15).

Male Rats

Studies in our laboratory have shown that sera of old male rats have lower concentrations of LH, FSH, and testosterone and higher concentrations of prolactin than in young mature male rats (Table 1). Although no changes in the spermatogenic cycle have been detected in the testes of old male rats (16), total sperm count is probably decreased. The aged rat testes show a thickening

Table 1. Serum Concentrations of Hormones in Young and Old Male Rats

Hormone concn (mean ± SD), μg/L

	Study 1		Study 2	
	Young	Old	Young	Old
Luteinizing hormone	20.0 ± 3	6.0 ± 2	18.0 ± 4	9.0 ± 2
Follicle-stimulating hormone	220.0 ± 10	166.0 ± 14	330.0 ± 26	186.0 ± 48
Prolactin	10.0 ± 1	29.0 ± 8	15.0 ± 2	37.0 ± 8
Testosterone	3.2 ± 0.3	1.1 ± 0.2	3.2	0.6

of the basement membrane, pigmentation of interstitial cells, and fibrous atresia of the seminiferous tubules. There appears to be no decline in testicular LH binding in the aging male rat (16), but the testosterone increase in response to injections of gonadotropin is less in old than in young males (17).

Hypothalamic LHRH content in the pituitary of 26-month-old male Long–Evans rats was about one-half that in four-month-old male rats of the same strain (18). The pituitary of old male rats also is less responsive to LHRH stimulation than the pituitary of young male rats, as in elderly human subjects. Thus multiple injections of synthetic LHRH into 21-month-old Wistar rats produced a significantly smaller release of LH, FSH, and testosterone than in four-month-old Wistar rats (19). This may reflect a diminished capacity of the pituitary of old male rats to synthesize and release gonadotropins. As in aging female rats, the hypothalamus of old male rats shows a decreased turnover of catecholamines and an increased turnover of serotonin (10), which undoubtedly contributes to the decreased secretion of gonadotropins by the pituitary.

Other indications that the hypothalamo-pituitary system of aging male rats is less responsive than in young males to stimuli that normally produce release of gonadotropins are: (a) castration elicited a much smaller increase in LH in serum in 24- to 28-month-old male rats than in five- to six-month-old male rats (20); and (b) acute stress markedly increased serum LH in four- to six-month-old, but not in 22- to 30-month-old male rats (21). We can conclude, therefore, that the hypothalamo-pituitary system is primarily responsible for the reproductive decline in the aging male rat, and the testes contribute to this process.

Conclusions

Obviously, there are similarities as well as differences in the changes that promote reproductive senescence in aging rats and human subjects. In female rats approaching the end of normal estrous cycles and in women approaching menopause, the cycles become irregular, the follicles tend to become cystic, and there are fewer ovulations. However, in aging female rats cessation of regular estrous cycles appears to be caused mainly by a decline in the ability of the hypothalamo-pituitary system to induce cyclic release of gonadotropins; the ovaries remain responsive to gonadotropin stimulation throughout the life span of the rat. The hypothalamus appears to be mainly at fault, because it no longer responds adequately to cues that normally induce release of gonadotropins. This appears to result mainly from deficiencies in catecholamines, particularly norepinephrine, and from an excess of serotonin activity. The main source of norepinephrine neurons is in the locus ceruleus, and of serotonin neurons the raphe nucleus, both in the mid-brain. Why these changes occur in activity of these biogenic amines in aging male and female rats is unknown, but may result from changes in the enzyme systems that synthesize and metabolize these neurotransmitters. It also is possible that there is a loss of neurons that synthesize catecholamines, and an increase in neurons that synthesize serotonin.

I have mentioned observations of a decrease in brain catecholamines in old humans similar to that in old rats, as well as an increase in monoamine oxidase, an enzyme that metabolizes catecholamines and serotonin (3). However, the hypothalamus does not appear to be primarily responsible for cessation of menstrual cycles in women nor for the gradual decline in sexual function in men. In aging women, the primary cause lies in the ovaries, which lose their ability to respond normally to gonadotropic stimulation by FSH and LH. Why they fail to respond is not entirely clear, but is related to the loss of follicles, follicular epithelium, and stroma, which result in a decline in estrogen secretion. The menopausal ovary contains primordial and small or medium-sized follicles, some in various stages of cystic atresia. By the early to mid-50 years of age, most of these follicles disappear. However, the stromal tissue may retain some capacity to secrete estrogen and androgens in the postmenopausal period (1, 2). Luteal failure is common in women approaching the menopause, and ovulation and formation of fresh corpora are rare after menopause.

The changes in the ovaries of aging, non-cycling female rats are different from those in the ovaries of menopausal and postmenopausal women. Although rat ovaries also show a marked loss of follicles, the follicles that remain retain their capacity to respond to gonadotropic stimulation. Even in old anestrous rats, the atrophic ovaries, containing mainly primary or small follicles, can be reactivated upon transplantation to young ovariectomized rats (Huang and Meites, unpublished). Reinitiation of cycling and even pregnancies have been induced by us in old, non-cycling rats, but there appear to be no such possibilities in postmenopausal women. This is fortunate, because of the increased risks involved in late pregnancies.

In aging men and male rats, the changes in the neuroendocrine system that lead to reproductive decline appear to show many similarities. In both species, the decline in male reproductive functions is more gradual than in females, and the capacity of the testes to produce sperm and testosterone often continues into advanced age. Although sex drive declines with aging, there are documented reports of men in their 70's and 80's, and at least one man aged 94 (12), who achieved paternity. The reproductive capacity of old male rats has not yet been tested, to our knowledge.

The decrease in testicular function in aging male rats appears to be due primarily to a decrease in gonadotropic secretion, which in turn is related to the decreased hypothalamic turnover of catecholamines and increased turnover of serotonin. The rat pituitary also is less responsive to stimulation by LHRH, and the testes to gonadotropic stimulation. The decreased testicular responsiveness to gonadotropins appears to be associated with a decrease in number of seminiferous tubules and Leydig cells in the testis. In aging men, the pituitary also is less responsive to LHRH, and the testes to choriogonadotropic stimulation. However, LH and FSH concentrations in blood increase while testosterone concentrations decrease, suggesting that the primary cause for the reproductive decline in men may lie in the testes rather than in the hypothalamo-pituitary system. If this is so, then changes in the gonads are mainly responsible for reproductive senescence both in aging men and women, whereas the hypothalamo-pituitary system is primarily responsible for the reproductive decline in aging male and female rats.

Many questions about the causes and possible treatments of reproductive senescence remain to be answered. Why, in the rat, mouse, and perhaps in other animal species, do the ovaries remain potentially functional for most or all of the animal's life span, whereas the ovaries of women lose their capacity to develop the follicles that are present at the onset of the menopause? Are there means by which the steroid-secretory capacity of the ovaries can be extended? Why is there a decrease in brain catecholamines in aging rats and humans, and an increase in hypothalamic serotonin in aging rats? Why do the pituitaries of aging humans and rats apparently become less responsive to LHRH stimulation?

Let me emphasize that not all the retrogressive changes in the gonads and reproductive tracts of aging rats and humans are due solely to changes in the hypothalamus and pituitary. Losses in structural and functional capacity of the ovaries and testes also may have other causes, including nutritional and environmental factors, use of drugs, and various illnesses and pathological changes. Changes in the neuroendocrine system may, to some extent, be the consequence rather than the cause of aging processes. In other words, hypothalamic and pituitary function may show a decline in function similar to that of other organs, such as the heart, kidneys, and lungs, during aging. However, reinitiation of estrous cycles in old rats by direct hypothalamic stimulation or by treatment with brain-active drugs and hormones suggests that the neuroendocrine system retains a remarkable degree of plasticity in regulating reproductive functions, at least in this species. The debate continues on the advisability of administering estrogens to women in the menopausal and postmenopausal states, and of using androgens in elderly men, but the possibilities of utilizing neuroendocrine approaches to problems of the aging reproductive system in humans remain to be explored.

Work from this laboratory was supported by USPHS grants AG00416 from the National Institute on Aging; AMO4784 from the National Institute of Arthritis, Metabolism, and Digestive Diseases; and CA10771 from the National Cancer Institute; and by the Michigan Agricultural Experiment Station.

We also thank the Macmillan Co., New York, NY, for permission to use Figure 1, and *Excerpta Medica,* Amsterdam, for permission to use Figures 3 and 4.

References

1. Schiff, J., and Wilson, E., Clinical aspects of aging in the female reproductive system. In *The Aging Reproductive System,* E. L. Schneider, Ed., Raven Press, New York, NY, 1978, pp 9–28.
2. Talbert, G. B., Aging of the reproductive system. In *Handbook of the Biology of Aging,* C. E. Finch and L. Hayflick, Eds., Van Nostrand Reinhold Co., New York, NY, 1977, pp 318–356.
3. Robinson, D. S., Nies, A., Davis, J., Bunney, W. E., Davis, J. M., Colburn, R. W., Bourne, H. R., Shaw, D. M., and Coppen, A. J., Aging monoamines and monoamine oxidase levels. *Lancet* i, 290–291 (1972).
4. Meites, J., Simpkins, J., Bruni, J., and Advis, J., Role of biogenic amines in control of anterior pituitary hormones. *IRCS J. Med. Sci.* 5, 1–7 (1977).
5. Kruse-Larson, C., and Garde, K., Postmenopausal bleeding: Another side effect of L-DOPA. *Lancet* i, 707–708 (1971).
6. Dilman, V. M., Age associated elevation of hypothalamic threshold to feedback control, and its role in development, aging and disease. *Lancet* i, 1211–1219 (1971).
7. Meites, J., Huang, H. H., and Simpkins, J. W., Recent studies on neuroendocrine control of reproductive senescence in rats. In *The Aging Reproductive System* (see ref. *1*), pp 213–236.
8. Meites, J., Huang, H. H., and Reigle, G. D., Relation of the hypothal-

94

amo–pituitary–gonadal system to decline of reproductive functions in aging female rats. In *Hypothalamus and Endocrine Functions*, F. Labrie, J. Meites, and G. Pelletier, Eds., Plenum Publishing Co., New York, NY, 1976, pp 3–20.

9. Huang, H. H., Steger, R. W., Bruni, J. F., and Meites, J., Patterns of sex steroid and gonadotropin secretion in aging female rats. *Endocrinology* **103**, 1855–1859 (1978).

10. Simpkins, J. W., Mueller, G. P., Huang, H. H., and Meites, J., Evidence for depressed catecholamine and enhanced serotonin metabolism in aging male rats: Possible relation to gonadotropin secretion. *Endocrinology* **100**, 1672–1678 (1977).

11. Peng, M. T., and Huang, H. H., Aging of hypothalamic–pituitary–ovarian function in the rat. *Fertil. Steril.* **23**, 535–542 (1972).

12. Harman, S. M., Clinical aspects of aging of the male reproductive system. In *The Aging Reproductive System* (see ref. *1*), pp 29–58.

13. Albeaux-Fernet, M., Bohler, C. S. S., and Karpes, A. E., Testicular function in the aging male. In *Geriatric Endocrinology*, R. B. Greenblatt, Ed., Raven Press, New York, NY, 1978, pp 201–216.

14. Vekemans, M., and Robyn, C., Influence of age on serum prolactin levels in women and men. *Br. Med. J.* **iv**, 738–739 (1975).

15. Farnsworth, W. E., Prolactin and the prostate. In *Prolactin and Carcinogenesis*, A. R. Boyns and K. Griffiths, Eds., Alpha Omega Alpha Publishing, Cardiff, U.K., 1972, pp 217–228.

16. Steger, R. W., Peluso, J. J., Bruni, J. F., Hafez, E. S. E., and Meites, J., Gonadotropin binding and testicular function in old rats. *Endokrinologie* **83**, 1–5 (1979).

17. Riegle, G. D., and Miller, A. E., Aging effects on the hypothalamic–hypophyseal–gonadal control system in the rat. In *The Aging Reproductive System* (see ref. *1*), pp 159–192.

18. Riegle, G. D., Meites, J., Miller, A. E., and Wood, S. M., Effect of aging on hypothalamic LH-releasing and prolactin-inhibiting activity and pituitary responsiveness to LHRH in the male laboratory rat. *J. Gerontol.* **32**, 13–18 (1977).

19. Bruni, J. F., Huang, H. H., Marshall, S., and Meites, J., Effect of single and multiple injections of synthetic GnRH on serum LH, FSH and testosterone in young and old male rats. *Biol. Reprod.* **17**, 309–312 (1977).

20. Shaar, C. J., Euker, J. S., Riegle, G. D., and Meites, J., Effects of castration and gonadal steroids on serum LH and prolactin in old and young rats. *J. Endocrinol.* **66**, 45–51 (1975).

21. Riegle, G. D., and Meites, J., Effects of aging on LH and prolactin after LHRH, L-DOPA, methyldopa and stress in male rats. *Proc. Soc. Exp. Biol. Med.* **151**, 507–511 (1976).

22. Timiras, P. S., *Developmental Physiology and Aging*, Macmillan Co., New York, NY, 1972, p 531.
23. Baker, H. W. G., Burger, H. G., deKrester, D. M., and Hudson, B., Endocrinology of aging: Pituitary testicular axis. *Clin. Endocrinol.* **5**, 349–372 (1976).

Discussion—Session I

DR. LEVINE: Dr. Strehler, you mentioned ribosomal RNA, especially in the heart and the brain, and then you mentioned the fact that the cells fill with lipofuscin to such an extent that RNA may be lost; can these two observations be correlated?

DR. STREHLER: Yes. It is very astute to note that when you see a correlation, you can not tell what is causal. There is a very nice study by Mann and Yates (*Brain* **97**: 481–488, 1974) in which they did in fact measure the amount of cytoplasmic RNA and lipofuscin. Which is primary one cannot say, but on the basis that unprotected membranes are susceptible to auto-oxidation processes, the absence of RNA ribosomes may be primary. However, that is a question that should be answered experimentally.

DR. NATELSON: Dr. Shock, has the variance of the amount of exercise by adults had an influence on the measurements you reported?

DR. SHOCK: The answer is, of course, yes. We were trying to look at the range of values one might anticipate among a group of normal subjects. The issue involved is the extent to which exercise and activity contribute to this variance among individuals of the same chronological age. They do contribute. As we are able to identify more and more of these factors that contribute to the total variance, we will be in a better position to identify the characteristics of individuals.

DR. GRANNIS: Dr. Shock, what do you anticipate will be future changes in the shape of the mortality curve in the United States? Will it go higher and higher, showing a tighter and tighter distribution of deaths at age 80 or 85, or will the curve begin to extend beyond 100 years?

DR. SHOCK: I can only comment and, really, I do not feel competent because I have not worked with survivorship curves to any great extent. But if you look at the data on humans for

97

the United States, in particular, you find that the average age of death for men has not increased much since 1960. In contrast, the average age for death in women has continued to rise at almost the same rate as before 1960. The difference between the average age of death for men and women has increased from about two years in 1900 to about eight years in 1979. There is no question that women in general live longer than men. This is also true for most mammals, so I think we have to look for some biological mechanisms to explain that sex difference in mortality. I think that the distribution of the average age of death will become more symmetrical, particularly for women, and the average age of death will continue to increase but at a slower rate. You will note that the curve for men is already skewed and this will probably continue. I don't think it is going to change a great deal. This is, obviously, the basis of concern of many in regard to the social problems being generated by changes in mortality patterns: the number of very old women will greatly exceed the number of old men.

DR. GRANNIS: Dr. Timiras mentioned experiments with rats where they appeared to be quite young and healthy until a late age and then declined rapidly. Dr. Strehler, can we expect mortality curves to become more rectangular or can we expect them to move to the right? How does this relate to the theories of aging?

DR. STREHLER: With respect to whether the curve is going to become more sharply focussed or whether the maximum is going to move to the right, which would be tantamount to slowing down the aging process, it is too early to say. I think that when we understand the essence of the process in greater detail we will be in a better position to make appropriate predictions.

Dr. Felicio, I would like to know whether in those cases where the Aschheim experiments were repeated and you obtained a high rate of cycling, a high efficiency of cycling, was the time between cycles decreased? One of the things you described early in your talk was an increase in the time between cycles at the onset of reproductive decline. When you transplanted young ovaries into older, previously ovariectomized animals, did they cycle more rapidly?

DR. FELICIO: Yes, they showed five to six cycles per month. Also, in contrast to the minimal response of the short-term ovariectomized old mice, the long-term ovariectomized animals showed a very marked response of the external genitalia to the young transplanted ovaries.

Dr. Nelson: Probably a more complete answer to that question will emerge when the hormone concentrations are measured. Then we will be able to determine if these subtle changes in the pattern of estrogen secretion that mark the onset of reproductive aging in this strain of mouse are reversed by this treatment.

Dr. Levine: I would like to first of all thank Dr. Meites for this very clear exposition of the similarities and the differences between rats and man. I ask him one serious question and one perhaps facetious one. The serious question is, what maintains estrous during this prolonged estrous period? What hormonal situation maintains it that the rats do not immediately go into anestrous?

Dr. Meites: As you may have seen, the serum concentration of follicle-stimulating hormone (FSH; follitropin) in these constant-estrous rats is rather high. It is higher than in any of the other categories of old rats. However, although FSH stimulates and maintains follicular development, it does not exhibit any cyclic surge; hence, there is no ovulation. In other words, the fault lies in the hypothalamus.

Dr. Levine: That does not hold for the human female because the ovary lies down on the job, is that it?

Dr. Meites: The ovary lies down on the job, that is correct.

Dr. Levine: Now the facetious one. I was stimulated by your statement linking the length of reproductive activity to the length of life. Do I interpret that correctly? In mammals?

Dr. Meites: Yes. This is in an article by Dr. G. B. Talbert (*Am. J. Obstet. Gynecol.* **102:** 451, 1968) and pertains to some submammalian species.

Dr. Levine: I am anxious to know whether this applies to individuals.

Dr. Meites: Certainly not to humans; but apparently this is the situation in many lower species.

Dr. Strehler: The answer is sort of obvious: if you are not alive, you cannot reproduce; but to be serious, Dr. Meites, do you have any idea whether the decreased release of testosterone by the old testes when stimulated with FSH is a decreased response per cell or a decreased number of cells or a combination of the two? I recall that Sertoli and Leydig cells become quite packed, for example, with lipofuscin granules in very old or perhaps moderately old individuals. Do you have any idea of whether this is a decrease in the number of live cells?

DR. MEITES: I am not sure there is a full answer to your question, but there is fairly good evidence, based on the aging testes in the human and in the rat, that there is a decrease in the number of Leydig cells. Whether there is a diminished capacity of the Leydig cells that remain to respond to gonadotropin remains to be answered. However, recent preliminary work suggests a decreased response per Leydig cell to choriogonadotropin (hCG) hormone stimulation under in vitro conditions (Varma et al., in *Endocrine Aspects of Aging*, S. E. Korenman, Ed., Sepulveda, CA, Oct. 1979).

DR. ADELMAN: Dr. Meites, I am under the impression that the nature of the testosterone data in aging humans is somewhat controversial in light of the fact that it was derived from male populations that were maintained in isolation, and that some of the decreases seen in these populations are not seen when the men are exposed to women. Considering a degree of sexual promiscuity of your experimental animals, would you comment on this?

DR. MEITES: It is certainly an interesting question to raise. As you are well aware, there are studies indicating an effect of female presence on stimulation of testosterone secretion. Apparently, behavioral stimuli can influence testosterone production in rats, but I do not know of any definite studies that have been done along this line in humans.

DR. SHOCK: Dr. Harman has assayed free and bound amounts of testosterone in the plasma of several hundred participants in the Baltimore Longitudinal Study and has no evidence of any change in the amounts in blood, even in our 80- and 90-year-old subjects (Harman, S. M., Martin, C. E., and Tsitouras, P. D., abstract no. 132 in *Abstracts of the 61st Annual Meeting of the Endocrine Society, Anaheim, CA, June 1979*, p 105). This, again, is a reflection of the nature of the population since we limited the study to active people who are still living in the community.

DR. NELSON: With the C57BL/6J mouse as an animal model for male reproductive aging, one of the early studies we did looking for age-related hormone changes was to measure plasma testosterone in older mice. We were unable to identify any decrement in testosterone unless the animals showed gross pathology. This is another factor that needs to be taken into consideration in addition to the sexual behavior of the male—the pathological status of the individuals being studied.

DR. NINO (Fullerton, CA): Dr. Timiras, your animals on low tryptophan diets showed decreased weight gains and neurological syndromes. Could this result from niacin deficiency?

DR. TIMIRAS: The tryptophan-deficient animals had some neurologic symptoms, but as far as the vitamins were concerned, we compounded the diets in collaboration with our nutritional sciences department and were assured that no other deficiencies were possible. There was a supplementation with vitamins, as the animals, generally, do not like their diet and eat less. There was no possibility of a niacin deficiency. The reduction in the tryptophan content had originally been to about 20% of the optimum; recently we have decreased the severity of the neurological symptoms by using a diet with 35 to 40% of the normal amount of tryptophan.

DR. NINO: Dr. Felicio, did you notice the development of mammary tumors in the older animals?

DR. FELICIO: No, the C57BL/6J female mouse does not develop mammary tumors.

DR. TIMIRAS: As I was thinking about the question on niacin, I can, perhaps, answer another way by saying that the animals that were not fed the tryptophan-deficient diets but given *p*-chlorophenylalanine (PCPA), which inhibits serotonin synthesis, showed effects similar to those from tryptophan deficiency. Thus, the effect we observed is more likely to be attributed to the tryptophan deficiency itself than to any possible vitamin deficiency.

DR. RATNER (Montreal, Canada): I would like Dr. Timiras to elaborate on the use of L-DOPA in prolongation of life in her rats, or in humans.

DR. TIMIRAS: We have not done work using L-DOPA, but there are several publications in addition to the work from Dr. Meites's laboratory. Cotzias demonstrated that high doses of L-DOPA administered for long periods of time to mice would prolong the life span (Cotzias, G. C., Miller, S. T., Nicholson, Jr., A. R., Matson, W. H., and Tang, L. C., *Proc. Natl. Acad. Sci.* **71**: 2466, 1974; and Cotzias, G. C., Miller, S. T., Tang, L. C., Papavasiliou, P. S., and

Wang, Y. Y., *Science* **196:** 549, 1977). There is some evidence for reestablishing the reproductive function in aging, as is the case with use of L-DOPA in Parkinson's disease.

DR. MEITES: If I may raise a question with Dr. Timiras that I wanted to ask after she finished her talk? The results with tryptophan are very intriguing, but I wonder whether they could not be as well explained on the basis of the general loss of appetite that a deficiency of tryptophan induces, as it is an essential amino acid. The animals that you showed lost weight, and it has been shown that reduced food intake can induce a condition called pseudohypophysectomy. In other words, are tryptophan deficiency and the effects that you attribute to it due to starvation? How can you differentiate the two?

DR. TIMIRAS: Whether tryptophan as such is responsible for the prolongation of physiologic competence in advanced age and, more importantly, whether it acts by specifically lowering the concentration of serotonin in the brain or by reducing food intake is not yet established. So far, we have conducted parallel experiments in which the animals were given a complete diet and also injected with PCPA and have observed effects similar to those of tryptophan deficiency in terms of growth retardation and alterations in the length of reproductive competence. On the other hand, reducing food intake only, i.e., giving so-called pair-fed rats the same amount of food consumed by the tryptophan-deficient animals but complete in all its constituents, induced retardation of growth as well, but both physiologic competence and brain neurochemistry were quite different. Finally, we have now in progress experiments in which decreases in tryptophan are graded in such a way as to minimize reduction in food intake and body growth and yet alter brain serotonin concentrations. Whether these animals in which we have tried to separate the neurochemical from the protein-synthesizing effects of tryptophan will also show a delayed maturation and aging remains to be determined. Clearly, the approach we have suggested requires further experimentation. Nevertheless, because of the outstanding progress in the pharmacology of neurotransmission in recent years, the possibility of devising animal models for testing the hypothesis that aging may be the consequence of synaptic deficits in specific brain areas, and that these deficits may be modified by drugs, is attractive enough to justify continuing study.

DR. STREHLER: Dr. Meites, you indicated that in the aging female rat there is continued production of follicles but they do not rupture and do not form corpus lutea. Is there anything about the anatomy that you notice; that is, are later-produced follicles deeper within the ovary? Is there more connective tissue that might interfere with easy rupture or anything else that you could point to that would act as a limiting factor in the release of the ovum and the continuation of the cycle?

DR. MEITES: I can tell you that when we administer the pituitary hormone LH (lutropin) or the hypothalamic hormone LHRH (luliberin) to these old, constant-estrous rats, with their numerous ovarian follicles and no ovulation, they do ovulate in response to these hormones. We have not determined if these follicles are less or more responsive. The cystic follicles we see in old rats definitely do not respond, and there are a fair number of them. Cystic follicles also are reported to be very numerous in women approaching menopause. We have measured LH and FSH receptors in the ovaries of the aging female rat, and they do not appear to be less numerous except in the cystic follicles. Cystic follicles show almost no LH and FSH receptors (Steger, R. W., Peluso, J. J., Huang, H., Hafez, E. S. E., and Meites, J., *J. Reprod. Fert.* **48:** 205, 1976).

II

METABOLIC CHANGES IN AGING

A description of age-related changes and of techniques used in studies of aging humans—Edward W. Bermes, Jr., Moderator

When Bismarck arbitrarily chose 65 as a retirement age 100 years ago, most workers died before attaining it.

Carbohydrate and Lipid Metabolism in the Aged

Rachmiel Levine

Aging is, of course, inevitable. It begins with fertilization and ends with death. Whatever the still-hidden molecular genetic mechanisms that set it in motion, the aging process is associated in the complex mammalian (and human) organism with a continuous decline in physiological performance, most noticeably from the time of completion of bodily growth or maturation. Figure 1 portrays the age changes in a set of various physiologic functions (1). These changes are especially striking if one measures maximum performance possible, in response to challenges. The older organism does not adapt as efficiently as it once could. Homeostatic regulation becomes gradually more sluggish and less precise.

Glucose and Insulin

An influence of age on the average concentration of fasting blood sugar has been noted and amply documented over the years, increasing by approximately 50 mg/L per decade after the age of 50. This increase is magnified considerably in the non-fasting state, such as after a meal, after a glucose challenge, or during a cortisone–glucose tolerance test. Apparently, therefore, aging brings with it a progressive diminution in the body's capacity to adjust to an acute metabolic load (2–9).

Thus, there is a gradually progressive significant diminution in glucose tolerance with age. This loss of assimilative capacity is evident in both the oral and the intravenous tests, and hence is not due to changes in the intestinal absorption of sugar (10, 11).

The principal regulator of the blood sugar concentration is, of

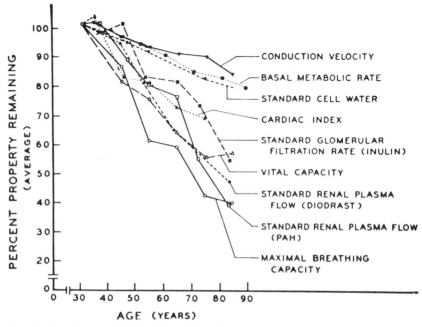

CONDUCTION VELOCITY

BASAL METABOLIC RATE

STANDARD CELL WATER

CARDIAC INDEX

STANDARD GLOMERULAR
FILTRATION RATE (INULIN)

VITAL CAPACITY

STANDARD RENAL PLASMA
FLOW (DIODRAST)

STANDARD RENAL PLASMA FLOW
(PAH)

MAXIMAL BREATHING
CAPACITY

Fig. 1. Age changes in physiologic functions, expressed as the percent change from the mean value at age 30

From Masoro et al. *(1)* and derived from the data obtained by Shock *(26)*

course, insulin. A survey of the data on the course of insulin secretion after a glucose stimulus in older subjects reveals a confusing picture. Normal *(12–14)*, delayed *(15–17)*, and even increased secretion rates have been measured *(18, 19)*. This state of affairs may well be due to the many factors (in addition to "aging" itself) that influence the secretory response, and that may co-exist in the older population groups. For example, body composition shifts in the direction of adipose tissue and away from lean-body mass (virtual obesity); and the frequent uncertainty of the nutritional state and of the dietary habits of the elderly may also influence the results,[1] as may the undetected presence of chronic degenerative disorders.

There is much more consistency in the data relating to insulin sensitivity (endogenous and exogenous). The majority of workers find a decreased effectiveness of insulin in the peripheral tissues

---

[1] See, for instance, the paper by Weir in this volume—*Ed.*

(10, 20, 21). The exact mechanism of this insulin resistance has not been ascertained. Theoretically, it could be due to a loss of insulin receptors, to changes in receptor affinity, or to the slowing of a post-receptor step in the metabolism of carbohydrates. The review by Davidson *(22)* is both thorough and thoughtful, and should be consulted by all interested in the carbohydrate–aging relationships.

If one were to apply the "normal" standards derived from a young and healthy control population to the glucose tolerance and insulin data obtained in older age groups, an uncomfortably high percentage of individuals in their sixth and seventh decades of life would be labeled "diabetic." One can get around this dilemma by setting the cutoff values higher for fasting blood sugar and the glucose tolerance test, as dictated by data derived from population surveys of the aged who do not exhibit any of the known symptoms and signs of diabetes or any indications of the specific complications of the disease such as small-vessel disease of the eyes and kidney or typical neuropathy. Nomograms have been constructed for this purpose *(8)*.

This approach is reasonable on the surface, in that it seems to distinguish between the "physiological" state of aging and a "pathological" entity, called diabetes.

However, this intellectual maneuver raises far more questions than it solves. Granted that aging is inevitably associated with a decline in the accurate regulation of function and the quick adaptation to loads, it is also evident that the rate of decline of each function depends upon a large number of genetic and environmental factors. Modern medical approaches have extended the life span for an ever-increasing percentage of the population. Not all of this "pushing back" of mortality and morbidity is related simply to the eradication of epidemics and the sharp decline in infant and child mortality. The question we confront in relation to the "worsening" of glucose tolerance with age is simply this: Are postprandial relative hyperglycemias, coupled with some insulin resistance, risk factors for the population after the sixth decade? The exact labels—"diabetes" or "abnormal glucose tolerance"—are semantic devices and do not answer this question.

In the section of the population who survive beyond their 70's, the degree of prevalence of "diabetes" and of "abnormal" tolerance appears to decline *(19)*, as if the survivors have aged "more normally"; i.e., the rate of physiological decline was slowed.

We have in recent years learned that the concentration of blood sugar determines the degree of glycosylation of hemoglobin and of other proteins (23) by a spontaneous, non-enzymatic reaction. If it turns out that protein glycosylation of catalytically important molecules leads to changes in their activities, this may account for the slow production of "pathological" changes, especially in the blood vessels and nerve tissues, and may well explain the evolutionary development of the very tight apparatus for blood sugar regulation, which in humans under normal conditions of food intake rarely allows the blood sugar to reach more than 1.2 g/L after a meal.

Is the decrease in glucose tolerance in the aged associated with chronic increases in their glycosylated hemoglobins (and other proteins), and could such changes over the years be injurious to blood vessels, nerves, and the lens of the eye? Under whatever label we choose to work (diabetes, disturbed glucose tolerance, age-adjusted glucose tolerance, etc.), should we endeavor to "correct" the disturbed tolerance of the aging population, perhaps by attention to nutritional factors and by muscular exercise? Can acceptable environmental intervention slow the decline in regulatory function, and would this reduce morbidity? These appear to be legitimate concerns, and they will require much careful experimental work and clinical observation before one can decide on the propriety and possible efficacy of therapeutic intervention.

Lipids and Lipoproteins

The available data in relation to lipids and lipoproteins in the aging population lead to very similar conclusions and considerations. Plasma cholesterol values increase with age from 20 to 65 years and then plateau or fall. Triglyceride values follow an almost identical curve, as does the cholesterol associated with the low-density lipoprotein (LDL) fraction. The concentration of high-density lipoprotein (HDL) cholesterol increases slowly and plateaus after age 65 (24, 25).

Again, as in the case of carbohydrate metabolism, the picture presented by aging is almost identical to that shown by a truly "diabetic" population of the adult-onset type. In a recent paper from Glueck's group in Cincinnati (25), 137 octo- and nonagenarians were studied and the following results reported: In the eighth and ninth decades of life there is a decrease in LDL cholesterol, no change in HDL-cholesterol, and a slight decrease in triglycerides and in the cholesterol associated with the very-low-density fraction (VLDL).

Two alternative explanations are possible for the "improvement" of the lipid values in the 70- to 90-year age range. It may be that (a) the individuals with higher cholesterol and LDL values had already succumbed to coronary disease, or that (b) the octo- and nonagenarians are from families with genetically lower LDL and higher HDL values.

The question arises, would a concerted attempt at influencing cholesterol and lipoprotein values from age 60 on improve longevity and favorably affect the mortality and morbidity of the aging population?

In experimental animals (especially rodents) chronic, prolonged reduction of the caloric intake extends the life span very significantly, and decreases the severity of pathological states usually associated with age. Although such procedures may not be directly applicable to humans, these studies show that the degree of "aging" changes can be influenced by environmental factors. It therefore seems possible that research directed at the bodily mechanisms responsible for the decrease with age of particular physiological functions may point the way to correction and slowing of the functional declines, with a consequent hoped-for decrease in morbidity.

The goal of geriatric medicine is not the mere chronological extension of age. The aim is the best possible maintenance of physiological parameters during the final years of life, especially the functioning of the cardio-respiratory, neurological, metabolic, and musculo-skeletal systems.

References

1. Masaro, E. J., Bertrand, H., Liepa, G., and Yu, B. P., Analysis and exploration of age-related changes in mammalian structure and function. Fed. Proc. **38**, 1956 (1979).
2. Spence, J. C., Some observations on sugar tolerance, with special reference to variations found at different ages. Q. J. Med. **14**, 314–326 (1920–21).

3. Streeten, D. H. P., Gerstein, M. M., Mamor, B. M., and Doisy, R. J., Reduced glucose tolerance in elderly human subjects. *Diabetes* **14**, 579–583 (1965).

4. Balodimos, M. C., Balodimos, P. M., and Davis, C. B., Abnormal carbohydrate tolerance and diabetes in elderly patients. *Geriatrics* **22**, 159–166 (1967).

5. Albanese, A. A., Higgons, R. A., Orto, L., Belmont, A., and DiLallo, R., Effect of age on the utilization of various carbohydrates by man. *Metabolism* **3**, 154–159 (1954).

6. Hayner, N. S., Kjelsberg, M. D., Epstein, F. H., and Francis, T., Carbohydrate tolerance and diabetes in a total community, Tecumseh, Michigan. 1. Effects of age, sex, and test conditions on one-hour glucose tolerance in adults. *Diabetes* **14**, 413–423 (1965).

7. O'Sullivan, J. B., Mahan, C. M., Freedlender, A. E., and Smith, G., Effect of age on carbohydrate metabolism. *J. Clin. Endocrinol. Metab.* **33**, 619–623 (1971).

8. Andres, R., Aging and diabetes. *Med. Clin. North Am.* **55**, 835–845 (1971).

9. O'Sullivan, J. B., Age gradient in blood glucose levels. *Diabetes* **23**, 713–715 (1974).

10. Silverstone, F. A., Brandfonbrener, M., Shock, N. W., and Yiengst, M. J., Age differences in the intravenous glucose tolerance tests and the response to insulin. *J. Clin. Invest.* **36**, 504–514 (1957).

11. Streeten, D. H. P., Gerstein, M. M., Woolfolk, D., and Doisy, R. J., Measurement of glucose disposal rates in normal and diabetic human subjects after repeated intravenous injections of glucose. *J. Clin. Endocrinol. Metab.* **24**, 761–774 (1964).

12. Palmer, J. P., and Ensinck, J. W., Acute-phase insulin secretion and glucose tolerance in young and aged normal men and diabetic patients. *J. Clin. Endocrinol. Metab.* **41**, 498–503 (1975).

13. Dudl, R. J., and Ensinck, J. W., Insulin and glucagon relationships during aging in man. *Metabolism* **26**, 33–41 (1977).

14. Feldman, J., and Plonk, J. W., Effect of age on intravenous glucose tolerance and insulin secretion. *J. Am. Geriat. Soc.* **24**, 1–3 (1976).

15. Metz, R., Surmaczynska, B., Berger, S., and Sobel, G., Glucose tolerance, plasma insulin and free fatty acids in elderly subjects. *Ann. Inter. Med.* **64**, 1042–1048 (1966).

16. Crockford, P. M., Harbeck, R. J., and Williams, R. H., Influence of age on intravenous glucose tolerance and serum immunoreactive insulin. *Lancet* **i**, 465–467 (1966).

17. Jaffe, B. I., Vinik, A. I., and Jackson, W. P. U., Insulin reserve in elderly subjects. *Lancet* **i**, 1292–1293 (1969).

18. Welborn, T. A., Stenhouse, N. S., and Johnstone, C. C., Factors

determining serum insulin response in a population sample. *Diabetologia* **5**, 263–266 (1969).

19. Smith, M. J., and Hall, M. R. P., Carbohydrate tolerance in the very aged. *Diabetologia* **9**, 387–390 (1973).
20. Himsworth, H. P., and Kerr, R. B., Age and insulin sensitivity. *Clin. Sci.* **4**, 153–157 (1939–42).
21. Dyck, D. R., and Moorhouse, J. A., A high dose intravenous glucose tolerance test. *J. Clin. Endocrinol. Metab.* **26**, 1032–1037 (1966).
22. Davidson, M. B., The effect of aging on carbohydrate metabolism. *Metabolism* **28**, 688–705 (1979).
23. Dollrofer, R., and Wieland, O. H., Glycosylation of serum albumin, *FEBS Lett.* **103**, 282 (1979).
24. Kritchevsky, D., How aging affects cholesterol metabolism. *Postgrad. Med.* **63**, 133 (1978).
25. Nicholson, J., Gartside, P. S., Siegel, M., Spencer, W., Steiner, P. M., and Glueck, C. J., Lipid and lipoprotein distributions in octo- and nonagenarians. *Metabolism* **28**, 51 (1979).
26. Shock, N. W., The science of gerontology. In *Proceedings of Seminars, 1959–61, Durham, NC, Council on Gerontology*, E. C. Jeffers, Ed., Duke University Press, Durham, NC, 1962, pp 123–140.

The Effect of Age on the Lung

William M. Thurlbeck

The best-studied aging phenomena in the human lung are the alterations in lung mechanics. This is because for many years clinical respiratory physiology was the main thrust of research in chest medicine. Surprisingly little is known about the effect of aging in animal lungs. The fundamental changes in mechanics are due to alterations in elastic properties of the lung, which in turn are related to collagen, elastin, and perhaps glycosaminoglycans of the lung. The way in which these substances are altered and the mechanisms by which this is brought about are unknown.

The key changes are an increase in the resting length of the alveolar-wall tissue and a decreased distensibility of the alveolar walls. Sugihara et al. (1) studied stress–strain relationships in strips of human alveolar wall approximately $300 \times 30 \times 30$ μm and expressed strain as an extension ratio of final length to initial length of their strips, i. e., $\lambda_{max} = L_{max}/L_o$, where λ_{max} is the extension ratio, L_{max} the maximum length of the strip, and L_o the resting length.[1] Figure 1 compares stress–strain relationships for an alveolar-wall strip of a young person and that of an old person. The maximum extensibility ratio is much less in the older person. Figure 2 shows that there is a significant decrease of λ_{max} with age ($r = -0.74$), λ_{max} being 2.04 at age 20 and 1.74 at age 70 in subjects without chronic airflow limitation. λ_{max} is further decreased in subjects with irreversible chronic airflow limitation but not in those with reversible chronic airflow limitation.

λ_{max} may be decreased either because L_{max} is decreased or L_o is increased. Sugihara et al. (1) have argued that L_o is increased

---

[1] Abbreviations used: λ_{max}, maximum extension ratio of extended (L_{max}) to resting (L_o) length of human alveolar wall: V_o, volume of the lung at rest, or V_{max}, fully expanded; V_{exp}, lung volume at infinite transpulmonary pressure.

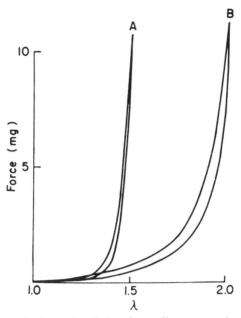

Fig. 1. λ, the extensibility ratio of alveolar-wall strips, is decreased in subject *A*, an 80-year-old man, compared with subject *B*, a 22-year-old woman

L_o, the resting length, is 280 μm for *A* and 300 μm for *B*. A_o, the resting area, is 4.4 × 10^{-6} cm² for *A* and 9.9 × 10^{-6} cm² for *B*. Courtesy of Dr. Jim Martin and the Editor-in-Chief, *Journal of Applied Physiology*

because the resting volume of the lung (V_o) is increased with age. Because morphologic studies have shown that air-space dimensions are increased with age when the lung is fully inflated (see below), Sugihara et al. also argue that absolute L_{max} is increased with age and therefore L_o is even more increased than expected. Whether maximum lung volume increases with age is not clear because of the complex interaction between lung and chest wall (see below). No data are available concerning age and the maximum lung volume of excised lungs at apparent full inflation (V_{max}) in humans, but a study in mice has indicated an increasing V_{max} with increasing age in female mice *(2)*. Thus it may be that V_{max} and L_{max} may increase with age.

For some time investigators have sought to explain many of the mechanical properties of the lung on the basis of a model of two connective-tissue networks *(3)*. One, the elastic fiber net-

115

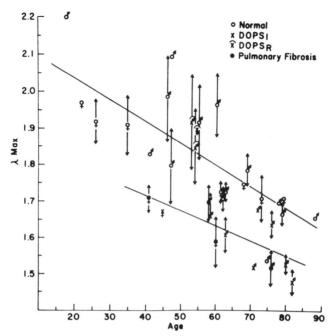

Fig. 2. $\lambda_{\max}$, the maximum extensibility ratio, is negatively related to age

$DOPS_I$ = irreversible airflow limitation; $DOPS_R$ = reversible airflow limitation. Courtesy of Dr. Jim Martin and the Editor-in-Chief, *Journal of Applied Physiology*

work, exhibits a high degree of distensibility: individual elastic fibers can be stretched to 130% of their resting lengths *(4)*. Single fibers are much less distensible than aggregates of fibers, in the same way as a nylon stocking is more distensible than a nylon thread. In addition, the elastic fibers are spirally arranged *(5)* so that the elastic net in the lung is more distensible than elastic tissue in other organs. The second connective-tissue element is the network of collagen fibers. Collagen fibers have a very high elastic modulus and can be stretched only 2% before yielding. Thus Mead *(3)* has suggested that the pressure–volume curve can be separated into two parts—at medium and low lung volumes, where the stretched elastic fibers provide the recoil force, and at high lung volumes, where the stretched collagen network provides the recoil force and limits further lung distensibility.

Several experiments have supported this hypothesis by showing that elastase (EC 3.4.21.11) alters the pressure–volume curves at medium and low lung volumes, whereas collagenase (EC 3.4.24.3) affects the lung at high lung volumes *(6–12)*. However, the relationship is probably not quite so simple: Collagen and elastin are intimately related to each other in the lung, and elastase may produce an increase in V_{max} when experiments are performed in vitro *(13, 14)*. Glycosaminoglycans may also play an important role in lung elasticity, functioning as a "glue" between the collagen and elastin network *(13)*.

Changes in Static Lung Mechanics

An increase in resting length of alveolar walls implies an alteration in the elastic-tissue network, decreasing elastic recoil at medium and low lung volumes; if maximum distensibility is also increased, this would imply a change at high lung volumes as well. The relationship between stress and strain cannot be predicted from the available data. The corresponding measurement in the whole lung is compliance, which is the change in volume per unit change in pressure, usually 1 cm H_2O. Depending on various arguments, one might or might not predict an increase in compliance at various lung volumes. We must thus look at studies of elastic properties of the lungs to see whether they are consonant with the hypothesis of an increase of resting length.

These studies suffer from a number of difficulties. Earlier studies did not exclude smokers *(15–19)*, so that many older subjects may have had emphysema. Because the most characteristic feature of emphysema is loss of elastic recoil, inclusion of such subjects would falsely imply that aging was associated with loss of recoil. Secondly, and more importantly, interaction between lung and chest wall affects interpretations of the elastic properties of the lung. For example, most observers have found a decrease in the recoil pressure of the lung at total lung capacity *(15–18, 20, 21)*. In some studies only men were studied *(17,18)*, and in others only women *(21)*; and in one study changes were apparent only in women *(20)*.

Total lung capacity is determined by the point at which the respiratory muscles can no longer generate sufficient force to fur-

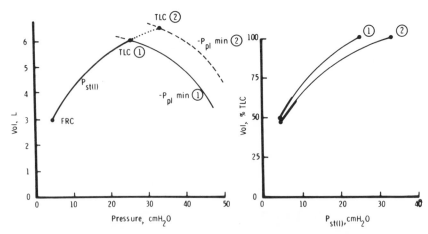

Fig. 3. Two hypothetical subjects, 1 and 2, have identical elastic pulmonary properties, but subject 2 has stronger respiratory muscles and generates a more negative intrapleural pressure and a higher total lung capacity (TLC) *(left)*; when the pressure–volume curves of the two subjects are expressed as a percentage of TLC *(right)*, subject 1 has a curve shifted upwards and to the left, a change that could be interpreted as loss of elasticity of the lung

$P_{st(l)}$ = static transpulmonary pressure, P_{pl} = pleural pressure. Courtesy of Dr. Neil Pride, and Editor-in-Chief, *Journal of Applied Physiology*

ther distend the lung. As lungs get larger, they get stiffer; and as the chest wall gets larger, the less effectively it generates inspiratory force. However, the chest wall becomes stiffer with age *(22)*. Although these observations *(22)* apply to the tidal volume range, the chest wall may be as stiff or stiffer at high lung volumes. Under these circumstances the respiratory muscles may not be able to generate a sufficiently negative intrapleural pressure to expand the lungs fully. Weakening of the respiratory muscles will have the same effect. Thus, age-related changes in the chest wall may result in a falsely low recoil pressure at total lung capacity, even if the elastic properties of the lung are unchanged. What is not so intuitively obvious is that stiffness or weakness of the chest wall may bring about apparent changes in elastic properties of the lung throughout the whole lung volume range *(21)*. This is shown in Figure 3, which portrays two hypothetical subjects with identical elastic properties of their lungs. Subject 2 has strong respiratory muscles and can generate a high negative intrapleural pressure at total lung capacity. The respiratory muscles of subject 1 are weaker and can generate a less-negative intrapleural pressure; thus his total lung capacity is smaller. When the curves are ex-

118

pressed as a percentage of total lung capacity, as is normally done to correct for differences due to stature, the shape of the curves are quite different, and subject 1 appears to have lost elastic recoil. With this method of expressing data, investigators have shown decreased recoil pressures with age in women at between 80 and 100% of total lung capacity *(20)*, in men at between 50 and 90% *(20)*, in women at between 60 and 100% *(21)*, in men at between 40 and 80% *(23)*, and in women at 80% *(23)*.

In trying to avoid the problems of lung and chest wall interaction, investigators have applied various methods to describe the pressure–volume curve mathematically *(24)*. The most popular method has been to apply an exponential fit. Above 50% of total lung capacity, the pressure–volume curve is well described by the equation $V = A - Be^{-KP}$ *(25)* where V is lung volume, A the predicted volume of the lung at infinite transpulmonary pressure (V_{exp}), K is the shape constant that reflects the rate at which the slope of the pressure–volume curve changes, and B is a constant that reflects absolute lung volume. When pressure–volume curves are expressed as percentages of V_{exp}, there are still alterations in the pressure–volume curves of old women *(21)*, indicating a true loss of recoil between 50 and 90% of V_{exp} (Figure 4). K, the shape constant, increases with age, indicating an upward shift of the pressure–volume curve; as K increases, the expression Be^{-KP} decreases and V at any pressure increases.

Another approach is to use excised lungs. In the only available comprehensive study, Niewoehner et al. *(26)* described the shape of the pressure–volume curve below a recoil pressure of 15 to 20 cm H_2O transpulmonary pressure by an empirical equation $P = \alpha_1 e^{\alpha_2 V}$. Because α_1 was very closely related to age $(r = -0.94)$, for a given volume, recoil pressure would be less with age.

Compliance is less affected by lung and chest wall interactions because it is usually measured in the tidal volume range, where the pressure–volume curve is relatively linear. As a measurement of elasticity, it suffers in that it is often expressed as an absolute value, thus portraying normal large lungs as having a greater compliance than normal small lungs. However, there have not been great differences in lung size in comparisons between young and old subjects. Some observers have found no change in compliance *(15, 17, 20, 21, 23)*, but others have noted increased compliance *(16, 19, 27)*.

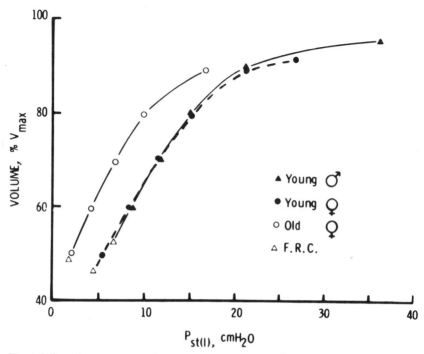

Fig. 4. When the pressure–volume curves are expressed as a percentage of volume at infinite transpulmonary pressure (V_{max}), old women have lower recoil pressure between 50 and 90% of V_{max}

$P_{st(l)}$, static transpulmonary pressure; FRC, functional residual capacity. Courtesy of Dr. Neil Pride, and Editor-in-Chief, *Journal of Applied Physiology*

Changes in Dynamics

Forced expiratory flow below 80% of vital capacity is independent of effort and depends on the force applied to the lungs, which is the recoil pressure of the lungs *(28)*. Because recoil is lost with age, flow should diminish with age, and in fact has been reported to decrease with age as assessed by the forced expiratory volume in 1 s *(29)*, forced expiratory flow at between 25 and 75% of vital capacity *(29)*, and maximum flow at 50 and 25% of vital capacity *(23)* and at 80 and 60% of total lung capacity *(23)*. Often the correlations were relatively poor; however, in two studies, changes in expiratory flow were noted only after 70% of vital capacity had been expired *(20,21)*. Because recoil pressure was lost in these subjects at higher lung volumes even though the flow remained unchanged, a lowered upstream resistance, due to an increase in dimensions of the upstream airways at large lung volumes, was indicated.

This suggests that upstream airways have lost their recoil properties (or have a greater unstressed length) at least as much as the lung parenchyma have (Figure 5). A corollary to this notion

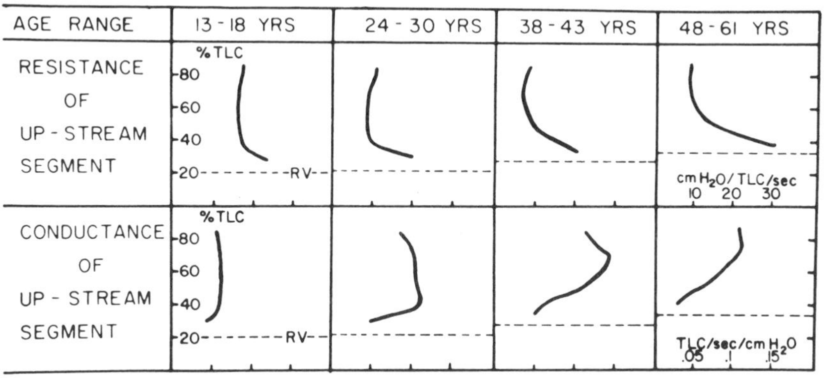

Fig. 5. The resistance is lower and the conductance is higher in older subjects at high lung volume, where elastic recoil of the lung is lost

TLC, total lung capacity. Courtesy of Dr. Jere Mead, and Editor-in-Chief of *Journal of Applied Physiology*

is that downstream events from the equal-pressure point must play an important part at low lung volumes. Exactly what happens is obscure, but it is worth noting that the trachea and bronchi become hypercompliant with age *(30)*.

Lung Volumes

As indicated, total lung capacity represents the balance between the maximum pressure that respiratory muscles can generate and the recoil pressure of the lung. Because recoil pressure is diminished with age, one might anticipate a corresponding increase in total lung capacity. Such is not the case *(15–19, 21)*, which suggests that there is stiffness or weakness of the respiratory muscles at high lung volumes.

Functional residual capacity is determined by the balance of forces between the lung (which tends to collapse inwards) and the chest wall (which tends to spring outwards). With loss of recoil, the chest wall can move further outwards, resulting in an increase in functional residual capacity. However, this might be counterbalanced by increased chest wall stiffness or weakness. Functional residual capacity has been increased in some studies *(15, 16, 18, 19)*, but not in others *(17, 21)*.

Residual volume is determined primarily by airway closure. The lumen of non-cartilaginous airways is determined by the recoil pressure applied to it. With loss of recoil, the distending pressure at any given volume will decrease and thus these airways will be smaller at the contracted volume. A higher volume will be required to generate the appropriate pressure to maintain the same airway dimensions. Thus the pressure at which airways close will require increasingly larger volumes with age, and residual volume should increase. Vital capacity, the difference between total lung capacity and residual volume, should decrease because, as described above, total lung capacity is unchanged. Residual volume generally increases and vital capacity generally decreases with age *(15, 16, 18, 19, 21)*.

Gas Mixing and Transfer

Arterial p_{O_2} gradually decreases with age, according to the regression equation $p_{aO_2} = 104.2 - 0.27$ (age in years) *(31)*. However, there is such a wide scatter that a p_{aO_2} of 75 falls within the normal range of a 70-year-old person. The decline of arterial p_{O_2} is thought to be due to changes in elastic properties in the lung. Closing capacity (the lung volume at which airways begin to close during a slow expiratory maneuver) increases with age *(27,34)*. Airways begin to close in the lower parts of the lung because recoil pressure there is less. The pleural pressure gradient is approximately 0.2 cm H_2O per cm of vertical height *(32)*; consequently, the pleural pressure is about 6 cm H_2O more negative at the apex of the lung than at the base. With loss of recoil, progressively more of the lower part of the lung closes during an expiratory maneuver, until closing capacity exceeds functional residual capacity. At this stage, parts of the lung are not ventilated during normal, quiet breathing. Another test of gas mixing is the single-breath nitrogen test. The slope of phase III of the nitrogen washout increased with age in one study *(27)*, indicating poorer gas mixing, but was unchanged in another study (34). One of the most characteristic features of age is the loss of diffusing capacity (transfer factor). Because this is true of both steady-state diffusing capacity and the single-breath diffusing capacity (33), this likely represents a loss of capillary area with age, probably because of a loss of capillary bed.

Structural Changes with Age

Predictable changes occur in the lung with age, e.g., changes in shape (35). Up to the age of 59 years there is an increase in antero-posterior diameter and height of the lung, the antero-posterior diameter increasing more than height; after age 59 only the antero-posterior diameter increases. Thus the lateral aspect of the lung "rounds," a process that accelerates at age 60. On gross examination of the lung, a change with age is readily apparent, and it is often quite easy to assess the age of the patient from the appearance of the lung (Figure 6). The "core" of air internal to alveoli increases with age, whereas the relative proportion of air in alveoli decreases (Figure 7) (36–38). This change in internal geometry of the lung results in an increase in the average interalveolar wall distance (26, 39–41) and a loss of surface area (Figure 8). The precise age at which this change commences is uncertain, but is probably in the third decade.

A further change is loss of alveolar wall tissue (Figure 9), which also likely starts in the third decade (38). The loss of alveolar wall tissue probably in part represents a loss of capillary bed. Holes in the wall between adjacent alveoli are well recognized and are generally thought to be normal structures, the pores of Kohn. Starting at the age of 20 years, the size and number of these structures progressively increase (42).

A subjective description of the elastic tissue in humans suggested that elastic fibers became thinner and fewer with age (5), but a more recent, quantitative study of human lungs could not confirm this observation (26). In mice, total length of elastic fibers did not change with age, but the chemically measured amount of elastin did; this suggested that either the fibers were thinned or some fibers were lost and the remainder stretched (2). Examination with an electron microscope indicated that no alterations with age were apparent in collagen and elastin in humans (44).

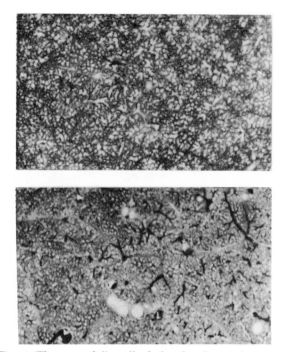

Fig. 6. The central "core" of alveolar duct is larger in an 85-year-old woman *(above)* than in a 45-year-old woman *(below)*

Source: ref. *38,* courtesy of W. B. Saunders Co.

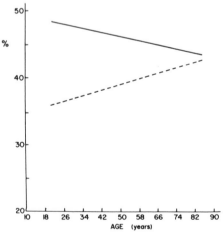

Fig. 7. The volume proportion of alveolar air (—) decreases and the volume proportion of alveolar duct and respiratory bronchiolar air (- - -) increases with age ($r = 0.4295$ and 0.4621, respectively)

y-axis, percentage of the volume of the lung. Source: ref. *38,* courtesy of W. B. Saunders Co.

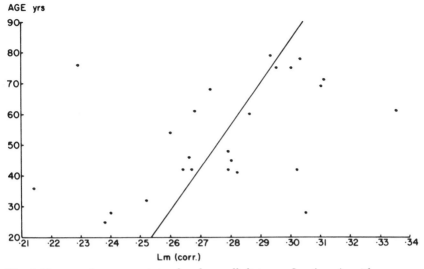

Fig. 8. Decrease in average interalveolar-wall distance, Lm (corr.), with age

Because surface area is reciprocally related to Lm (corr.), there is a loss of surface area
with age. Source: ref. *38*, courtesy of W. B. Saunders Co.

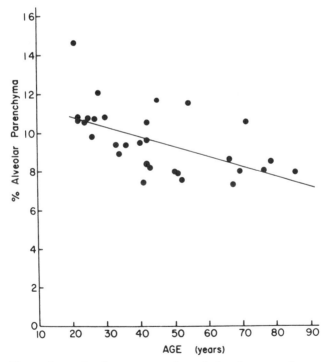

Fig. 9. Loss of volume proportion of alveolar parenchyma
with age ($r = 0.5809$)

Source: ref. *38*, courtesy of W. B. Saunders Co.

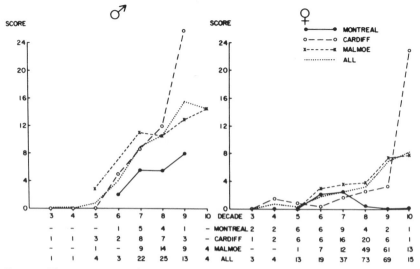

Fig. 10. The average emphysema score increases with age in nonsmoking men and women, and there is more emphysema in men

Numbers shown below the graph are the number of subjects. Source: ref. *38,* courtesy of W. B. Saunders Co.

Emphysema increases in frequency with age (Figure 10), even in nonsmokers *(45).* It is not clear whether this represents a normal part of the aging process or a response to abnormal environmental agents to which certain individuals have been exposed.

Alterations in Collagen, Elastin, and Proteoglycans with Age

Only scanty data on these components are available. The rate of collagen synthesis in the lung parenchyma decreases exponentially with age. In rabbits, by the time of weaning, adult rates have been reached (Figure 11); collagen thus accumulates rapidly in early life but appears to remain stable during adult life *(46).* In mice, collagen diminished with age in old females *(2).*

The effect of age on the elastin content of the human lung has been more frequently studied, but the techniques used are open to criticism *(47).* The total amount of elastin in the lung appears to increase with age *(48, 49),* but this is due to an increase in elastic tissue of the bronchi, blood vessels, septa, and pleura; the amount in the lung parenchyma remains the same *(50).* In

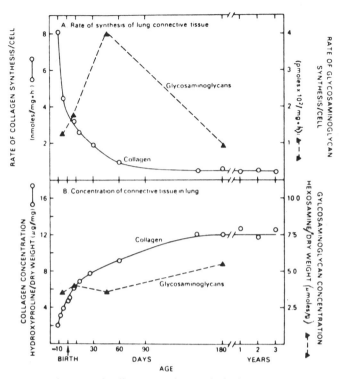

Fig. 11. The rate of collagen synthesis (A) declines exponentially and the amount of collagen in the lung (B) increases exponentially with age in rabbits

Courtesy of Dr. Ron Crystal, and the Editor-in-Chief of *American Review of Respiratory Disease*

old female mice the amount of elastic tissue decreases in the parenchyma with age (2).

Alterations in the Biochemical Functions of the Lung

Besides the exocrine secretion of surfactant into the alveolar spaces, the lung harbors a host of biochemical activities, including metabolism of vasoactive peptides and amines (51, 52). One might anticipate age-related phenomena, but it is unlikely that these would be of major biological significance because considerable shunting can occur in the lung without serious biochemical sequelae.

Supported by Medical Research Council of Canada Grant MA-6179.

References

1. Sugihara, T., Martin, C. J., and Hildebrandt, J., Length–tension properties of alveolar wall in man. *J. Appl. Physiol.* **30**, 874–878 (1971).
2. Ranga, V., Kleinerman, J., Ip, M. P. C., and Sorensen, J., Age-related changes in elastic fibers and elastin of lung. *Am. Rev. Resp. Dis.* **119**, 369–381 (1979).
3. Mead, J., Mechanical properties of lungs. *Physiol. Rev.* **41**, 281–330 (1961).
4. Carton, R. W., Dainauskas, J., and Clark, J. W., Elastic properties of single elastic fibers. *J. Appl. Physiol.* **17**, 547–551 (1962).
5. Wright, R. R., Elastic tissue of normal and emphysematous lungs—tridimensional histologic study. *Am. J. Pathol.* **39**, 355–367 (1961).
6. Johanson, W. G., Jr., and Pierce, A. K., Effects of elastase, collagenase, and papain on structure and function of rat lungs in vitro. *J. Clin. Invest.* **51**, 288–293 (1972).
7. Senior, R. M., Bielefeld, D. R., and Abensohn, M. K., The effects of proteolytic enzymes on the tensile strength of human lung. *Am. Rev. Resp. Dis.* **111**, 184–188 (1975).
8. Martin, C. J., and Sugihara, T., Stimulation of tissue properties of irreversible diffuse obstructive pulmonary syndrome: Enzyme digestion. *J. Clin. Invest.* **52**, 1918–1924 (1973).
9. Turino, G. M., Lourenco, R. V., and McCracken, G. H., Role of connective tissue in large pulmonary airways. *J. Appl. Physiol.* **25**, 645–653 (1968).
10. Hoffman, L., Mondshine, R. B., and Park, S. S., Effect of DL-penicillamine on elastic properties of rat lung. *J. Appl. Physiol.* **30**, 508–511 (1971).
11. Stanley, N. N., Alper, R., Cunningham, E. L., Cherniack, N. S., and Kefalides, N. A., Effect of a molecular change in collagen on lung structure and mechanical function. *J. Clin. Invest.* **55**, 1195–1201 (1975).
12. Fish, D. E., and Kuhn, C., Emphysema associated with defective cross linking of collagen and elastin in the blotchy mouse. *Am. Rev. Resp. Dis.* **111**, 918 (1975). Abstract.
13. Karlinsky, J. B., Snider, G. L., Franzblau, C., Stone, P. J., and Hoppin, F. G., Jr., *In vitro* effects of elastase and collagenase on mechanical properties of hamster lungs. *Am. Rev. Resp. Dis.* **113**, 769–777 (1976).
14. Polzin, J. K., Napier, J. S., Taylor, J. C., and Rodarte, J. R., Effect of elastase and ventilation on elastic recoil of excised dogs lungs. *Am. Rev. Resp. Dis.* **119**, 377–381 (1979).
15. Frank, N. R., Mead, J., and Ferris, B. J., Jr., The mechanical behaviour

of the lungs in healthy elderly persons. *J. Clin. Invest.* **36**, 1680–1687 (1957).

16. Turner, J. M., Mead, J., and Wohl, M. E., Elasticity of human lungs in relation to age. *J. Appl. Physiol.* **25**, 664–671 (1968).

17. Permutt, S., and Martin, H. B., Static pressure–volume characteristics of lungs in normal males. *J. Appl. Physiol.* **15**, 819–825 (1960).

18. Cohn, J. E., and Donoso, H. D., Mechanical properties of lung in normal men over 60 years old. *J. Clin. Invest.* **42**, 1406–1410 (1963).

19. Pierce, J. A., and Ebert, R. V., The elastic properties of the lungs in the aged. *J. Lab. Clin. Med.* **51**, 63–71 (1958).

20. Knudson, R. J., Clark, D. F., Kennedy, T. C., and Knudson, D. E., The effect of aging alone on mechanical properties of the normal adult lung. *J. Appl. Physiol.* **43**, 1054–1062 (1977).

21. Gibson, G. J., Pride, N. B., O'Cain, C., and Quagliato, R., Sex and age differences in pulmonary mechanics in normal non-smoking subjects. *J. Appl. Physiol.* **41**, 20–25 (1976).

22. Mittman, C., Edelman, N. H., Norris, A. H., and Shock, N. W., Relationship between chest wall and pulmonary compliance and age. *J. Appl. Physiol.* **20**, 1211–1216 (1965).

23. Bode, F. R., Dozman, J., Martin, R. R., Ghezzoh, H., and Macklem, P. T., Age and sex differences in lung elasticity, and in closing capacities in non-smokers. *J. Appl. Physiol.* **41**, 129–135 (1976).

24. Murphy, B. G., and Engel, L. A., Models of the pressure–volume relationship of the human lung. *Resp. Physiol.* **32**, 183–194 (1978).

25. Colebatch, H. J. H., Ng, C. K. Y., and Nikov, N., Use of an exponential function for elastic recoil. *J. Appl. Physiol.* **46**, 387–393 (1979).

26. Niewoehner, D. E., Kleinerman, J., and Liotta, L., Elastic behaviour of post-mortem human lungs: Effects of aging in mild emphysema. *J. Appl. Physiol.* **36**, 943–949 (1975).

27. Begin, R., Renzetti, A. D., Bigler, A. H., and Watanabe, S., Flow and age dependence of airway closure and dynamic compliance. *J. Appl. Physiol.* **38**, 199–207 (1975).

28. Mead, J., Turner, J. M., Macklem, P. T., and Little, J. B., Significance of the relationship between lung recoil and maximum expiratory flow. *J. Appl. Physiol.* **22**, 95–108 (1967).

29. Morris, J. F., Koski, A., and Johnson, L. C., Spirometric standards for healthy nonsmoking adults. *Am. Rev. Resp. Dis.* **103**, 57–67 (1971).

30. Croteau, J. R., and Cook, C. D., Volume–pressure and length–tension measurements in human tracheal and bronchial segments. *J. Appl. Physiol.* **16**, 170–172 (1961).

31. Mellemgaard, K., The alveolar-arterial oxygen difference: Its size and components in normal man. *Acta Physiol. Scand.* **67**, 10–20 (1966).

32. Agostoni, E., Mechanics of the pleural space. *Physiol. Rev.* **52,** 57–128 (1972).
33. Bates, D. V., Macklem, P. T., and Christie, R. V., *Respiratory Function in Disease. An Introduction to the Integrated Study of the Lung.* W. B. Saunders Co., Philadelphia/London/Toronto, 1971.
34. Buist, A. S., Ghezzo, H., Anthonisen, N. R., Cherniack, R. M., Ducic, S., Macklem, P. T., Manfrieda, J., Martin, R. R., McCarthy, D., and Ross, B. B., Relationship between the single-breath N_2 test and age, and smoking habit in three North American cities. *Am. Rev. Resp. Dis.* **120,** 305–318 (1979).
35. Anderson, W. F., Anderson, A. E., Jr., Hernandez, J. A., and Foraker, A. G., Topography of aging and emphysematous lungs. *Am. Rev. Resp. Dis.* **90,** 411–423 (1964).
36. Weibel, E. R., *Morphometry of the Human Lung.* Springer-Verlag, Berlin, 1963.
37. Ryan, S. F., Vincent, T. N., Mitchell, R. S., Filey, G. F., and Dart, G., Ductectasia: An asymptomatic pulmonary change related to age. *Med. Thorac.* **22,** 181–187 (1965).
38. Thurlbeck, W. M., *Chronic Airflow Obstruction in Lung Disease.* W. B. Saunders Co., Philadelphia/London/Toronto, 1976.
39. Thurlbeck, W. M., The internal surface area of non-emphysematous lungs. *Am. Rev. Resp. Dis.* **95,** 765–776 (1967).
40. Butler, C., Lung surface area in various morphologic forms of human emphysema. *Am. Rev. Resp. Dis.* **114,** 347–352 (1976).
41. Hasleton, P. S., The internal surface area of the adult human lung. *J. Anat.* **112,** 391–400 (1972).
42. Pump, K. K., Emphysema and its relation to age. *Am. Rev. Resp. Dis.* **114,** 5–13 (1976).
43. Niewoehner, D. E., and Kleinerman, J., Morphometric study of elastic fibers in normal and emphysematous lungs. *Am. Rev. Resp. Dis.* **115,** 15–21 (1977).
44. Adamson, J. S., An electron microscopic comparison of the connective tissue from the lungs of young and elderly subjects. *Am. Rev. Resp. Dis.* **98,** 399–406 (1968).
45. Thurlbeck, W. M., Ryder, R. C., and Sternby, N., A comparative study of the severity of emphysema in necropsy populations in three different countries. *Am. Rev. Resp. Dis.* **109,** 239–248 (1974).
46. Bradley, K. H., McConnell, S. D., and Crystal, R. G., Lung collagen composition in synthesis: Characterization and changes with age. *J. Biol. Chem.* **249,** 2674–2683 (1974).
47. Hance, A. J., and Crystal, R. G., The connective tissue of the lung. *Am. Rev. Resp. Dis.* **112,** 657–711 (1975).

48. Pierce, J. A., and Hocott, J. B., Studies on the collagen and elastin content of the human lung. *J. Clin. Invest.* **39,** 8–14 (1970).

49. Johnson, R., and Andrews, F. A., Lung scleroproteins in age and emphysema. *Chest* **57,** 239 (1970).

50. Pierce, J. A., and Ebert, R. V., Fibrous network of the lung and its change with age. *Thorax* **20,** 469–476 (1965).

51. Kuhn, C., III, Ultrastructure and cellular function in the distal lung. In *The Lung. Structure, Function and Disease,* W. M. Thurlbeck and M. R. Abell, Eds., Williams and Wilkins Co., Baltimore, MD, 1978.

52. Bakhle, Y. S., and Vane, J. R., Eds., *Metabolic Functions of the Lung,* **4,** Marcel Dekker, Inc., New York, Basel, 1978.

Regulation of the Availability and Effectiveness of Hormones during Aging[1]

Richard C. Adelman

One feature that probably characterizes all aging populations is the progressive loss of adaptability to challenges of the surrounding environment. This feature may be expressed in numerous ways, including changes in neurological reaction, immunological response, and regulation of intermediary metabolism. The major interest of my laboratory is to focus on one example of the altered ability to adapt—to study its cellular origin, to understand the phenomenon in biochemical terms, and to pursue the reasons why and how such features of aging populations are expressed.

I will present highlights of some of our experiments on changes in the capability for enzyme adaptation, focusing on changes in liver enzymes. These changes are not intrinsic to liver but instead reflect disturbances in the availability and effectiveness of several circulating hormones. In particular, my focus will be insulin. As I will show, we are close to identifying the specific cell populations in which the initial biochemical modifications of aging cell populations are expressed.

The ability to initiate adaptive increases in the activities of more than 60 enzymes is known to be impaired in a variety of tissues from several different species and in response to a broad spectrum of environmental challenges. Some enzyme adaptations are altered in the time course of response, some in magnitude, and some in both ways; and some are not altered at all. These age-dependent adaptabilities are subject to differences in sex, strain, species, and conditions of environmental maintenance of the animal model. (This speaks to a crucial issue of gerontological research—the need for rigorous definition of the environmental

---

[1] Abstracted from a recording of the presentation.

conditions for maintaining colonies of animals into old age. For our work, Sprague–Dawley rats are maintained throughout their life in a specific pathogen-free environment on a diet of constant composition and component source.)

After the intragastric injection of an aqueous solution of glucose into two-month-old rats that have been fasted for three days, the activity of hepatic glucokinase (EC 2.7.1.2) increases with time. When 24-month-old rats are used in this experiment, they require more time to adapt to the same degree. The time elapsed between the application of the stimulus (glucose) and the increase in glucokinase activity lengthens progressively and is proportional to the chronological age, between two and at least 24 months. This has been demonstrated for a large number of enzymes and biochemical adaptations. We conclude that these changes are not intrinsic to the hepatocyte, on the basis of the following results:

1. The capability for hormone-stimulated adaptivity is not impaired by aging. In experiments where glucokinase is measured after insulin injection into two- and 24-month-old rats, both the time course and the magnitude of the response are identical. Similarly, both the time course and the magnitude of the increase of hepatic tyrosine aminotransferase (EC 2.6.1.5) are identical after the injection of corticosterone into two-, 12-, and 24-month-old rats.

2. The binding of insulin to its receptors on hepatic plasma membranes, or of adrenal glucocorticoids to their receptors in cytosol, shows no difference, in rats older than 12 months, in the molar dissociation constant or in binding capacity.

3. In experiments where hepatocytes are isolated from livers of two- to 24-month-old rats and incubated with hydrocortisone, the activities of tyrosine aminotransferase as a function of time after incubation with the hormone are identical in terms of time course and response.

Thus, there is no impairment at the level of hepatic response, and changes in the regulation of hepatic enzyme activity probably involve regulatory activities of extrahepatic mechanisms. The availability and effectiveness of key circulating hormones are important in liver enzyme adaptation. To clarify the complexities of the interplay of circulating hormones and liver enzymes, I will focus on the regulation of hepatic glucokinase by insulin.

Insulin is an absolute requirement for the liver cell to express itself fully in terms of glucose-stimulated synthesis of glucokinase. Other hormones required include adrenal glucocorticoids and thyroid hormones. In adrenalectomized or thyroidectomized rats, glucose does not stimulate the adaptation of hepatic glucokinase, even in the presence of insulin; replacement of the hormone will restore the response in these rats. Certain hormones will negate the response; i.e., sufficient quantities of glucagon or catecholamines will totally prevent the glucose-stimulated synthesis of glucokinase.

To study the effect of age on the adaptive regulation of hormones, we used the same experimental conditions as for our glucokinase experiments. The concentration of immunoreactive insulin in portal vein blood was monitored as a function of time after the administration of glucose to two-, 12-, and 24-month-old rats. In the two-month-old animals the response was biphasic. In the initial phase, the response in the 12- and 24-month-old rats was greater than in the two-month-olds; moreover, the response was longer in the older animals, an expression of hyperinsulinemia. The second phase began after about 30 min in the two-month-old rats, 3 to 4 h in the 12-month-old rats, and 5 to 7 h in the 24-month-old rats.

Under similar experimental conditions, we noted marked differences in immunoreactive glucagon concentrations in serum from portal vein blood. Circulating glucagon was suppressed by glucose for 2 h in two-month-old rats. There was no suppression in the 12-month-old rats, but in the 24-month-olds there was an enormous stimulation of circulating glucagon. Because glucagon is a physiological antagonist to the action of insulin in liver, the molar ratios of glucagon/insulin in the first 2 h of response become so high in the aging animals that the insulin concentrations probably are ineffective.

In the young adult rat there is an increase in the circulating amounts of corticosterone and other adrenal glucocorticoids. In each, the ability to increase the amounts circulating is diminished as a function of age.

Elderly humans and animals are characterized by a hypothyroid stage. A possible explanation in aging rats is an inactivation of pituitary thyrotropin (TSH). In separation of serum from portal blood on Sephadex G-100, immunoreactive thyrotropin is eluted at two different times. In two-month-old rats, most is isolated at the point expected for purified thyrotropin, a form with low relative molecular mass; small amounts are eluted as a species with high relative molecular mass. With serum from 24-month-old animals, the reverse is true. When tested in Swiss mice, the high-mass material acts as a potent inhibitor of thyrotropin-stimulated thyroxine production. The accumulation of this high-mass immunoreactive thyrotropin may represent an important factor in the hypothyroid state of the elderly.

The hyperinsulinemia expressed in the initial phase of glucose stimulation is associated with the appearance of an aberrant hyperplasia of the pancreatic islet population, which becomes more apparent as the rats grow older. The delayed second phase of the response can be expressed in an in vitro system. Isolated islet of Langerhans cells are perifused with buffered medium containing 0.3 to 3.0 g of glucose per liter. With islets from the two-month-old rats, fasted for three days, the secretion of insulin over a 2-h period when challenged with 3.0 g of glucose per liter is stimulated. When islet cells of 24-month-old rats are perifused with high concentrations of glucose, there is virtually no response in the early period, although a delayed response occurs, demonstrating the phenomenon shown in vivo.

This problem is not necessarily restricted to the β cells of the pancreatic islets of Langerhans. The islets are a very complicated multicellular conglomerate, of which at least two other cell types secrete polypeptide hormones capable of interacting with β cells and influencing the rate of glucose-stimulated insulin secretion. The α cells secrete glucagon, an enhancer of glucose-stimulated insulin secretion. The δ cells contain somatostatin, which under certain conditions inhibits glucose-stimulated insulin secretion. Thus even this in vitro system is very complicated. The limiting factor appears to be the production of somatostatin by the δ cells. In preliminary experiments, when islet cells are incubated in vitro with specific antibodies to somatostatin, the islets from 24-month-old animals show a completely restored response, possibly better than those from the younger animals.

A complicated problem of the effects of aging on whole-animal biology can therefore be reduced to the level of cell biology. For example, one feature of all aging populations is the progressively modified ability to adapt to changes in the surrounding environment. An example of this is the changes in the capability for hepatic enzyme adaptation. These changes probably do not originate within the hepatocyte, but are reflections of disturbances in the availability and effectiveness of circulating hormone molecules such as insulin and glucagon.

For insulin, a major problem has to do with the capability of the β cells of the islets of Langerhans to secrete insulin in response to glucose. However, it is clear that this is a complex problem related to cell-to-cell communication and to the ability of somatostatin and glucagon, at least, to influence the pattern of glucose-stimulated insulin secretion. If the results of these experiments are correct, we have isolated a cell population in which we may seek one biochemical event, the modification of which is responsible for the expression of the alteration in glucose-stimulated insulin release. This event may contribute to the delayed adaptation of hepatic glucokinase. We are a long way from understanding the origin of a fundamental aging process; however, these results open the door to the type of experiment and questions the gerontologist must now begin to ask, such as:

1. At what age in the life span is the biochemical modification expressed for the first time?

2. What is the nature and the sequence of events responsible for the appearance of this modification?

3. How do the events relate to other findings in gerontology?

4. How do the events relate to age-associated diseases such as maturity-onset diabetes?

5. How do the events relate to potential longevity?

References

Adelman, R. C., Loss of adaptive mechanisms during aging. *Fed. Proc.* **38,** 1968–1971 (1979).

Adelman, R. C., An age-dependent modification of enzyme regulation. *J. Biol. Chem.* **245,** 1032–1035 (1970).

Kitahara, A., and Adelman, R. C., Altered regulation of insulin secretion in isolated islets of different sizes in aging rats. *Biochem. Biophys. Res. Commun.* **87,** 1207–1213 (1979).

Klug, T. L., and Adelman, R. C., Regulation of glucagon levels in rats during aging. *Biochem. Biophys. Res. Commun.* **89,** 907–912 (1979).

Discussion—Session II

DR. GOLDMAN: I would like to take this opportunity to present a concept that implies that many of the so-called diseases of aging may be based on the natural effects of risk factors. For example, if we examine data based on blood pressure, rather than glucose tolerance (for which the conclusions could be similar), we find an essentially normal distribution of both systolic and diastolic pressures. At the same time, mortality ratios show an accelerating increase with increases in either the systolic or diastolic blood pressure. This leads us to the concept that blood pressure is a risk factor for which there is a normal distribution, considerable evidence of a constitutional basis, and the possibility of modification by such factors as salt intake, physical conditioning, drug administration, and so forth. There is a broad curve for risk-factor distribution (Figure 1), yet there is a continuous and geometric increase in the mortality with increasing blood pressure, rather than two separate distributions. Thus blood pressure is considered a risk factor.

The Framingham study showed that blood pressure, blood glucose, blood uric acid, and some other parameters are risk factors. Individual risk factors appear to have a constitutional basis modified by environment. Mortal risk increases with each unit of unfavorable change in the risk factor, even within standard ranges. Therefore, is it not possible that most of the "diseases" of aging and associated causes of death are due to the combination of a given set of constitutional risk factors, modified by environment, and accelerating with time to produce a critical event? Would this not make diabetes and its complications a natural phenomenon, depending on heredity and distribution, rather than a disease in the classic sense?

DR. LEVINE: There is nothing artificial about the natural phenomenon. There is a tendency among the diabetologists to say

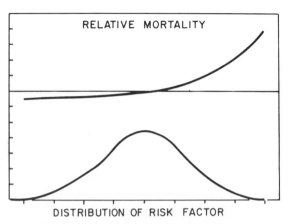

Fig. 1. Relating mortality to the distribution of a risk factor

Note that the relative risk is below average on the favorable limb of the distribution and increases continuously at an accelerated rate in the unfavorable limb. Source: Goldman, R., The relationship of individual risk factor status to mortal risk. In *Health Care of the Aged*, University of Virginia Press, Charlottesville, VA, 1980. Used by permission of the publisher

that it does not make any difference, so do not call it diabetes until it reaches 1.50–2.00 g of glucose per liter.

DR. GOLDMAN: This is the same argument as to whether or not you treat hypertension.

DR. LEVINE: Right. Exactly.

DR. GOLDMAN: Let me ask one corollary question. The basement membrane increases in thickness with age from an average of about 7 μm at birth to about 11 μm at age 75.

DR. LEVINE: It depends on the tissue. In muscle it increases for only two or three years and then stops. In kidney you are correct.

DR. GOLDMAN: Let us take the kidney. It has been dichotomized because apparently the rate of thickening doubles in diabetics. Has anybody related the rate of thickening of the basement membrane to the blood sugar concentration?

DR. LEVINE: No. It has not been done, mainly because there still is an outstanding quarrel as to how you measure basement membrane thickness.

DR. NATELSON: I have a question bothering me that none of

the people this morning addressed, though they talked around it, and that is, what happens to the growth hormone, somatotropin, on aging? This is important because somatotropin passes through the liver and becomes somatomedin or the sulfation factor. The most obvious symptom in any adult, or I should say any old person, is the shifting of his teeth, peridontal disease, the various collagen diseases, and as someone pointed out, various lung diseases. Somatotropin affects the medium in which the cells grow, and if you do not have sulfation factor, you can not make proper support for the collagen. In other words, you do not have the cross linking due to condrotin sulfate. Has anyone on the panel measured changing amounts of somatotropin in aging or sulfation factor in aging?

DR. ADELMAN: There are a number of measurements, predominantly clinical measurements, in the literature. Generally speaking, these hormone concentrations, as is the case with many other hormone and enzyme concentrations, go up, down, or remain the same depending on whom you want to believe. However, to be a little more serious, there is a laboratory that is very actively pursuing this right now. The name is Jim Florini, Department of Biology at the University of Syracuse.

DR. LEVINE: A very active group working with somatomedins is that of Kirsten Hall and of Luft in Sweden, and they have studied this topic. The results for growth hormone itself are not spectacular. As a matter of fact, nobody seems to understand the levels of growth hormone because when the growth is fastest the level of growth hormone is low, and when you think you do not need growth hormone, as in sleep, you have a lot of it. Therefore, I just do not know how to interpret their findings. Dr. Natelson, do we know more about somatomedin than that it is a sulfation factor in cartilage, or is it the sulfation factor everywhere?

DR. NATELSON: It is a sulfation factor everywhere.

DR. GOLDSTEIN:[1] I think it is pretty clear now that sulfation factor is not the only entity that is released through somatotropin stimulation—there are at least five somatomedins that have already been proposed, and there are probably a few other insulin-

---

[1] Dr. Goldstein presented his paper during the second session of the conference and hence participated in this discussion session. For the purposes of this book, however, he preferred that his paper be included with the papers of Session IV.—Ed.

like growth factors that may turn out to be mediated (Gospoda-rowicz, D., and Moran, J. S., *Ann. Rev. Biochem.* **45:** 531–558, 1976). It is too early to know what these amounts are at any time of life because they are only just now being purified. Before they can be measured, we need to purify them and make ^{125}I-labeled materials and specific antibodies.

DR. ADELMAN: I would like to add something to that. I implied from the TSH (thyrotropin) data I showed you, as most clinical chemists are undoubtedly aware anyway, that, as powerful a tool as immunoassay is, you must take the results with a grain of salt. There is an increasing amount of evidence, particularly in the case of the polypeptide hormones, that these things are enormously heterogeneous. Under a variety of physiological conditions, let alone increasing age, the distribution of this heterogeneity in several cases changes rather dramatically. So it does not suffice to say what the amount of an immunoreactive species in circulation is; it is very complicated.

DR. NATELSON: In that connection, are you dealing with a high molecular weight substance such as an antigen/antibody complex? It is well known that an antigen/antibody complex will inhibit the activity of the particular material you are dealing with. In other words, as we are aging, are we making antibodies to TSH?

DR. ADELMAN: Based on what we have purified thus far, I would say no. And we also may be able to generate this substance in an in vitro protein-synthesizing system, so the odds are that it is a high molecular mass precursor of TSH. But even more to the point, do not be misled by the Sephadex elution profile because TSH is known to be a glycoprotein and its behavior on that type of column is mind-boggling, to say the least.

DR. LEVINE: Dr. Adelman, I followed your arguments up to the time of somatostatin. It is very difficult for me to see glucose acting on insulin via somatostatin. It is not the way I picture it. May I ask whether to resolve this you have attempted or will attempt to use a culture of pure beta cells?

DR. ADELMAN: That is an elegant way to do the experiment, but I do not believe anyone yet is capable of getting the cultured beta cells out of young and old normal animals.

DR. LEVINE: Well, you know, you have done other things.

DR. ADELMAN: I appreciate your faith.

DR. LEVINE: Dr. Goldstein, now that the organelle hypothesis is limping, so to speak, from your exposition, would you care to think or speculate about whether aging does have something to do with polymer formation of unit protein molecules so that the function of the protein is altered?

DR. GOLDSTEIN: If you mean covalent bonding, then the answer is no, at least in the fibroblast system, where we are looking at two-dimensional O'Farrell gels [see ref. 7–9 in my paper, this book] and where we do not see any differences between protein patterns from young cells and those from old cells. If you mean more subtle kinds of dissociable polymeric forms, that is possible. In fact there is some evidence in tissue culture from Bob Dell'Orco's group that there may be, at least in one enzyme, a tendency in late-passage cells to have more of the tetramer glucose-6-phosphate dehydrogenase, which may be a relatively inactive form and the one that is more easily denatured with heat (Duncan, M. R., Dell'Orco, R. T., and Guthrie, P. L., *J. Cell. Physiol.* **93**: 49–56, 1977). So that may be a possibility. But it would still mean that there have to be some changes in the basic unit (monomer) to bring about a change in the polymeric association, unless there is an ionic difference between the young and the old cell or, let us say, co-factor or substrate differences in terms of enzymes that tend to favor higher aggregates.

DR. ADELMAN: There is another way of answering that. The whole business of accumulation of altered enzymes during aging, which now is being suggested as a consequence of a slowdown in the rate of protein turnover, provides the possibility of another answer. Part of Fred Goldberg's work on protein turnover suggests that an important intermediate involves the accumulation of a material with a high relative molecular mass (M_r), although it is not clear how this is formed. So maybe there are high M_r materials that reflect either changes in protein synthesis or degradation. It is a wide-open field for a biochemist.

DR. GOLDSTEIN: Could I add a little to that? You have to be cautious about systems used to define this. Goldberg has defined the high M_r aggregate form in two systems, one bacterial and the other mammalian (rabbit) reticulocyte [ref. *14*, my paper]. These are two specific and limited systems that cannot be extrapolated to all cells.

DR. GRANNIS: Dr. Adelman, you seemed quite willing to extrapolate some results from rat experiments to elderly people. Considering that life events in the rat are measured in months and the same events in humans in years, could you tell us the type of aging process or mechanism you would conceive as being common to both rat and man but that could still operate on vastly different time scales?

DR. ADELMAN: I never have any particular problem extrapolating, as those who know me can attest. Be that as it may, I can say this with a certain amount of authority, as I have an active role on the National Academy of Science's committee whose major responsibility is to determine the suitability of different animal models for aging research: there are a number of physiological, biochemical, and pathological characteristics that are quite similar between the rat and the human, and there are a number that are quite different. I do not think there is any particular problem with that. There are probably a number of very fundamental happenings in regard to the aging process that are in common to each species and that express themselves in similar proportions of the total life span, if not in similar periods of time. Dr. Hart, when he speaks tomorrow, will have greater insight into the nature of species differences. Let me focus on one specific age-associated disease here, if I am allowed to call maturity-onset diabetes an age-associated disease. There are a number of manifestations that are similar in both species, such as alterations in the pattern of insulin secretion, and the failure to suppress glucagon. Both are common features of maturity-onset diabetes in man and in the rat. Yet there are a number of differences, particularly in the pathological features. I would hasten to add that there are small-vessel changes in the rat. There are certain changes that resemble neuropathies, and changes in the eyes of rats with increasing age that are very similar to what is seen in man. I do not feel we should make it a major problem.

DR. FORMAN (Chapel Hill, NC): Dr. Thurlbeck, would you comment on some of Dr. Adelman's ideas regarding the altered ability for enzyme adaptation in the synthesis of the type-2 alveolar-cell surfactant, which might be decreasing in the aging patient?

DR. THURLBECK: There are, as far as I know, no data. The pressure–volume change that occurs in the lung also occurs in the saline-filled lung, which indicates that these are tissue forces rather than surface forces. There are no real indications that there are alterations in the surface forces of the lung with age.

DR. FORMAN: Like the acyltransferase?

DR. THURLBECK: I am talking only about the data I know. It would be very interesting if investigators would report data that had anything to do with the surfactant secretion. I would predict that there should be an effect of age on surfactant secretion.

DR. LEVINE: Dr. Thurlbeck, in the last 10 years the gastrointestinal tract has become the premier endocrine organ of the body. The peptide hormones of this dispersed endocrine system are found in the brain and pancreas as well as in the gut. Has anyone detected dispersed endocrine cells on the surfaces of the respiratory system?

DR. THURLBECK: All the lung is is a bit of gut modified for gas exchange. There are cells in the airway that are called K cells (K for Kultschitsky) that have all the features of neuroendocrine cells. The only question is, what do they do, what do they secrete? The analog we know about is tumors of these cells, the carcinoid- and the small oat-cell cancer, which make a variety of polypeptides.

DR. LEVINE: ACTH (adenocorticotropin) comes from these?

DR. THURLBECK: Yes, they make ACTH, choriogonadotropin, parathormone, and antidiuretic hormone-like substances; they also make a variety of vasoactive amines. Thus these cells have a potential for producing a variety of hormone-like substances. No one has found a specific substance that is peculiar to them.

DR. FORLANO (Eldorado, TX): Dr. Adelman, in the last experiment you described somatostatin antibody and you showed an increase in insulin release. Did you do any experiments to determine the effect of somatostatin antibody on glucagon release?

DR. ADELMAN: We have not looked at its effect on glucagon release, but all these cross experiments, as well as the effects of donor age, on glucose-stimulated secretion of somatostatin, glucagon, and insulin are underway.

DR. MEACHUM (Shrevesport, LA): Dr. Thurlbeck, did your studies include persons who were deficient in α_1-antitrypsin?

DR. THURLBECK: One study in which we looked at the findings at necropsy in patients who had various phenotypes of α_1-antitrypsin came out negative. However, the study was too small, smoking histories were poor, and we could not show an increased frequency of emphysema in MZ subjects—with the ZZ type, there was no problem. From my understanding of the literature (it is a very controversial subject), it appears that with proper epidemiologic surveys, the MZ phenotypes are not predisposed to lung disease. However, if you start with patients and then study their relatives with what you think are matched controls, you will find that MZ phenotypes have an increased frequency of lung disease. What this represents is a socioeconomic grouping, as the relatives tend to come from the same part of town and have the same smoking habits. This may be the cause of the apparent increase in lung cancer.

DR. MEITES: One of the theories that Dr. Levine referred to is that aging is essentially a disease process. This is hard for people like Dr. Timiras and me to accept. We are more optimistic and believe that favorable intervention might be possible. For example, I ask that you explain our demonstration that in old female rats, both constant-estrous and old, pregnant rats, we can by hormonal means, by altering the hypothalamic picture, initiate normal cycling—despite the fact that we cannot detect disease in the ovaries, pituitary, or hypothalamus?

DR. LEVINE: We agree 100%, but I think we have a semantic difficulty. The reason that I put it bluntly as a disease process was to alert the physician to do something about it. I am advocating that you do the same thing for high blood sugar and high lipids that you are doing for the reproductive tract. Secondly, finding no clinical disease in the ovaries does not mean that there is no dysfunction.

DR. MEITES: We have tested the function, as you have seen, and we can make the organ function normally.

DR. LEVINE: Yes, when you added the missing link. It does not have to be in the organ. I did not refer to the disease of an organ; I referred to the disease of an organism.

DR. MEITES: I was talking with Dr. Hazzard at lunch, and he told me that even in healthy humans that go to a ripe old age, often disease can not be found at autopsy. Would you agree with this, Dr. Levine?

DR. LEVINE: Of course.

DR. STEENBLOCK (El Toro, CA): Dr. Levine, could you try to tie together all the data on increased blood sugar, free and bound tryptophan amounts in the blood, and serotonin in the brain in relation to the aging process?

Dr. Levine: Not in the time available.

Dr. Nelson: Dr. Adelman, you said that if time permitted you would talk a little about hyperplastic changes that might be related to this insulin phenomenon. Could you, please?

Dr. Adelman: As a function of increasing age in the Sprague–Dawley rat model system, we have pancreatic islets of Langerhans that are extremely heterogeneous in size. As a function of increasing age, the size distribution changes rather dramatically so that there is a much greater proportion of the larger hyperplastic islets. If you wait long enough, the older animals are characterized by an enormous incidence of insulin-secreting islet-cell tumors. These are not detectable until 24–30 months of age. One way of interpreting this, and it is sheer speculation and not based on data, is that because the major population of islets, the smaller islets, are losing their capabilities of secreting insulin rapidly in response to glucose, a compensatory response ensues and this is the hyperplasia, resulting in the islet population that makes much more insulin in such a way that it is not impaired during aging. That is a religious conviction and why I really did not want to discuss it.

Dr. Nelson: Your last results on the NV 2 measurements were in 24-month-old animals. Have you looked at the 12-month-old rats?

Dr. Adelman: At the moment, we have limited the in vitro islet work to two- and 24-month-old rats.

III

DEGENERATIVE CHANGES IN AGING

A discussion of major diseases that occur with age and whose pathological features are superimposed on the normal aging process—Samuel Natelson, Moderator

Whatever poet, orator, or sage
May say of it, old age is still old age.
LONGFELLOW

Renal Changes with Age

Ralph Goldman

The conquest of most of the acute diseases and the control of many chronic diseases have resulted in greater survival to old age and have increased our need to know the characteristics of the aging organism. An important consequence is the recognition that the nature of the aging process itself must be identified. A fundamental question still to be resolved is to what extent are age changes intrinsic, and thus are normal and expected (although not necessarily unalterable) phenomena, and to what extent are they due to environmental exposure? Age-related changes should be universal, although they could occur at variable rates, whereas disease phenomena should be unique, and attack only selected populations. Moreover, we need not assume that all aging phenomena are manifestations of the same mechanism, although this possibility cannot be excluded.

The kidney, as an organ, offers many features that can be utilized for research on aging: it is complex, yet many renal functions can be conveniently evaluated; it is paired, which provides greater flexibility in animal study; and its failure is not a predominant cause of death either by disease or in senile individuals.

Anatomic Changes

The size of human kidneys increases markedly from birth to a maximum during the fourth decade of life, then decreases with increasing rapidity (1). Similar changes have been reported for rat kidneys, with the maximum size at 150 days (2). By the ninth decade in humans and 500 days in rats, the decrease in renal weight from maximum values is on the order of 20 to 30%.

149

The number of glomeruli per human kidney has been reasonably established at about one million, and all are present at birth *(3)*. A few are lost in utero and the rate of loss gradually increases, so that by the eighth decade the number may be decreased by one-third or more *(4–7)*. Despite the loss of nephron units, there is little increase in scarring or infiltration in the cortex. Although the number of scarred and obsolescent glomeruli increases with age, the fraction is generally less than would be expected, and is reported in terms of residual, rather than original glomeruli *(8)*. The glomerular loss is diffuse, and seems to be distributed evenly throughout the kidney. Typically, there are no characteristic changes of glomerulonephritis, pyelonephritis, or focal, wedge-shaped scarring to which nephron loss could be attributed.

Interestingly, unlike in humans, glomeruli form for a time after birth in rats *(2)* and presumably in other species as well. In addition, glomerular size in rats appears to increase with age, which may also be contrary to observations of the human kidney *(9)*.

At birth the tubules in human kidneys are quite short, but there is an immediate development, primarily of the proximal convoluted portions *(1)*. However, microdissections show that this development is later partially reversed with a one-third decrease in proximal tubular length and volume from maturity to old age *(10)*. Distal tubular diverticuli appear in the region of attachment to the macula densa *(10)*. They are unusual before the age of 16 years, then increase linearly in number until in the tenth decade they average three per nephron. These diverticuli contain bacteria and detritus, which may have implications for the increasing frequency of urinary tract infections with age.

A variety of evidences points away from lesions of the major arteries as the cause of age-related nephron decrements. The characteristic decreases in renal function with age are still observed in extensive studies of potential renal-transplant donors, who have been carefully selected for the absence of significant vascular abnormality or overt evidence of atherosclerosis *(11, 12)*.

Muscular arteries show increased collagen between the intima and the internal elastic lamina, replacement of muscular cells with collagen, fragmentation of elastin, and calcium deposits. Although these changes decrease vascular elasticity, there is no evidence that they reduce blood flow. At postmortem, kidneys can be injected with radio-opaque media and radiographed to reveal fine vascular detail *(5, 13)*. Before age 40 the renal vessels taper gradually from hilum to cortex, and the arcuate arteries curve smoothly. Abnormalities begin to appear after age 40, and all kidneys show some abnormality beyond age 80. The changes in the arcuate arteries are most consistently related to age, and show angulation, tortuosity, and notching at the bifurcations. The most common observation is failure of vessels to taper. Tortuosity, spiraling, and luminal irregularity may be seen in the interlobar arteries.

Mild arteriolar hyalinization is consistently age-related, but intimal proliferation, medial hypertrophy, and necrosis are rare in the absence of hypertension, being seen in the kidneys of fewer than 15% of normotensive individuals but reported in 58–97% of persons with hypertension *(14–16)*. In a comparison of the ability of the small artery and arteriole to carry an adequate blood flow in normal elderly persons and in hypertensive individuals (Table 1), the ratios of lumen diameter to wall thickness in the small arteries and arterioles are unaffected by age unless hypertension is present *(17)*.

A large body of data now details the sequence of glomerular obsolescence *(5, 7)*, which differs for cortical and juxtamedullary nephrons (Figures 1 and 2). In the former, there is a gradual glomerular sclerosis, without an inflammatory reaction, and eventual reabsorption of the scar. Injection studies reveal that the afferent arteriole may remain patent after complete loss of the nephron. The pattern in the juxtamedullary nephrons differs in that one of the glomerular capillaries remains patent, enlarges, and becomes

Table 1. Effects of Age and Hypertension on the
Lumen Diameter:Wall Thickness Ratios of Small
Renal Arteries and Arterioles

Ratio of diameter to thickness

	Normal	Hypertensive
Arteries		
Young	3.91	2.26
Old	3.84	2.52
Arterioles		
Young	2.52	1.51
Old	2.66	1.97

Adapted from Yamaguchi et al. *(17)*.

151

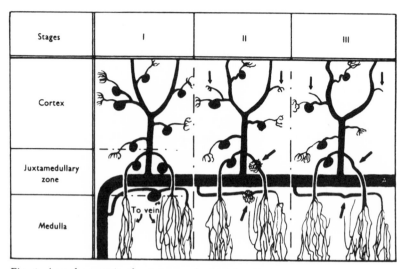

Fig. 1. Age changes in the intrarenal arterial pattern

I, Normal adult pattern. *II*, Partial degeneration of some glomeruli: two cortical afferent arterioles ramify into remnants of glomerular tufts *(upper arrows)*, two juxtamedullary arterioles pass through partially degenerated glomeruli *(lower arrows)* and interlobular arteries and afferent arterioles show slight spiraling. *III*, Two cortical afferent arterioles end blindly *(upper arrows)*, two juxtamedullary arterioles are aglomerular *(lower arrows)*, and the corresponding glomerular tufts have degenerated completely. There is pronounced spiraling of interlobular arteries and afferent arterioles. Source: Ljundqvist and Lagergren *(5)*, by permission of the publisher

Forms of communication between the arterioles and the glomeruli at the vascular pole			
I	II	III	IV

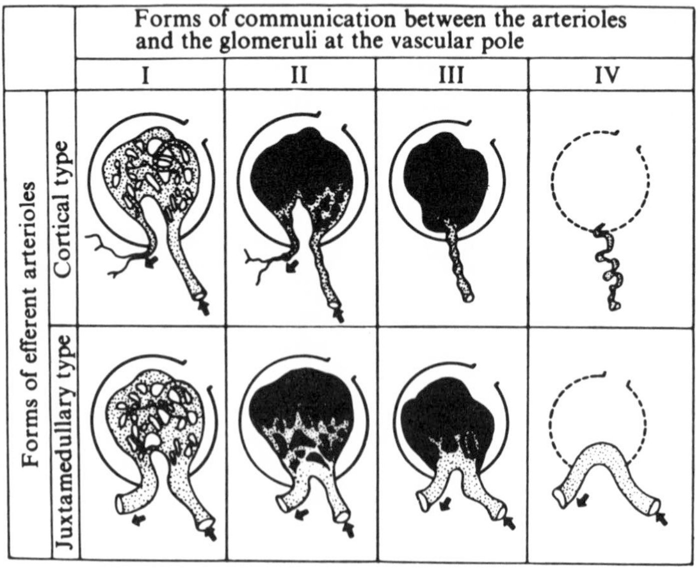

Fig. 2. Diagram of the degenerative process in the cortical and juxtamedullary nephrons

Reprinted from *Kidney International (7)*, by permission of the publisher

a shunt connecting the afferent and efferent arterioles. This unit becomes a vasa recta of Ludwig, and the shunt remains as a kink and a reminder of the lost glomerulus. In view of these observations it is difficult to ascribe the glomerular loss to ischemia. Because of its function, the kidney is an extremely vascular organ, receiving much more blood than should be needed for normal nutrition; yet it is possible that locally reduced flow to the small vessels could account for the observed phenomena.

The basement membrane in both the glomerulus and the tubule has been noted to thicken with age (8, 10), and may in some way be related to the nephron involution. Basement-membrane thickening has been noted in other capillaries and may be a universal phenomenon of aging (19).

Physiologic Changes

Lewis and Alving (20) were probably the first to document the age-related decrease in renal function and to report the effect on urea clearance. The decrease in the glomerular filtration rate, measured with inulin, was reported by Davies and Shock (21) and has been extensively confirmed. Although the decrement accelerates with age, it is about 0.6% per year after the third decade.

Cross-sectional studies have always been suspect, and longitudinal studies have not been available. Recently, however, the Baltimore group has reported on the changes in a large group of men observed for more than 10 years (22). As shown in Figure 3, the changes occurring during this period had essentially the same slope as was predicted from the cross-sectional study (the actual values for the two studies should be in close agreement, having been derived from the same data). Note that the decrease in creatinine clearance between the ages of 20 and 80 years is associated with an increase in serum creatinine only from 8.08 to 8.43 mg/L. Creatinine is an end-product of creatine metabolism; the amount produced and requiring excretion is determined by the amount of creatine, which is in turn dependent on the muscle-cell mass. The decrease in muscle mass and creatine production, which is almost proportionate to the decrease in renal function, prevents the increase in serum creatinine values. Because the concentration of creatinine in serum is often used to estimate renal clearance for assessing drug dose requirements, obviously age *must*

153

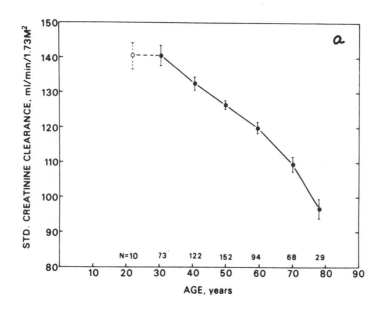

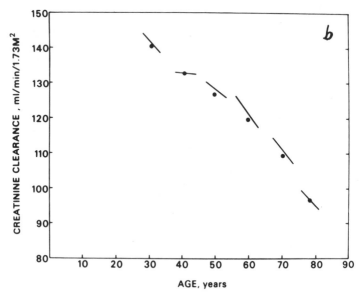

Fig. 3. The relationship of standard true creatinine clearance (mL/ min per 1.73 m² of body surface) and age: *a*, values determined by age only; *b*, values and slopes established by multiple determinations in the same subjects over time, a longitudinal survey

Source: Rowe et al. *(22)*, by permission of the publisher

be introduced as a factor. The wide range of normal values makes it necessary to determine the actual amount of clearance if this information is to be used to prepare accurate dose estimates.

Renal blood flow decreases with age, and the consensus is that it decreases at a rate even more rapid than that of the filtration rate (21). The validity of renal blood flow estimates depends upon the renal extraction ratio of the test substance. Studies by Miller et al. (23) showed an extraction ratio for p-aminohippurate of 91.8% for those less than 50 years old and of 91.1% for those over 50. Thus, not only does the method continue to be valid, but also the vasa rectae verae, if they carry any significant amount of blood, must be as well-cleared of p-aminohippurate as are the vessels still functionally related to intact nephron units.

Based upon the available data, the filtration fraction (the ratio of the glomerular filtration rate to the renal plasma flow) appears to increase with age. The reported magnitudes at different ages are quite variable; however, the observation that there is a greater loss in blood flow than in function implies a causal sequence, and one that in some way involves all of the nephrons.

Two contradictory studies bear on the problem. The first, by McDonald et al. (24) compared renal function in 20 young men, mean age 37 years; 20 middle-aged men, mean age 59 years; and 14 old men, mean age 77 years. The respective filtration fractions were 0.189, 0.206, and 0.232 (Figure 4). The subjects then received intravenous pyrogen (killed typhoid organisms) after the pyretic effect had been blocked with aminopyrine. There was no effect on the glomerular filtration rate, but the renal plasma flow increased in all groups, with a resultant decrease in the filtration fractions to 0.115, 0.123, and 0.122, respectively. The disappearance of the age-related differential in filtration fraction suggested that the relative reduction in blood flow was physiologic, not anatomic, in origin. By implication, if nephron loss is due to reduced blood flow, it should be possible to reduce the rate of nephron loss.

The second study was performed by Hollenberg et al. (12), who had the unique opportunity to examine potential kidney donors in great detail and identify overt abnormalities. They confirmed the decrease in creatinine clearance with age and demonstrated with xenon-washout techniques a decreased perfusion per unit of renal mass. They then observed the effect of acetylcholine

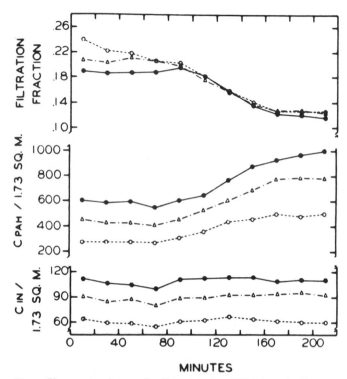

Fig. 4. Changes in glomerular filtration rate (CIN, *bottom*) effective
renal plasma flow (CPAH, *middle*), and filtration fraction *(top)*
during the pyrogen reaction

O, mean values for 14 subjects aged 70–85 years; △, mean values for
20 subjects aged 50–69 years; ●, mean values for 20 subjects aged
20–49 years. Source: McDonald et al. *(24)*, by permission of the
publisher

and angiotensin infused directly into the renal artery. Although
they state that the maximum dilatation achieved with the administration of 100 μg of acetylcholine per minute was less in the
aged than in younger subjects, examination of the data shows
the dilatation to be almost identical as a fraction of initial values.
The response to angiotensin (30 ng/min) was identical in the
two groups, but fractionally greater in the aged. Thus, in contrast
to the work of McDonald et al., Hollenberg's group seems to
have shown that the renal vessels of the aged are more responsive
than the young to vasoconstrictive, rather than to vasodilatory,
stimuli. Yet in both instances the total fractional range of responsiveness was greater in the aged than in the young.

Unfortunately, the Hollenberg data cannot be related directly to the usual data for filtration rate and plasma flow. However, the diminished perfusion per unit volume of tissue may be evidence that decreased blood flow is the primary factor decreasing renal mass. As a corollary, the renal plasma flow should decrease more rapidly, because an increasing filtration fraction implies either arteriolar luminal adjustment or a specifically greater anatomic reduction of the efferent than of the afferent arteriolar lumen. Because their study showed a proportionately greater inner cortical (juxtamedullary) flow in the aged, and this area is reported to have a higher filtration fraction than the outer cortex, Hollenberg et al. attribute the increased filtration fraction to the greater relative loss of cortical nephrons.

I find these studies confusing. First, although they demonstrate responsiveness in different directions, both studies show an increased physiologic response with age that seems incompatible with the known anatomical changes. Second, the increased shunting would increase the relative juxtamedullary blood flow, but reduce the filtration fraction. The shunting, the increased total juxtamedullary blood flow, and the increased filtration fraction would seem to require a much larger proportional loss of cortical nephrons than is observed. In addition, the efferent arteriole of the juxtamedullary nephron is relatively larger than that of the cortical nephron, and on anatomic grounds seems less likely to be associated with an increased filtration fraction. Because of the significance of these observations, it is clear that further examination is necessary.

Several tubular functions also decrease with age at a rate that parallels the decrease in the filtration rate: the secretory maxima for iodopyracet (21) and p-aminohippurate (25), maximum reabsorption of glucose (26), free-water clearance (27), and total acid excretion (28). The persistence of function, which parallels residual nephron mass, is surprising in view of experiments showing that tubule cells have fewer mitochondria (29), lower enzyme concentrations (30), and less transport capacity (31) than younger cells.

Although the ratio of the free-water clearance to residual renal mass remains constant, a similar relationship has not been established for maximum concentrating ability, which in a recent study was found to decrease from 1109 mosmol/kg H_2O in young subjects (mean age 33 years) to 882 mosmol/kg H_2O in old subjects (mean age 68 years) *(32)*. Because this decrease does not seem to be related to a relative osmotic diuresis, attention is now focussed on medullary changes. The same mechanism, still unknown, is probably why old kidneys fail to respond fully to maximum doses of vasopressin, although less complete responsivity is retained.

The renal response to an acid load is impaired with age, although the urinary pH is the same as in young adults *(28)*. However, the ability to produce ammonia is decreased, and although there is an increase in the titratable acidity, excretion of the acid load requires a longer time. Ultimately, the aging organism maintains the same distribution and concentrations of fluids, electrolytes, and hydrogen ions; the ability to respond to acute or sustained overload, however, is progressively decreased, which must be recognized in proper management.

Compensatory Renal Hypertrophy

Although the remaining kidney tissue will hypertrophy after tissue loss, this capacity is inversely proportional to age *(33)*. Recent interest has been fueled by the use of kidney transplants, where ultimately function in both the donor and the recipient will be affected by this ability. Current evidence indicates that when one kidney is removed, the remaining kidney will increase in size and function by 48% if the donor is aged 20 years, and by 30% if aged 60 years, with a linear decrease with age between *(11)*. Compensation results from enlargement of the residual nephrons, not from new nephron formation *(34)*, and although in the younger individual cellular hyperplasia may be significant, in the older individual cellular hypertrophy is predominant *(35)*. Kidney cells of newborn rats grow well in culture, but cells from eight-month-old rats show poor and poorly sustained growth *(36)*.

Conclusions

There are undoubted decremental renal changes with age, yet these changes are never so severe as to threaten life except under unusually stressful conditions. My bias is that the preponderance of evidence supports a universal and intrinsic mechanism(s), which may be alterable by external maneuvers. The role of the vascular system as the site of primary or secondary change is not yet known, but should be subject to further resolution. The important changes are probably at the capillary or arteriolar level. Forty years ago, Oliver (37) noted that renal obsolescence was known to every individual, having been experienced in the successive development and regression of the pronephros and then the mesonephros before the final appearance of the metanephric kidney. Because these are essentially normal phenomena, it should not be surprising to find a similar regression in the metanephric kidney as well.

References

1. Dunnill, M. S., and Halley, W., Some observations of the quantitative anatomy of the kidney. *J. Pathol.* **110**, 113–121 (1973).
2. Arataki, M., On the postnatal growth of the kidney, with special reference to the number and size of the glomeruli (albino rat). *Am. J. Anat.* **36**, 399–450 (1926).
3. Moore, R. A., Total number of glomeruli in the normal kidney. *Anat. Rec.* **48**, 153–168 (1931).
4. Ljungqvist, A., Fetal and postnatal development of the intrarenal arterial pattern in man. A microangiographic and histologic study. *Acta Paediat.* **52**, 443–454 (1963).
5. Ljungqvist, A., and Lagergren, C., Normal intrarenal arterial pattern in adult and aging human kidney. A microangiographical and histological study. *J. Anat. Lond.* **96**, 285–298 (1962).
6. Ljungqvist, A., Structure of the arteriole-glomerular units in different zones of the kidney. *Nephron* **1**, 329–337 (1964).
7. Takazakura, E., Wasabu, N., Handa, A., Takada, A., Shinoda, A., and Takeuchi, J., Intrarenal vascular changes with age and disease. *Kidney Int.* **2**, 224–230 (1972).
8. McLachlan, M. S. F., Guthrie, J. C., Anderson, C. K., and Fulker, M. J., Vascular and glomerular changes in the ageing kidney. *J. Pathol.* **121**, 65–78 (1977).
9. Moore, R. A., and Hellman, L. M., The effect of unilateral nephrectomy on the senile atrophy of the kidney of the white rat. *J. Exp. Med.* **51**, 51–57 (1930).
10. Darmady, E. M., Offer, J., and Woodhouse, M. A., The parameters of the aging kidney. *J. Pathol.* **109**, 195–207 (1973).
11. Boner, G., Shelp, W. D., Neton, M., and Rieselbach, R. E., Factors influencing the increase in glomerular filtration rate in the remaining kidney of transplant donors. *Am. J. Med.* **55**, 169–174 (1973).

12. Hollenberg, N. K., Adams, D. F., Solomon, H. S., Rashid, A., Abrams, H. L., and Merrill, J. P., Senescence and the renal vasulature in normal man. *Circ. Res.* **34,** 309–316 (1974).
13. Davidson, A. J., Talner, L. B., and Downs, W. M., A study of the angiographic appearance of the kidney in an aging normotensive population. *Radiology* **92,** 975–983 (1969).
14. Jackson, J. G., Puchtler, H., and Sweat, F., Investigation of staining, polarization and fluorescence—microscopic properties of pseudoelastic fibers in the renal arterial system. *J. R. Microsc. Soc.* **88,** 473–485 (1968).
15. Moritz, A. R., and Oldt, M. R., Arteriolar sclerosis in hypertensive and non-hypertensive individuals. *Am. J. Pathol.* **13,** 679–728 (1937).
16. Bell, E. T., *Renal Diseases,* 1st ed., Lea and Febiger, Philadelphia, PA, 1946, p 322.
17. Yamaguchi, T., Omae, T., and Katsuki, S., Quantitative determination of renal vascular changes related to age and hypertension. *Jpn. Heart J.* **10,** 248–258 (1969).
18. Farquhar, M. G., Vernier, R. L., and Good, R. A., The application of electron microscopy in pathology. Study of renal biopsy tissues. *Schweiz. Med. Wochenschr.* **87,** 501–510 (1957).
19. Kilo, C., Vogler, N., and Williamson, J. R., Muscle capillary basement membrane changes related to aging and diabetes mellitus. *Diabetes* **21,** 881–905 (1972).
20. Lewis, W. H., Jr., and Alving, A. S., Changes with age in the renal function in adult men. I. Clearance of urea. II. Amount of urea nitrogen in the blood. III. Concentrating ability of the kidneys. *Am. J. Physiol.* **123,** 500–515 (1938).
21. Davies, D. F., and Shock, N. W., Age changes in glomerular filtration rate, effective renal plasma flow, and tubular excretory capacity in adult males. *J. Clin. Invest.* **29,** 496–507 (1950).
22. Rowe, J. W., Andres, R., and Tobin, J. D., et al., The effect of age on creatinine clearance in men: A cross-sectional and longitudinal study. *J. Gerontol.* **31,** 155–163 (1976).
23. Miller, J. H., McDonald, R. K., and Shock, N. W., The renal extraction of p-amino-hippurate in the aged individual. *J. Gerontol.* **6,** 213–216 (1951).
24. McDonald, R. F., Solomon, D. H., and Shock, N. W., Aging as a factor in the renal hemodyamic changes induced by a standardized pyrogen. *J. Clin. Invest.* **30,** 457–462 (1951).
25. Watkin, D. M., and Shock, N. W., Agewise standard value for C_{IN}, C_{PAH} and Tm_{PAH} in adult males. *J. Clin. Invest.* **34,** 969 (1955).
26. Miller, J. H., McDonald, R. K., and Shock, N. W., Age changes in

the maximal rate of renal tubular reabsorption of glucose. *J. Gerontol.* **7**, 196–200 (1952).

27. Lindeman, R. D., Lee, T. D., Jr., Yiengst, M. J., and Shock, N. W., Influence of age, renal disease, hypertension, diuretics, and calcium on the antidiuretic responses to suboptimal infusions of vasopressin. *J. Lab. Clin. Med.* **68**, 206–223 (1966).

28. Adler, S., Lindeman, R. D., Yiengst, M. J., Beard, E., and Shock, N. W., Effect of acute acid loading on urinary acid secretion by the aging human kidney. *J. Lab. Clin. Med.* **72**, 278–289 (1968).

29. Barrows, C. H., Jr., Falzone, J. A., Jr., and Shock, N. W., Age differences in the succinoxidase activity of homogenates and mitochondria from the livers and kidneys of rats. *J. Gerontol.* **15**, 130–133 (1960).

30. Burich, R. L., Effects of age on renal function and enzyme activity in male C57BL/6 mice. *J. Gerontol.* **30**, 539–545 (1975).

31. Beauchene, R. E., Fanestil, D. D., and Barrows, C. H., The effect of age on active transport and sodium–potassium activated ATPase activity in renal tissues of rats. *J. Gerontol.* **20**, 306–310 (1965).

32. Lindeman, R. D., VanBuren, H. C., and Raisz, L. G., Osmolar renal concentrating ability in healthy young men and hospitalized patients without renal disease. *N. Engl. J. Med.* **262**, 1306–1309 (1960).

33. MacKay, E. M., MacKay, L. L., and Addis, T., The degree of compensatory hypertrophy following unilateral nephrectomy. I. The influence of age. *J. Exp. Med.* **56**, 255–265 (1932).

34. Kaufman, J. M., Hardy, R., and Hayslett, J. P., Age-dependent characteristics of compensatory renal growth. *Kidney Int.* **8**, 21–26 (1975).

35. Mandache, E., and Repciuc, E., Microautoradiographic study of cell proliferation in compensatory renal growth. *Morphol. Embryol.* **21**, 71–78 (1975).

36. Soukupova, M., Holeckova, E., and Cinnerova, O., Behaviour of explanted kidney cells from young, adult and old rats. *Gerontologia* **11**, 141–152 (1965).

37. Oliver, J. R., Urinary system. In *Problems of Aging: Biological and Medical Aspects*, E. V. Cowdry, Ed., Williams and Wilkins, Baltimore, MD, 1939, pp 257–277.

Aging and Cardiovascular Disease: Coping with Success

William R. Hazzard

The spectrum of diseases encountered by the geriatric physician is a result of three forces:

1. Factors that have allowed the patient to live into old age.
2. Disease processes superimposed upon or interrelated with the basic aging process.
3. The aging process itself.

Advances in nutrition, hygiene, public health, and medicine have dramatically affected the first of these forces. The second, especially with regard to atherogenesis, shows signs of having been affected by secular trends in life-style in the past 15 years. With regard to the third, however, few advances can be counted, and understanding awaits basic, clinical, and epidemiological research.

A universal characteristic of underdeveloped nations is a high birth rate coupled with a high infant death rate attributable to poor hygiene and malnutrition. As such nations develop economically, both of these trends tend to abate, allowing greater survival into middle and old age and, consequently, a greatly increased life expectancy at birth. The United States has experienced these changes in this century, with a resulting shift in population distribution from one that was predominantly younger than 20 (as in 1891) to one in which the proportion of those under 20 has been reduced from 46% to 34%, and the proportion of older than 55 (12% in 1891) has increased to 20%. In the next 50 years, however, the proportion of those over 55 will increase to 27%, of those between 20 and 55 will be 46%, and of those under 20 will decline further to 27% of the total. Only in recent years has the birth rate declined substantially, most of 20th-century

America having been characterized by a population explosion. The greater longevity of that increased population will give rise to an explosion of the elderly population in the 21st century. Such advances—better health and greater longevity from improved socioeconomic conditions—represent remarkable achievements for our society. The challenge of the future will be how to cope with such success.

The probability of cardiovascular disease in any given individual is strongly correlated with age. Of note, advances in diagnosis, anesthesiology, and surgery have resulted in a sharp decline in

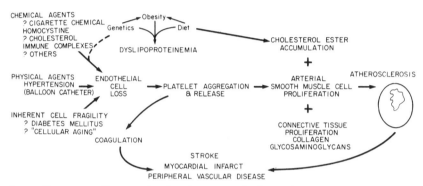

Fig. 1. Processes affecting the development of atherosclerosis

congenital heart disease, which has decreased by 38% since 1948 *(1)*. Simultaneously, rheumatic fever and rheumatic heart disease have also decreased by 65% *(1)*, not only because of improved surgical treatment but also because of earlier treatment of the antecedent streptococcal infections and almost certainly because of better nutrition and hygiene in the population at large. These advances, which primarily affect children and young and middle-aged adults, serve to increase the proportion of cardiovascular disease in the elderly population.

The close correlation between age and cardiovascular disease is related most clearly to the insidious, prolonged course of atherogenesis and hence the time required for its clinical expression as myocardial infarction, stroke, or peripheral arterial disease. At the cellular level (Figure 1), atherogenesis appears to involve disruption of the arterial endothelium by such forces as mechanical stress, e.g., hypertension; chemical agents, e.g., homocystine in hereditary homocystinuria and possibly the cholesterol-rich low-density lipoproteins (LDL) in the patient with familial hypercholesterolemia; and immunological factors (atherosclerosis is vastly accelerated in cholesterol-fed rabbits immunized with bovine serum albumin), and may well be affected by inherent instability of the endothelial cells, which may in turn be related to disease processes such as diabetes mellitus or aging per se *(2)*. Platelet aggregates form at sites of endothelial denudation, releasing various factors, including one that appears to stimulate replication of arterial smooth muscle cells, the principal cellular component of atherosclerotic lesions. These cells migrate from media to intima and appear to represent an early repair process. However, in the presence of high concentrations of circulating cholesterol-rich LDL and remnant lipoproteins (as seen in cholesterol-fed animals), complicated atherosclerotic lesions occur at such sites, characterized by well-known constituents, including cholesterol-laden foam cells, extracellular cholesterol clefts, calcified cellular debris, collagen, and glycosaminoglycans.

If these findings from basic research can be extrapolated to human atherogenesis, they have profound implications for both preventive cardiology and cardiovascular disease in the elderly. First, they give a basic rationale for the well-known association between certain risk factors and premature coronary disease, e.g., hypertension, hypercholesterolemia, and even homocystinuria. Second, they open important new avenues for epidemiological and clinical investigation; for example, because vasectomy, which is associated with high titers of circulating anti-sperm antibodies, is correlated with accelerated atherosclerosis in cholesterol-fed non-human primates, an epidemiological study of the association between vasectomy and coronary disease in humans is being planned. Third, this pathogenetic model underscores the infinitely complex nature of the atherogenic process, producing an appropriate humility in clinicians and investigators alike, some of whom have expected far more from risk-factor analysis in the given patient than could ever be reasonable.

Nevertheless, population studies indicate some value of risk-factor analysis, at least as applied to groups of subjects. These studies have clearly defined the roles of age, sex, serum cholesterol, cigarette smoking, and blood pressure in predicting premature cardiovascular disease *(3)*. They have proved less reliable in predicting cardiovascular disease among those who survive into old age. More important, they do not yield the critical information as to the risk/benefit ratio of intervention designed to reduce risk by reduction of risk factors. For example, cessation of cigarette smoking clearly appears to confer substantial benefit in both primary and secondary coronary disease prevention even as late as middle age. No such benefit, however, has clearly been shown in elderly subjects. Even more difficult is the issue of hypertension. Treatment of moderate and severe hypertension has been clearly demonstrated to have a favorable risk/benefit ratio in middle-aged patients, especially with regard to renal failure, congestive heart failure, and complications of the central nervous system. Treatment of hypertension in the elderly, however, is clearly a double-edged sword, and the experienced geriatrician all too often encounters the adverse results of such treatment—notably, falls from orthostatic hypotension secondary to diuretic-induced hypovolemia. Regarding hypercholesterolemia, the association between cholesterol concentrations, especially LDL cholesterol, and premature coronary disease gradually declines with increasing age, to the point where no clear correlation exists between cholesterol and cardiovascular risk above the age of 60. Moreover, although LDL cholesterol appears clearly to correlate only with premature coronary heart disease, high-density lipoprotein (HDL) cholesterol continues to be inversely correlated with cardiovascular risk, even into old age. Thus undue attention to treatment of hypercholesterolemia in elderly patients is not warranted, though measurement of HDL cholesterol concentrations may remain useful in establishing prognosis. Measures to increase HDL cholesterol, apart perhaps from vigorous aerobic exercise, have not been validated in any age group. Hence, direct intervention to increase HDL cholesterol in the elderly is currently not widely possible even if it were warranted.

On balance, the greater risk to elderly patients would appear to be the consequences of malnutrition, a problem of emerging national significance, given the decreased caloric intake of the elderly. This problem is related in turn to a mix of factors, including decreased physical activity and caloric expenditure and decreased appetite due to diminished gustatory perception, depression, social deprivation, and superimposed disease.[1] Even obesity, commonly singled out as that characteristic of middle-aged Americans most responsible for our high incidence of premature atherosclerosis, should not be treated in the elderly patient without careful consideration of possible adverse effects.

What emerges from this discourse is a different pattern of cardiovascular disease prevention in youth and middle age vs what is appropriate in old age. All evidence to date suggests that for atherosclerosis prevention to be of greatest impact it must be started early, in youth or young adulthood, and be maintained on a lifelong basis. At the other end of the age spectrum, those who have lived into old age in spite of their antecedent diet, blood pressure, cigarette-smoking status, LDL and HDL cholesterol concentrations, etc. are by definition the survivors, and may have far less to gain and far more to lose from aggressive intervention.

While the debate has raged among clinicians and epidemiologists over the relationships among diet, serum cholesterol, and other risk factors potentially affecting cardiovascular disease over the past three decades, the public appears to have voted in favor of moderating life-styles. Between 1963 and 1975 (4) U.S. per capita consumption declined for all tobacco products by 22.4%, fluid milk and cream by 19.2%, butter by 31.9%, eggs by 12.6%, and animal fats and oils by 56.7%, while consumption of vegetable fats and oils increased by 44.1%. During these same years coronary disease mortality declined in all age groups, by 13% in those aged 75 to 84, to as much as 27% in those aged 35 to 44. Cerebrovascular disease mortality declined to an even greater extent, by 19% in 35- to 44-year-olds, to as much as 34% in 55- to 64-year-olds. Even for the very old, those over 85 years of age, both forms of atherosclerotic disease mortality declined, by 19% for coronary disease and by 29% for cerebrovascular disease. Those who have analyzed these decreases suggest that parallel changes in the population distribution of the traditional risk factors are sufficient to account for these decreases in cardiovascular disease.

The implications of these trends for longevity and hence the proportion of the present population living into old old age are

---

[1] See also the paper by Weir, this volume—*Ed.*

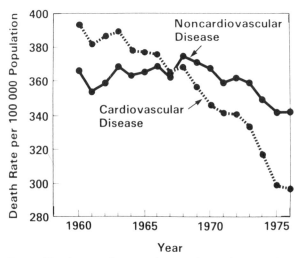

Fig. 2. Death rates from cardiovascular and noncardiovascular disease

Source: Levy *(1)*; used with permission of the American Heart
Assoc., Inc.

enormous. Whereas between the years of 1960 and 1975 death
rates from noncardiovascular disease declined almost impercepti-
bly (Figure 2), those for cardiovascular disease plummeted to the
point where the total deaths from cardiovascular disease decreased
to less than one million in 1975 and in 1976, despite the larger
number of elderly persons in the population *(1)*.

As a result of these trends, we have witnessed in the 1970's
an increase in expected longevity at birth that applies to old age
as well as the rest of the life span (Figure 3). For some subgroups
this increase in life expectancy has been spectacular; e.g., life expectancy among black men between the years of 1970 and 1975
was increased by three years *(1)*.

The implications of these trends for the health-care system
of the future cannot be dismissed. These trends of decreasing
premature atherosclerosis may only defer the problem of cardiovascular disease until it emerges in the elderly patient, who, because of parallel disabilities in other spheres (social and economic
as well as mental and physical), may be far more difficult to restore
to a life of satisfactory quality. Thus the elusive qualities of judg-
ment, compassion, and administrative ability (to manage a com-

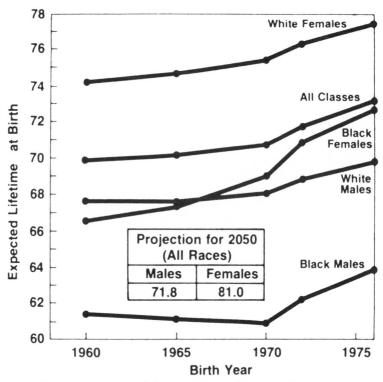

Fig. 3. Recent increases in life expectancies, by sex and race

Source: Levy *(1)*; used with permission of the American Heart Assoc., Inc.

plex system of health and social supports), rather than a command of numerical data from a cardiac catherization or clinical chemical laboratory, may characterize the distinguished cardiologist of the future.

References

1. Levy, R. I., Progress toward prevention of cardiovascular disease. A 30-year retrospective. *Mod. Concepts Cardiovasc. Dis.* **47,** 103–108 (1978).
2. Ross, R., and Glomset, J. A., Studies of primate arterial smooth muscle cells in relation to atherosclerosis. *Science* **180,** 1332 (1973).
3. Stamler, J. V., and Epstein, F. H., Coronary heart disease: Risk factors as guides to preventive action. *Prev. Med.* **1,** 27 (1972).
4. Walker, W. J., Changing United States lifestyle and declining vascular mortality: Cause or coincidence? *N. Engl. J. Med.* **297,** 163–165 (1977). Editorial.

Prevention of Age-Related Bone Loss

Gilbert S. Gordan and Cynthia Vaughan

Age-related bone loss has been noted frequently since antiquity. In the sixth century, Paulus Aeginata described a bone disease that was typically osteoporosis. In 1824, Sir Astley Cooper noted that in old age, "the bones become thin in their shell and spongy in their texture." Despite these and many other similar observations, very little was known of the cause and course of this condition (1). Today there is still much to learn, particularly about bone loss in men, but it is also true to say we now know a good deal of the mechanism and natural history of bone loss in the largest group affected, i.e., ethnically predisposed postmenopausal women. Therefore, our comments will be largely directed to this type of bone loss, because postmenopausal osteoporosis constitutes a major public health problem and is one of the few serious complications of aging that we can easily detect and prevent by several innocuous methods.

The general term *osteoporosis* means "too little bone." Normally, bone formation and bone breakdown, or resorption, are homeostatically coupled and, except in growth and in certain pathologic states, these two mechanisms balance each other. In osteoporosis, however, bone resorption exceeds bone formation so that, ultimately, there is a net loss of bone mass. What bone tissue remains is normally calcified, but the decreased mass results in a brittle, porous, and fragile skeleton.

Bone loss occurs in both sexes with advancing years; however, in men the onset is much later and the rate of loss is much slower than in women. In addition, in all races men start off with a heavier skeleton than women. The cause of age-related bone loss is not known except in certain pathologic conditions, notably hypercorticism, immobilization, chronic alcoholism, cirrhosis, chronic obstructive pulmonary disease, and eunuchoidism. Otherwise, no significant loss of bone occurs in men before age 70. Also, because American men have a lower life expectancy than women, fewer men live long enough to permit age-related bone loss to progress to the stage of skeletal fragility and osteoporotic fractures often seen in women after age 65. Thus, osteoporotic fractures, especially of the vertebrae, wrists, and hips, are much more frequent in women than in men.

Epidemiologic data and measurements of bone mass both show that predisposed women start losing bone after the menopause or oophorectomy (Figures 1 and 2) *(2)*. Age itself is not the critical factor because women who undergo early bilateral oophorectomy, or suffer a premature menopause for any reason, immediately start to lose bone mass. Conversely, women who have a late menopause in their fifties show no significant bone loss until their periods stop. Numerous studies have now confirmed that in women bone loss is directly related to loss of ovarian function. We prefer to call this bone loss in elderly women *postmenopausal osteoporosis,* a time-honored term coined in 1940 by the great pioneer endocrinologist Fuller Albright, who was the first to associate this bone loss with estrogen deficiency. This term accurately delineates both the cause and the population at greatest risk of developing severe bone loss and fractures.

We have already mentioned sexual dimorphism in bone loss in the elderly. In addition, there is an ethnic polymorphism (Figure 3). Bone mass parallels skin pigmentation, blacks having the greatest amount and whites the least. We do not yet have definitive data on bone loss in brown- and yellow-skinned populations, but we can assume from having seen many osteoporotic fractures in older women of these groups that their bone-mass measurements also decrease after loss of ovarian function. We do not know the reason for the ethnic protection of bone in black people, but it appears to be ethnic and not the result of greater activity or the influence of diet. For example, the Bantu of South Africa are a poor people with a grossly deficient diet, by our standards, and a high incidence of lactase deficiency, which deprives them of milk and milk products, their best source of calcium. Moreover, Bantu women have frequent pregnancies and prolonged periods of lactation, both of which drain the mother's skeleton. Despite these adverse factors, the incidence of hip fractures in elderly

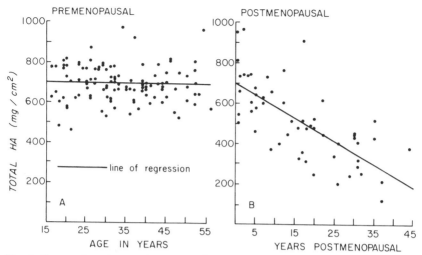

Fig. 1. Bone mineral mass in women by radiodensitometry before and after a natural menopause, expressed as total hydroxyapatite (HA) in mg/cm²

Note that there is no significant loss before the menopause. Source: Meema and Meema *(2)*, by kind permission of the authors and the editor

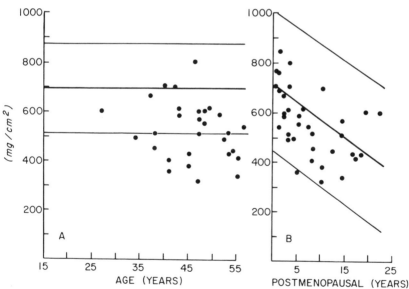

Fig. 2. Bone mineral mass in women by radiodensitometry before and after oophorectomy

Source: Meema and Meema *(2)*, by kind permission of the authors and the editor

171

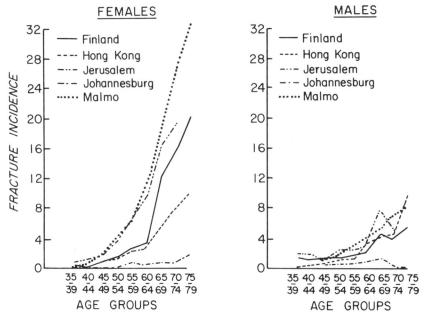

Fig. 3. Fractures of the upper end of the femur in both sexes in five geographical areas

Note that increase after age 50 is far greater in women than in men. The Bantu of Johannesburg do not show the great increase seen in other areas. Source: Alhava and Puittinen *(3)*, by kind permission of the authors and the editor

Bantu women is very low and contrasts conspicuously with the great increase seen in aging white women *(3)*. Osteoporotic fractures are also extremely rare in American blacks of all ages and in both sexes. Therefore, despite considerable interbreeding in this country, the ethnic protection persists *(4)*.

Accurate statistics of morbidity and mortality of osteoporotic hip fractures are difficult to obtain and must be extrapolated, often with considerable misgiving, from available data. Osteoporosis is the most common metabolic bone disease, and postmenopausal osteoporosis is the most common type. Urist *(5)* has shown that at age 60, 26% of white women in California have pathologic osteoporosis with vertebral deformity, compression, and wedging. Knoweldon et al. *(6)* report that by age 75, 50% of white women have vertebral fractures. Hip fractures are, of course, a serious complication of osteoporosis and cause prolonged invalidism and many deaths. Our Bureau of Vital Statistics records deaths only from the secondary causes, e.g., thromboembolism, atelectasis, pneumonia, etc., and not the precipitating cause, the hip fracture, which usually requires anesthesia, surgical repair, and prolonged hospitalization.

In 1881 Bruns noted that, although fractures of the femur before age 50 occur six times more frequently in men than in women, after age 50 hip fractures are more common in women. This seemed strange because one usually associates fractures with trauma, and certainly in 1881 occupational exposure to trauma was more frequent in men. Bruns therefore postulated that elderly women tripped over their long skirts. However, the long-skirt hypothesis is clearly no longer defensible, and recent epidemiologic data are even more impressive: after age 65 hip fractures in the United States are now *eight* times more common in women than in men *(7)*. Alhava and Puittinen *(3)* have shown that the frequency of hip fracture in Scandinavian women *doubles every five years after age 65* and reaches the remarkably high rate of 40% after age 80. Using data from three separate sources [Rochester, MN *(8)*, North Carolina vital statistics, and the National Health Survey *(9)*], we estimate that between 113,000 and 120,000 hip fractures occur in elderly white women in the United States each year, resulting in 12,000 to 15,000 deaths. Thus, hip fracture ranks as the twelfth leading cause of death.

Postmenopausal women with vertebral or hip fractures have significantly less bone mass than is normal for women of their age (Figure 4) *(10)*. Although early bone loss is asymptomatic, it eventually goes on to skeletal depletion, fragility, and fractures. In this context, asymptomatic bone loss is like increased intraocular pressure; both conditions can now be detected and treatment prescribed long before irreparable damage occurs. Just as one no longer waits for optic atrophy and blindness to recognize and treat glaucoma, bone loss can now be accurately demonstrated years before fractures ensue. If we prevent the bone loss that leads to osteoporotic fractures, we shall not only spare thousands of women great suffering and disability but also save at least a billion dollars in hospital and nursing home costs every year.

Identifying Postmenopausal Osteoporosis

Vertebral fractures are usually the first evidence of *pathologic osteoporosis* and the most frequent complication of this disease. The

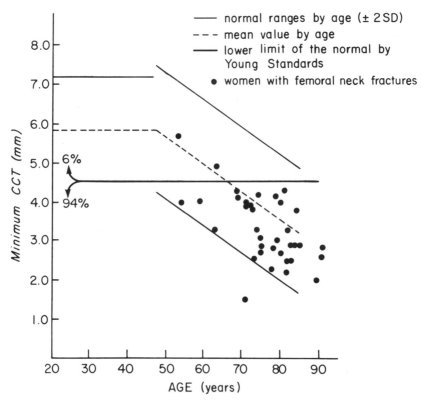

Fig. 4. Combined cortical thickness (CCT) in normal white women *(dotted line)* and in women with hip fractures (●)

Note that after age 70 women with hip fractures are all more than two standard deviations below the youthful normal value. Source: Meema and Meema *(10)*, by kind permission of the authors and the editor

first compression fractures usually occur in the weight-bearing vertebrae, below T-7. These fractures cause acute localized pain, deformity, loss of height, and, eventually, dorsal kyphosis ("dowager's hump"). Vertebral fractures usually heal spontaneously with bed rest, local applications of heat, and mild analgesics. However, with each succeeding fracture the osteoporotic patient becomes more shrunken, deformed, and incapacitated. Pain and the fear of another fracture may result in complete invalidism, and the immobilization of prolonged bed rest can exacerbate the condition with additional osteoporosis of disuse.

Before compression fractures occur, the spongiosa is almost entirely lost so that the vertebrae look like biconcave empty boxes.

This appearance can also occur in metastatic cancer (most commonly breast cancer), in myeloma, and sometimes in osteomalacia or in osteitis fibrosa (hyperparathyroid bone disease), so that one cannot rely solely on the conventional roentgenogram but must examine the patient and the blood chemistry as well. The essential chemical examination includes determination of calcium, phosphate, and alkaline phosphatase and examination of the electrophoretic protein pattern in serum. All of these will give normal values in most cases of postmenopausal osteoporosis, but not in the conditions that can mimic it. The value of these determinations in differential diagnosis is probably well known to clinical chemists, though some details have not been well publicized outside this specialty.

The serum calcium is about 2 to 3 mg/L lower in women during the reproductive years than in men of the same age; after menopause or oophorectomy, calcium concentration in women's sera increases while that of men actually decreases with aging. We have now seen over a dozen postmenopausal women in whom the increase resulted in a hypercalcemic concentration, which had, unfortunately, been misinterpreted as evidence of hyperparathyroidism and led to unnecessary operations, including sternum splitting. Attention to the serum phosphate, which also increases after the menopause, and measurement of the tubular reabsorption of phosphate, which is normal in postmenopausal women but almost always low in patients with hyperparathyroidism, would have spared these women unnecessary surgery. The postmenopausal increase in serum calcium and phosphate reflects the loss of estrogenic restraint on bone breakdown. In all cases we have tested, these increased values have come back to the premenopausal norm when estrogen replacement therapy was introduced.

Alkaline phosphatase, of course, is of enormous differential diagnostic value. It is not increased in osteoporosis or myeloma, but is very often increased in metastatic cancer and almost always in osteomalacia. Alkaline phosphatase increases temporarily in osteoporotic women after hip fractures but usually does not exceed the wide range of normal. The electrophoretic protein pattern identifies most but not all cases of myeloma, which can simulate the roentgenographic appearance of osteoporosis with great fidelity. Repeated examinations are necessary in "idiopathic osteoporosis," which usually turns out to be something else, often myeloma.

One other frequent and sometimes difficult differential diagnosis is epiphysitis (Scheuermann's disease), which can superficially resemble osteoporosis with wedged vertebrae and kyphosis. However, epiphysitis starts in adolescence, and the radiologic data and physical appearance show large osteophytes and thick, irregular vertebral plates, and the classic "coffin-cover"-shaped back is obvious clinically. Radiologic artifacts may also commonly be mistaken for osteoporosis. Fluctuating voltage or amperage is usually the culprit; overpenetration gives the false appearance of decreased bone density in normal bones. Apparent biconcavity can be produced when the roentgen tube is positioned incorrectly, so that the vertebrae are viewed obliquely.

Measuring Bone Mass

Bone mass can now be accurately measured by several techniques, and we can now identify those women at risk of developing postmenopausal osteoporosis. Serial measurements showing a sequential loss of bone identify those individuals who will eventually progress to vertebral fractures and those groups (but not, at present, individuals) who will progress to hip fracture *(11)*. Lindsay et al. *(12)* in 1976 and Horsman et al. *(13)* in 1977 found that bone loss after oophorectomy averages 3% per year for the first six years and then decreases to about 1% per year thereafter. Overall bone loss after a natural menopause averages 1 to 2% per year. Serial bone mass measurements can tell the clinician in three years whether a patient requires treatment to avoid the risk of subsequent osteoporotic fractures.

The most readily available and cheapest way to measure bone mass is measurement of cortical thickness. The only equipment needed is a standard roentgenogram of a tubular bone (e.g., phalanx, metacarpal, or radius) and a pair of calipers. The inside diameter is subtracted from the outer diameter, giving the sum of the width of the right and left cortices, the combined cortical thickness (CCT). Another commonly used technique is photon absorptiometry, which involves small exposure to a radioactive isotope, usually ^{125}I or americium. The bone to be measured (again, usually a phalanx, metacarpal, or radius) is placed over the isotope and below a counter that records how many photons pass through the bone; the photon count is inversely proportional to bone density. Careful technique permits accuracy within 2% and requires minimum radiation exposure. The critical factor is exact positioning; otherwise, serial measurements will not be comparable. More complex methods are valuable in research but are not generally available to the clinician. We are currently using computed tomography with very satisfactory results; preliminary data indicate this method reveals early loss of vertebral spongiosa after oophorectomy before any change can be seen in the peripheral skeleton. Other methods to measure bone mass or bone mineral content include measurements of total or partial body calcium by neutron activation analysis, and dual-beam spectrophotometry. X-ray densitometry, one of the first methods to be developed, is now less commonly used. This method involves a known standard, usually a series of step-wedges placed in the cassette at the time the roentgenogram is taken; the bone to be assessed is then compared with the standard to determine density.

Prophylaxis

Several methods are effective in preventing or retarding post-menopausal bone loss, including low-dose estrogens, a long-acting progestogen, high-dose oral calcium supplements, and short-acting calcitonin injections. Prophylactic treatment is, of course, advocated only for those women known to be at risk of developing osteoporotic fractures. Now that we can objectively measure bone mass, we can ascertain which women are actually losing a significant amount of bone; then we can institute an appropriate regimen of prophylaxis before irreparable damage has occurred to the skeleton, just as we can detect and correct hypertension.

In 1973, Aitken et al. *(14)* reported that small doses of oral estrogen are effective in preventing bone loss in white women after oophorectomy. This study has been continued by Lindsay et al. *(12)* and is now in its tenth year (Figure 5). These workers found that as little as 20 μg of mestranol daily not only prevents the bone loss that occurs in untreated oophorectomized women, but actually increases bone mass to a small but significant extent. Similar prevention of bone loss in women after natural menopause was provided by Recker et al. *(15)*, who used 0.6 mg of natural conjugated estrogens with 5 mg of methyltestosterone daily, the estrogenic equivalent of 19 μg of ethynyl estradiol daily *(16, 17)*.

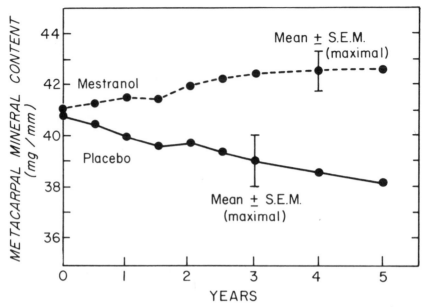

Fig. 5. Bone mineral mass by photon absorptiometry at two sites in 120 oophorectomized white women

In a study involving the double-blind technique 63 received 20 μg of mestranol daily, while 57 received a lactose placebo. At one year the mestranol-treated women had significantly greater bone mass than the controls. At three years of mestranol treatment bone mineral mass was significantly increased. Source: Lindsay et al. *(12)*, by kind permission of the authors and the editor

We are conducting a prospective study, using the double-blind technique, to determine the minimum *osteotrophic* dose of estrogens in postmenopausal and oophorectomized women. Preliminary data indicate that this dose is lower than that found effective by Lindsay, Recker, Heaney, and others. Low-dose estrogen prophylaxis is, in our opinion, the treatment of choice to prevent postmenopausal bone loss. Estrogens are well tolerated if the patient hasn't been terrified by adverse publicity. Minimum effective doses do not produce endometrial hyperplasia and, therefore, there is no bleeding; moreover, these doses are much lower than the doses of estrogen implicated, rightly or wrongly, in the etiology of endometrial cancer. We must emphasize, however, that after bone loss has progressed to the stage of skeletal fragility and osteoporotic fractures, these low prophylactic doses of estrogen no longer suffice and full replacement doses are needed to prevent further fractures. In a 25-year prospective study we successfully managed 220 women with advanced osteoporosis on this regimen (18).

Prevention and treatment of postmenopausal bone loss demands a lifelong commitment from the patient and her physician; therefore, education of patients is absolutely essential. Lindsay et al. (19) found that when estrogen replacement was stopped in 14 of their oophorectomized patients, these women promptly started to lose bone and soon were indistinguishable from the placebo-treated control subjects (Figure 6). Similarly, we found that when full replacement doses of estrogen were decreased or stopped, our osteoporotic women promptly began to fracture again. Resumption of full replacement doses of estrogen effectively prevented further fractures (18). Consequently, if estrogen prophylaxis must be stopped, for whatever reason, another type of treatment must be instituted.

A significant number of women at risk of postmenopausal osteoporosis either cannot or will not take estrogens. Fortunately we now have alternative therapies for such women. A recent report indicates that a long-acting progestogen can help protect the skeleton against bone loss after oophorectomy (20). Two other recent studies have shown that high-dose oral calcium supplements are almost as effective as estrogens in preventing postmenopausal bone loss. Recker et al. (15) prescribed calcium carbonate, 2.6 g daily, in addition to the normal dietary intake. Horsman et al. (21) gave their patients two calcium gluconate tablets daily, equivalent to 800 mg of calcium. Neither group reported any ill effects during the short-term study period. However, high-dose calcium therapy is not without risk; the development of hypercalciuria and even hypercalcemia is a real hazard. Despite these concerns, with careful instruction, hydration, and monitoring, high-dose calcium supplements are a useful alternative to estrogens to prevent postmenopausal osteoporosis. Finally, three separate groups have had some success in treating established osteoporosis with calcitonin, with or without added calcium (22–24). Calcitonin must be given frequently because of its short duration of action; it must be given by injection; and it can stimulate the formation of antibodies. Patients can be taught to administer their own calcitonin injections, but the antibody problem requires considerable further study. Despite these drawbacks we can reasonably assume

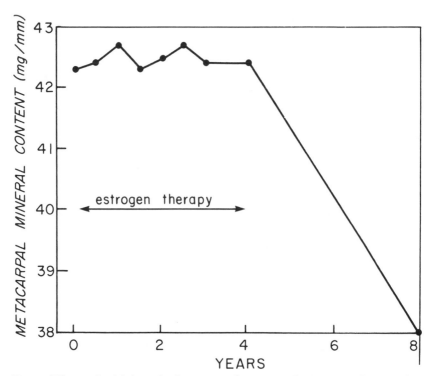

Fig. 6. Effects of withdrawal of estrogen therapy on bone mineral mass after four years of active treatment

Termination of estrogen treatment is followed by loss of bone similar to that seen in lactose-treated controls. Source: Lindsay et al. *(19)*, by kind permission of the authors and the editor

that, for some women, calcitonin will provide some protection against postmenopausal bone loss.

Summary

Although both sexes lose bone with aging, only in women does this bone loss start early, proceed rapidly, and lead to an enormous number of deforming, painful, and even fatal fractures of the vertebrae, wrists, and hips. For some reason black-skinned people, both in Africa and in the United States, are ethnically protected from osteoporosis. Bone loss can now be measured accurately and conveniently, long before skeletal fragility and fractures occur. The best news is that surprisingly small doses of estrogens prevent this bone loss. Where estrogens cannot be given, large doses of calcium, calcitonin, or a progestational agent may be substituted; therefore, it is now feasible to prevent osteoporotic fractures with their heavy toll of human suffering and financial outlay. Unhappily, for the infrequent problem of age-related osteoporosis in men, less is known of its pathophysiology, prevention, and treatment. Similarly, the osteoporosis of disuse and of Cushing's syndrome is also poorly understood. However, the greatest public health problem is postmenopausal osteoporosis, a condition for which we now have effective, innocuous prophylaxis.

Incidence and mortality data on hip fractures in the United States were obtained with the collaboration of Drs. J. R. Abernathy and B. G. Greenberg of the School of Public Health, University of North Carolina, Chapel Hill; the Division of Health Services of the State of North Carolina; and the National Center for Health Statistics, Hyattsville, MD. We also thank Dr. J. C. Gallagher for the use of his data prior to publication.

References

1. Gordan, G. S., and Vaughan, C., Clinical Management of the Osteoporoses. Publishing Sciences Group, Acton, MA, 1976, pp 6–8.
2. Meema, S., and Meema, H. E., Menopausal bone loss and estrogen replacement. Israel J. Med. Sci. 12, 601 (1976).
3. Alhava, E. M., and Puittinen, J., Fractures of the upper end of the femur as an index of senile osteoporosis in Finland. Ann. Clin. Res. 5, 398 (1973).
4. Gyepes, M., Mellins, H. Z., and Katz, I., The low incidence of fracture of the hip in the Negro. J. Am. Med. Assoc. 181, 133 (1962).
5. Urist, M. R., Observations bearing on the problem of osteoporosis. In Bone as a Tissue, J. Nicholson, Ed., McGraw Hill Co., New York, NY, 1960, pp 18–45.
6. Knowelden, J., Buhr, A. J., and Dunbar, O., Incidence of fractures in persons over 35 years of age. Br. J. Prev. Soc. Med. 18, 130 (1964).
7. Iskrant, A. P., The etiology of fractured hips in females. Am. J. Pub. Health 58, 485 (1968).
8. Gallagher, J. C., Melton, L. J., Riggs, B. L., and Bergstrath, E., Epidemiology of fractures of the proximal femur in Rochester, Minnesota, U.S.A. Clin. Orthop. (in press, June–July 1980).
9. National Center for Health Statistics, Inpatient utilization of short-stay hospitals by diagnosis, United States, 1975, Vital and Health Statistics. Series 13-No. 35. DHEW Pub. No. (PHS) 78–1786. Washington, DC, U.S. Govt. Printing Office, April 1978.

10. Meema, H. E., and Meema, S., Involutional (physiologic) bone loss in women and the feasibility of preventing structural failure. *J. Am. Geriatr. Soc.* **22,** 443 (1974).
11. Hagberg, L., and Nilsson, B. E., Can fractures of the femoral neck be predicted? *Geriatrics* **32,** 55 (1977).
12. Lindsay, R., Aitken, J. M., Anderson, J. B., Hart, D. M., MacDonald, E. B., and Clarke, A. C., Long-term prevention of post-menopausal osteoporosis by oestrogen: Evidence for an increased bone mass after delayed onset of oestrogen treatment. *Lancet* **i,** 1038 (1976).
13. Horsman, A., Simpson, M., Kirby, P. A., and Nordin, B. E. C., Nonlinear bone loss in oophorectomized women. *Br. J. Radiol.* **50,** 504 (1977).
14. Aitken, J. M., Hart, D. M., and Lindsay, R., Oestrogen replacement therapy for prevention of osteoporosis after oophorectomy. *Br. Med. J.* **iii,** 515 (1973).
15. Recker, R. R., Saville, P. D., and Heaney, R. P., Effect of estrogens and calcium carbonate on bone loss in postmenopausal women. *Ann. Int. Med.* **87,** 649 (1977), and Letter to Editor, *ibid.,* **89,** 149 (1978).
16. Heaney, R. P., Recker, R. R., and Saville, P. D., Menopausal changes in calcium balance performance. *J. Lab. Clin. Med.* **92,** 953 (1978).
17. Heaney, R. P., Recker, R. R., and Saville, P. D., Menopausal changes in bone remodelling. *J. Lab. Clin. Med.* **92,** 964 (1978).
18. Gordan, G. S., Picchi, J., and Roof, B. S., Antifracture efficacy of long-term estrogens in osteoporosis. *Trans. Assoc. Am. Phys.* **86,** 326 (1973).
19. Lindsay, R., Hart, D. M., and MacLean, A., Bone response to termination of oestrogen treatment. *Lancet* **i,** 1325 (1978).
20. Lindsay, R., Hart, D. M., Purdie, D., Ferguson, M. M., Clark, A. S., and Kraszewski, A., Comparative effects of oestrogen and a progestogen on bone loss in postmenopausal women. *Clin. Sci. Molec. Med.* **54,** 193 (1978).
21. Horsman, A., Gallagher, J. C., Simpson, M., and Nordin, B. E. C., Prospective trial of oestrogen and calcium in postmenopausal women. *Br. Med. J.* **ii,** 789 (1977).
22. Wallach, S., Cohn, S. H., Atkins, H. L., Ellis, K. J., Kohberger, R., Aloia, J. F., and Zanzi, I., Effect of salmon calcitonin on skeletal mass in osteoporosis. *Curr. Ther. Res.* **22,** 556 (1977).
23. Chestnut, C. H., Baylink, D. J., Matthews, M., Ivey, J., and Nelp, W. B., Calcitonin therapy in postmenopausal osteoporosis. Preliminary results. *Clin. Res.* **27,** 85A (1979).
24. Milhaud, G., Talbot, J. N., and Coutris, G., Calcitonin treatment of postmenopausal osteoporosis. Evaluation of efficacy by principal components analysis. *Biomedicine* **23,** 223 (1975).

Aging Brain and Dementia

Leopold Liss

The title of my presentation can easily be paraphrased: "Is Senility a Condition Normally Encountered in Aging?" The physiological aging of the brain as well as other tissues results in a "change of tissue to a lower or less functionally active form" (1), the definition of a degenerative process, a pathological entity. Thus, this question, which may appear to be semantic hair-splitting, actually represents the key problem of the issue at hand.

The present impetus of research on aging is the potential to extend the human life span, which until now has been regarded as predestined and therefore impregnable to any manipulations. While this boldest of endeavors is progressing, we must address ourselves to the quality of life within the survival limits available to us.

Dementia represents a high risk to a large percentage of our aged population. By its nature it is the most dehumanizing of diseases, leaving a functioning organism without a mind. Naming this condition "senility" implies that it is a "natural" phenomenon occurring with advancing age (senium); it has been so accepted by all cultures and races. The clear understanding that we are dealing with a disease process should, therefore, lead to the determination of the predisposing and etiologic factors, and subsequently open the way to develop tools for diagnosis, treatment, and prevention.

"Regressive" Changes in Aging

Lipofuscin is the pigment of aging, the "wear and tear" pigment that increases with age. It begins to accumulate in some regions of the brain during adolescence, achieving impressive deposits by middle age *(2)*. On the other hand, increased accumulation of lipofuscin granules in neuronal groups, which normally occurs only with advanced age, can also be observed in cases where the nature of injury is known. For example, extensive amounts of lipofuscin were found in almost all areas of the brain of a 16-year-old severely retarded girl (Figure 1). Her brain had been damaged by maternal disease during pregnancy and subsequently

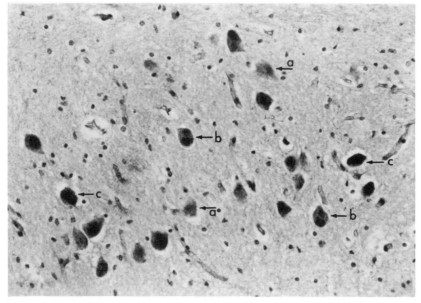

Fig. 1. A group of neurons from a 16-year-old mentally retarded girl who suffered severe pre- and perinatal cerebral anoxia

The deposition of lipofuscin in some neurons is mild *(a)*, other neurons show significant accumulation of lipofuscin granules *(b)*, and some are densely filled *(c)*

by prolonged labor. The decreased ability of the neurons to perform their physiological function of storing and transmitting information is apparently concomitant with damage to their metabolic activity, preventing disposal of the metabolized material and therefore resulting in extensive lipofuscinosis. This correlation between hypoxic neuronal damage and lipofuscin deposition represents only one of the modes of neuronal injury leading to lipofuscinosis, which in some cases can be associated with environmental factors.

The lack of adequate perfusion of blood is assumed to be the reason for clinical symptomatology in cases of normal-pressure hydrocephalus (3). In my own limited experience with cerebral biopsies of patients with low-pressure hydrocephalus, I consistently found an increased lipofuscin deposition in the cortical neurons. After a shunting procedure, which by lowering the pressure of cerebrospinal fluid facilitated better perfusion of the cortex, some patients were clinically improved. There remains a valid question: If the preoperative symptoms were related to lipofuscin accumulation, was the improvement related to a decrease in lipofuscin, and is this process a reversible one?

Another morphological finding related both to "aging" and to cerebral hypoxia are the "amyloid bodies"; these begin to appear in adulthood, becoming more numerous and involving more regions with increasing age. These unspecific changes are also encountered in abundance in the brains of young persons with a history of hypoxic, traumatic, or postinflammatory brain injury (Figure 2).

These unspecific aging changes, in the form of lipofuscin and the amyloid bodies, are abundant in injured brains of young individuals and occur regularly in old brains. The mechanisms responsible for the occurrence of these "aging" changes have to be viewed as a pathological process, most likely resulting from decreased metabolic activity in the old cells, which may respond to normal demands or to minimum stress the way a young cell would respond to a catastrophic event.

Cerebrovascular Disease

The widely accepted explanation for "senility" is either simply "aging" or the arteriosclerotic disease of the brain, popularly referred to as "hardening of cerebral arteries." This latter process is regarded as being unavoidable with age and thus responsible for the feebleness of many of the elderly. As many as 90% of elderly individuals suffering from various degrees of dementia used to be diagnosed routinely as having hardening of the arteries (4). Studies on the prevalence of Alzheimer's disease (5) also indicate the importance of vascular disturbances that lead to changes in higher nervous activity. An estimated 10 to 25% of all dementias are caused by cerebrovascular disease and another 10 to 25% by mixed vascular lesion and Alzheimer's disease.

185

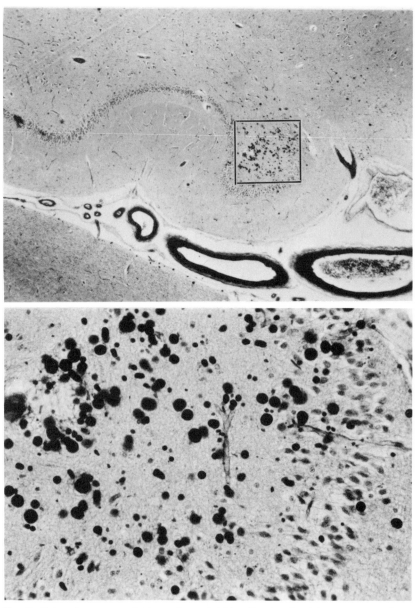

Fig. 2. Extensive accumulation of amyloid bodies in the hippocampus of an 18-year-old retarded man with a history of severe perinatal anoxia

Bottom, enlargement of outlined area in the *upper* frame

Vascular lesions responsible for the clinical picture of dementia with insidious onset result from continuous nutrient starvation of areas of the brain. The ischemic episode that results from occlusion of a major artery, most frequently from obstruction at the carotid bifurcation, will often lead to obvious neurological changes that affect the motor activity but impair cognitive abilities little or not at all. Therefore, the vascular dementias, or (as they are more appropriately termed) multi-infarct dementias, are characterized by widespread lesions that affect large areas of the cerebral cortex and result in general oxygen and glucose starvation. This starvation is frequently sufficient to injure the neurons, yet permits maintenance of the tissue structure and even facilitates glial response and astrocytic scarification. These conditions can be insidious without any clinical evidence of cerebral ischemia, or may be accompanied by transient ischemic episodes with temporary symptoms of weakness, speech, or visual difficulties. Although apparent to the individual, these episodes do not result in permanent impairment of these functions; in many cases, however, the slow deterioration of neurons leads to a depletion of their number.

The catastrophic event of a major obstructive cerebrovascular disease may have little effect on mental performance. Examples of these processes are quite common. Figure 3 shows the brain of an individual in his 80's who had suffered from occlusion of major arteries and multiple infarcts, which resulted in paralysis. On histological examination, however, his cortex showed no evidence of Alzheimer-type changes. Apparently, sufficient tissue was preserved that, despite considerable physical impairment, his mental abilities remained intact. Contrast this case with findings in an individual who suffered from a cardiovascular disease and had no clinical evidence of cerebrovascular disease and no motor loss, either transient or permanent. He had only a continuously progressing dementia, which resulted in severe mental deterioration. As the postmortem examination showed (Figure 4), there was a considerable loss of neurons in the cortex, which occurred in a diffuse and lacunar fashion, did not produce any tissue-matrix destruction, and resulted in diffuse and focal astrocytic gliosis. This process, which was not accompanied by Alzheimer-type changes, illustrates pure ischemic disease of the brain resulting in dementia.

Another example shows combined vascular disease and Alz-

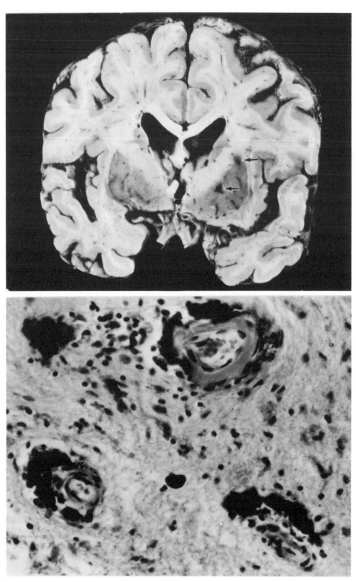

Fig. 3. Brain of 82-year-old man with history of stroke and subsequent paralysis but no clinical evidence of dementia

Top, multiple old cysts resulting from ischemic infarcts *(arrow); (bottom)* evidence of small-vessel disease with thickening walls and calcium deposits. Histologically, there was no evidence of neurofibrillary tangles or neurogenic plaques

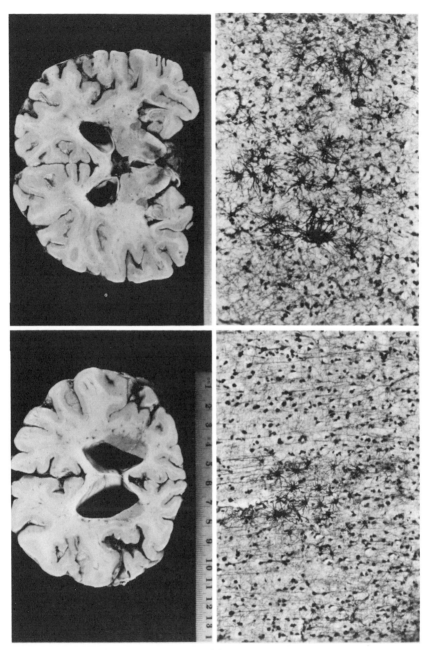

Fig. 4. Multiple infarcts in an 80-year-old man, resulting in progressive dementia

(Left) Marked cerebral atrophy without any gross evidence of infarcts microscopically; *(right)* multiple foci of astroglial scars, which are the response of lacunar loss of neurons in the cortex and vary considerably in size

189

heimer-type changes (Figure 5). In this individual a cerebrovascular disease resulting from numerous embolic episodes randomly destroyed several cortical areas and resulted in complete deterioration of motor as well as mental functions. This type of pathology represents a vascular dementia of the multi-infarct type, combined with Alzheimer-type changes.

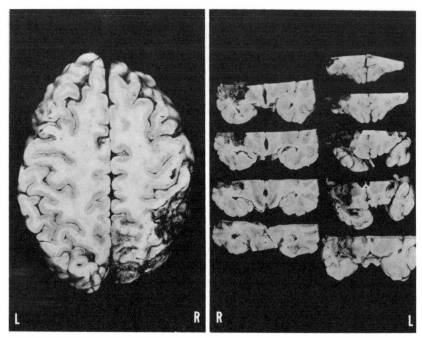

Fig. 5. Vascular occlusive disease resulted in multiple large and small infarcts involving frontal, parietal, occipital, and temporal areas

This individual was demented; histology showed a moderate degree of neurofibrillary tangles and neurogenic plaques

Vascular changes represent, therefore, an important but not the leading cause of dementia, and are etiologically unrelated to Alzheimer-type dementia.

Cerebral Atrophy and Dementia (Alzheimer-Type)

The cerebral substance, expressed as total weight, decreases in senium *(6)*. This finding, which has been demonstrated with autopsy material, can now be studied in live individuals with use of computerized tomography *(7, 8)*. The progressive loss of brain weight had been erroneously correlated with the assumption that the cerebral neurons in all areas of the brain were dying continuously, so that this process of programmed, neuronal loss was the cause of both brain atrophy and dementia in senium. Current evidence, however, indicates that variations in brain size among the general population do not account for individual variation in learning, memory, or special talents. More recently, the hypothesis linking the neuronal loss with decrease in brain mass and cognitive functions, which are impaired in dementia, has been abolished. The loss of neurons is indeed a function of advancing age, but has a localized, limited character *(9)*.

Examination of the importance of cerebral atrophy in the progression of Alzheimer-type dementia can help us understand the role of cerebral atrophy in normal aging. The data illustrated are based on extensive studies of 17 controls and 44 individuals suffering Alzheimer-type dementia. The progression of Alzheimer-type dementia has been classified into five stages.

Stage I, preclinical: The first clinical symptoms of onset of the disease can be reconstructed only in retrospect, the forgetfulness and deviation from the individual's normal behavior pattern having been earlier attributed to preoccupation, stress, or a temporary condition.

Stage II, independent: At this point medical help is usually sought. The coworkers, family, or the individual has become aware of difficulty with memory or occasional confusion. The ability to maintain gainful employment is lost, but the social graces persist and a casual observer may be unaware of a pathological condition.

Stage III, dependent: The confusion progresses, making possible performance of simplest tasks only. There is a need for continuing supervision, help with personal care, and assistance in feeding. With further progression, incontinence develops. In many instances the family situation may warrant placement in an extended-care facility.

Stage IV, demented. The loss of interaction with surroundings is advanced. The patient is unable to recognize family members and has no evidence of cognitive function. Ambulation is maintained, but continuous supervision is needed.

Stage V, advanced: At this terminal stage, the patient is bedridden

Table 1. Comparison of Alzheimer-Type Dementia, Presenile Form, with Normal, Aged Controls

	CAT	EEG	NFT–NP
Controls[a]	++/+++	+/−	+/−
Alzheimer-type dementia[b]			
I, preclinical	−	−	+/−
II, self-sufficient	−	+/−	+/++
III, dependent	+	+	++/+++
IV, demented	++/+++	++	+++/++++
V, advanced	+++/+++++	+++	++++

[a] Mean age, 75 years.
[b] Mean age, 61 years.
CAT, results of computerized tomography; EEG, electroencephalograms; NFT–NP, neurofibrillary tangles and neurogenic plaques. Each column indicates the presence (+) or absence (−) of confirming evidence with the method or factor shown; the number of +'s indicates strength of correlation. Information on morphological changes is extrapolated for early stages, where the data are least reliable. The morphological data for Stages II and III are derived from a limited biopsy material, and Stages IV and V from autopsy material. The changes of brain size, as measured by computerized tomography, illustrate the importance of age-related cerebral atrophy.

and requires complete care. On the basis of postmortem examinations, which by their nature are limited to evaluation of the end-stage of the disease, this stage of Alzheimer's disease is associated with extensive brain atrophy and weight loss of 400–500 g.

These findings are now being augmented with the use of computerized tomography, which as a noninvasive technique permits measurement of the brain mass, the subarachnoid compartment, and the ventricular size in a live patient, and allows a follow-up of the progression of the disease. These new findings have modified current views as follows.

The correlation of the clinical performance, electroencephalographic findings, and degree of cerebral atrophy (Table 1) shows that in Stages I and II of Alzheimer's disease, there is no evidence of cerebral atrophy but occasional evidence of unspecific electroencephalographic abnormalities. In Stage III cerebral atrophy becomes more apparent, and late in Stage III can be used as a diagnostic criterion. In the last two stages the atrophy progresses significantly (Figure 6). The normal controls used in our study were older (mean, 75 years) than patients with Alzheimer-type dementia (mean, 61 years), which resulted in overcompensation, to the detriment of the control group, and made the findings even more impressive. Individuals in the control group scored high on the extensive test battery, which confirmed the high intel-

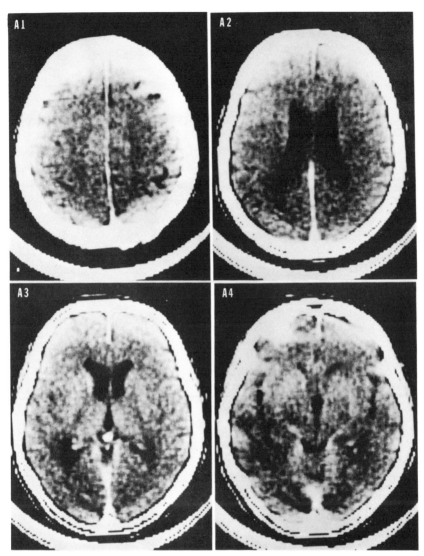

Fig. 6. Computerized tomographic scans *A1* to *A4* show a moderate degree of ventricular dilation in a 55-year-old woman classified at time of scanning as late third or early fourth stage of dementia

lectual performance demonstrated by their active life-style. Nonetheless, the size of the controls' brains showed significant decreases in mass (Figure 7).

The correlation of clinical manifestations, electro-physiological

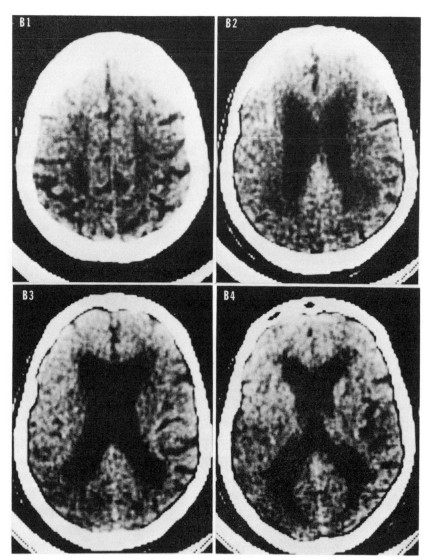

Fig. 7. *B1* to *B4*, computerized tomographic scans of an 87-year-old woman who volunteered as control; she is intellectually active and has scored high on the psychometric battery

Comparison of Figs. 6 and 7 shows dilation of sulci on cut *1*. Cuts *3* and *4* show little dilation of the ventricles and minimal atrophy of the island and temporal lobe sulci despite dementia

194

findings, and brain size indicates that physiological aging involves a considerable loss of tissue without a significant loss of function. In contrast, in cases of total incapacitation due to loss of function (cases requiring constant supervision of confused patients who may not be able to take care of their daily essential needs), brain atrophy was moderate or absent. Postmortem examination of advanced cases of Alzheimer's disease, as a rule, has dealt with brains weighing 1000 g or less and having an estimated weight loss of 25% or more. Thus atrophy follows an advanced loss of function, progresses rapidly in the last stages of the disease, and cannot be used as an indicator of function in the early stages of the disease. We should not, therefore, accept cerebral atrophy as the cause of, or a finding preceding, dementia.

The striking difference between the normal-sized brain of a demented individual and the severely atrophic brain of a normal, aged person makes imperative a critical reevaluation of the relationship between brain atrophy and function. Yet one may occasionally see a case in which brain weight remains normal, even though clinical deterioration is profound and morphologic changes (plaques and tangles) are diagnostic for advanced Alzheimer's disease (Figure 8). Although such observations are very unusual, it is important to underscore the fact that, in the general population, the relationship between brain size and performance has long been discredited. I will state it more strongly: the extensive loss of brain weight observed in aged individuals is compatible with some loss of performance, normal for their age (10). The patient dying in advanced stages of Alzheimer's disease, however, will show a massive atrophy unlike those seen in normal, aged individuals.

The presence of Alzheimer-type histological changes in normal, aged individuals is difficult to understand fully on the basis of available information (11). It is premature to state unequivocally what the "physiological" alteration of mental performance of the elderly represents. Numerous individuals in the seventh decade, more in their eighth decade, and the majority of those in the ninth decade show at least some evidence of neurofibrillary tangles and plaques on routine postmortem examination. The conclusion is, therefore, that these changes, because they are almost ubiquitous, represent a normal aspect of aging. The question is, Are

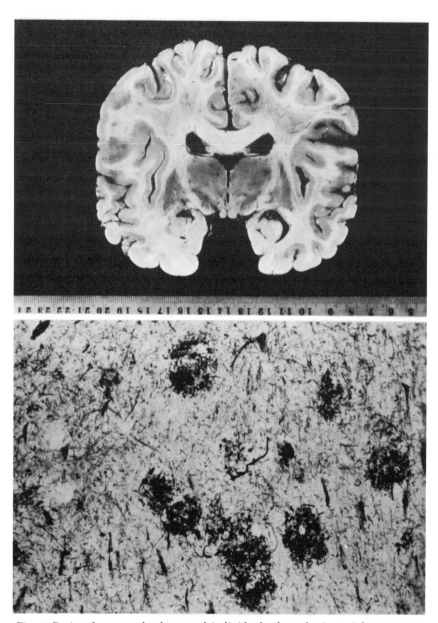

Fig. 8. Brain of a severely demented individual whose brain weight was 1500 g and showed no evidence of gross atrophy despite marked Alzheimer-type changes; abundant neurofibrillary tangles and neurogenic plaques in hippocampus, frontal, and temporal lobes

these changes inevitable, even if quantitatively they are age related?

The inevitability concept is questionable, given the sporadic occurrence of cases such as the following. The oldest individual examined in this autopsy material was 116 years old. His mental performance was quite difficult to evaluate, in that he had been schizophrenic for the last 80 years of his life; however, there were no obvious clinical indications that he had become feeble toward the end of his life. Extensive examination of his brain failed to show any evidence of neurofibrillary tangles or neurogenic plaque. This finding, as well as others with similar results, could seriously challenge the assumption that development of Alzheimer-type changes is inevitable at a certain age and represents an almost physiological function of age. My current hypothesis, which I will discuss later, is that Alzheimer's disease might instead be related to the decrease of other functions, such as immune surveillance, with resulting loss of natural defenses against the entry of aluminum into the central nervous system.

What is of essential importance is the classification of these changes either as "normal aging" or as "early Alzheimer's disease," which increases in frequency with age, similar to other conditions such as arteriosclerosis and cancer that are maintained in proper perspective and classified as disease processes. This clarification is essential for the scientific community to be able to establish appropriate priorities for research.

Neurofibrillary Tangles and Aluminum

The neurofibrillary tangles represent a finding characteristic for Alzheimer's disease. This type of neuronal degeneration, which has been associated with the original description of the presenile dementia by Alzheimer in 1907, represents accumulation of argentophil fibers in the neurons and is referred to as "Alzheimer-type" neurofibrillary degeneration. Numerous observations, on both humans and experimental animals, have shown that this neurofibrillary degeneration of neurons represents an unspecific type of pathological response of the neurons to numerous chemical toxins and biological agents [12]. Despite the reports of the nonspecificity of the neurofibrillary degeneration observed in an ever-increasing number of pathological situations, the undeniable fact remains that there is a quantitative correlation between the mental deterioration of patients with presenile or senile forms of Alzheimer's dementia and the density of neurofibrillary degeneration; both are related to severity of clinical manifestations (13). It is, therefore, significant that this particular degenerative process occurs consistently in Alzheimer's disease and that the severity of brain involvement can be correlated with the functional state of the patient.

Among the physiological factors capable of injuring neurons by stimulating production of abnormal protein, as suggested originally by Alzheimer, aluminum produces neurofibrillary tangles when applied in the form of aluminum gel to the cortex of experimental animals to produce an epileptogenic focus (14). The morphological correlation between Alzheimer's disease and the aluminum-produced neurofibrillary tangles has been challenged through ultrastructural analysis, which shows that, in contrast to the paired helical filaments that form the "neurofibrillary tangles" in Alzheimer's disease, the experimentally produced argentophil tangles are composed of straight filaments and therefore apparently represent a different entity (15, 16).

Crapper et al. (17), despite these findings, analyzed the aluminum content in brains of individuals with Alzheimer's disease; they found increased concentration of aluminum and correlated aluminum content with severity of neurofibrillary degeneration of the neurons in the examined areas. Their scientific curiosity laid the foundation of important research in this area into causative factors of Alzheimer's disease. Subsequently, aluminum injection into the cerebral substance has been found to result in formation of neurofibrillary tangles composed of straight filaments; the injection also decreases learning ability, as demonstrated in avoidance-response studies with cats (7). The aluminum produces neurofibrillary tangles only in large cells of the cerebral hemispheres, showing distinct preference for specific areas.

The large neurons of the supraoptic nucleus do not develop neurofibrillary tangles in Alzheimer's disease; neither do the Purkinje cells of the cerebellum. The large motor cells and periaqueductal neurons, however, are frequent targets, in addition to the usual hippocampal, frontal, and temporal areas of predilection. In vitro studies show that neurons from the spinal ganglia subjected to high aluminum concentrations undergo toxic changes but will not produce neurofibrillary tangles.

Observation of a focal disturbance of the blood–brain barrier, unrelated to Alzheimer's disease, with concomitant increases in aluminum and transformation of all neurons into elements with neurofibrillary tangles of the human paired-helical variety *(18)*, brings forth a hypothesis that the neurotoxic effect of aluminum, which results in formation of neurofibrillary tangles, can be of at least three and possibly more types. In certain neurons in humans, aluminum causes formation of neurofibrillary tangles composed of paired helical filaments. Aluminum acting upon the neurons of experimental animals, however, produces neurofibrillary tangles composed of straight filaments. Aluminum deposited in high concentrations in neurons that are not capable of producing neurofibrillary tangles may either lead to unspecific degeneration or produce damming of axonal flow, as proposed for the Purkinje cells in humans *(19)*. Recent observations with x-ray diffraction have confirmed preferential accumulation of aluminum in the neuronal nuclei of cells in which neurofibrillary tangles are present. This indicates a very specific preferential attraction and also suggests an extremely high concentration of aluminum attached to the nuclear DNA, which results in synthesis of abnormal proteins.

This concept, in which aluminum is the final triggering factor in producing neurofibrillary tangles in presenile and senile forms of Alzheimer's disease, poses an important question as to the natural defense mechanism of human brain: Did it perhaps evolve to counter this ubiquitous, most common of metals, the third most common element of the earth's crust?

Another important point to consider is the artificially increased contact with aluminum, which has been demonstrated to result in increased uptake in body tissues, including the brain. Increased exposure to aluminum is expected in individuals engaged in industries processing aluminum, by inhaling aluminum dust as silicosis prophylaxis, and in others who are in contact with the aluminum in baking powder, antacids, deodorants, cookware, and food-storage containers—to name only some. Presumably the brain has a natural barrier against invasion of aluminum, and excessive intake will, in normal individuals, result in increased excretion *(20)*.

Role of Intrinsic Factors

Alzheimer-type changes, specifically the neurofibrillary tangles and the plaques, are subject to environmental modifications. Presumably individuals have various degrees of susceptibility to developing these kind of changes. Recent studies indicate that a group with 100% risk to develop Alzheimer-type changes and Alzheimer's disease (Figure 9) are the patients with Down's syndrome *(21)*. These individuals, who have trisomy 21 and suffer from various degrees of retardation, also show evidence of changes in the enzymes superoxide dismutase, gluthathione peroxidase, and hexose monophosphate shunt. Enzyme activity has been shown to correlate with mental performance in patients with Down's syndrome *(22)*.

There is also a genetically determined higher risk for individuals from families with a history of Down's syndrome and Alzheimer's disease to develop Alzheimer-type dementia *(23)*. Therefore, the state of immune mechanism, the enzymes controlling superoxides, and other factors may represent variations of the risk level for an individual to develop the Alzheimer-type changes or dementia. One of the highest research priorities should be the determination of the type of changes governing susceptibility and increasing the risk factor. A laboratory test that could identify these individuals would be most valuable for identification of susceptible individuals and application of preventive or therapeutic measures.

Viral Etiology

Gajdusek *(24)* elucidated the role of transmissible agents that, after long latency, produce neurological disorders; such diseases had previously been classified as degenerative diseases or abiotrophies. His pioneer work on kuru, a disease occurring in New Guinea, showed it to be caused by an agent transmitted by the practice of ritual cannibalism. The transmission of this agent to primates has created in human neuropathology the category of diseases referred to as slow or latent virus diseases. Several animal models of these conditions occur in nature, such as scrapie in sheep.

One of the dementias, which is characterized by rapid progression of mental deterioration and extrapyramidal signs, was de-

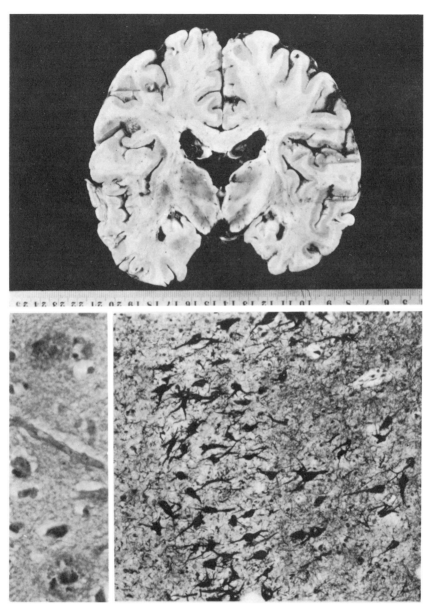

Fig. 9. Brain of a 50-year-old retarded man with Down's syndrome; his frontal lobe shows extensive neurogenic plaques and neurofibrillary tangles

scribed by Jakob and Creutzfeldt and bears their name (it is classified as spongiform encephalopathy) (25). This condition is caused by a transmissible agent, and after a considerable latency, which in humans apparently lasts for years or even decades, produces rapidly progressing deterioration.

This agent is resistant to the usual sterilization procedures; to inactivate it, special measures must be taken. Consider that brain specimens fixed and processed for histology can be used successfully to transmit the disease to an experimental animal. In pathology laboratories many people handle highly infectious material, which when injected into the nervous system could produce a disease. People who handle blood and other body fluids are exposed to a similar risk; yet infections of this type fortunately are rare, considering the resistance of this kind of agent to deactivation. A few convincing reports of transmission of Jakob–Creutzfeldt disease to or by health professionals warrant a set of precautionary rules when dealing with material from patients (25, 26).

Determination of the viral etiology of spongiform encephalopathy has stimulated studies to elucidate the role of viruses in diseases such as amyotrophic lateral sclerosis, Alzheimer's disease, Huntington's chorea, and others. In the case of Alzheimer's disease, an infectious nature is extremely difficult to accept, in view of the epidemology of the disease. Let me cite only three well-verified observations, which question the infectious nature of the disease. First, there is the 100% risk factor to develop Alzheimer's disease or at least Alzheimer-type pathological changes in individuals with Down's syndrome after age 30. In more than 30 autopsy cases I and coworkers have observed, every one older than age 30 showed involvement; the youngest in our series who showed unequivocal early changes was 16 years old. Secondly, another group at high risk to develop Alzheimer's disease is the aged; from age 60, the risk factor for this group increases with every succeeding decade. Thirdly, there are infrequent but definite familial occurrences of Alzheimer's disease, which both clinically and pathologically appear to be identical to the sporadic cases.

If we analyze these three groups with highest risk to develop Alzheimer's disease, we cannot accept an infectious hypothesis of etiology on the basis of random infection from communication with other individuals or transmission by some other means. There might, however, be an agent that is not transmissible but is attached to the genome. This risk factor could affect the entire population of the world equally.

The condition that aging and Down's syndrome have in common is decreased immune competence. Desuppressions of the causative agent might affect the blood–brain barrier or some other protective mechanism of the brain designed to prevent deposition of aluminum in nerve cells. Because protection at the neuronal level is less likely, we should consider a more generalized decrease of resistance, possibly at the blood–brain barrier, as the result of the decrease of the immunologic competence. Let us, therefore, look at this hypothetical virus as an agent facilitating the entrance into the central nervous system of substances that are toxic and capable of damaging neurons.

The etiology of the neurogenic plaques, the histological structures found consistently in the presenile and senile forms of Alzheimer's disease, is not known. These structures are represented by persisting debris of cells; their processes stimulate a vigorous glial response, resulting in the dense accumulation of cell bodies and processes in the periphery of the plaques *(27)*. The centers of the plaques contain amyloid and increased concentrations of immune proteins, especially immunoglobulin. Obviously this response has some characteristics similar to those of granulomas in the body, being of immune etiology and having a persisting nature. The plaque structure, unique to the central nervous system, has been experimentally reproduced by injection of a scrapie virus into mice *(28)*. The nature of the plaques requires further studies, especially from the standpoint of their development and the expression of the initial stimulus to form them. It is likely that the initial trigger occurs in the neuronal element, because the plaques occur only in the gray matter and frequently in the same region in which an abundance of neurofibrillary tangles can be observed. A causative relationship between neurofibrillary tangles and plaques is unlikely, however, because of the cases in which the plaques almost totally dominate the entire brain or some regions of it. Moreover, there is frequently topographic separation of areas severely affected by neurofibrillary degeneration and those dominated by neurogenic plaques, whereas in other regions they might be intermingled.

Therefore, the etiologic factors responsible for neurofibrillary tangles and neurogenic plaques have to be viewed at least at the present time as separate; alternatively, the etiologic agent for plaque formation may be the predisposing factor for neurofibrillary degeneration. This suggests that the etiology of Alzheimer's disease may have a dual nature. To what extent factors responsible for each of these two morphologic changes represent prerequisites for one another is an important area for future investigations.

This investigation was supported in part by the General Clinical Research Center Grant RR-34, Division of Research Resources, NIH, and a grant from the Ohio Department of Mental Health and Mental Retardation.

References

1. *Stedman's Medical Dictionary*, Williams and Wilkins, Baltimore, MD, 1974, pp 32 and 327.
2. Mann, D. M. A., and Yates, P. O., Lipoprotein pigments—their relationship to ageing in the human nervous system. *Brain* **97**, 481 (1974).
3. Adams, R. C., Fisher, C. M., Hakim, S., Ojemann, R. G., and Sweet, W. H., Symptomatic occult hydrocephalus with "normal" cerebro-spinal-fluid pressure. *N. Engl. J. Med.* **273**, 117 (1965).
4. Butler, R. N., Alzheimer's disease—senile dementia and related disorders. In *The Role of NIFT in Alzheimer's Disease: Senile Dementia and Related Disorders*, R. Katzman, R. D. Terry, and K. L. Dick, Eds., Raven Press, New York, NY, 1978, pp 5–9.
5. Malamud, N., A comparative study of neuropathologic findings in senile psychosis and in "normal senility." *J. Am. Geriatr. Soc.* **13**, 113 (1965).
6. Pakkenberg, H., and Voigt, J., Brain weight of the Danes. *Acta Anat.* **56**, 297 (1964).
7. Oxman, T. E., The use of computerized axial tomography in neuroradiologic diagnosis in psychiatry. *Compr. Psychiatry* **20**, 177 (1979).
8. Roberts, M. A., McGeorge, A. P., and Caird, F. I., Electroencephalography and computerized tomography in vascular and non-vascular dementia in old age. *J. Neurol. Neurosurg. Psychiatry* **41**, 903 (1978).
9. Brody, H., Structural changes in the aging nervous system. In *Interdisciplinary Topics in Gerontology*, H. T. Blumenthal, Ed., Karger, New York, NY, 1970, pp 9–21.
10. Potvin, A. R., Syndulko, K., Tourtellotte, W. W., Lemmon, J. A., and Potvin, J. H., Human neurologic function and the aging process. *J. Am. Geriatr. Soc.* **28**, 1 (1980).
11. Kaszmiak, A. W., Garron, D. C., Fox, J. H., Bergen, O., and Huckman, N., Cerebral atrophy, EEG slowing, age education and cognitive function of suspected dementia. *Neurology* **29**, 1273 (1979).

12. Wisniewski, K., Jervis, G. A., Moretz, R. C., and Wisniewski, H. M., Alzheimer neurofibrillary tangles in diseases other than senile and presenile dementia. *Ann. Neurol.* **5,** 288 (1979).

13. Blessed, G., Tomlinson, B. E., and Roth, M., The association between quantitative measures of dementia and of senile change in the cerebral gray matter of elderly subjects. *Br. J. Psychiatry* **114,** 797 (1968).

14. Kopeloff, L. M., Barrera, S. E., and Kopeloff, N., Recurrent convulsive seizures in animals produced by immunologic and chemical means. *Am. J. Psychiatry* **98,** 881–902 (1942).

15. Klatzo, I., Wisniewski, H., and Streicher, E., Experimental production of neurofibrillary degeneration. *J. Neuropathol. Exp. Neurol.* **24,** 187 (1965).

16. Kidd, M., Paired helical filaments in electron microscopy of Alzheimer's disease. *Nature* **197,** 192 (1963).

17. Crapper, D. R., Krishnan, S. S., and Dalton, A. J., Brain aluminum distribution in Alzheimer's disease and experimental neurofibrillary degeneration. *Science* **180,** 511–513 (1973).

18. Liss, L., Ebner, K., and Couri, D., Neurofibrillary tangles induced by sclerosing angioma. *Hum. Pathol.* **10,** 104–108 (1979).

19. Liss, L., and Long, T. F., Axonal swellings in Purkinje cells. An aluminum encephalopathy? *J. Neuropathol. Exp. Neurol.* **38,** 329 (1979).

20. Gorsky, J. E., Dietz, A. A., Spencer, H., and Osis, D., Metabolic balance of aluminum studied in six men. *Clin. Chem.* **25,** 1739–1745 (1979).

21. Burger, P. C., and Vogel, S. F., The development of the pathologic changes of Alzheimer's disease and senile dementia in patients with Downs's syndrome. *Am. J. Pathol.* **73,** 457 (1973).

22. Sinet, P., Lejeune, J., and Jerome, H., Trisomy 21 (Down's syndrome) glutathione peroxidase, hexose monophosphate shunt and IQ. *Life Sci.* **24,** 29–34 (1979).

23. Heston, L. L., and Mastri, A. R., The genetics of Alzheimer's disease. *Arch. Gen. Psychiatry* **34,** 976 (1977).

24. Gadjusek, D. C., Unconventional viruses and the origin and disappearance of kuru. *Science* **197,** 943–958 (1977).

25. Gadjusek, D. C., Gibbs, C. J., Asher, D. M., Brown, P., Diwan, A., Hoffman, P., Nemo, G., Rohwer, R., and White, L., Precautions in medical care of and in handling materials from patients with virus dementia (Creutzfeldt–Jakob disease). *N. Engl. J. Med.* **297,** 1253–1258 (1977).

26. Liss, L., Safety precautions with spongiform encephalopathy. *Arch. Neurol.* **36,** 451 (1979). Letter.

27. Liss, L., Senile brain changes. *J. Neuropathol. Exp. Neurol.* **19,** 559–571 (1960).

28. Bruce, M. E., Fraser, H., Dickinson, A. G., and Wisniewski, H. M., Factors involved in the occurrence of amyloid and neuritic plaques produced by scrapie infection in mice. *Neuropathol. Appl. Neurobiol.* **3**, 399 (1975).

Recent Advances in Management of Breast Cancer

O. H. Pearson and Andrea Manni

Breast cancer is the most common cancer in women between the ages of 40 and 60 years. The incidence of the disease has been increasing slightly each year for the past decade, and it is estimated that about 90 000 new cases will occur this year in the United States. About 35 000 deaths from breast cancer are recorded each year, a rate that has remained fairly constant over the past decade. The majority of women who contract this disease will eventually die from it, despite treatment of the primary lesion by surgery, radiation therapy, or both, indicating that it is usually a disseminated disease when first diagnosed. A major effort has been made during the past several years to determine whether earlier diagnosis of breast cancer can improve the results of treatment of the primary lesion. Screening women in the age groups of peak incidence by regular physical examinations of the breasts and the use of mammography has resulted in detection of smaller primary lesions, and treatment of these smaller lesions seems to result in a somewhat better prognosis after five years. However, because many patients apparently have disseminated disease even at an early stage of diagnosis, this approach does not appear promising for the ultimate control of breast cancer.

Discovery of the etiology of human breast cancer and of means to prevent it would obviously be the best solution to this problem, but promising leads for accomplishing this are not available. Another approach, which has received a great deal of attention, has been the development of systemic treatment capable of inducing regression of tumors in patients with advanced disease. Two general types of systemic treatment have effectively induced temporary tumor regression and prolonged survival in some patients with advanced disease: endocrine treatment and cytotoxic chemotherapy.

Endocrine Treatment

More than 80 years ago, Beatson *(1)* reported the first therapeutic ovariectomies in two premenopausal women with inoperable breast cancer and described significant regression of the primary tumors in both patients. This observation was confirmed at the turn of the century, remissions being reported in 30 to 40% of premenopausal women with breast cancer after ovariectomy; this remission lasted about one year, after which the disease reactivated. These findings were made before there was any knowledge of hormones, but Beatson undertook his study because of some observations that the ovaries had an effect on lactation in animals. This therapeutic procedure was used only sporadically over the next 50 years, perhaps because it was effective in only a fraction of the patients and because the beneficial effects were temporary.

With the discovery of the sex steroids and cortisone more than 30 years ago, there was a renewed interest in the endocrine treatment of women with breast cancer. Administering pharmacological doses of estrogens or androgens to women with advanced breast cancer was in some instances found to induce regression of the metastatic tumor. With the availability of cortisone, it became possible to ablate the adrenal glands and the pituitary gland, which induced remissions in about 40% of the cases. Table 1 summarizes the results of various treatments in women with stage IV breast cancer. Some patients may respond to multiple endocrine treatments; thus, a postmenopausal patient who responds to estrogen therapy may benefit again from androgen therapy, and a premenopausal patient who responds to ovariectomy is very likely to obtain a second remission through adrenalectomy or hypophysectomy. Survival of these patients is prolonged for about the duration that tumor growth is controlled by the endocrine treatment. This prolonged survival is worthwhile: most patients can enjoy normal, productive lives during the periods of remission.

The mechanism by which the various endocrine treatments induce tumor regression in patients is not well established, and the development of these therapies has been based primarily on an empirical approach. The physiological basis for endocrine abla-

Table 1. Results of Endocrine Therapy and Chemotherapy in Women with Stage IV Breast Cancer

Treatment	Remission rate, %	Duration of remissions, months	Patient's menopausal status
Additive endocrine treatment			
Estrogen	35	12	Post
Progestin	30	8	Post
Androgen	20	6	Post
Cortisone	30	3	Post
Ablative endocrine treatment			
Ovariectomy	40	12	Pre
Adrenalectomy	40	12	Post
Hypophysectomy	40	18	Pre or post
Anti-estrogen treatment			
Tamoxifen	40	18	Pre or post
Cytotoxic chemotherapy			
Five-drug combination	70	12	Pre or post
Adriamycin	35	6	Pre or post

tive therapy has been the concept that various steroid and peptide hormones play a role in the growth and maintenance of normal breast epithelium, and that the growth of hormone-responsive breast cancers may be dependent upon such endocrine stimuli. Thus, ablation of ovaries, adrenals, and the pituitary would lower the circulating titers of these hormones and induce tumor regression in a manner similar to the atrophy of normal mammary epithelium after endocrine ablation. The mechanisms by which pharmacological doses of steroid hormones induce tumor regression have not been elucidated, but recent studies suggest that large doses of estrogens may depress the amount of receptors in the target tissue and thus induce local hormonal deprivation. This subject has been discussed in detail elsewhere *(2, 3)*.

Anti-Estrogen

The development of the anti-estrogen drug, tamoxifen, which has produced results similar to those of surgical hypophysectomy (Table 1), constitutes a major advance in the endocrine therapy of women with breast cancer *(4)*. Tamoxifen is a nonsteroidal, triphenylethylene compound with very little estrogenic activity, and yet it binds with high affinity to the cytosol estrogen-receptor. It apparently blocks the entry of estrogens into target organs rather than suppresses the secretion of estrogens. Given orally and in therapeutic doses, it is nontoxic, producing minimum side effects. The use of this drug appears to eliminate the need for surgical procedures such as ovariectomy and adrenalectomy *(3)*.

The effectiveness of the anti-estrogen in women with stage IV breast cancer has also provided insight into the endocrinology of human breast cancer. The antitumor effects of anti-estrogen appear to be related to its action as an anti-estrogen and not to some other mechanism. If this is the case, then estrogens must play a major role in maintaining the growth of hormone-responsive tumors in women. It has been shown that tamoxifen can induce remissions in some patients after surgical ablation of the ovaries and adrenal glands, as well as in some patients after total ablation of the pituitary *(5)*. Estradiol, estrone, and estriol are still detectable in the blood after these endocrine ablations; thus, if tamoxifen can block the entry of these small amounts of estrogen into the tumor and induce regression, then these estrogens may be directly stimulating the growth of the tumors. On the other hand, hypophysectomy can induce remissions in some patients who were initially treated with tamoxifen and whose disease had reactivated. This suggests that a pituitary hormone, or hormones, may play a role in the growth of some breast cancers. Further studies of this type may provide more insight into the endocrine factors that may play a role in the growth of human breast cancer.

Estrogen Receptors

Only about 40% of women with breast cancer respond to endocrine therapy. Until recently there was no way to predict which patients would respond to this therapy. With the discovery of a specific estrogen-binding protein in the cytosol of estrogen target tissues, Jensen et al. *(6)* reported that some breast cancers contained cytosol estrogen-receptors and that their presence correlated with the response of patients to adrenalectomy. This observation has now been confirmed by many other investigators *(7)*. In our experience, about 70% of primary or metastatic breast cancers in women contain detectable estrogen receptors. In patients with estrogen-receptor-negative tumors, the response rate to hypophysectomy or to anti-estrogen is virtually nil. In patients with estrogen-receptor-positive tumors the response to hypophysectomy *(5)* and anti-estrogen therapy *(4)* is favorable in 65% of the patients. Thus, estrogen receptors are a useful marker for hormone-responsive breast cancer, and this constitutes an important advance in the management of patients with this disease.

Other hormone receptors have been found in some human breast cancers, such as progesterone-, androgen-, glucocorticoid-, and prolactin-receptors, and are being studied for their potential usefulness as markers for hormone responsiveness.

Cytotoxic Chemotherapy

When the alkylating drug, nitrogen mustard, was first evaluated as an antitumor agent in patients with malignant disease, it was found to induce short-term remissions in a small percentage of patients with advanced breast cancer. Subsequently, other cytotoxic drugs, such as 5-fluorouracil, methotrexate, vincristine, and Adriamycin were found to have similar effects. A major advance in the cytotoxic chemotherapy of advanced breast cancer occurred when combinations of these drugs were used. Cooper *(8)* introduced a five-drug combination of prednisone, Cytoxan (cyclophosphamide), vincristine, 5-fluorouracil, and methotrexate, which we have found to be quite effective (Table 1). We have used this treatment particularly in patients who have already been treated with endocrine modalities, although we now use it as an initial treatment of choice in patients who have estrogen-receptor-negative breast cancers. This five-drug chemotherapy induces objective improvement in about 70% of our patients with an average duration of about one year *(9)*. The results of chemotherapy were quite similar in patients who initially responded to endocrine treatment and then relapsed, and in those who failed to benefit from prior endocrine treatment. Adriamycin has been used as a secondary form of chemotherapy with some worthwhile results (Table 1).

In those patients who have responded to sequential endocrine therapy and chemotherapy we have obtained an average survival from onset of metastases of nearly five years. In those patients who failed to respond to endocrine treatment but responded to chemotherapy, the average survival is slightly more than two years. In patients who respond to neither treatment, the average survival after onset of metastases is about six months. Thus, these treatments are very useful for those patients who obtain a favorable response, even though they are of limited effectiveness.

Early Systemic Treatment

Many investigators are actively studying the possibility that systemic treatments might be more effective at an earlier stage of breast cancer (stage I and II), when presumably only micrometastases are present, than when the disease is more advanced. After mastectomy for primary operable breast cancer, most of the patients will still develop metastatic disease. If four or more axillary nodes are involved with cancer at the time of surgery, 80% of the patients will have recurrence within five years; if one to three axillary nodes are involved, about 60% of these patients will have recurrence; if no axillary nodes are involved, about 20% of patients will have recurrence within five years. Some studies indicate that systemic treatments can at least delay recurrence.

Three prospective, randomized studies of the effects of radiation castration in premenopausal women with stage I and II breast cancer have shown a delay in the appearance of metastases in castrated vs untreated patients. Cole *(10)* and Nissen-Meyer *(11)* have reported 15-year follow-up results that show that delayed recurrence from castration may persist for up to 15 years. Meakin et al. *(12)*, reporting 10-year results of a study in which prednisone therapy was added to radiation castration in an attempt to suppress adrenal as well as ovarian function, found a highly significant delay in the appearance of recurrence as well as an improvement in crude survival in treated vs nontreated patients.

The use of chemotherapy as adjuvant treatment has delayed recurrence in premenopausal patients with stage II breast cancer. Fisher et al. *(13)* reported that administration of L-phenylalanine mustard for two years after mastectomy for stage II breast cancer significantly delayed the appearance of metastases in premenopausal patients but not in postmenopausal patients. Bonnadonna et al. *(14)* administered a three-drug chemotherapy (CMF: Cytoxan, methotrexate, and 5-fluorouracil) for one year after mastectomy in patients with stage II and III breast cancer. They also found that the three-drug therapy significantly delayed the appearance of metastases in premenopausal patients, whereas in postmenopausal women, although there was an initial delay in recurrence, after three years of follow-up the relapse rate was the same as in untreated patients.

We have also made a prospective, randomized study of the effects of CMF therapy vs CMF plus tamoxifen given for one year after mastectomy to women with stage II breast cancer (15). Over a four-year period, we have studied 300 patients, measuring estrogen receptors in the primary tumors and stratifying the patients according to whether their tumors were estrogen-receptor positive or negative and according to the number of axillary nodes involved. The preliminary results show a significantly higher relapse rate in patients with estrogen-receptor-negative cancers than in those with estrogen-receptor-positive tumors, for both pre- and postmenopausal women. In addition, there is no significant difference in recurrence rate with CMF vs CMF plus tamoxifen therapy in estrogen-receptor-negative patients. On the other hand, in estrogen-receptor-positive patients, the recurrence rate after 30 months is significantly lower ($p = 0.02$) with CMF plus tamoxifen than with CMF therapy alone. This beneficial effect of tamoxifen appears to occur in both pre- and postmenopausal women.

These findings indicate that anti-estrogen therapy is exerting an antitumor effect in this subgroup of patients, over and above any effect from the cytotoxic chemotherapy. Further periods of observation are needed to determine how long such beneficial effects may last.

Summary

The therapeutic management of women with breast cancer has significantly improved in the past few years. The introduction of anti-estrogens provides an optimum form of endocrine treatment that is nontoxic and may eliminate the need for certain surgical procedures. The measurement of estrogen receptors in breast cancer tissue provides a useful marker that has improved selection of appropriate therapy for patients. Early systemic treatment of patients with less-advanced disease shows promise of long-term control of the disease in some patients.

This work is supported by grants from the USPHS, CA–05197–20, RR-80, and the American Cancer Society, Inc., PDT-48U.

References

1. Beatson, G. T., On the treatment of inoperable cases of carcinoma of the mamma: Suggestions for a new method of treatment with illustrative cases. *Lancet* ii, 104–107 (1896).
2. Pearson, O. H., and Manni, A., Hormonal control of breast cancer growth in women and rats. In *Current Topics in Experimental Endocrinology*, L. Martini and V. H. T. James, Eds., Academic Press, New York, NY, 1978, pp 75–92.
3. Pearson, O. H., and Manni, A., Endocrine ablative procedures for breast cancer. In *Commentaries on Research in Breast Disease*, 1, R. D. Bulbrook and D. J. Taylor, Eds., Alan R. Liss, New York, NY, 1979, pp 147–164.
4. Manni, A., Trujillo, J. E., Marshall, J. S., Brodkey, J., and Pearson, O. H., Antihormone treatment of stage IV breast cancer. *Cancer* 43, 444–450 (1979).
5. Manni, A., Pearson, O. H., Brodkey, J., and Marshall, J. S., Transsphenoidal hypophysectomy in breast cancer: Evidence for an individual role of pituitary and gonadal hormones in supporting tumor growth. *Cancer* 44, 2330–2337 (1979).
6. Jensen, E. R., Block, G. E., Smith, S., Kyser, K., and DeSombre, E. R., Estrogen receptors and breast cancer response to adrenalectomy. *Natl. Cancer Inst. Monogr.* 34, 55–70 (1971).
7. McGuire, W. L., Carbone, P. P., and Vollmer, E. P., Eds., *Estrogen Receptors in Human Breast Cancer*. Raven Press, New York, NY, 1975.
8. Cooper, R., Combination chemotherapy in hormone-resistant breast cancer. *Proc. Am. Assoc. Cancer Res.* 10, 15 (1969).
9. Manni, A., Trujillo, J. E., and Pearson, O. H., Sequential use of endocrine treatment and chemotherapy in metastatic breast cancer: Effects on survival. *Cancer Treat. Rep.*, 1980 (in press).
10. Cole, M. P., A clinical trial of an artificial menopause in carcinoma of the breast. In *Hormones and Breast Cancer*, 55, l'Institut National de la Santé et de la Recherche Médicale (INSERM), Paris, May 1975, pp 143–150.
11. Nissen-Meyer, R., Ovarian suppression and its supplement by additive hormonal treatment. In *Hormones and Breast Cancer* (see ref. *10*), pp 151–158.
12. Meakin, J. W., Allt, W. E. C., Beale, F. A., Brown, T. C., Bush, R. S., Clark, R. M., Fitzpatrick, P. J., Hawkins, N. V., Jenkin, R. D. T., Pringle, J. F., and Rider, W. D., Ovarian irradiation and

prednisone following surgery for carcinoma of the breast. In *Adjuvant Therapy of Cancer*, W. E. Salmon and S. E. Jones, Eds., Elsevier/North-Holland Biomedical Press, Amsterdam, 1977, pp 95–99.

13. Fisher, B., Carbone, P., Economou, S. G., Frelick, R., Glass, A., Lerner, H., Redmond, C., Zelen, M., Band, P., Katrych, D. L., Wolmark, N., and Fisher, E. R., L-Phenylalanine mustard (L-PAM) in the management of primary breast cancer. *N. Engl. J. Med.* **292,** 117–122 (1975).

14. Bonnadonna, G., The value of adjunctive chemotherapy. *Program of the 12th International Cancer Congress.* Buenos Aires, Oct., 1978. Panel 5 abstract, p 103.

15. Hubay, C. A., Pearson, O. H., Marshall, J. S., Rhodes, R. S., Debanne, S. M., Mansour, E. G., Hermann, R. E., Jones, J. C., Flynn, W. J., Eckert, C., McGuire, W. L., and 27 participating investigators, Adjuvant chemotherapy, antiestrogen therapy and immunotherapy for stage II breast cancer. In *Breast Cancer—Experimental and Clinical Aspects* (Proceedings of the 2nd European Organization for Research on Treatment of Cancer, Breast Cancer Working Conference, Copenhagen, 1979), H. T. Mouridsen and T. Palshof, Eds., 1980.

Discussion—Session III

DR. HARRIS (Hays, KS): Dr. Pearson, I have not heard much about progesterone-receptor assays recently. Are they showing any additional value or are they not worth the money to do them?

DR. PEARSON: At a recent consensus meeting in Washington it was decided that progesterone-receptor assays did add a little to estrogen-receptor assays in predicting hormonal responsiveness. Unfortunately, contrary to initial hopes, its use has not eliminated that group of perhaps 25 to 30% of the patients who have abundant receptors but do not respond to endocrine treatment.

DR. FORMAN (Chapel Hill, NC): Dr. Liss, in patients with aluminum encephalopathy syndromes resulting from dialysis, in whom aluminum exceeds 200 μg/L, studies indicate that it is not so much the amount of aluminum in the blood of patients, but the malnutrition state or the amount of protein in the blood that tends to keep aluminum from penetrating the blood–brain barrier. Some of these older patients do not synthesize protein as would be expected. This might be related to some of the encephalopathic dementias. Would you comment on this?

DR. LISS: This is a very interesting situation because the dialysis dementia from the beginning was a very complex entity. To begin with, we had observed higher concentrations of aluminum than you ever see in cases of Alzheimer's disease and yet nobody was ever able to show neurofibrillary tangles. Also, the location of aluminum in these cases was different because in cases of Alzheimer's disease, the aluminum is definitely intranuclear, attached to chromatin; in dialysis dementia, it is deposited in the cytoplasm. I believe that you are absolutely correct. It is agreed now that in dialysis dementia we are dealing with multifactor conditions and aluminum is only one factor.

DR. STREHLER: Dr. Liss, do you know whether anybody is

attempting to differentiate between the type of mongolism that is due to a translocation in which trisomy occurs, as compared with improper segregation?

DR. LISS: In a study by Sinet (*Life Sci.* **24:** 29–34, 1979), a number of enzymes that control the superoxides were found to be deficient in patients with Down's syndrome. They examined 50 individuals with trisomy as well as translocation. In our own material there is one case of translocation. As far as the chromosomal defect and occurrence of morphological changes are concerned, there appears to be no difference.

DR. STREHLER: The reason I asked is that the latest results I had seen on the chemical characterization of the twisted neurofibrils/neurotubules indicated a mixture of neurofibrillary and neurotubular material. Neurotubules are involved in the separation of chromosomes, and I wondered whether the abnormality might be in that category. But one case you had, did it have neurofibrillary tangles, the one that involved a translocation?

DR. LISS: Yes.

DR. STREHLER: Dr. Pearson, is there any epidemiological study to show that women who had been breast-fed have a lower probability of developing breast cancer? I understand from one of the other speakers that the converse is true, that is that women who breast-feed tend to have a lower incidence of breast cancer.

DR. PEARSON: I cannot answer the question about the mother having been breast-fed. However, if a woman breast-feeds her children, there is no protection against breast cancer. There was thought to be some in the past, but the more recent epidemiological studies show that is not the case. It does turn out, though, that the earlier the woman becomes pregnant, the more protection she has. In other words, if she becomes pregnant after the age of 25, the incidence is two times greater than if she became pregnant before 25.

DR. STREHLER: Is there any relationship between breast size and the probability of developing breast cancer?

DR. PEARSON: I am not really sure about that. I do not think so. The prognosis is different because it is sometimes more difficult to detect a tumor in a very large breast.

DR. FREE (Elkhart, IN): Dr. Gordan, in relation to your observations with the older women, does the amount of exercise have an influence? It is my impression that in some instances in both men and women the lack of exercise may cause a significant hypercalcuria.

DR. GORDAN: Clearly, disuse can produce osteoporosis, although it is quite a different kind of osteoporosis, often associated with an increase of alkaline phosphatase and with changes that you see in the cortex of tubular bones—the striated lines we call "busy bone." You see this in rapid turnover states, as in hyperthyrodism and hyperparathyroidism. The question of whether postmenopausal women can be protected against bone loss by exercise alone is not completely answered. It is something we are quite interested in because Dr. Eisenberg and I were the first to show back in 1961 that the San Quentin football team had a bigger calcium pool and more rapid accretion rates than their colleagues of the same ethnic background and on the same diet (*J. Clin. Invest.* **40:** 1809–1825, 1961). The Swedes have shown quite recently that weight lifters and ballet dancers have denser bones than appropriate controls. On the other hand, when post-menopausal women were introduced to cross-country running as an attempt to increase their bone mass, nothing happened in the six months that their bone mass was followed. I should emphasize that the proper way of evaluating treatment is by bone-mass measurements. This is rather recent, and we do not have all the information we should have. I certainly do not advocate a sedentary life—it has lots of complications. On the other hand, I do not believe I can prevent the deleterious effects of loss of estrogen upon the bone by exercise alone.

DR. NINO (Fullerton, CA): Dr. Gordan, in the prevention or treatment for bone loss, would you find it advisable to use some of the new, highly active forms of vitamin D?

DR. GORDAN: The question of using vitamin D for osteoporosis is being investigated rather widely at the moment. To me it seems a bit irrational. After all, vitamin-D deficiency causes rickets or osteomalacia in man; it does not cause osteoporosis. In osteoporosis the bone is normally calcified. The one point in favor of this approach is that calcium absorption is decreased in elderly women and the blood concentrations of 1,25-dihydroxy-D_3 are lower, as reported by Gallagher, Riggs, and DeLuca (*Clin. Res.* **27:** 366, 1979). Now the crux of the situation is that when you give estrogen alone, in small doses, calcium absorption improves and the blood 1,25-dihydroxy-D_3 concentration comes up to normal, all without having to administer the D_3 form. I am rather alarmed at what is going on now. People are using a lot of very toxic agents like large doses of fluoride and large doses of vitamin D. At the vitamin D conference two years ago a person from Denmark, who shall be nameless, reported treating 48 post-menopausal osteoporotic women with 1 μg per day of 1,25-dihydroxy-D_3. Fourteen hypercalcemias and four deaths resulted. That is in contrast to the kind of innocuous treatment I have been urging.

DR. FLEISHER (New York, NY): We have studied well over a thousand women who presented with cystic mastopathy, in an attempt to relate it to a higher cancer rate. One of the things we did find, in a demographic evaluation, was a delay in menopause in those women who did develop breast cancer and who had presented initially with cystic mastopathy, compared with those women with cystic mastopathy who did not develop breast cancer. That delay was some five to six years. Dr. Pearson, would you care to speculate on what this may mean in relation to the menopausal status in women?

DR. PEARSON: I am afraid I do not have any erudite comments about that. It is true, of course, that women who develop breast cancer tend to have late menopause. So I suspect your cystic mastitis patients with a later menopause would fit that concept.

DR. FORMAN: I believe it is the patients with hypertriglyceridemia, such as diabetics or patients with poor handling of endogenous carbohydrates, who develop most of the occular, cerebral, and other abnormal manifestations related to hyperviscosity syndromes. Do you not think that hypertriglyceridemia is a greater predisposing factor than hypercholesterolemia in patients with hyperlipidemias?

DR. HAZZARD: In population studies there is at present no strong evidence that the triglyceride concentration is predictive of premature coronary disease. On the other hand, if one looks at those who have premature coronary disease, one can see a rather high prevalence of hypertriglyceridemia. This illustrates two different approaches: taking a very large population with a relatively small incidence of atherosclerosis in any given year vs looking at those who already have complications of atherosclerosis. The mechanism whereby the hypertriglyceridemia might be associated with premature coronary disease requires consideration of the inverse relationship between the concentrations of triglycerides and of high-density lipoprotein cholesterol. Were there a patho-physiological connection between the two, there would probably be a closer relationship of risk to hypo-α-lipoproteinemia than to hypertriglyceridemia. Hyperviscosity occurs at extremely high triglyceride concentrations, but is not much of a problem at the moderate yet more prevalent concentrations. As far as diabetes and premature atherosclerosis are concerned, there is intense interest in the relationship between lipid abnormalities in diabetes and the increased incidence of atherosclerosis in diabetes. The most prominent form of hyperlipidemia in diabetes is, as you pointed out, hypertriglyceridemia, but there again we do not know if it is a cause-and-effect relationship or whether the triglyceride, like blood sugar, is a marker of a person who has increased risk rather than a direct mediator of atherogenesis.

DR. MEITES: Dr. Goldman, why is there hypertrophy of the remaining kidney after one is removed? What are the mechanisms involved?

DR. GOLDMAN: I am not sure that anyone knows. The presence of growth hormone or some growth-hormone-like substance is presumably necessary, but has not been clearly established.

DR. MEITES: Has anyone actually hypophysectomized rats and then removed one kidney to see whether the other would hypertrophy?

DR. GOLDMAN: You know I am embarrassed? I did that once but at this moment I cannot remember how the experiment came out.

DR. MEITES: Dr. Pearson, how do you explain, considering the importance of estrogen in breast cancer, the fact that estrogen declines in women at the same time that the incidence of breast cancer goes up?

DR. PEARSON: I do not think that estrogen has anything to do with the etiology of breast cancer. It has a function after you have breast cancer as to whether it will grow, or whether its growth will be affected by estrogen. From the data on the use of the birth-control pill for the last 10 to 15 years, there has been no increase in the incidence of breast cancer. Dr. Gordan spoke about this too, and he did not find an increased incidence of breast cancer.

DR. MEITES: I am really astonished to hear you say that estrogen has nothing to do with the development of breast cancer.

DR. PEARSON: I think you have to have some hormones, i.e., you have to have breast tissue, but I suspect there is a carcinogen or something else that causes the cancer. I do not think it is endocrine-induced. Do you not agree with that?

DR. MEITES: One has to talk about the sex first.

DR. NATELSON: Dr. Goldman, does the glomerulus increase in the hypertrophied kidneys? What does increase?

DR. GOLDMAN: Primarily, the increase is in the size of the glomerulus; the proximal tubular cells either increase in size or number, depending on the age of the individual. Clearly, there are no new glomeruli that form, and many years ago it was demonstrated that this compensatory hypertrophy had no effect on the number of residual glomeruli. In other words, they are lost at the same rate that they would have been, even had the compensatory hypertrophy not occurred.

DR. NATELSON: The shunt that forms on aging and is wiped out, is it the same as the Trueta shunt, which in cases of shock becomes positive but quiescent?

DR. GOLDMAN: The Trueta shunt died 25 to 30 years ago and, as far as I know, was never clearly demonstrated except in the rabbit. In this species, the portal vascular situation is eliminated by the enlargement of one blood vessel. This has been very clearly demonstrated to be an anatomic change because the new vessel that connects the afferent and efferent arterioles is no longer a capillary but has all the characteristics of an arteriole.

DR. NATELSON: Dr. Liss, one of the most common symptoms to be seen in older men, who keep secret the fact that they are having prostate trouble, is that they develop severe uremia and become disoriented. In your studies, what effect does the decrease in kidney function have to do with dementia?

DR. LISS: We go back to the criteria for diagnosis of Alzheimer's disease, which is diagnosed by exclusion. It is extremely important to determine in a demented individual whether there is an abnormality of kidney function, glucose metabolism, or endocrine function. The other extremely important factor is whether the drugs used by the patient can induce dementia. In other words, a host of different factors can induce dementia; these have to be ruled out because many cases are treatable when the offending cause is dealt with.

DR. DIETZ: Dr. Gordan, is there any reason why, when the

bones break in elderly women, they break in certain places? Is there selective loss of bone in those areas?

DR. GORDAN: The three places that are most likely to fracture are the vertebrae, the wrist, and the hip. These areas are characterized by a very large preponderance of spongy or trabecular bone. The first good study of what happens after an oophorectomy was done by a very complicated technique, dual-beam x-ray spectrophotometry, which is one of the few methods by which you can measure trabecular bone. It was shown that oophorectomized women specifically lost their bone in these three sites, the vertebrae, the wrist, and the hips (Dalen et al., *J. Bone Jt. Surg.* **56A:** 1235–1238, 1974). The reason why the vertebrae fracture early is that once their sponginess is gone, they can no longer resist the normal biomechanical stress of weight. Usually the first fractures you see are in T 8, 9, 10, 11, 12, and L 1, the areas that bear the most weight. The fractures of the wrist usually occur with very slight trauma: a woman trips, catches herself, and the bone breaks. The woman who has lost her estrogen and now has mobilized trabecular bone and thin bone cortex, no longer has sufficient support and fractures with little or no trauma. The hip, of course, takes a longer period of time. You can predict which women are going to fracture their hips. There has been a very good series of studies on this. Singh at the Mayo Clinic had proposed that the trabecular pattern, used with what is called a Singh Index, will tell you those who may suffer broken bones. Hagberg and Nilsson at Malmö, Sweden, have done a prospective study in a group of women in whom cortical thickness and the Singh Index were measured; they showed that the Singh Index did not give an accurate prediction but cortical thickness did (*Geriatrics* **32:** 55, 1977). You see, they all lose trabecular bone; what really makes the difference here is whether they have enough cortex to withstand normal weight and physiological biomechanical stress.

DR. GOLDMAN: In my experience the humerus at the neck has also been a very vulnerable spot. Is this not actually the case statistically?

DR. GORDAN: We have epidemiologic data on fractures in a large number of areas, and it is true that other areas are involved. It is also true that the humerus is susceptible, particularly in the upper portion, which has a large proportion of spongy bone, but it does not approach the really astronomical figures that we see with vertebrae, wrists, and hips. It also does not produce the severe morbidity found for vertebral fractures or the severe mortality from hip fractures. I am emphasizing the three where we think we know pretty well what is going on, the three that constitute the biggest public health problems because they are the ones where we can actually make life better for people. I have a very old-fashioned idea of medicine—that it is supposed to make life better—which is one of the reasons why I am not so interested in giving toxic agents when I can get by with things that make women feel better at the same time.

DR. HAZZARD: I simply want to close the loop among the various presentations and suggest an hypothesis that is consistent with Dr. Goldman's remarks; namely, that it may be more desirable for elderly women to be overweight or obese than underweight.

DR. GORDAN: I want to make it clear that I am not advocating obesity. Blacks do not get osteoporosis, and most American blacks have mixed white and black ancestry, so obviously the black superiority holds as far as bone is concerned. On the other hand, obesity has many other disadvantages, including diabetes and cardiovascular disease. It is true that bone loss is less in obese women than it is in slender women, but they all lose. It is also true that we picture slender, light-boned, North European women as being most susceptible to very severe osteoporosis, but I have seen a lot of osteoporosis is obese women, even with brown or yellow skin.

DR. GOLDMAN: I cannot resist that. I certainly do not advocate obesity, but Dr. Reubin Andres ("Influence of obesity on longevity in the aged," to be published in vol. 7, Advances in Cancer Biology Series, *Aging, Cancer, and Cell Membranes,* Stratton Intercontinental Medical Book Corp., New York, NY) has been reviewing statistics recently, and from a number of studies found that there is no support for the idea that weight is inversely related to longevity except in the *extremes* of high and low weight, on the order of 20% above or below the optimum. Thus those of us who are just a little heavy need not give up hope yet.

DR. GORDAN: If we were not neurotic about 10 pounds, we would probably all have 25 extra pounds.

IV

EXPERIMENTAL APPROACHES TO AGING RESEARCH

An account of basic research techniques developed to investigate and test various hypotheses concerning the fundamental cause(s) of aging—Robert L. Habig, Moderator

Old age is respectable so long as it asserts itself, maintains its rights, is subversive to no one, and retains its sway to the last breath.

CICERO

The Expression of Human Aging at the Cellular Level

Leonard Hayflick

Studying biological aging by using cultured cells is a relatively recent discipline. This field, called cytogerontology, had its origins 50 years ago when the "growth rates" of chicken-embryo fibroblasts grown in plasma clots were found to be inversely related to the age of the chicken supplying the plasma *(1)*. A few years later, investigators learned that the latent period preceding the first appearance of migrating cells from small, cultured tissue explants increased with advancing donor age *(2, 3)*. A third observation, made before the renaissance in the 1950's of cell-culture techniques, was the finding of Carrel that cultured fibroblasts grown from chicken-heart tissue purportedly could proliferate indefinitely *(4, 5)*. Since 1950 the first two observations have been confirmed, but the last, and by far the most important to gerontologists, has not; in fact, quite the opposite is true.

The notion that isolated animal cells in culture are capable of unlimited proliferation profoundly influenced thinking on many fundamental biological questions, not the least of which were theories of aging. It was once thought that animal cells placed in culture would multiply indefinitely if proper culture conditions were provided; this is now known not to be the case. Indeed, it is a rare event when human or animal cells are found to acquire, spontaneously, the properties of unlimited capability for division in vitro. Furthermore, such cells are inevitably abnormal in one or more properties and often resemble cancer cells. Because aging is the fate of normal cells in vivo, we should therefore be studying normal cells in vitro. Immortality in vitro is a property of abnormal cells, not normal ones.

Probably the major impetus to further research has been the finding by Moorhead and me that cultured normal human fibroblast cells have a finite capacity to replicate and that this capacity is age-related (6, 7). In the 20 years since this phenomenon was first described, a large literature has been published that substantially supports our original notion. Early debates centered around the possibility that the cause of the cessation of normal cell proliferation in vitro was an artifact, attributable to the techniques used to grow cells. Although this possibility can never be excluded absolutely, conditions have yet to be found that will permit normal cell populations to replicate indefinitely.

Suppose, as is most likely, that conditions for the indefinite replication of normal cells might best be found in vivo; even under in vivo conditions of serial transplantation, normal cells do not proliferate indefinitely, as will be discussed subsequently. Thus the proliferative finitude of cultured normal cells must be regarded as a biological phenomenon that has no trivial explanation.

The fact that highly differentiated normal epithelial cell populations double only a few times in vitro has been offered as evidence for the inadequacy of cell-culture conditions. Yet it is at least equally plausible to suggest that such cell populations are as incapable of many rounds of cell division in vitro as they are in vivo, and for the same inherent reasons. The likelihood of finding in vitro conditions that would permit many rounds of division in highly differentiated cells is thus as unlikely as finding similar conditions that would permit the indefinite proliferation of normal fibroblasts, and the search for conditions permitting extended proliferation of normal differentiated cells may be just as futile as the search for conditions that would allow normal fibroblasts to replicate indefinitely.

Cells Derived From Adult Donors

In the past few years more attention has been given to the properties of human diploid cell strains derived from older donors. Because most of what is known about the biology of cultured normal human cells has come from studies of strains derived from tissue of fetal or embryonic origin, studies of adult strains are clearly warranted. Comparative data between these strains and those derived from fetal or embryonic donors are likely to yield significant new insights in the field of cytogerontology.

The first comparative studies on these two classes of cell populations suggested that population-doubling potential was inversely
related to donor age (7, 8). Recently, three additional studies on
different human tissues [LeGuilly et al. (9) used human liver tissue,
Schneider and Mitsui (10) studied fibroblasts from skin biopsies,
and Bierman (11) examined arterial smooth muscle cells] also support the original contention that the number of population doublings achievable by cultured normal human cells is inversely
proportional to donor age. These findings must be tempered, however, with observations that the relationship may be clouded when
different tissue sites are compared (12) or where the physiological
state of the donor is abnormal. For example, strains derived from
diabetics have been found to undergo fewer doublings in vitro
than their non-diabetic age-matched counterparts (13).

The suggestion that there may be a direct correlation between
species life span and population-doubling potential of cultured
cells has been discussed previously (14, 15). More recently, species
life span has been found to be inversely correlated with the ability
of their cultured normal cells to metabolize polycyclic hydrocarbons (16, 17).

Dividing vs. Nondividing Cells

Since our suggestion was made that the finite capacity of normal
cell proliferation (called Phase III) might be an expression of aging
in cells, some have suggested that this capacity cannot be regarded
as a useful subject for gerontological inquiry, because the major
age-related changes in animals are believed to be an expression
of events that occur in nondividing or slowly dividing highly
differentiated cells. This notion is predicated on the implied prem-
ise that fibroblast cell division is not a function, or that it is
somehow quantitatively less so than that of functioning neuron,
kidney, or liver cells. Our contention is that whatever causes functional decrements in nondividing or slowly dividing cells is equally
likely to cause that functional decrement recognized as cessation
of proliferative ability. There is no justification for distinguishing
between slowly or nondividing cells on the one hand and dividing
cells on the other hand, on the basis that the former cells function
and the latter do not; cell division is, after all, a functional property
for which the likelihood for change with age is just as probable
as change in any other cell function.

We do not contend that aging in animals is necessarily the result of the loss of proliferative capacity in those cells capable of division. What is more likely is that the determinants that lead to decreased cell function with time also decrease replicative capacity. Such determinants are likely to repose in the cell genome (14).

Aging or Differentiation?

Although the idea is not new, the suggestion has been made again that the Phase III phenomenon may not be a manifestation of aging but of differentiation (19). Until an unambiguous and testable distinction can be made between these two terms, the notion that the Phase III phenomenon represents one and not the other will not be meaningful. The processes of differentiation and aging are so inextricably interwoven that it would be futile to make any fundamental distinction. In its simplest relationship, aging may be regarded as a constellation of physiological decrements that follow the processes that result in differentiation. Yet these processes represent a continuum of cell changes, all of which are probably governed by the same fundamental mechanism. Indeed, it is well documented that even during embryogenesis, phenomena indistinguishable from cell aging occur. The death of cells and the destruction of tissues and organs is a normal part of developmental sequences in animals (19).

The fact is, normal cells cultured in vitro or serially transplanted in vivo ultimately incur physiological decrements and die. Whether one regards this as aging or "differentiation to death" is more likely to interest semanticists than to lead to meaningful experimentation.

Functional and Biochemical Changes in Cultured Normal Human Cells

As previously indicated, the likelihood that animals age because one or more important cell populations lose their proliferative capacity is unlikely. Normal cultured cells have a finite capacity for replication, and I have proposed that this finite limit is rarely, if ever, reached by cells in vivo. I would therefore suggest that many of the functional losses that occur in cultured cells before their loss of division capacity also may occur in vivo much before replicative capacity is lost. These functional decrements that herald the loss of mitotic capability may be the causes of in vivo age changes.

Presumably, not all functional decrements occur in cells at the same time or at the same rate. Loss of division capacity by mitotically active cells occurs well after the occurrence of many other decrements. Indeed, cytogerontologists are now becoming aware of a plethora of functional changes in normal human cells grown in vitro and expressed well before the capacity to replicate is lost. These changes have been reported by many laboratories. An exhaustive, but undoubtedly incomplete, listing of these increments and decrements as found by various workers is given in Tables 1 and 2. Table 3 lists variables that have *not* been observed to change as normal human cells approach Phase III. It is more likely that the changes that herald the approach of loss of division capacity (described in Tables 1 and 2) play the central role in the expression of aging and result in death of the individual animal well before replicative failure of its somatic cells.

The measurement of loss of cell division potential is, after all, one of many cell functions that could be studied. If the manifestations of age changes are due to loss of cell function other than loss of cell division, as we believe is likely, then in vitro systems are all the more useful for gerontological research.

Irradiation, DNA Repair, and Effects of Visible Light

One of the major theories of age changes involves decreased or less efficient mechanisms for cells to repair DNA damage as a function of age. Much work has been done on cultured cells in the past five years to elucidate this phenomenon.

An early study by Lima et al. *(20)* on chick-embryo fibroblasts was one of the first to show the effects of ^{60}Co irradiation on cell longevity in vitro. Saturation densities were unaffected, but Phase III was initiated earlier in the irradiated cultures; also, the percentage of dividing cells was unchanged, but the number of population doublings reached was less in the irradiated cultures. The decrease in the total number of cells produced was directly

Table 1. Properties That Increase as Different Normal Human Diploid Cell Strains Approach the End of Their In Vitro Life Span (Phase III)

RNA
RNA content
RNA turnover
Proportion of RNA and histone in chromatin

Enzymes
Lysosomes and lysosomal enzymes
Heat lability and activity of glucose-6-phosphate dehydrogenase and 6-phosphogluconate dehydrogenase
Activity of "chromatin-associated enzymes" (RNAase, DNAase, protease, nucleoside triphosphatase, DPN pyrophosphorylase)
5'-MNase activity
Esterase activity
Acid phosphatase, band 3
Acid phosphatase
β-Glucuronidase activity
Membrane-associated ATPase activity
pH 3.4 protease activity (decreased in middle population doublings)
N-Acetyl-β-glucosaminidase
5'-Nucleotidase
Cytochrome oxidase
Tyrosine aminotransferase activity
Acid hydrolases:
    α-D-Mannosidase
    N-Acetyl-β-D-galactosaminidase
    N-Acetyl-β-D-glucosaminidase
    β-L-Fucosidase
    β-D-Galactosidase
    γ-Glutamyltransferase (5-glutamyl)-peptide: amino-acid 5-glutamyltransferase activity
Monoamine oxidase activity

Lipids
Lipid content
Lipid synthesis
Requirement for delipidized serum protein for stimulation of lipid synthesis

Carbohydrates
Glucose utilization
Glycogen content

Proteins and amino acids
Protein content
Proteins with increased proteolytic susceptibility (only at last population doubling)
Protein component P8
Breakdown rate of proteins when treated with an amino-acid analog
Albumin uptake
Stimulatory activity of polyornithine on protein uptake
Proportion of rapidly degradable proteins
Amino-acid efflux

Table 1 (cont.).

Proteins and amino acids (cont.)
Error level for misincorporation of methionine into histone H1
Number of methionine residues
Complexity of H1 polypeptide chains

Cell cycle
Prolongation of doubling time
Heterogeneity in length of division cycle
Slow or non-replicating cells
Mitotic cycle
Cell longevity with certain fractions of cigarette smoke condensate

Morphology
Cell size and volume
Number and size of lysosomes
Number of residual bodies
Cytoplasmic microfibrils
Endoplasmic reticulum, constricted and "empty"
Particulate intracellular fluorescence
Nuclear size of the slow or non-replicating cell component
Mean nuclear area in cells from donors aged 8, 40, and 84 years
Cell sizes in both G1 and G2 + M
Particles on freeze-fracture face E
Microvilli on cell surfaces, chromatin condensation, and dense bodies
Cells containing long, thin, dense mitochondria and bizarre shapes, cells exhibiting filamentous degeneration
Blebs and marginal ruffling
Fraction of cells with one large nucleolus per nucleus
Mean nucleolar dry mass and area

Unclassified
Cyclic AMP per milligram of protein
Tolerance to sublethal radiation damage
Time needed to respond to proliferative stimulus by medium change
Reversion rate of herpesvirus temperature-sensitive mutant E
DNA repair in cells arrested by low serum concentration
Rate of uridine transport
Cyclic AMP concentration

See ref. *65* for references to each item.

proportional to the total number of rads received. Lima et al. concluded that even very small doses of irradiation may have long-term damaging effects on cultured normal cells.

Epstein et al. *(21–23)* reported deficient DNA-strand rejoining after x-ray irradiation of Phase III normal human cells, but Regan and Setlow *(24)* and Clarkson and Painter *(25)* could not confirm this. Goldstein *(26)* and Painter et al. *(27)* showed decreased repair

Table 2. Properties That Decrease as Different Normal Human Diploid Cell Strains Approach the End of Their In Vitro Life Span (Phase III)

DNA
DNA synthesis
Nucleic acid synthesis
Rate of DNA chain elongation
Rate of DNA strand rejoining and repair rate
Induced sister-chromatid exchanges
DNA polymerase activity

RNA
Rate of RNA synthesis
Ribosomal RNA content
RNA-synthesizing activity of chromatin
Chromatin-template activity
Incorporation of tritiated uridine into cellular RNA
Template activity of isolated nuclei (only in late Phase III)

Enzymes
Lactic dehydrogenase isoenzyme pattern
Glycolytic enzymes
Transaminases
Alkaline phosphatase
Specific activity of lactic dehydrogenase
Response to induction of ornithine decarboxylase
pH 7.8 neutral protease activity
Prolyl hydroxylase activity
Ornithine decarboxylase activity
Ascorbate dependence of the prolyl hydroxylase system
Glutamine synthetase specific activity and heat lability

Proteins
Collagen synthesis
Collagen synthesis and collagenolytic activity
Rate of histone acetylation
Total protein and hydroxyproline
Proteolytic capacity
Incorporation of isotope into histone

Synthesis, incorporation, and stimulation
Mucopolysaccharide synthesis
Pentose phosphate shunt
Cyclic AMP (moles)
Stimulation of growth with putrescine
Radioactive uridine, thymidine, protein-hydrolysate, acetate, oleic acid, cholesterol
Synthesis of glycosaminoglycans
Interferon production
Number of cells responding to proliferative stimulus by medium change
Ability to synthesize proteins and amino acids

Cell cycle
Numbers of cells in proliferating pool

234

Table 2 (cont.).

Cell cycle (cont.)
Cell saturation density
Population-doubling potential as a function of donor age
Incorporation of tritiated thymidine
Synchronous division, constancy of interdivision time, and motility
Growth potential
Percent of colonies exceeding a given colony size
Cell longevity decreased by one fraction of cigarette smoke condensate

Morphology
Proportion of mitochondria with completely transverse cristae
Distribution and development of specialized structures for intercellular contact
    and communication
Particles on freeze-fracture face P
Number of mitochondria and granular endoplasmic reticulum

Unclassified
HLA specificities (cloned cells)
Adherence to polymerizing fibrin and influence on fibrin retraction
Electrophoretic mobility (net negative cell-surface change)
Life span after chronic exposure to above-normal partial pressures of oxygen
Reversion rate of herpesvirus temperature-sensitive mutant G

See ref. 65 for references to each item.

in ultraviolet-induced damage in Phase III human fibroblasts, but Mattern and Cerrutti *(28)* found that isolated nuclei from Phase II WI-38 cells lost their capacity to excise damaged bases from γ-irradiated DNA. In 1974 Hart and Setlow *(29)* made the important observation that cultured skin fibroblasts from long-lived species have a greater capacity to repair ultraviolet-induced damage than do cells from shorter-lived species. In 1976 they also reported *(30)* that the average amount of unscheduled DNA synthesis decreases as cultured human cells approach Phase III.

Bowman et al. *(31)*, working with WI-38 cells, showed that unscheduled DNA synthetic capacity was significantly decreased in Phase III cultures. This was a result of decreased repair capacity, correlating well with a similar decrease in the proportion of dividing cells in the population.

The Finite Lifetime of Normal Cells In Vivo

If the concept of the finite lifetime or aging of cells grown in vitro is related to aging in the whole animal, then it is important

Table 3. Properties That Do Not Change as Different Normal Human Diploid Cell Strains Approach the End of Their In Vitro Life Span (Phase III)

DNA and RNA
Soluble RNAase, soluble DNAase, soluble seryl tRNA synthetase, soluble and chromatin-associated DNA polymerase
Mean temperature of denaturation of DNA and chromatin
Histone/DNA ratio
Rate of DNA strand rejoining and ability to perform repair replication
Chromatin template activity
Nucleoplasmic synthesis of RNA
Heat lability in relative profiles of DNA, RNA, and protein precursors (minor increase at last doubling)
Amount of unscheduled DNA synthesis in confluent cultures

Enzymes
Respiratory enzymes
Glutamic dehydrogenase
Alkaline phosphatase
Superoxide dismutase activity
Heat stability of glucose-6-phosphate dehydrogenase
Catalase activity
Lysyl hydroxylase activity
Enzymes of the "γ-glutamyl cycle"
Specific activity or thermostability of phosphoglucose isomerase
Glucose-6-phosphate dehydrogenase alterations
N-Acetyl-α-D-galactosaminidase
N-Acetyl-β-D-glucosaminidase-D-glucosidase
Sulfite cytochrome c reductase

Cell cycle
S phase of cell cycle
Generation time of selected mitotic cells

Karyology
Diploidy (only changes in late Phase III)
Prematurely condensed chromosomes
Proportion of colchicine-induced polyploid cells

Synthesis and degradation
Glycolysis
Mis-synthesized or post-translationally modified proteins
Conversion of glutamate to proline or hydroxyproline
Hydralazine inhibition of hydroxylation
Increase in V_{max} of uridine transport with serum stimulation
Ability to degrade normal or analog-containing proteins

Cyclic AMP, GMP
Cyclic AMP concentration
cAMP-cAMP phosphodiesterase activity
Decrease in K_m of cyclic AMP phosphodiesterase with serum stimulation
cAMP and cGMP concentrations

Morphology
Number of mitochondria
Number of intramembrane particles

Table 3 (cont.).

Virology
Virus susceptibility
Poliovirus and herpesvirus titer, mutation rate, and protein chemistry
Chromosome 21-directed anti-viral gene(s)
Reversion rate of herpesvirus temperature-sensitive mutant D
Synthesis of vesicular stomatitis virus RNA
Susceptibility to interferon

Unclassified
Irreversible absorption/uptake of foreign macromolecules
Membrane fluidity
Phospholipid and neutral fat content
Effect of nicotine
Effect of polynuclear hydrocarbon carcinogens
Cell viability at sub-zero temperature (17 years)
Respiration
HLA specificities (mass cultures)

See ref. *65* for references to each item.

to know whether normal cells, given the opportunity, can proliferate indefinitely in vivo. If all of the multitude of animal cell types were continually renewed, without loss of function or capacity for self-renewal, we would expect that the organs composed of such cells would function normally indefinitely and that their host would live on forever. Unhappily, however, renewal-cell populations do not occur in most tissues, and when they do, a proliferative finitude is often manifest. Although this important question has been discussed previously *(32),* much new information has become available in recent years.

Most animals are generally believed to have a species-specific life span. The normal somatic cells composing their tissues obviously die as well. An important question arises: Is it possible to circumvent the death of normal animal cells, which results from the death of the "host," by transferring marked cells to younger animals seriatim? If such experiments could be conducted, we would have an in vivo counterpart of the in vitro experiments and would predict that normal cells transplanted serially to proper inbred hosts would, like their in vitro counterparts, senesce. Such experiments would largely rule out those objections to in vitro findings that are based on the artificiality of in vitro cell cultures. The question could be answered by serial orthotopic transplantation of normal somatic tissue to new, young, inbred hosts each time the recipient approaches old age.

Data from seven different laboratories in which mammary tissue (33), skin (34), and hematopoietic cells (35–40) were transplanted indicate that normal cells, serially transplanted to inbred hosts, do not survive indefinitely. The trauma of transplantation does not appear to influence the results (34); furthermore, in heterochronic transplants, survival time is related to the age of the grafted tissue (34). Under similar conditions of tissue transplantation, cancer cell populations can be serially passed indefinitely (41–43), which implies that the acquisition of potential for unlimited cell division or escape from senescent changes by mammalian cells in vitro or in vivo can only be achieved by somatic cells that have acquired some or all properties of cancer cells. Paradoxically, this leads to the conclusion that, for mammalian somatic cells to become biologically "immortal," they first must be induced to an abnormal or neoplastic state either in vivo or in vitro, at which time they can then be subcultivated or transplanted indefinitely. Krohn (44) found some transplants capable of surviving several years beyond the maximum life span of the mouse, but all were ultimately lost. Long survival time is *not* equivalent to proliferation time or rounds of division; hence, these long-surviving grafts consist of cells that have a very slow rate of reproductive turnover. This is analogous to maintaining cell cultures at room temperature, which also extends calendar time for cell survival but does not increase the number of population doublings.

A series of experiments (33, 45, 46) recently reviewed (47) shows that the birth rate of mouse mammary epithelium clearly declines during in vivo serial transplantation. When mouse mammary epithelium was propagated in isogenic female hosts by periodic transplantation of tissue samples into the mammary fat pads from which the host gland was surgically removed (33), normal mammary epithelium, unlike cancerous and precancerous mammary tissue, repeatedly displayed a characteristic decline in proliferative capacity with repeated transplantations. When transplants that were allowed to proliferate continuously were compared with transplants in which growth was restricted, the decrease in cell proliferation was related to the number of population doublings undergone rather than to the passage of metabolic time (45). This represents the first in vivo confirmation of our in vitro data (6,

7), in which Moorhead and I suggested that somatic cells have an intrinsic, predetermined capacity for division under the most favorable environmental conditions. Although others (48) have invoked the passage of "metabolic time" as the determinant of in vitro senescence, it has been recently demonstrated rigorously that the number of population doublings, rather than metabolic time, is the governing factor (49, 50).

The in vivo finding that population doublings and not "metabolic time" dictate cell senescence is especially significant in that it results from studies on cells grown entirely in situ, which circumvents arguments leveled at similar data obtained from the alleged "artificial" conditions of in vitro cell culture. Young et al. (51) conclude that "the ability of grafts from old donors to proliferate rapidly in young hosts suggests that the life span of mammary glands is influenced primarily by the number of cell divisions rather than by the passage of chronological or metabolic time."

Studies of single-antibody-forming cell clones in vivo show that these cells are also capable of only a limited capacity to replicate after serial transfer in vivo (52, 53). Harrison (38, 54) reports that when marrow-cell transplants from young and old normal donors are made to a genetically anemic recipient mouse strain, the anemia is cured. He further reports that such transplants to anemic mice ultimately expire, exhibiting once again the finitude of normal cell proliferation in vivo (39).

In connection with findings that bear upon the proliferative capacity of cells in vivo as a function of age, I should mention several other intriguing reports here. The most informative of such studies are those bearing upon the major cell-renewal systems: the hematopoietic cells of the bone marrow, the epidermis, the lymphatic cells of the thymus, the spleen and lymph nodes, the sperm cells in the seminiferous tubules of the testes, and the epithelial cells lining the gastrointestinal tract and in the crypts of the epithelial lining of the small intestine. In the last-named system, for example, cell generation time in the mouse increases with age (55–57). The increase in generation time is not a linear increase from early youth to extreme old age (58); rather, it increases up to approximately one year of age and levels off during the second year, increasing again between 675 and 825 days. The intestinal crypt of a three-month-old mouse contains a population of about 132 dividing cells, whereas the proliferative compartment of a 27-month-old animal contains only 92 cells. These data support the finding of Thrasher and Greulich *(57)*, who also found in older animals a decrease in the number of crypt cells that are capable of dividing and synthesizing DNA. Lesher and Sacher *(58)* conclude that "because of the increase in generation time and the decrease in the proliferating cell population, production of new cells in old animals is approximately 50% less than the production in 100-day-old BCF_1 mice."

Post and Hoffman *(59)* find in rats that after birth the rate of body and liver growth as well as the number of cells engaged in DNA synthesis and mitosis decreases exponentially. Furthermore, the size of the replicating pool decreases, and time for replication and for its component processes (DNA synthesis, G_2, mitosis, and G_1) lengthens. As the rat reaches maturity (six months of age), there is a marked decline in the percentage of hepatic cells and hepatocytes engaged in DNA synthesis and mitosis, after which a low amount of each activity is maintained.

Schneider and Fowlkes *(60)* find an increased proportion of human diploid cells in the G_1 period as they approach Phase III. Suzuki and Withers *(61)* make the significant finding that even mouse spermatogonial stem cells decrease exponentially with age under circumstances in which tissue transplantation is avoided.

Thus there is a wide variety of examples of in vivo constraints on the proliferative capacity of replicating cell cohorts, and different proliferating cell systems will likely display variations on this general theme. On the basis of in vitro data, the fibroblast may represent the upper limit of proliferative potential; however, one should not exclude placing a higher limit on such cell-renewal systems as hematopoietic cells or skin epithelium, neither of which has been shown to proliferate in vitro for long periods of time while still retaining normal characteristics and functional capacities.

Organ Clocks

Is it possible that a limit on cell proliferation or function in some strategic organ could orchestrate the entire phenomenon of senescence? Burnet *(62, 63)* has speculated that, if this is so, the most likely organ is the thymus and its dependent tissues.

He reasons that aging is largely mediated by autoimmune processes that are influenced by progressive weakening of the function of immunological surveillance, and argues that the weakening of immunological surveillance may be related to weakness of the thymus-dependent immune system. He concludes that the thymus and its dependent tissue are subject to a proliferative limit similar to the Phase III phenomenon or senescence in vitro described by us for human cells. Whether the role played by the thymus and its dependent tissues as the pacemaker in senescence is important remains to be established.

Theories of Aging

Most gerontologists agree that there is probably no single cause of aging. A phenomenon that probably comes closer to a unifying theory consists of concepts based on genetic instability as a cause of aging *(64)*. The genetic contribution to the aging process is likely to be foremost in the determination of a life span that is characteristic of each species. This contribution is effective because the range of variation in the maximum life span among different species is obviously much greater than the range of individual life spans within the species. One fundamental problem in relating genetic processes to aging is the attempt to separate the genetic basis of differentiation from a possible genetic basis for aging, or the concept of "first we ripen, then we rot."

Genetic instability as a cause of age changes might include the progressive accumulation of faulty copying in dividing cells or the accumulation of errors in information-containing molecules.

The progressive accumulation of errors in the functions of either fixed post-mitotics or in actively dividing cells could act as a clock. This process would initiate secondary types of mischief, which would ultimately be manifest as biologic aging as it is known. Thus, aging could be a special case of morphogenesis: cells may be programmed simply to run out of program.

Probably no other area of biologic inquiry is susceptible to so many theories as is the science of biogerontology. This proliferation of theories has occurred not only because of a lack of sufficient fundamental data but also because manifestations of biologic changes with time affect almost all biological systems, from the molecular level up to that of the whole organism. It is therefore easy to construct a theory of aging based on a biological decrement that may be observed to occur in time in any system, at the level of the cell, tissue, organ, or whole animal. The important question will always be: Is the change observed a direct cause of aging, or is it the result of changes that may be occurring at a more fundamental level?

If, as modern concepts have it, biological development is based on signals originating from information-containing molecules, then post-developmental changes can reasonably be attributed to a similar system of signals at the molecular level. This notion assumes that the switching on and off of genes during developmental processes also determines age changes; that is, age changes, like developmental changes, are "programmed" into the original pool of genetic information and are "played out" in an orderly sequence just as developmental changes are. The graying of the hair, for example, is not generally thought of as a disease associated with the passage of time; rather, it is regarded as a highly predictable event that occurs later in life after the genetic expression of many other programmed developmental events that occur in orderly sequences.

This example might be analogous to the attribution of aging to a similar series of orderly, programmed genetic events that shut down or slow down essential physiological phenomena when post-reproductive age is reached. The programming may be the result of specific gene determinants that, like the end of a tape recording, simply trigger a sequence of events to shut the machine down.

Alternatively, the universality of aging might be attributed to functional failures arising from the random accumulation of "noise" in some vulnerable parts of the system, which ultimately interferes with optimum function and produces all the well-known physiological decrements. But, if the "noise" is randomly accumulated, why do members of each species appear to age at specific, highly predictable times? One may call the span of time during which "noise" accumulates and becomes manifest in some functional decrement, "the mean time to failure." This concept is applicable to the deterioration of mechanical as well as biological systems and can be illustrated by a consideration of the mean time to failure of, for example, automobiles. The mean time to failure of the average machine may be five to six years, which may vary as a function of the competence of repair processes. Barring total replacement of all vital elements, deterioration is inevitable. Similarly, failure of cell function may occur at predictable times that depend on the fidelity of the synthesizing machinery and the degree of perfection of cellular repair systems. Because biological systems do not appear to function perfectly and indefinitely, one is lead to the conclusion that the ultimate death of a cell or loss of function is genetically programmed and has a mean time to failure. The mean time to failure may be applicable to a single cell, tissue, or organ, or to the intact animal itself. If the genetic apparatus simply runs out of accurate programmed information, that might result in different mean times to failure for all the dependent biological systems. The existence of different life spans for different species may reflect better repair systems in animals of greater longevity.

Finally, one must consider the two cell lineages that seem to have escaped from the inevitability of aging or death: the germ cells (precursors of egg and sperm cells) and the continuously reproducing cancer-cell populations. The immortality of cancer-cell populations may be related to a possible exchange of genetic information between somatic cells or viruses and somatic cells, in the same way that the genetic cards are reshuffled when egg and sperm fuse. Thus, exchange of genetic information may serve to reprogram or reset the biologic clock. By this mechanism, species survival is guaranteed, but the individual members are ultimately programmed to failure.

Supported, in part, by the Glenn Foundation for Medical Research, Manhasset, NY, and Grant RO1 AG 00850 from the National Advisory Council on Aging, National Institute on Aging, National Institutes of Health, Bethesda, MD.

References

1. Carrel, A., and Ebeling, A. H., Age and multiplication of fibroblasts. *J. Exp. Med.* **34,** 599 (1921).
2. Suzuki, Y., *Mitt. Allg. Path. Sendai* **2,** 191 (1925).
3. Goldschmidt, J., Hoffman, R., and Doljanski, L., Etude comparative sur la durée de la péroide de latence pour la croissance des tissus embryonnaires et adultes explantés in vitro. *Compt. Rend. Soc. Biol. (Paris)* **126,** 389 (1937).

4. Ebeling, A. H., The permanent life of connective tissue outside of the organism. *J. Exp. Med.* **17,** 273 (1913).
5. Parker, R. C., *Methods of Tissue Culture,* Harper and Row, New York, NY, 1961.
6. Hayflick, L., and Moorhead, P. S., The serial cultivation of human diploid cell strains. *Exp. Cell Res.* **25,** 585 (1961).
7. Hayflick, L., The limited in vitro lifetime of human diploid cell strains. *Exp. Cell Res.* **37,** 614 (1965).
8. Martin, G. M., Sprague, C. A., and Epstein, C. J., Replicative life-span of cultivated human cells. Effect of donor's age, tissue, and genotype. *Lab. Invest.* **23,** 86 (1970).
9. LeGuilly, Y., Simon, M., Lenoir, P., and Bourel, M., Longterm culture of human adult liver cells: Morphological changes related to in vitro senescence and effect of donor's age on growth potential. *Gerontologia* **19,** 303 (1973).
10. Schneider, E. L., and Mitsui, Y., The relationship between in vitro cellular aging and in vivo human aging. *Proc. Natl. Acad. Sci. USA* **73,** 3584 (1976).
11. Bierman, E. L., The effect of donor age on the in vitro lifespan of cultured human arterial smooth-muscle cells. *In Vitro* **14,** 951 (1978).
12. Schneider, E. L., Mitsui, Y., Aw, K. S., and Shorr, S. S., Tissue-specific differences in cultured human diploid fibroblasts. *Exp. Cell Res.* **108,** 1 (1977).
13. Goldstein, S., Moerman, E. J., Soeldner, J. S., Gleason, R. E., and Barnett, D. M., Chronologic and physiologic age affect replicative life-span of fibroblasts from diabetics, prediabetics, and normal donors. *Science* **199,** 781 (1978).
14. Hayflick, L., The cell biology of human aging. *N. Engl. J. Med.* **295,** 1302 (1976).
15. Hayflick, L., The cellular basis for biological aging. In *Handbook of the Biology of Aging,* C. Finch and L. Hayflick, Eds., Van Nostrand Reinhold Co., New York, NY, 1977, pp 159–179.
16. Schwartz, A. G., and Moore, C. J., Inverse correlation between species lifespan and capacity of cultured fibroblasts to bind 7,12-dimethyl-benz(a)anthracene to DNA. *Exp. Cell Res.* **109,** 448 (1977).
17. Moore, C. J., and Schwartz, A. G., Inverse correlation between species lifespan and capacity of cultured fibroblasts to convert benzo(a)pyrene to water-soluble metabolites. *Exp. Cell Res.* **116,** 359 (1978).
18. Bell, E., Marek, L. F., Levinstone, D. S., Merrill, C., Sher, S., Young, I. T., and Eden, M., Loss of division potential in vitro: Aging or differentiation? *Science* **202,** 1158 (1978).

19. Saunders, J. W., Jr., Death in embryonic systems. *Science* **154**, 604 (1966).
20. Lima, L., Malaise, E., and Macieira-Coelho, A., Aging in vitro. *Exp. Cell Res.* **73**, 345 (1972).
21. Epstein, J., Williams, J. R., and Little, J. B., Deficient DNA repair in progeria and senescent human cells. *Radiat. Res.* **55**, 527 (1973).
22. Epstein, J., Williams, J. R., and Little, J. B., Rate of DNA repair in human progeroid cells. *Proc. Natl. Acad. Sci. USA* **70**, 977 (1973).
23. Epstein, J., Williams, J. R., and Little, J. B., Rate of DNA repair in progeric and normal human fibroblasts. *Biochem. Biophys. Res. Commun.* **59**, 850 (1974).
24. Regan, J. D., and Setlow, R. B., DNA repair in human progeroid cells. *Biochem. Biophys. Res. Commun.* **59**, 858 (1973).
25. Clarkson, J. M., and Painter, R. B., Repair of x-ray damage in aging WI-38 cells. *Mutat. Res.* **23**, 107 (1974).
26. Goldstein, S., The role of DNA repair in aging of cultures of fibroblasts from xeroderma pigmentosum and normals. *Proc. Soc. Exp. Biol. Med.* **137**, 730 (1971).
27. Painter, R. B., Clarkson, J. M., and Young, B. R., Ultraviolet-induced repair replication in aging diploid human cells (WI-38). *Radiat. Res.* **56**, 560 (1973).
28. Mattern, M. R., and Cerutti, P. A., Age-dependent excision repair of damaged thymidine from γ-irradiated DNA by isolated nuclei from fibroblasts. *Nature* **254**, 450 (1975).
29. Hart, R. W., and Setlow, R. B., Correlation between deoxyribonucleic acid excision-repair and life-span in a number of mammalian species. *Proc. Natl. Acad. Sci. USA* **71**, 2169 (1974).
30. Hart, R. W., and Setlow, R. B., DNA repair in late-passage human cells. *Mech. Ageing Dev.* **5**, 67 (1976).
31. Bowman, P. D., Meek, R. L., and Daniel, C. W., Decreased synthesis of nucleolar RNA in aging human cells in vitro. *Exp. Cell Res.* **101**, 434 (1976).
32. Hayflick, L., Aging under glass. *Exp. Gerontol.* **5**, 291 (1970).
33. Daniel, C. W., DeOme, K. B., Young, J. T., Blair, P. B., and Faulkin, L. J., Jr., The in vivo lifespan of normal and preneoplastic mouse mammary glands: A serial transplantation study. *Proc. Natl. Acad. Sci. USA* **61**, 53 (1968).
34. Krohn, P. L., Review lectures on senescence. II. Heterochronic transplantation in the study of ageing. *Proc. R. Soc. (London) Ser. B* **157**, 128 (1962).
35. Ford, C. E., Micklem, H. S., and Gray, S. M., Evidence of selective

proliferation of reticular cell-clones in heavily irradiated mice. *Br. J. Radiol.* **32,** 280 (1959).

36. Cudkowicz, G., Upton, A. C., Shearer, G. M., and Hughes, W. L., Lymphocyte content and proliferative capacity of serially transplanted mouse bone marrow. *Nature* **201,** 165 (1964).

37. Siminovitch, L., Till, J. E., and McCulloch, E. A., Decline in colony-forming ability of marrow cells subjected to serial transplantation into irradiated mice. *J. Cell. Comp. Physiol.* **64,** 23 (1964).

38. Harrison, D. E., Normal production of erythrocytes by mouse marrow continuous for 73 months. *Proc. Natl. Acad. Sci. USA* **70,** 3184 (1973).

39. Harrison, D. E., Normal function of transplanted marrow cell lines from aged mice. *J. Gerontol.* **30,** 279 (1975).

40. Hellman, S., Botnick, L. E., Hannon, E. C., and Vigneulle, R. M., Proliferative capacity of murine hematopoietic stem cells. *Proc. Natl. Acad. Sci. USA* **75,** 490 (1978).

41. Stewart, H. L., Snell, K. C., Dunham, L. J., and Schylen, S. M., *Transplantable and Transmissible Tumors of Animals.* Armed Forces Institute of Pathology, Washington, DC, 1959.

42. Till, J. E., McCulloch, E. A., and Siminovitch, L., Isolation of variant cell lines during serial transplantation of hematopoietic cells derived from fetal liver. *J. Natl. Cancer Inst.* **33,** 707 (1964).

43. Daniel, C. W., Aidells, B. D., Medina, D., and Faulkin, L. J., Jr., Unlimited division potential of precancerous mouse mammary cells after spontaneous or carcinogen-induced transformation. *Fed. Proc.* **34,** 64 (1975).

44. Krohn, P. L., *Topics in the Biology of Aging,* Interscience Publishers, John Wiley, New York, NY, 1966.

45. Daniel, C. W., and Young, L. J. T., Influence of cell division on an aging process. *Exp. Cell Res.* **65,** 27 (1971).

46. Daniel, C. W., Finite growth span of mouse mammary gland serially propagated in vivo. *Experientia (Basel)* **29,** 1422 (1973).

47. Daniel, C. W., Cell longevity: In vivo. In *Handbook of the Biology of Aging* (see ref. *15*), pp 122–158.

48. McHale, J. S., Moulton, M. L., and McHale, J. T., Limited culture lifespan of human diploid cells as a function of metabolic time instead of division potential. *Exp. Gerontol.* **6,** 89 (1971).

49. Dell'Orco, R. T., Mertens, J. G., and Kruse, P. F., Jr., Doubling potential, calendar time, and donor age of human diploid cells in culture. *Exp. Cell Res.* **84,** 363 (1974).

50. Harley, C. B., and Goldstein, S., Cultured human fibroblasts: Distribution of cell generations and a critical limit. *J. Cell Physiol.* **97,** 509 (1978).

51. Young, L. J. T., Medina, D., DeOme, K. B., and Daniel, C. W., The influence of host and tissue age on the life span and growth rate of serially transplanted mouse mammary gland. *Exp. Gerontol.* **6**, 49 (1971).

52. Williamson, A. R., Extent and control of antibody diversity. *Biochem. J.* **130**, 325 (1972).

53. Williamson, A. R., and Askonas, B. A., Senescence of an antibody-forming cell clone. *Nature* **238**, 337 (1972).

54. Harrison, D. E., Normal function of transplanted mouse erythrocyte precursors for 21 months beyond donor life spans. *Nature New Biol.* **237**, 220 (1972).

55. Lesher, S., Fry, R. J. M., and Kohn, H. I., Age and the generation time of the mouse duodenal epithelial cell. *Exp. Cell Res.* **24**, 334 (1961).

56. Lesher, S., Fry, R. J. M., and Kohn, H. I., Aging and the generation cycle of intestinal epithelial cells in the mouse. *Gerontologia (Basel)* **5**, 176 (1961).

57. Thrasher, J. D., and Greulich, R. C., The duodenal progenitor population. I. Age-related increase in the duration of the cryptal progenitor. *J. Exp. Zool.* **159**, 39 (1965).

58. Lesher, S., and Sacher, G. A., Effects of age on cell proliferation in mouse duodenal crypts. *Exp. Gerontol.* **3**, 211 (1968).

59. Post, J., and Hoffman, J., Changes in the replication times and patterns of the liver cell during the life of the rat. *Exp. Cell Res.* **36**, 111 (1964).

60. Schneider, E. L., and Fowlkes, B. J., Measurement of DNA content and cell volume in senescent human fibroblasts utilizing flow multiparameter single cell analysis. *Exp. Cell Res.* **98**, 298 (1976).

61. Suzuki, N., and Withers, H. R., Exponential decrease during aging and random lifetime of mouse spermatogonial stem cells. *Science* **202**, 1214 (1978).

62. Burnet, F. M., *Immunological Surveillance,* Pergamon Press, New York, NY, 1970, pp 224–257.

63. Burnet, F. M., An immunological approach to aging. *Lancet* **ii**, 358 (1970).

64. Hayflick, L., Current theories of biological aging. *Fed. Proc.* **34**, 9 (1975).

65. Hayflick, L., Cell aging. In *Annual Review of Gerontology and Geriatrics,* **1**, C. Eisdorfer, Ed., Springer Publishing Co., New York, NY, 1980.

247

Fidelity of Protein Synthesis in Aging Human Fibroblasts

Samuel Goldstein, Roman I. Wojtyk, Calvin B. Harley,
Jeffrey W. Pollard, John W. Chamberlain,
and Clifford P. Stanners

Cultured human fibroblasts have a finite replicative life span
(1) inversely proportional to the age of the donor (for a recent
review, see ref. *2*). Moreover, physiological rather than chronological aging is the prime determinant of this replicative limit, in
that fibroblasts derived from donors with syndromes of premature
aging show curtailed life spans *(2)*. Several explanations have been
promulgated to account for the loss of replicative ability, but
the most widely tested in recent years has been the "error-catastrophe" theory of Orgel *(3, 4)*. According to this theory, errors
in protein synthesis lead to an increasingly error-prone translational machinery and an autocatalytic augmentation of errors that
will kill the cell when the proportion of abnormal proteins exceeds
a critical threshold.

Here we describe results from two different experimental systems that directly examine the fidelity of protein synthesis during
cellular aging. In the first, we have used a cell-free system in
which proteins ordered by the artificial mRNA poly(U) are
synthesized.[1] Because the UUU-codon codes for phenylalanine,
phenylalanine alone should be incorporated into the nascent polypeptide, poly(Phe) *(5)*. However, other amino acids, particularly
leucine (with codons UUA, UUG, and CUU), could become misin-
corporated into the poly(Phe) chain if errors occurred by codon–
anticodon mispairing *(6)*. Thus, the leucine/phenylalanine ratio

---

[1] Abbreviations used: mRNA, tRNA, messenger and transfer ribonucleic acid; U, uracil;
C, cytosine; A, adenine; G, guanine; Phe, phenylalanine; Leu, leucine; his, histidine; S-
30, supernate of ruptured cells after centrifugation at 30 000 × *g*.

within poly(Phe), as directed by poly(U), provides a measure of translational infidelity.

In the second technique *(7–9)*, intact cells were used, so that the natural mRNAs and other components of protein synthesis were preserved. Specific errors were induced at histidine sites by starving the cells for histidine, both by omitting this amino acid from the medium and by simultaneously adding histidinol, an analogue of histidine that competes with histidine for histidyl-tRNA synthetase *(10)*. Our present evidence supports the view that histidyl-tRNA becomes depleted, and glutaminyl-tRNA, most closely related in its two anticodons to those of histidyl-tRNA, binds to the specific histidine codons CAU and CAC. The net result is the substitution of glutamine for histidine. Because glutamine is a neutral amino acid, substituting it for the basic histidine will result in synthesis of proteins with decreased isoelectric points. Thus, on two-dimensional gel electrophoresis, where proteins are resolved according to isoelectric point and relative molecular mass, a series of satellite spots with masses corresponding to one, two, three, etc. substitutions of glutamine for histidine will appear on the acidic side of the native proteins.

Using these two techniques, we have compared the accuracy of protein synthesis in normal fibroblasts at early and late passage, i.e., "young and old" cells in vitro, as well as in cells from donors with disorders or premature aging: progeria (Hutchinson-Gilford syndrome) and Werner's syndrome. Because a corollary of the Orgel hypothesis predicts that permanent lines of "immortal" cells should have lower error frequencies, we have also examined SV40-transformed fibroblasts. Our findings are contrary to the predictions of the Orgel hypothesis in all respects.

Fidelity of Protein Synthesis in a Cell-Free System

We derived fibroblasts from normal and prematurely aged subjects from skin biopsies of the anterior forearm and cultured them at 37 °C (see ref. *11*). MRC5 and WI38 cells were developed from fetal lung and their SV40-transformed derivatives were obtained as described *(9, 12)*. All cells were subcultured routinely in a 1.25 g/L solution of trypsin in phosphate-buffered saline and passaged each time they achieved confluence. Young cells were subdivided at eightfold dilutions, counting three mean population doublings

249

with each such manipulation (1, 2). Old cells were subcultured at fourfold or twofold dilutions, counting two or one mean population doubling, respectively, each time. The cumulative life span (in total mean population doublings) was thus obtained when each culture failed to reach confluence at advanced stages of passage after three weeks of growth with feeding at weekly intervals (1, 2).

To obtain cell-free extracts, the cells were harvested, washed, swollen in hypotonic buffer, and homogenized in a Dounce apparatus (12). This method ruptured virtually all cells and left the nuclei intact, as monitored by phase-contrast microscopy. After restoring isotonicity, we centrifuged the lysate at 30 000 $\times$ g for 30 min and removed the supernate (S-30). The S-30 was then incubated for 45 min at 37 °C to run the ribosomes off the natural mRNAs (13). The S-30 was then dialyzed, adjusted to a concentration of 10 A_{260} units/mL, and used immediately without freezing and thawing. We optimized conditions for poly(U) translation with respect to Mg^{2+}, KCl, poly(U), and amino acid concentration. Aliquots were incubated with the appropriate ^{3}H-labeled amino acid (phenylalanine, leucine, or lysine), then prepared for liquid scintillation counting as before (12).

In the absence of poly(U), small quantities of phenylalanine were incorporated into acid-precipitable material (Table 1). Upon addition of poly(U), incorporation of phenylalanine increased up to 1000-fold, and all cell extracts showed approximately equal stimulation. Leucine incorporation, which was also low in the absence of poly(U), increased somewhat upon addition of poly(U), but this increment was considerably less than the poly(U)-stimulation of phenylalanine incorporation. Leucine incorporation without poly(U) was inhibited by more than 90% by puromycin or by pretreatment of extracts with micrococcal nuclease (12), which suggests that this amount of incorporation represents protein synthesis resulting from translation of residual amounts of endogenous mRNA. To confirm this by an independent means and to ensure that poly(U) did not affect leucine or phenylalanine incorporation directed by endogenous mRNA, we monitored lysine incorporation with and without poly(U) (Table 1). The lysine codons AAA and AAC are remote in the genetic code from the phenylalanine codon UUU. Lysine incorporation, therefore, should not be stimulated by poly(U) and can serve as a marker

Table 1. Poly(U)-Stimulation of Phenylalanine and Leucine Incorporation

	Amino acid incorporated (cpm)[a]			Amino acid incorporated due to poly(U), fmol	Error frequency, %[b]
Amino acid	−Poly(U)	+Poly(U)	Increase due to poly(U)		
Phe	51	18800	18749	4128	
Leu	70	267	197	6	0.15
Lys	310	306	—	0	

[a] Counts per minute; hot acid-insoluble counts incorporated after subtraction of background counts.
[b] Error frequency = (Δleu/Δphe) × 100.
Data, derived from S-30 extracts of A$_2$ cells at 37 mean population doublings, represent the mean of duplicates (which agreed within 5%) of aliquots of S-30 equivalent to 250 000 cells. Counts per minute have been corrected for the variable specific radioactivities of each amino acid to give molar incorporation.

for residual protein synthesis directed by endogenous mRNA. As shown, poly(U) did not stimulate lysine incorporation, and we can conclude that poly(U) has no effect on endogenous mRNA-directed protein synthesis.

We also found no proteolysis of poly(U)-directed proteins in the cell-free extracts. This is an important negative finding because proteolytic degradation (14) of either poly(Phe) or leucine-containing poly(Phe) could have confounded estimates of infidelity.

To calculate error frequencies, we took the ratio of the increment in leucine incorporation upon addition of poly(U) (Table 1) to the increment of poly(U)-stimulated incorporation of phenylalanine. Error frequencies varied considerably among the normal cell strains (Table 2). The highest values were found in extracts of A25 at early passage, and the lowest were in extracts of late-passage A2 cells. However, consistent results were observed within a given cell strain at a given passage level. Error frequencies of strains from an old donor (J089), from subjects with progeria or Werner's syndrome, and from the fetal lung strain MRC5 and its SV40-transformed derivative fell within this range. We observed no correlation between replicative life span of cell strains and their error frequencies. Most important in terms of the Orgel hypothesis, late-passage cells of all normal and fetal strains did not have higher error frequencies than their early-passage counterparts. Indeed, unexpectedly but reproducibly, early-passage cells displayed higher error frequencies than the corresponding late-passage cells.

Table 2. Error Frequency of Poly(U)-Directed Synthesis in Cell-Free Extracts of Cultured Human Fibroblasts as a Function of Passage Level

Cell strain	Donor age, yr	Replicative life span[a]	Passage level[b]	Percent error frequency[c]	n
Normal					
A2	10	65	early	0.25 ± 0.03	3
			late	0.05 ± 0.02	3
A25	9	50	early	1.15 ± 0.21	2
			late	0.24 ± 0.04	3
J089	67	55	mid	0.13 ± 0.01	2
			late	0.06 ± 0.01	2
Progeria					
P18	4	53	mid	0.23 ± 0.01	3
P5	9	42	mid	0.23 ± 0.03	2
Werner's syndrome					
WS-2	37	27	mid	0.17 ± 0.06	2
Other					
MRC5	fetal lung	70	mid	0.42 ± 0.04	2
			late	0.10	1
MRC5-SV40	transformed	∞	immortal	0.30 ± 0.01	2

[a] Replicative life span is defined as the number of mean population doublings accruing until cultures fail to reach confluence under normal growth conditions after three weeks with weekly refeedings.
[b] Early, < 50% of life span consumed; mid, 50–90% consumed; late, > 90% consumed.
[c] Error frequency shown as the mean ± standard deviation (SD) of fresh extract preparations from n separately grown lots of cells.

Histidine Starvation Leading to Mistranslation in Intact Cells

This method has been described in detail (7, 9). Briefly, cells growing in plastic dishes were rinsed with medium minus histidine and methionine and incubated for 40 min in the same medium plus either 0.15 mmol of histidine per liter (unstarved) or 2 to 20 mmol of histidinol per liter (starved). We then replaced media with identical media containing either [³H]phenylalanine for measurement of the protein synthesis rate or [³⁵S]methionine for labeling of proteins by two-dimensional gel electrophoresis with isoelectric focusing in the first dimension (final linear pH range 4–7) followed by the second-dimension electrophoresis on sodium dodecyl sulfate polyacrylamide gel slabs. These gels were then dried and exposed to roentgenogram film for appropriate periods to identify [³⁵S]methionine-containing proteins. We scanned autoradiograms with a microdensitometer and quantified

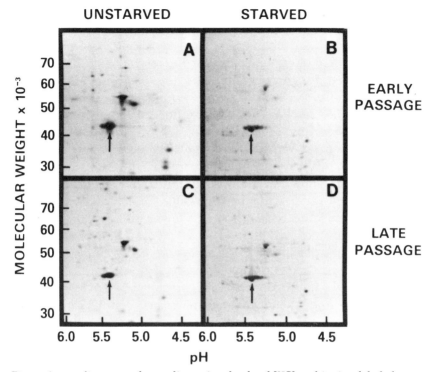

Fig. 1. Autoradiograms of two-dimensional gels of [^{35}S]methionine-labeled proteins.

Early- and late-passage human fibroblasts from a normal donor (A2, Table 3) were grown in complete medium (unstarved), or in medium lacking histidine but containing histidinol at 10–20 mmol/L. The most prominent protein spot at relative molecular mass 44 000 and pH 5.4–5.5 represents β-actin *(arrow)*, and the smaller adjacent spot on the basic side is γ-actin. Satellite spots can be discerned on the acid side of the native γ- and β-actin species in the starved fibroblasts, with a corresponding decrease in intensity of the native spots. Reproduced from ref. *9* with permission of the publisher.

both the native and substituted (satellite) proteins by integrating the curves. Because there are nine histidine residues in both native actins (β and γ) synthesized by human fibroblasts, the possible range of substitution varies from one to nine residues per actin molecule. In practice, however, only two to five substituted actin species were found *(9)*.

Under normal (unstarved) conditions no differences were evident in either charge or molecular mass of proteins from "aged" cells (Figure 1). This includes late-passage normal fibroblasts, as well as cells from an old donor and subjects with progeria or Werner's syndrome. On the other hand, when cells were starved for histidine to induce mistranslation, satellite spots were visible on the acidic side of the native actin species. We quantified the native and satellite proteins at protein synthesis rates of from 2 to 10% of normal rates, using actin as the reference protein. There are three reasons for choosing actin: it is the most abundant protein in the human fibroblasts, it contains nine histidine residues, and it can be readily resolved from surrounding proteins on two-dimensional gels.

Error frequencies were determined after normalizing induced mistranslation to the protein synthetic rate (Table 3). Late-passage cells from fetal, young, or old normal donors did not have greater error frequencies than early-passage cells. As before, two young-donor strains at late passage showed a lower error frequency than their early-passage counterparts ($p < 0.05$). Additionally, cells from old donors and subjects with progeria or Werner's syndrome did not have greater error frequencies. In striking contrast, SV40-transformed fibroblasts showed a significantly greater error frequency than either their own untransformed counterparts or all normal fibroblasts combined. Again, we found no correlation between the in vitro life span and the error frequency.

Implications and Conclusions

Evidence for and against the error-catastrophe hypothesis has come entirely from indirect studies (for recent reviews, see ref. 15 and 16). Therefore, the significance of the present data is that they directly contradict the Orgel hypothesis in several respects. First, fidelity of protein synthesis measured by either technique does not decline at late passage. Second, cells from old donors do not show an increased error frequency. Third, fibroblasts derived from subjects with two inherited disorders of premature aging, which contain a diversity of abnormal proteins (17), show error frequencies within the normal range. Fourth, although a corollary of the Orgel hypothesis predicts that escape from "mortality" and development of an immortal cell line should be associated with a *decrease* in synthetic errors, this was not observed in either assay, and indeed, error frequencies by the intact system assay were increased.

It is unclear why the cell-free system fails to reveal the greater infidelity of SV40-transformed cells. However, poly(U)-directed

Table 3. Error Frequencies of Cultured Human Cells as a Function of Passage Stage

Cell type	Donor age, yr	Replicative life span[a]	Error frequency per 10 000 (mean ± SEM)[b] Early passage	Late passage
Young donors				
WI38	fetus	55	0.6 ± 0.1 (7)	0.4 ± 0.1 (4)
MRC5	fetus	65	1.5 ± 0.2 (2)	
A$_2$	11	65	1.2 ± 0.2 (10)	0.9 ± 0.2 (8)
GM37	18	50	1.6 ± 0.1 (3)	
Mean of young donors			1.0 ± 0.1 (22)	0.7 ± 0.2 (12)
Old donors				
J069	69	50	0.8 ± 0.2 (3)	0.8 ± 0.1 (3)
J088	76	48	1.0 ± 0.3 (4)	
Progeria				
P5	9	42	1.2 ± 0.2 (6)	
P18	5	53	1.3 ± 0.3 (4)	
Werner's syndrome				
WS2	37	37	1.3 ± 0.3 (2)	
WS4	41	ND	0.5 ± 0.1 (3)	
Mean of old, progeria, and Werner's syndrome donors			1.1 ± 0.1 (22)	0.8 ± 0.1 (3)
Mean of diploid cells			1.1 ± 0.1 (44)	0.8 ± 0.1 (15)
Immortal cells				
WI38–SV40			2.8 ± 0.2 (10)[c]	

[a] See Table 2.
[b] The error frequency was derived by normalizing the fraction of substituted sites to the calculated step time of ribosomes at the histidine codon (ref. 9 and Harley et al., in preparation). Numbers in parentheses are the number of separately analyzed extracts of proteins labeled during histidine starvation.
[c] SV40-transformed WI38 cells have significantly greater ($p < 0.0001$) error frequency than either normal WI38 cells or all diploid cells combined at early or late passage.
ND, not determined.

synthesis is unnatural in that it does not carry out normal initiation or termination. In contrast, the intact system appears normal in these functions and preserves the normal cell architecture, at least before histidine starvation. This may also account for the apparently higher frequencies of errors in the poly(U)-directed system—on the order of 10^{-3} to 10^{-2} per amino acid site vs 10^{-4} in the intact system. A differential effect of protein degradation of these estimates of error frequency seems unlikely; the cell-free system did not have significant proteolytic activity, and we were unable to show increased turnover of the substituted actin species in the intact cell system (9). Other estimates of error frequency in vivo have also been reported to be about 10^{-4} (18–20).

The errors observed with both of these techniques have been interpreted to be the result of codon–anticodon mispairing, and it is possible that misacylation of the relevant tRNA (tRNA^{phe} or tRNA^{his}) could be involved. However, it is unlikely that misacylation of tRNA^{phe} with leucine or of tRNA^{his} with a neutral amino acid could occur, and misacylation of a cognate amino acid with noncognate tRNA is relatively rare (21). Moreover, recent genetic evidence overwhelmingly supports the idea of mistranslation based on ribosomal ambiguity, leading to codon–anticodon mispairing (22–24). In any case, the comparisons made here between the cell types would still be valid because our assays measure errors from all causes under standardized conditions.

Although it is still possible that a small increase in the error frequency of old cells may have gone undetected and could still, therefore, be responsible for error catastrophe and senescence, we believe this is unlikely for three reasons. First, induction of error frequencies about 50-fold greater than normal in *Escherichia coli* exposed to streptomycin did not produce loss of bacterial viability (25, 26). Second, both *Drosophila* (27) and cultured human cells (28) tolerate substantial incorporation of amino acid analogues into protein without reducing their life span. Third, in neither of our systems could we find a correlation between error frequency and the replicative life span. Indeed, the immortal SV40-transformed cells had the greatest error frequency of all cells examined. It is tempting to speculate that the high error frequency in these virally transformed fibroblasts may play a role in transformation to permanent cell lines and perhaps by analogy to carcinogenesis and tumor progression. However, other studies (Pollard et al., in preparation) indicate that this phenomenon may be more closely related to SV40 virus per se rather than a general property of permanent lines. Further work is required to determine the significance of the increased error frequency in SV40-transformed human cells.

Finally, neither of these two systems of determining fidelity of protein synthesis has been reported before in cultured human fibroblasts. Both techniques should be useful in further studies of diploid cells derived from subjects with disorders that may involve translational infidelity. Our present results, however, fail to show a decline in the fidelity of protein synthesis during fibro-blast aging in vitro, and thus fail to support the Orgel hypothesis of cellular senescence.

References

1. Hayflick, L., The limited in vitro lifetime of human diploid cell strains. *Exp. Cell Res.* **37**, 614–636 (1965).
2. Goldstein, S., Senescence. In *Endocrinology*, **3**, L. J. Degroot et al., Eds., Grune & Stratton, New York, NY, 1979, pp 2001–2028.
3. Orgel, L. E., The maintenance of the accuracy of protein synthesis and its relevance to ageing. *Proc. Natl. Acad. Sci. USA* **49**, 517–521 (1963).
4. Orgel, L. E., Ageing of clones of mammalian cells. *Nature* **243**, 441–445 (1973).
5. Matthei, J. H., and Nirenberg, M. W., Characteristics and stabilization of DNAase-sensitive protein synthesis in *E. coli* extracts. *Proc. Natl. Acad. Sci. USA* **47**, 1580–1587 (1961).
6. Davies, J., Gorini, L., and Davis, B., Misreading of RNA code words induced by aminoglycoside antibiotics. *J. Mol. Pharmacol.* **1**, 93–106 (1965).
7. Parker, J., Pollard, J. W., Friesen, J. D., and Stanners, C. P., Stuttering: High level mistranslation in animal and bacterial cells. *Proc. Natl. Acad. Sci. USA* **75**, 1091–1095 (1978).
8. O'Farrell, P. H., The suppression of defective translation by ppGpp and its role in the stringent response. *Cell* **14**, 545–557 (1978).
9. Harley, C. B., Pollard, J. W., Chamberlain, J. W., Stanners, C. P., and Goldstein, S., Protein synthetic errors do not increase during aging of cultured human fibroblasts. *Proc. Natl. Acad. Sci. USA*, 1980 (in press).
10. Hansen, B. S., Vaughan, M. H., and Wang, L., Reversible inhibition by histidinol of protein synthesis in human cells at the activation of histidine. *J. Biol. Chem.* **247**, 3854–3857 (1972).
11. Goldstein, S., and Littlefield, J. W., Effect of insulin on the conversion of [^{14}C]glucose to $^{14}CO_2$ by normal and diabetic fibroblasts in culture. *Diabetes* **18**, 545–549 (1969).
12. Wojtyk, R. I., and Goldstein, S., Fidelity of protein synthesis does not decline during aging of cultured human fibroblasts. *J. Cell. Physiol.*, 1980 (in press).
13. Villa-Komaroff, L., McDowell, M., Baltimore, D., and Lodish, H. F., Translation of reovirus mRNA, poliovirus RNA, bacteriophage Qβ RNA in cell-free extracts of mammalian cells. *Methods Enzymol.* **30**, 709–723 (1974).

14. Goldberg, A. L., and St. John, A. C., Intracellular protein degradation in mammalian and bacterial cells. *Ann. Rev. Biochem.* **45**, 747–803 (1976).

15. Gershon, D., Current status of age altered enzymes: Alternative mechanisms. *Mech. Ageing Dev.* **9**, 189–196 (1979).

16. Rothstein, M., The formation of altered enzymes in aging animals. *Mech. Ageing Dev.* **9**, 197–202 (1979).

17. Goldstein, S., and Moerman, E., Defective proteins in normal and abnormal human fibroblasts during aging in vitro. *Interdiscip. Top. Gerontol.* **10**, 24–43 (1976).

18. Loftfield, R. B., The frequency of errors in protein biosynthesis. *Biochem. J.* **89**, 82–92 (1963).

19. Loftfield, R. B., and Vanderjagt, D., The frequency of errors in protein biosynthesis. *Biochem. J.* **128**, 1353–1386 (1972).

20. Edelmann, P., and Gallant, J., Mistranslation in *E. coli. Cell* **10**, 131–137 (1977).

21. Loftfield, R. B., The mechanism of aminoacylation of transfer RNA. *Prog. Nucl. Acid Res.* **12**, 87–128 (1972).

22. Gorini, L., Streptomycin and misreading of the genetic code. In *Ribosomes,* M. Nomura et al., Eds., Cold Spring Harbor Laboratory, Long Island, New York, 1974, pp 791–803.

23. Parker, J., and Friesen, J. D., "Two out of three" codon reading leading to mistranslation in vivo. *Mol. Gen. Genet.,* 1980 (in press).

24. Gallant, J., and Foley, D., On the causes and prevention of mistranslation. In *Ribosomes, Structure, Function, and Genetics,* G. Chambliss, G. R. Craven, J. Davies, K. Davis, L. Kahan, and M. Nomura, Eds., University Park Press, Baltimore, MD, 1980, pp 615–638.

25. Edelmann, P., and Gallant, J., On the translational error theory of aging. *Proc. Natl. Acad. Sci. USA* **74**, 3396–3398 (1977).

26. Gallant, J., and Palmer, L., Error propagation in viable cells. *Mech. Ageing Dev.* **10**, 27–38 (1979).

27. Shmookler Reis, R. J., Enzyme fidelity and metazoan aging. *Interdiscip. Top. Gerontol.* **10**, 11–23 (1976).

28. Ryan, J. M., Duda, G., and Cristofalo, V. J., Error accumulation and aging in human diploid cells. *J. Gerontol.* **29**, 616–662 (1974).

The Comparative Biology of Longevity-Assurance Mechanisms

Ronald W. Hart and Ralph E. Stephens

Throughout their evolutionary history, prokaryotic and eukaryotic systems have been subject to numerous physical, chemical, and biological agents that alter the information content and flow of their cellular systems. The origin of these agents can be either internal or external. Thus, to maintain speciation, organisms have had to develop systems that will maintain the genetic integrity of cellular DNA and control its functional expression. Although the endpoint required by evolution may be the same, the methods to achieve this endpoint may vary as a function of kingdom, phylum, and class, and depend both upon the environmental milieu in which the organism finds itself and its need to meet other requirements such as reproduction, motility, and feeding. Hence, whereas nature must be adequate, it must not necessarily be fancy; as long as the products of nature satisfy the requirements for survival of the species and the perpetuation of evolution, all evolutionary requirements have been met. Thus, although it might aid conceptualization to believe that longevity will be achieved in all systems by the same physiological method, such may not necessarily be the case, nor is the onset of senescence or death necessarily due to alterations of the same processes in all systems. Variability in methods of attaining longevity should be greater when one considers differences between classes and phyla than when one considers difference between species, subfamilies, and families within the same class. Therefore, modifications within a class will probably be more closely related to one another for accomplishment of a given endpoint than will modifications between different classes or phyla. Placental mammals, for example, apparently use several interacting mechanisms to prevent, repair, or repress the induction or the expression of genetic damage from a number of agents; this maintains or decreases the risk per cell per unit time from alteration in the information content of the cellular DNA *(1)*. Failure to maintain the integrity of the genetic material results in the alteration of numerous physiological processes *(2)* and can be reflected in the rate of spontaneous transformations per cell per unit time *(3)*, which appears to decrease with an increase in maximum achievable life span of the species.

Approaches to the Study of Longevity-Assurance Systems

All research on aging and longevity is circumscribed by two basic paradigms: *(a)* the ontogenetic approach, which examines age-related changes during the lifetime of an organism, and *(b)* the evolutionary-comparative or phylogenetic approach, which examines the genetic differences in the race history of an organism, to ascertain which differences in the observed characteristics of defined populations could account for the observed differences in species' maximum achievable life spans.

Although both approaches are useful, the ontogenetic approach, which currently dominates contemporary research, does not by itself easily permit a determination of the causes of aging. The evolutionary-comparative approach, by concentrating on those physiological and biochemical factors that may contribute to the evolution of longevity, seeks to determine cause by asking what it is that the longer-lived organism does better than the shorter-lived organism by way of protection, repair, and stabilization of its systems. Because aging can be defined as a loss of homeokinesis, most of the attention of this approach has been focused on those systems that protect, repair, or stabilize the information content of those cells composing the major rate-limiting steps of activity of the higher systems within an organism (i.e., the neural and immune systems).

All placental mammals have similar morphological, physiological, and biochemical characteristics, yet differ from one another in maximum achievable life span by approximately 50-fold *(4, 5)*. To maximize the probability of finding what leads to this difference, we can examine differences and similarities between closely related species exhibiting different specific life spans. For

this purpose, randomly bred populations are preferred, to minimize the effects of genetic selection evident in inbred animals.
The fact that life span varies even within closely associated families—for example, in the primates and mytomorph rodents it varies by more than 20-fold *(6)* and threefold *(7)*, respectively—demonstrates that whatever governs the life span of a species must
have been modified over a relatively short period of time and
thus be under the control of relatively few gene products *(7)*.
This is supported not only by primate DNA-DNA hybridization
studies but also by the observation that within the primates, which
are of relatively recent evolutionary occurrence, life spans vary
greatly, and yet physiological, morphological, and biochemical
characteristics are quite similar. Moreover, the rapidity of the
evolution of life span in hominid evolution has occurred at a
rate approaching 1000 millidarwins (1 millidarwin is the normal
rate of evolution that occurs in the absence of positive or negative
selective pressures), thus imposing rigid constraints on any possible mechanism(s) that might be hypothesized.

Regardless of the exact nature of the longevity-assurance mechanisms suggested to explain these molecular and biochemical observations, such mechanisms must also account for certain physiological observations:

1. The time-dependent, universal, and progressive alteration
of all functional processes in the body at all levels of biological
organization.

2. The similar rate of occurrence of age-related changes in all
species when measured as a fraction of maximum life span.

3. The rapid rate of evolution of longevity in closely related
species such as the hominids.

4. The relationship between cancer and aging, on an inductive
but not necessarily expressive level.

5. The apparent lack of syndromes that uniformly mimic the
aging process or of agents that uniformly and proportionally accelerate the aging process.

6. The stability of maximum life spans of species, and the identical rates of aging in identical but not fraternal twins *(8,9)*.

Such a mechanism will not only have to explain how rapid
evolution of longevity as seen in the hominids and certain other
subfamilies can occur but must also be consistent with basic molecular genetics.

DNA as a Primary Target for Senescence

From the factors outlined above, DNA is reasonably the target for aging; further, the processes controlling the integrity of DNA could serve as a longevity-assurance mechanism. Thus, even though RNA, protein, and lipid membranes are each possible targets for molecular senescence, they are not as suitable as DNA because they turn over, are present in multiple copies, and have a limited number of functions per molecule. Thus these cellular constituents are probably not the primary targets or directors of senescence. DNA, on the other hand, can be expected to be a major physiological target in the aging process because of its multifunctional nature; its lack of turnover; its presence as a unique copy; its function as the ultimate template for synthesis of all DNA, RNA, protein, carbohydrates, and lipids; and its large size (8). Further, damage to DNA can result in such age-related alterations as changes in cell growth, cell division, transcription, and respiration, as well as cell death, mutation, and malignant transformation (10). In comparisons between carcinogenesis (presumably a phenomenon of damage to DNA) and aging, most similarities between these two processes can be related to either inducing or modifying factors, and all differences between them can be related to expressive factors (9).

At the organism level, agents that induce DNA damage also produce organ atrophy; alter endocrine, neural, and muscular response time or function; suppress the immune system; and cause cancer. Because these phenomena are also characteristic in many cases of the aging process (11), alterations in DNA structure and function may reasonably play a significant role in the aging process. Indeed, the most recent evidence suggests not only that DNA damage shortens life spans (12, 13) but additionally that the direct reversal of DNA damage overcomes both the carcinogenic and life-span-shortening effects of such damaging agents (13, 14).

Alterations in DNA can again be useful from a conceptual basis, in explaining the six physiological observations mentioned on the previous page, which must be considered by any general mechanism for explaining the progressive loss of function as results of age (8). Specifically:

1. The laws of random functional integrity of DNA would be

expected to alter progressively all functional processes at all levels of biological organization.

2. Modification of factors controlling the integrity and fidelity of DNA could explain species differences and rates of aging without requiring extensive differences in the pathway for expression of events of senescence.

3. If the genes controlling genome integrity were active to different extents, depending on the state of differentiation, the rates of evolution of longevity could be modified rapidly by altering the degree of activity of such genes. This could well explain the rapid rate of evolution of longevity in primates.

4. The relationship between cancer and aging could result from the similarity of the primary target (DNA) and the difference in location of the damage within the target.

5. If aging were due to a composite of various forms of DNA damage, and if the maintenance of genetic integrity resulted from a series of interlocking but separate longevity-assurance mechanisms that controlled the rate of loss of DNA fidelity, then presumably neither a single agent nor syndrome would mimic in all aspects the normal aging process.

6. The stability of maximum life span within the same species and between identical twins must be related directly or indirectly to the inheritance of genetic factors controlling longevity.

Finally, the rapid rate of evolution of longevity, with the concurrent input of relatively few genes, becomes more reasonable in light of recent studies indicating that, although the number of factors that can damage DNA is extremely large and the expression or number of methods by which such damage can be expressed is even larger, the genetic factors that control whether this damage will result in some alteration of function are relatively few and appear to be related somehow to the differentiation process during embryogenesis (8). The possibility that all genes may be present during embryogenesis for the maintenance of information fidelity, and that they are altered in such a way as to correlate with the maximum achievable life span of the species, is indicative of the fact that they may be under similar control at the level of differentiation, perhaps through the control of DNA super-helicity. Such group-to-group unifying models as control of longevity assurance through modifying the amount of DNA superhelicity thus become attractive models for investigation (Lipetz and Hart, unpublished data).

Longevity-Assurance Requirements

At the subcellular level, at least four properties have been identified that could maintain the fidelity of the genetic information (regulate the amount of "noise" accumulated) and thus maintain the stability of cellular systems:

1. The ability of a system to detoxify electrophilic agents that may damage DNA; or, conversely, the inaction of a system to activate chemicals metabolically to their electrophilic form.

2. The scavenging potential of enzymic systems for electrophilic agents.

3. The ability of cellular systems to remove damage, whether from exogenous or endogenous sources, from their information-containing macromolecules.

4. The location and degree of control over expression of damaged regions within the cell's genetic material.

Each of these is under genetic control and has been shown to correlate well, in cultures of fibroblast cells, with the maximum achievable life span of the species from which such cultures were derived (3). Thus, these properties can be viewed as stabilizing forces that maintain the operational range of the genetic information of cellular systems. Failure of these forces to operate can result in the onset of senescence in a healthy organism, if an initiating event is permitted to nudge the system away from the center of its operational range. The relative significance of any particular form of stress will depend upon its permanency and location within the genetic structure. The fact that susceptibility to stress appears to increase with age may imply either a repeated appearance of initiating events, a steady progression of or numerous sequels to such events, or the combined expression of present and previous stress factors.

Depending upon the mitotic potential of the tissue considered, the manifestation of differences between species and tissues in the first three properties above would lead to the differential rate of accumulation of DNA damage as a function of time and species. Manifestation of differences in the fourth property would be reflected in differential expression of alterations in genetic function.

Both damage and programmed theories of aging have as their basis the belief that initiating events are causal *(8)*. Damage theories are based on the inadequacy of protection and restoration systems: failure of these systems initiates events that result from incompletely restored alterations after stress. Subsequent expression of such interactions can thus be modulated by control over the altered region. Originally, the stresses were considered to be internal obligatory stresses, such as free radicals formed as by-products of metabolism, alterations of amounts of hormones because of organism development, or massive (T-cell) death accompanying infection *(8)*. Recently, damage theories have come to include exogenous stresses such as radiation, toxic substances, and endogenous molecular errors of protein or DNA synthesis.

In programmed aging, the initiating event is generally not thought to be related to an inadequate design, but rather to the appearance of a destructive agent that overwhelms an adequate design. Because the destructive factor is optimal, its appearance is presumably governed by a clock. Three elements are required for conceptualization of such a timed event: a clock that varies with time but does not age; a trigger that is sensitive to some aspect of the clock; and the stress mechanism. The clock and trigger are usually postulated to be at the organ level in the neural network or at the molecular level in the developmental program. Two proposed stress mechanisms are a death hormone and the release of a degenerative enzyme *(8)*. The destruction caused by the distress mechanism would then propagate further impairments, just as in damage theories, leading eventually to the death of the organism.

Clearly, damage to system components does not occur in certain internally timed events such as maturation. Further, internal clocks such as the biological rhythms do exist; indeed, both of these processes may reasonably be involved in aging. Because a critical component of the programmed aging concept is the timing event itself, which is believed to vary in its rate of expression among species and potentially among tissues, the modulating factors mentioned above (metabolism of toxic substances, scavenging, repair, and control over gene expression) could, through the efficacy and variation of efficacy between systems, serve as a multicomponent clock that would determine the rates of accumulation of various forms of damage in the genetic information within cellular systems. There is evidence to support such a contention, and at the molecular level damage and programmed theories of aging may converge.

This does not eliminate the fact that simpler clock systems do exist, such as in plants and embryos and during metamorphosis. For example, at a particular time in chick limb morphogenesis, certain cells undergo differentiation that leads to morbidity and engulfment by leukocytes. With increasing differentiation these cells exhibit a decrease in both DNA and protein synthesis. The differentiation of this system may be reversed by diffusible molecules from other tissues. Such behavior is typical of embryogenesis, where, for example, primitive skin tissues differentiate to primitive nervous system tissue upon stimulation by molecules diffusing from primitive backbone and muscle. In more advanced systems, however, the evidence for such a simplistic clock is slim. If the potential longevity-assurance systems are viewed as complex sets of interacting modulators that control the rate of accumulation and the expression of various forms of alterations in cellular DNA, then essentially the notion is fulfilled regarding a control over timed events that could be modulated between species and that would be amenable to rapid rates of evolution under times of proper environmental and evolutionary stress.

Longevity-Assurance Mechanisms

Each information-fidelity system has several subcomponents that may vary in their ability to maintain the integrity of cellular DNA. Ideally, we would describe the various mechanisms and their effectiveness relative to their ability to control the fidelity of the genetic material in different species and classes for various physical and chemical agents; however, such data are not yet available. The data we do have, however, indicate that there is a relationship between many of these systems in fibroblast-cell cultures and the maximum achievable life span of the species from which they were derived. These data are described below.

Detoxification and Activation

DNA damage arises primarily as the result of (a) the interaction of exogenous or endogenous electrophilic agents with cellular

DNA and *(b)* thermal denaturation of cellular DNA. The latter route is the most ubiquitious, but so far has not been examined relative to life span.

It has been proposed (reviewed in ref. *9* and *11*) that the DNA-damaging metabolites resulting from microsomal oxidation of 7,12-dimethylbenz*(a)*anthracene and other polycyclic aromatic hydrocarbons (PAHs) are derived from an epoxide intermediate. The major metabolic products of benzo*(a)*pyrene oxidations are *trans*-dihydrodiols, phenols, and glutathione conjugates *(11)*. For PAHs with exocyclic methyl functions, the situation is considerably more complex, because these compounds form metabolites from

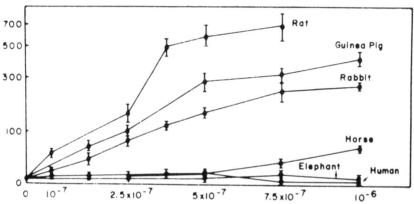

Fig. 1. Mutagenicity of 7,12-dimethylbenz*(a)*anthracene to V-79 cells cocultivated with fibroblasts from various mammalian species irradiated with x-rays

Abscissa: 7,12-dimethylbenz*(a)*anthracene concentration (mol/L); *ordinate:* number of mutants per thousand viable cells, Source: Schwartz *(15)*, used by permission

both ring oxidations and methyl hydroxylations *(9)*. Cultured cells metabolize both DNA-binding and non-DNA-binding PAHs at roughly equal rates; human cells, however, generally oxidize PAH more slowly than rodent cells *(9)*.

There appear to be species-specific differences with regard to cell-mediated chemical activation among fibroblast cultures from different species. As shown in Figure 1, there is an inverse correlation between species' maximum achievable life span and the capacity of cultured fibroblasts to activate the potent chemical carcinogen 7,12-dimethylbenz*(a)*anthracene to its mutagenic form *(15)*.

Subsequently, this group of researchers confirmed their observation with several independently isolated fibroblast strains from the same six species and demonstrated an excellent inverse correlation between species' life span and the rate and extent to which the metabolites of 7,12-dimethylbenz(a)anthracene bind to DNA (16).

In human populations, Kellerman et al. (17) have measured aryl hydrocarbon hydrolase activity in 3-methylcholanthrene mitogen-stimulated human lymphocytes and found that the lymphocytes fell into three groups: low (1.8-fold), medium (2.5-fold), and high (5.6-fold). Their subsequent studies on families and identical twins suggest that inducibility of aryl hydrocarbon hydrolase in humans is under genetic control (18). Similarly, aging rates appear to be the same in identical, but not fraternal, twins (4). Aryl hydrocarbon hydrolase, however, represents only one pathway for metabolic activation; alternative pathways unrelated to life span could exist. Further, comparative studies in vivo of metabolic activation in liver (the system primarily responsible for metabolic activation) are yet to be performed.

Scavenging of Electrophilic Species

The extent to which electrophilic agents damage cellular DNA is affected by factors that neutralize or inactivate these particles before their interaction with genetic material. Such factors include the ability of components of the cell to (a) scavenge free radicals (e.g., vitamin E); (b) break down nucleophilic molecules (e.g., epoxide hydrolase, glutathione 5-epoxide transferase, and superoxide dismutase); (c) absorb the action of electrophiles in macromolecules that turn over before their interaction with the genetic material (e.g., their attack on proteins, lipids, and RNA); and (d) modify the rate of breakdown or removal of electrophiles from cellular systems by enzyme induction. Of these, only superoxide dismutase has been examined with regard to an evolutionary-comparative approach to longevity assurance in primates; those studies indicate a positive correlation between the life span within primates and the intrinsic activity of superoxide dismutase in the tissues, after adjustment for metabolic factors.[1]

---

[1] Cutler, R. G., Dean, R., and Kator, K., Age-dependent derepression of specific genes in brain and liver of mice. 31st Annual Scientific Meeting of the Gerontological Society, Dallas, TX, 1978.

DNA Repair Processes

There may be as many as four general pathways of DNA repair: excision, strand-break, post-replication, and photoreactivation. Excision repair, the most widely examined form of repair, operates in four or five steps and can be classified into two forms, each of which removes bases that have been damaged by physical or chemical agents. The four-step form is nucleotide-excision repair and operates primarily on bulky distortions such as pyrimidine dimers. The second type, base-excision repair, has an additional step and appears to operate on bases damaged by alkylating agents or by thermal denaturation: an N-glycosidase cleaves off the altered purine base, and the resulting apurinic site is then nicked by an apurinic-site-specific endonuclease. The exonuclease, polymerase, and ligase then complete the repair (8).

Strand-break repair rapidly restores broken single strands and, in some organisms, double strands (9). Strand-breaks in DNA can arise from treatment of cells with either chemical or physical agents via direct or indirect chemical interactions with DNA, or from the action of enzymes on damaged DNA (9).

Though little is known about the mechanism of post-replication repair, the concept is derived from the observation that newly synthesized DNA in ultraviolet-irradiated cells initially has a lower molecular mass than after subsequent incubation (11). In bacteria, one form of post-replication repair operates by recombination and is mutagenic; in addition, bacterial systems also appear to have an error-prone form of post-replication repair (11).

In the photoreactivation repair system, which is specific for the monomerization of ultraviolet-radiation-induced cyclobutane-type pyrimidine dimers, an enzyme binds the irradiated DNA, presumably at the dimer site. In the presence of photoreactivating light (300–600 nm), the enzyme is activated, converting the dimer into two monomers. Thus, photoreactivation is a diagnostic tool for discerning the biological role of selected alterations in the secondary structure of DNA. Smith-Sonneborn (13) recently used photoreactivation as an exquisite tool to demonstrate that the life-span-shortening effects of ultraviolet light in the clonal Paramecium aging model system can be reversed.

Thus far excision repair of ultraviolet-induced DNA damage has been the most intensely studied. Human cells (19) and cow

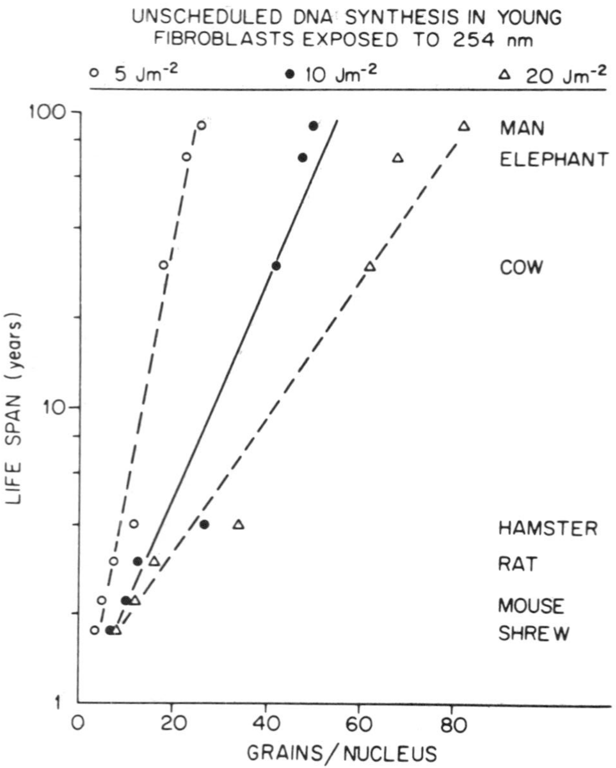

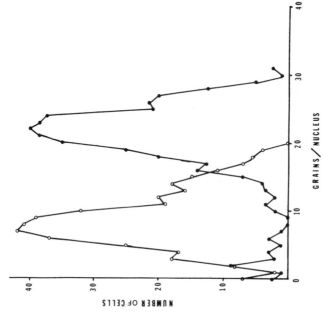

Fig. 3. Unscheduled DNA synthesis in the mytomorph rodents *Peromyscus leucopus* (●) and *Mus musculus* (○); distribution curves represent the number of cells with the indicated number of grains per nucleus

Source: Sacher and Hart (1), used by permission

Fig. 2. Correlation between the amount of unscheduled DNA synthesis measured 13 h after exposure to several fluences of ultraviolet light and the estimated life span of the species

Source: Hart and Setlow (2), used by permission

cells [20] are very efficient at dimer excision (a direct measure of DNA damage and repair); hamster cells [21] show less excision repair than cow or human cells but far more than mouse cells [21]. As shown in Figure 2, a subsequent study has shown an excellent correlation between the rate of unscheduled DNA synthesis induced by ultraviolet radiation, as measured by autoradiography, and the life span of seven species drawn from five orders of mammals [2].

Similar studies have confirmed this correlation in (a) a well-defined comparative system consisting of two mytomorph rodent species, Mus musculus and Peromycus leucopus (Figure 3) [1]; (b) 11 fibroblast-cell cultures derived from punch biopsies of primates of similar physiological age in a blind analysis of previously coded cultures (Figure 4)[2]; and (c) inbred rodent strains exhibiting approximately a threefold difference in life span under similar conditions. These results suggest that this correlation holds between strains of the same species with differing immune competencies [22].

Studies like these have not yet been done using chemical agents; however, certain reports are relevant to this discussion. The hamster cell line BHK21/C13, which excises ultraviolet-induced cyclobutane-type pyrimidine dimers, is more proficient in removing DNA adducts induced by benzo(a)pyrene than is the mouse cell line C57B1 over the same period after exposure to the same concentration of benzo(a)pyrene [23]; the Chinese hamster V-79 cell line appears to be as proficient as the human HeLa cell line for repairing damage from similar concentrations of 7-bromomethylbenz(a)anthracene-induced DNA damage [3]; and the rodent cell line A31–714 appears to remove the DNA damage induced by 4-nitroquinoline-1-oxide at approximately the same rate and to the same extent as SV-40-transformed human fetal lung cells in vitro [24]. A preliminary review of the literature suggests that permanent cell lines may not always reflect a correlation between maximum achievable life span of the species from which they were derived and excision repair; however, the reasons for this are unclear.

---

[2] Hall, K. Y., Albrightson, C., and Hart, R. W., A direct relationship among primates between maximum lifespan and DNA repair. Abstract, 11th Int. Congr. Gerontology, Tokyo, 1978.

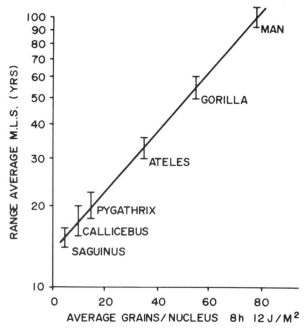

Fig. 4. Average autoradiographic grains per nucleus during unscheduled DNA synthesis, correlated with the maximum life span (M.L.S.) of six primate species

Source: Hall et al. (p 271, footnote 2, this volume), used by permission

Alteration of Gene Expression

Cell cultures taken from mouse embryos between the fifth and nineteenth days of gestation have a high degree of ultraviolet-induced excision repair, which subsequently decreases just before birth to the degree observed in the adult (25). Relative to this work is the hypothesis that the rate of senescence in animals is directly proportional to the rate of accumulation of damage in cellular DNA in terminally differentiating and senescent postmitotic cells, and to the accumulation of randomly placed mutations in mitotically active cells. Considerable evidence now exists that, in terminally differentiating and aging cells, excision repair and strand-break rejoining become defective as a function of age (9). Additionally, work in our laboratory done in conjunction with Dell'Orco suggests that human cells in late passage but mitotically active may exhibit an accumulation of damaged regions in their cellular DNA. On the basis of previously described studies, it would be interesting to determine *(a)* whether mitotically inactive cells from the same cell passage have accumulated more DNA damage than mitotically active cells, and *(b)* whether the rate of accumulation of such damage is species-specific and is related to the maximum life span of the species from which the cells were derived. How such damage may affect gene expression is as of yet undetermined. Such damage may preferentially accumulate in chromatin-associated regions of cellular DNA *(9)* and thus may ultimately be manifested in an increase in sister-chromatid exchanges upon promotion of these normally unexpressed regions of the genome. Whether the accumulation of damage in these regions, the action of endogenous or exogenous promoters, or a modification in chromatin structure might be responsible for a loss of control of gene expression is yet to be determined. However, because many nucleophilic agents interact not only with DNA but also with RNA and protein, the subunit structure of chromatin may control or at least partly modify both the location of DNA endonuclease-sensitive sites and the probability of expression of such sites.

If the accessibility of damaged sites and the expression of damaged regions are modulated by histone interactions with cellular DNA, and if the DNA in old postmitotic cells contains a greater degree of superhelicity than young postmitotic cells, as measured indirectly by staphylococcal nuclease digestion,[3] it would appear that the amount of DNA tightly associated with the chromatin increases as a function of both differentiation and age, thus potentially modifying gene expression. Other factors must also be taken into consideration in determining how chromatin exercises its influence on the expression of altered DNA regions: the ratio of protein in core particle to that in linker region; the conformational restraints exercised by formation of protein-DNA cross-links; the effects of polyamines on chromatin structure; the role of various hormones on the control of chromatin association with DNA; and the differential physiological effects of physical/chemical alterations in the DNA structure misinsertions during DNA replication.

---

[3] Modak, S. P., Gonet, C., Unger-Ullman, C., and Chappuis, M., Chromatin structure in aging mouse livers. Personal communication.

Looking Ahead

Thus far most studies in this area have depended upon cells in cultures. Recent discoveries now make it possible to evaluate DNA damage and repair of several forms in vivo. Preliminary evidence indicates that not only may the forms of damage induced in vivo vary from damage in vitro, but additionally, repair and expression may vary as a function of tissue type, stage of the cell cycle, mitotic classification, diet, and emotional state. Each of these factors may affect different longevity-assurance systems in different ways. Therefore, probably no single longevity-assurance system, regardless of its importance, will always correlate directly in all cases with life span, and all such systems must be evaluated concurrently in critical organ systems in vivo and in vitro if indeed the roles of these systems in longevity are to be determined.

This work was supported in part by the National Cancer Institute Grant No. CA21371.

References

1. Sacher, G. A., and Hart, R. W., Longevity, aging, and comparative and molecular biology of the house mouse, *Mus musculus,* and the white-footed mouse, *Peromuscus leucopus.* In *Genetic Effects on Aging,* **14,** D. Bergsma and D. Harrison, Eds., Alan R. Liss National Foundation, New York, NY, 1978, pp 71–96.
2. Hart, R. W., and Setlow, R. B., Correlation between deoxyribonucleic acid excision-repair and lifespan in a number of mammalian species. *Proc. Natl. Acad. Sci. USA* **71,** 2169–2173 (1974).
3. Hart, R. W., and Daniel, F. B., Genetic stability *in vivo* and *in vitro. Adv. Pathobiol.* **8** (in press, 1980).
4. Comfort, A., *Aging, the Biology of Senescence.* Holt, Rinehart and Wilson, New York, NY, 1964.
5. Hart, R. W., D'Ambrosio, S. M., Ng, K. G., and Modak, S. P., Longevity, stability and DNA repair. *Mech. Ageing Dev.* **9,** 203–223 (1978).
6. Cutler, R., Evolution of human longevity and the genetic complexities governing aging rate. *Proc. Natl. Acad. Sci. USA* **72,** 4664–4668 (1975).
7. Hart, R. W., Sacher, G. A., and Hoskins, T. L., DNA repair in a short- and a long-lived rodent species. *J. Gerontol.* **34,** 808–817 (1979).
8. Burki, K., Liebelt, A. G., and Bresnick, E., Induction of aryl hydrocar-

bon hydroxylase in mouse tissues from a high and low cancer strain and their F_1 hybrids. *J. Natl. Cancer Inst.* **50**, 369–380 (1973).

9. Hart, R. W., and Modak, S. P., Aging and changes in genetic information. In *Proceedings of the National Symposium on Interrelations among Different Levels of Biological Organization*, K. Oota and T. Makinodan, Eds., Tokyo Academic Publishing Co., Tokyo, Japan (in press).

10. Hart, R. W., Role of DNA repair in aging. In *Aging, Carcinogenesis and Radiation Biology*, K. C. Smith, Ed., Plenum Press, New York, NY, 1976, pp 537–556.

11. Hart, R. W., Hall, K. Y., and Daniel, F. B., DNA repair and mutagenesis in mammalian cells. *Photochem. Photobiol.* **28**, 131–155 (1978).

12. Hart, R. W., and Smith-Sonneborn, J., Molecular mechanisms of aging and carcinogenesis. *Excerpta Med.* (in press).

13. Smith-Sonneborn, J., DNA repair and longevity assurance in *Paramecium tetraurelia. Science* **203**, 1115–1117 (1979).

14. Hart, R. W., Setlow, R. B., and Woodhead, A. D., Evidence that pyrimidine dimers in DNA can give rise to tumors. *Proc. Natl. Acad. Sci. USA* **74**, 5574–5578 (1977).

15. Schwartz, A. G., Correlation between species lifespan and capacity to activate 7,12-dimethylbenz(a)anthracene to form mutagenic to mammalian cell. *Exp. Cell Res.* **94**, 445–447 (1975).

16. Schwartz, A. G., and Moore, C. J., Inverse correlation between species lifespan and capacity of cultured fibroblasts to bind 7,12-dimethylbenz(a)anthracene to DNA. *Exp. Cell Res.* **109**, 448–450 (1977).

17. Kellermann, G., Cantrell, T., and Shaw, C. R., Variations in extent of aryl hydrocarbon hydroxylase induction in cultured human lymphocytes. *Cancer Res.* **33**, 1654–1656 (1973).

18. Kellermann, G., Shaw, C. R., and Lugten-Kellerman, M., Aryl hydrocarbon hydroxylase inducibility and bronchogenic carcinoma. *N. Engl. J. Med.* **289**, 934–937 (1973).

19. Cleaver, J. E., Thomas, G. H., Trosko, J. E., and Lett, J. T., Excision repair (dimer excision, strand breakage and repair replication) in primary cultures of eukaryotic (bovine) cells. *Exp. Cell Res.* **74**, 67–80 (1972).

20. Cleaver, J. E., and Trosko, J. E., Absence of excision of ultraviolet-induced cyclobutane dimers in xeroderma pigmentosum. *Photochem. Photobiol.* **11**, 547–550 (1970).

21. Setlow, R. B., Regan, J. E., and Carrier, W. L., Different levels of excision repair in mammalian cell lines. *Biophys. Soc.* **12**, 19a (1972). Abstract.

22. Walford, R. L., Multigene families, histocompatability, transformation, meiosis, stem cells and DNA repair. *Mech. Ageing Dev.* **9**, 9–26 (1979).

275

23. Cerutti, P., Shinohara, K., and Remsen, J., Repair of DNA damage induced by ionizing radiation and benzo(a)pyrene in mammalian cells. *J. Toxicol. Environ. Health* **2**, 1375–1386 (1977).

24. Ikenaga, M., Ishii, Y., Tada, M., Kakunage, T., Takebe, H., and Kondo, S., Excision-repair of 4-nitroquinoline-1-oxide damage responsible for killing, mutation and cancer. In *Molecular Mechanisms for Repair of DNA, Part B*, P. C. Hanawalt and R. B. Setlow, Eds., Plenum Press, New York, NY, 1975, pp 763–772.

25. Ben-Ishai, R., and Peleg, L., Excision-repair in primary cultures of mouse embryo cells and its decline in progressive passages and established cell lines. In *Molecular Mechanisms for Repair of DNA* (see ref. *24*), pp 607–610.

Immunological Studies of Aging: CBA/N Immune Defect as a Delay Rather Than an Arrest of B-Lymphocyte Maturation

John M. Fidler, Edward L. Morgan, and William O. Weigle

The general outcome of the aging process, and one that recently has garnered the attention of researchers of numerous disciplines, is the gradual degradation of structure and function and a decrease in the overall integrity of the body and its systems. This loss of normal function has, because of increased survival and consequent recognition of infirmities associated with increasing age, been categorized as the "diseases of aging" (1). These are nowhere more apparent than in the increased susceptibility to disease (1, 2), one of the earmarks of the aged individual. Studies of the immune system with aging reveal a decline that may be responsible for the downturn in general immunity and for the emergence of diseases that, although affecting numerous body systems, appear to be temporally related to the alteration in immunity (3). Besides being involved directly in certain disorders, the immune system is largely dispersed through the body, and thus provides an excellent system for the study of organism-wide disturbances of homeostasis at virtually every level, from cell to organ system. Thus, the study of the immune system in the context of aging offers insight into a system that not only changes profoundly with age (2), reflecting alterations in a single system that occur throughout the body, but also appears to be intimately involved in both the surveillance against and the emergence of the diseases of aging (2, 3).

Whereas aging is accompanied by the decline and loss of function, ontogenic maturation is characterized by the acquisition and enhancement of function, especially in the immune system. A thorough understanding of cellular interaction, regulation, and recognition in the immune system is fundamental to any discussion of aging in the immune system, and information gained from studies of the maturation phase of immune function may contribute to the scrutiny of the aging process as it relates to immunity. Thus, although the loss of a particular function does not necessarily recapitulate in reverse order the events contributing to the acquisition of reactivity, the mechanistic and temporal manner in which the various requirements of a particular function are met may help us to understand the loss of the function with age and to design protocols to ameliorate or reverse the effects of aging. Moreover, maturation and aging may be affected by the same processes that control homeostasis or that contribute to the observed alterations in cellular immune reactivity.

Defective B-Cell Maturation of CBA/N Mice

The maturation of murine lymphocyte reactivity normally occurs rapidly after birth, with six-to-eight-week-old mice usually considered to be mature young adults. The CBA/N mouse subline, used extensively in studies of lymphocyte activation requirements and maturation, bears a defect in bone marrow (bursal equivalent)-derived (B) lymphocyte[1] reactivity, which has been interpreted to be an absolute blockage of B-cell maturation at a point reached in normal mice during the first two weeks of life (4–9). However, a study of mice significantly older than young adults (i.e., 12 to 14 months old rather than two to three months old) has led to a reassessment of the nature of the defect in B-cell differentiation characteristic of the CBA/N mouse. We will present here the data supporting this conclusion.

Derived from the CBA/H strain, the CBA/N subline bears an X-linked defect in the B-lymphocyte compartment (4–9). Initially described as an inability to mount a humoral immune response to pneumococcal polysaccharide (4), the immune deficit is characterized by unresponsiveness to certain thymus-independent (TI)

---

[1] Abbreviations used: B-cell, bone marrow (bursal equivalent)-derived lymphocyte; IgD, IgG, and IgM, immunoglobulins; LAP, lipid-associated polypeptide; poly(I-C), polyinosinic polycytidylic acid; TD, thymic-dependent; TI, thymic-independent; TNP-LPS and TNP-Ficoll, trinitrophenylated lipopolysaccharide and Ficoll, respectively.

antigens *(4–9)*, including haptenated Ficoll, levan, dextran, and polyinosinic polycytidylic acid [poly(I-C)]. In contrast, virtually normal humoral immune responses are obtained from another set of TI antigens, which includes trinitrophenyated lipopolysaccharide (TNP-LPS), TNP-*Brucella abortus,* and TNP-*Nocardia* water-soluble mitogen *(9–11)*. Mice of this strain are capable of mounting thymic-dependent (TD) antibody responses, but these are of somewhat less magnitude and appear to be of limited heterogeneity and with lower affinity than responses in controls *(11, 12)*. Hyporesponsiveness to some mitogens such as lipopolysaccharide, poly(I-C), and purified protein derivative is observed *(6, 13)*, whereas CBA/N spleen cells are refractory to stimulation with 2-mercaptoethanol *(13)*, anti-μ,κ *(14)*, and the polyclonal stimulating effects of concanavalin-A-induced factors.[2] Mutant mice exhibit deficient antibody-dependent cell-mediated cytotoxicity responses *(6)*, an inability to produce B-lymphocyte colonies in vitro *(15)*, a significantly decreased concentration of IgM in serum *(4)*, and a greatly reduced production of γ_3-antibody in immune responses *(16)*. Furthermore, the immune defects are paralleled by deficiencies at the cellular level. Not only are there fewer nucleated cells and surface-immunoglobulin-bearing B-cells in the spleen *(6)*, but also an increased percentage of high-density surface-immunoglobulin-bearing lymphocytes *(17)* and a decreased ratio of IgD to IgM heavy chains on B-cells *(7)* are observed in mutant spleens. One unusual feature of CBA/N spleen cells is the inability to stimulate mixed lymphocyte responses to minor lymphocyte-stimulating antigens *(18)*. This defect is not the result of a generalized and abnormal deficiency of the minor lymphocyte-stimulating cell-surface antigens, but is due rather to the absence of a specific subpopulation of late-maturing B-cells that bear these determinants *(19)*. Furthermore, there is an absence of cells exhibiting other surface antigens characteristic of mature B-lymphocytes, such as Lyb3 *(20)*, Lyb5 *(21)*, and Lyb7 *(22)*. These data on B-cell surface markers and the development of lymphocyte reactivity have been supported by ontogeny studies *(23–28)* and have led to the conclusion that the CBA/N defect reflects a

---

[2] Fidler, J. M., Polyclonal B cell activation by mitogen-stimulated lymphocytes. I. Concanavalin-A-induced antibody production by mature B cells. Submitted for publication.

maturational arrest of B-lymphocyte development, which leads to the absence of a subpopulation of relatively late-maturing B-cells (9, 11, 17).

In this report dealing with functional B-cell development in the CBA/N mouse, we demonstrate that the defect in B-lymphocyte maturation and responsiveness is not absolute, but age-associated. Spleen cells from 12-to-14-month-old (aged) CBA/N mice respond well to a number of immunological stimuli to which three-month-old (young adult) defective mice are refractory or markedly hyporesponsive. However, the acquisition of reactivity is incomplete, with some responses less than that displayed by histocompatible control CBA/CaJ spleen cells, and another that remained negative.

Mitogenic Reactivity: Effect of Age

The proliferative response to a range of lymphocyte mitogens arises sequentially both during ontogeny (13) and after the reconstitution of lethally irradiated adoptive hosts by fetal liver stem cells (13, 29). Moreover, the mitogenic reactivity of young adult CBA/N spleen cells to these nonspecific stimulators is consistent with the degree of maturation of responding cells in normal mice (13).

As an initial step in the investigation of the effects of aging upon reactivity of mice bearing the *xid* defect, we determined with previously described techniques (20–33) the proliferative response in microcultures to a panel of mitogens. As shown in Table 1, the mitogenic response of spleen cells from young adult CBA/N mice (12 weeks old) ranged from about background values with 2-mercaptoethanol to a normal uptake of [³H]thymidine with concanavalin A. In agreement with previous findings, the response to concanavalin A was similar to that observed with age-matched histocompatible CBA/CaJ control mice, indicating normal T-cell proliferative function in the CBA/N mouse[2] (13). Characteristically hyporesponsive to lipopolysaccharide, poly(I-C), and purified protein derivative, young adult CBA/N splenocytes failed to mount a significant proliferative response to 2-mercaptoethanol (13). Aged CBA/N spleen cells (from 12- to 14-month-old mice) produced improved responses to all B-cell activating substances

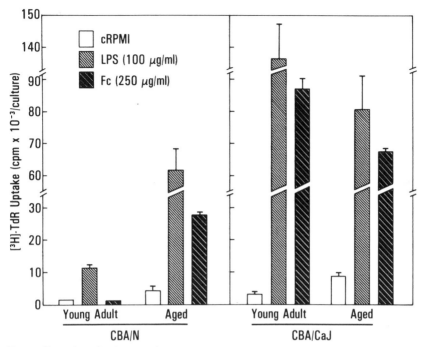

Fig. 2. Fc-induced mitogenesis

Spleen cells were cultivated in microcultures with Fc fragments of human immunoglobulin (250 mg/L) or with Boivin lipopolysaccharide (055:B5, 100 mg/L). [³H]Thymidine was added after two days of incubation, and the cells were harvested 18 h later to assess the proliferative response. Results are expressed as cpm of [³H]thymidine uptake per culture ± SE of triplicate cultures. cRPMI refers to culture medium

mitogen and polyclonal B-cell activator *(34, 35)*. Unlike those from conventional mice, B-cells from young adult CBA/N mice did not produce a proliferative response to Fc fragments of human immunoglobulin (IgG₁ class myeloma Fi) *(36)*. To further characterize the mitogenic reactivity of CBA/N spleen cells, we studied the effect of aging upon the Fc-fragment-induced proliferative response by using previously described techniques *(30, 31, 36–38)*. Young adult CBA/N spleen cells failed to respond to Fc fragments and had only moderate lipopolysaccharide-induced proliferation, compared with that of age-matched CBA/CaJ control splenocytes (Figure 2).

Mitogenesis of aged control spleen cells induced by both lipopolysaccharide and Fc fragments was somewhat less than the young adult response. Unlike the young adult mutant spleen cells, lymphocytes from aged CBA/N mice produced a proliferative response to both mitogens, with lipopolysaccharide-induced [³H]thymidine uptake more than fivefold greater than in young adult defective spleen cells. The Fc mitogenic response rose from background values to sixfold greater in the aged CBA/N mice. Fc fragments of human immunoglobulin appeared to stimulate mature B-lymphocytes, because young adult CBA/N spleen cells are refractory to stimulation by this polyclonal activator. Thus, reactivity to a mitogen that activates mature B-cells arises with age in CBA/N mice, which lack the capacity to mount a response when tested earlier in life. This finding is a clear demonstration that the CBA/N defect is not absolute.

Effects of Age upon Polyclonal Antibody Response

Next, we assessed the polyclonal antibody response of CBA/N mice to nonspecific stimulation with lipopolysaccharide, poly-(I-C), and purified protein derivative *(30–32, 39–43)*. The lypopolysaccharide-induced polyclonal antibody response of young adult CBA/N spleen cells is considerably decreased from that of age-matched CBA/CaJ control lymphocytes (Table 2).[2] Although the polyclonal response to poly(I-C) was even more greatly decreased in young adult CBA/N mice, the response stimulated by purified protein derivative constituted the greatest difference between the mutant and the control CBA/CaJ responses, the CBA/N response being about 2% of that of the positive control. The nonspecific antibody response was greater in aged CBA/N mice than in young adult defective mice. Lipopolysaccharide- and poly(I-C)-induced responses of aged mutant mice were double that of the young adults, but the greatest increase in reactivity was obtained with purified protein derivative. The nearly 20-fold increase with age, from barely significant in the young adult CBA/N mice to the highest of the three responses in the aged mice, is consistent with the recent suggestion that purified protein derivative stimulates the more mature B-cells to polyclonal antibody synthesis and proliferation *(40)*.

Response of Aged CBA/N Mice to TNP-Ficoll

One of the distinguishing characteristics of the CBA/N strain is the inability to respond (by the production of antibody) to a

Table 2. Polyclonal Antibody Response

TNP-HRC, plaque-forming cells/culture (mean ± SE)

	LPS (100 mg/L)	Poly(I–C) (250 mg/L)	PPD (250 mg/L)
Young adult CBA/N	174 ± 15	81 ± 8	23 ± 2
Aged CBA/N	340 ± 18	170 ± 14	441 ± 14
Young adult CBA/CaJ	584 ± 25	421 ± 26	1214 ± 71
Aged CBA/CaJ	520 ± 34	557 ± 10	1074 ± 28

Spleen cells were cultivated for three days with polyclonal activating substances. Cultures were harvested and the polyclonal antibody response was estimated by determining the number of cells producing antibody to heavily conjugated trinitrophenylated horse erythrocytes (TNP-HRC). Results are from three cultures per group, with data pooled from three experiments. Abbreviations as in Table 1.

number of polysaccharide antigens or to the haptenated form of these carriers *(4, 8, 44)*. Although the initial description of the CBA/N immune defect involved humoral responsiveness to pneumococcal polysaccharide *(4)*, the prototype antigen for definition of the genetic defect in B-cell reactivity to TI-2 immunogenic challenge has become TNP-Ficoll *(8)*. To further investigate the alteration of B-cell reactivity observed with increasing age, we tested the responsiveness of young adult and aged CBA/N mice to this antigen (38 TNP residues per 100 000 daltons of Ficoll) *(30–32, 39–42)*. We used the TI antigen Boivin TNP-LPS (9 TNP residues per 100 000 daltons of lipopolysaccharide) as a positive control because both CBA/CaJ and CBA/N mice are positive responders *(10)*.

The in vitro responses to TNP-LPS and to TNP-Ficoll are shown in Table 3. As expected, young adult CBA/N mice were capable of mounting an antibody response to TNP-LPS but not to TNP-Ficoll. The standard dose of the TI-2 immunogen for control CBA/CaJ mice and a 10-fold higher concentration were used to establish the unresponsiveness of the young adult defective splenocytes. The B-cell maturation defect characterized by nonreactivity to TI-2 antigens was apparently overcome with age: not only did the aged CBA/N spleen cells respond better to the TI-1 antigen TNP-LPS, but they also mounted an excellent antibody response to TNP-Ficoll. Thus, consistent with data presented above concerning other immunologic parameters, the B-lymphocyte maturation defect in responsiveness to TI-2 antigens is not absolute;

Table 3. In Vitro Antibody Response to TNP-LPS and TNP-Ficoll

Anti-TNP response, plaque-forming cells (mean ± SE)

	TNP-LPS (10 µg/L)	TNP-Ficoll (10 µg/L)	TNP-Ficoll (100 µg/L)
Young adult CBA/N	412 ± 18	0	0
Aged CBA/N	519 ± 25	696 ± 81	720 ± 26
Young adult CBA/CaJ	504 ± 33	963 ± 28	887 ± 69
Aged CBA/CaJ	623 ± 20	963 ± 76	869 ± 41

Spleen cells were cultivated in vitro with TNP-LPS or TNP-Ficoll. Three days later, the cultures were harvested and the number of TNP-specific plaque-forming cells was determined. Results are expressed for three cultures/group, assayed individually; data are pooled from three experiments.

rather, CBA/N mice acquire the ability to mount a response to TNP-Ficoll with age. Moreover, the enhanced reactivity does not reflect a generalized improvement of responsiveness with age, because only the TI-1- and not the TI-2-induced responses of control CBA/CaJ spleen cells were enhanced.

To investigate further the alterations in immune reactivity, to continue the characterization of the emergence of TNP-Ficoll responsiveness in CBA/N mice, and to avoid potential difficulty of interpretation with in vitro cultivation introduced by the requirement for fetal calf serum and 2-mercaptoethanol, we tested the effect of age upon adoptive responsiveness. Lethally irradiated young adult CBA/CaJ hosts were reconstituted with equivalent numbers of spleen cells from CBA/N or CBA/CaJ mice of the two age groups, and the adoptive recipients were challenged intraperitoneally with 1 µg of either Boivin TNP-LPS or TNP-Ficoll. As shown in Table 4, young adult defective spleen cells mounted a positive response to TNP-LPS, but less than that of control CBA/CaJ splenocytes. As expected, young adult mutant spleen cells failed to elaborate an adoptive plaque-forming-cell response to TNP-Ficoll. The aged CBA/N spleen cells responded to both antigens. Thus, although the TI-1 response of aged mutant mice more closely approached the control response, a positive and significant adoptive plaque-forming-cell response to TNP-Ficoll was produced by aged CBA/N spleen cells. Furthermore, similar to the in vitro response shown above (Table 3), the appearance with

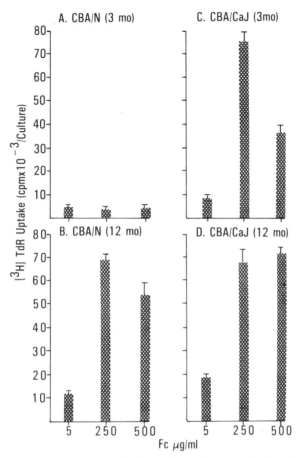

Fig. 3. Comparison of the ability of young adult and aged CBA/N and CBA/CaJ spleen cells to proliferate, given various concentrations of Fc fragments

Cultures of 5×10^5 spleen cells were incubated with Fc fragments for two days, pulsed with 1 μCi of [^{3}H]thymidine, and harvested 18 h later. Results are expressed as cpm of [^{3}H]thymidine uptake per culture ± SE of triplicate cultures (background cpm subtracted)

adult and aged CBA/CaJ splenocytes. Spleen cells from young adult defective mice failed to mount a significant proliferative response (Figure 3A), but the response of aged CBA/N spleen cells was 23-fold greater (Figure 3B). Young adult (Figure 3C) and aged (Figure 3D) CBA/CaJ control spleen cells, however, could proliferate in response to Fc fragments. Thus the difference in reactivity of young adult and aged CBA/N mice was not due to the concentration of Fc utilized in vitro.

Kinetics of Fc proliferation. To determine whether the inability of young adult CBA/N spleen cells to respond to Fc fragments was due to an alteration in the kinetics of the response, we assessed proliferation from day 1 to day 5 of cultivation in cultures stimulated with 250 mg of Fc fragments per liter. As shown in Figure 4*A*, young adult CBA/N spleen cells exhibited no proliferative response on any day tested. Cells from aged mutant mice proliferated significantly (Figure 4*B*), peaking on day 3. Splenocytes from both young adult (Figure 4*C*) and aged (Figure 4*D*) control CBA/CaJ mice proliferated optimally when assayed on day 3. Thus, the lack of proliferation in young adult CBA/N mouse spleen cells was not due to a shift in the kinetics of the response to Fc fragments.

Cell concentration and Fc response. Because the range of cell concentrations producing Fc-fragment-induced proliferation is rather restricted, we thought it possible that cell density was critical in the response of young adult defective mice. To test this, we compared the effect of three cell concentrations upon the ability of splenocytes to respond to Fc fragments. Optimum spleen cell concentration for aged CBA/N and CBA/CaJ control mice was 5×10^5 cells/culture (2.5×10^9 cells/L; results not shown). As is evident in Figure 5, optimum cell concentration was the same with young adult control splenocytes, whereas young adult defective cells failed to respond at any concentration tested.

Cell mixing and Fc response. To determine whether the failure of young adult CBA/N spleen cells to respond to Fc fragments was due to active suppression at the cellular level, we mixed the cells, as follows: Young adult defective spleen cells were cultured at various concentrations with aged CBA/N spleen cells, and the proliferative responses to Fc fragments were assessed three days later. As shown in Table 6, the addition of 1×10^5 young adult spleen cells to 4×10^5 aged cells did not significantly alter the response observed with the latter cells alone. Moreover, when equal numbers of young adult and aged splenocytes were mixed, the response was never less than that of the aged cells alone. Indeed, the response was enhanced when 2×10^5 young adult cells were added to an equal number of aged splenocytes (21 046 cpm vs 13 000 cpm). Because young adult cells were unrespon-

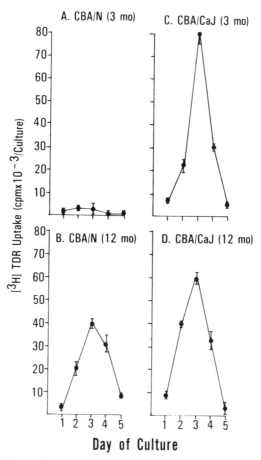

Fig. 4. Determination of the optimum day of Fc-fragment-induced proliferation for spleen cell cultures derived from young adult and aged CBA/N and CBA/CaJ mice

Cultures of 5×10^5 spleen cells with 250 mg of Fc fragments per liter were harvested after one to five days of incubation (background cpm subtracted from experimental cpm)

sive when tested alone, a filler-cell effect might account for this result *(47)*.

CBA/N Defect Not Absolute

The deficiency in B-cell responsiveness displayed by the CBA/N mouse strain is due to a delay in the appearance of reactivity

Table 6. Inability of Young Adult CBA/N Spleen Cells to Suppress the Fc Response of Aged CBA/N Spleen Cells

No. of CBA/N spleen cells		[³H]thymidine uptake, cpm/culture (mean ± SE)
12 months old	3 months old	
400 000	—	25 958 ± 25
400 000	100 000	26 449 ± 351
200 000	—	13 110 ± 98
200 000	200 000	21 046 ± 1300
500 000	—	28 553 ± 1521
—	100 000	<1000
—	200 000	<1000

Fc (250 mg/L) was added to the cultures and the response was assayed on day 3 of culture. Background cpm was subtracted from the experimental cpm.

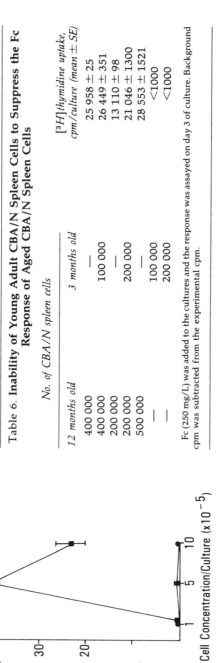

Fig. 5. Effect of cell concentration on the ability of CBA/N spleen cells to respond to Fc fragments

Spleen cells were cultivated with 250 mg of Fc fragments per liter at a concentration of 1, 5, or 10 (× 10⁵) cells/culture. The cultures were pulsed with [³H]thymidine after 48 h and harvested 18 h later (background cpm subtracted from experimental cpm)

rather than an absolute defect, as evidenced by the age-dependent acquisition of immunocompetence. We base this conclusion on the study detailed here of the responsiveness of young adult (three months old) and aged (12 to 14 months old) CBA/N mouse spleen cells to a variety of stimuli, including TI antigens and nonspecific polyclonal activators. CBA/N mice display an X-linked absence of a mature or late-appearing subset of B lymphocytes *(6, 7, 17, 18, 20–22)*. Although several responses are normal [i.e., T-cell mitogenesis[2] *(36)* and some T-cell helper activities (48)], certain other functions are diminished or absent entirely[2] *(4–9, 13, 37, 49–51)*. Nonspecific *(52)* and idiotype-linked (personal communication, D. E. Mosier) T-cell helper functions are abnormal, as is the B-cell polyclonal antibody response to a concanavalin-A-induced T-cell factor.[2] Mitogenesis and polyclonal activation by lipopolysaccharide and poly(I-C) are decreased, compared with the amounts of stimulation obtained with nondefective mice, and proliferative responses of young adult CBA/N mice to 2-mercaptoethanol *(13)*, Fc fragments of human immunoglobulin *(36)*, and anti-μ,κ *(17)* are absent. Moreover, humoral responses to haptenated polysaccharides, such as TNP-Ficoll, are not generated by the defective mice if tested either early in life, when reactivity is normally acquired, or at maturity (eight to 12 weeks of age) *(8)*.

To investigate the effect of aging upon the reactivity profile of CBA/N mice, and to determine whether the lack of responsiveness of these mutant mice was an absolute defect in maturation, as suggested by a number of reports *(1, 6–8, 26)*, we tested the proliferative, polyclonal antibody, and TI antigen-specific responses of aged CBA/N mouse spleen and compared them with those of young adult CBA/N and age-matched histocompatible control spleen cells. The positive responses for aged CBA/N splenocytes to TNP-Ficoll suggest that the deficiency in B-cell responsiveness is due to an extended delay in the acquisition of reactivity rather than an invariable defect. Moreover, the enhanced responses of spleen cells from aged CBA/N mice are not the result of a general increase in reactivity with age; rather, the age-related appearance of responsiveness appears to be directly associated with the B-cell defect of these mice.

Phenol TNP-LPS Immune Defect in CBA/N Mice

Young adult CBA/N mice responded by the production of antibody to Boivin TNP-LPS but not to phenol TNP-LPS. Thus, an immune-response defect encountered in the CBA/N strain involved an antigen generally considered to be in the TI-1 category (10). The extraction procedure is the major difference between these preparations, with LAP retained by Boivin lipopolysaccharide but absent from phenol lipopolysaccharide (45, 46). CBA/N mice are therefore deficient in responsiveness to haptenated lipopolysaccharide that lacks the LAP moiety. One possible explanation for this observation is that lipopolysaccharide is a TI-2 antigen, whereas LAP is a TI-1 immunogen. Accordingly, CBA/N mice responding to Boivin TNP-LPS would actually be reacting to haptenated LAP and remain unresponsive to TNP-LPS. Alternatively, LAP may exert an adjuvant effect, allowing the deficient mice to respond to TNP-LPS. Both explanations are based upon the unresponsiveness of young adult CBA/N mice to the TNP-LPS moiety in the absence of LAP, which was first noted in these experiments. A transition from unresponsiveness to positive reactivity with TNP-LPS is similar to the TNP-Ficoll result; young adult CBA/N spleen cells fail to respond to TNP-LPS lacking LAP, whereas aged defective splenocytes elaborate a marked response.

B-Lymphocyte Differentiation Sequence

Young adult CBA/N mice exhibit various proliferative responses to polyclonal-activating substances, ranging from normal for concanavalin A^2 to absent for 2-mercaptoethanol (13) and Fc fragments of human immunoglobulin (36). The amounts of mitogenic responsiveness and polyclonal-antibody production induced by B-cell polyclonal activators are generally increased with age in CBA/N mice without reaching the level of response by the control CBA/CaJ mice. Of the mitogens that stimulate the more mature B-cells, purified protein derivative induced a proliferative response that was increased significantly in the aged CBA/N splenocytes, and a polyclonal response that increased from the lowest initial amount and by the largest factor when young adult and aged CBA/N spleen cells were compared. Mitogenic reactivity to Fc fragments was acquired by the aged CBA/N splenocytes, with the response exceeding the background values in the young adult cells. 2-Mercaptoethanol, however, stimulated only an insignificant proliferative response in both young adult and aged CBA/N lymphocytes. On the basis of these results, 2-mercaptoethanol-reactive B cells appear to be more mature than lymphocytes responsive to Fc fragments, whereas purified protein derivative-responsive lymphocytes are not as far along the B-cell differentiation pathway as either of the other two subpopulations. This result has added significance in light of the similar sequence of B-cell maturation *(13)* suggested by the appearance of reactivity both during ontogeny and after reconstitution of lethally irradiated recipients with fetal liver stem cells *(13, 29)*.

Based upon the responsiveness of CBA/N mice and the ontogeny of B-cell reactivity, the sequence of maturation of reactivity may be summarized as shown in Figure 6. The mechanism of the acquisition of reactivity by the aged CBA/N mice to a number of immunological probes to which younger defective mice are unresponsive is not evident. However, the defect in B-cell responsiveness, which is characteristic of the CBA/N mouse strain, is obviously not absolute. Rather, positive responses were obtained in some, but not all, cases when the reactivity of aged mice was tested. Thus, B-lymphocyte development may be merely delayed rather than terminated prematurely by the X-linked B-cell defect. Accordingly, the maturation of B lymphocytes and the appearance of reactivity similar to that in nondefective control cells would occur at a much slower rate than normally observed, a concept consonant with the lag in the development of responses exhibited by young adult CBA/N mice *(53)*.

Although the deficiency in mature B-cells may be directly and solely responsible for the degree of responsiveness observed in young adult CBA/N mice, there are other possibilities. Because the reactivities that are defective in these mutant mice are nonuniformly remedied with age, there may be additional lesions and thus other factors that can enhance, modify, or regulate the observed reactivities. In terms of TI-1 and TI-2 antigens, the alteration of reactivity may depend upon physical properties of the antigens involved. In general, TI-1 immunogens have rather large molecular dimensions, being particulate (TNP-*Brucella abortus*) or highly aggregated (TNP-LPS); TI-2 antigens are of intermediate size. However, differences in the polyclonal-activating ability of

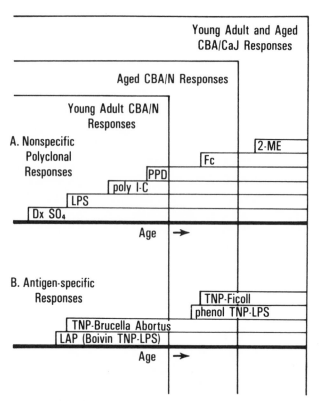

Fig. 6. B-lymphocyte maturation sequence

B-cell subsets indicated by the antigen or nonspecific activator to which they are reactive. DxSO$_4$, dextran sulfate

TI antigens do not offer a basis for differentiating between the B-cell subsets stimulated by them. Although it has been suggested that antigens must possess polyclonal-activating ability in order to be TI antigens *(54)*, some TI antigens are either extremely poor polyclonal activators or are unable to stimulate nonspecific antibody formation or proliferation *(55, 56)*. Thus levan is reportedly an excellent polyclonal B-cell activator, whereas TNP-*Brucella abortus* is a very weak stimulator of polyclonal-antibody synthesis *(11)*.

Lymphocytes Carry CBA/N Defect

The inability of young adult CBA/N mice to respond humorally to TI-2 antigens is clearly a property of the lymphocytes bearing the immune defect and not of the environment, in which they either differentiate from stem cells or are confronted with antigen. In reciprocal reconstitutions of lethally irradiated adoptive recipients with marrow cells of phenotypically normal female or defective male (CBA/N ♀ × DBA/2 ♂) F_1 mice, the reactivity to TNP-Ficoll developed in recipients of normal cells eight weeks after repopulation, regardless of the phenotype of the host (8). Furthermore, the recipients of marrow from mice bearing the *xid* mutation expressed the CBA/N defect (8). CBA/N spleen cells failed to mount primary plaque-forming-cell responses to TNP-Ficoll in vitro, whereas histocompatible control cells displayed positive reactivity (Table 3). Moreover, B-lymphocytes (but not T-cells or macrophages) from phenotypically normal mice reconstitued the in vitro responsiveness in mutant spleen cells (57). Thus, removing splenocytes from the environment of the mutant mouse to the neutral tissue-culture milieu fails to result in positive reactivity. Additionally, transferring immunoglobulin-bearing (B) cells from normal mice into nonirradiated defective recipients allowed the defective mice to respond to TNP-Ficoll (8, 11). Thus, the environment appears to prejudice neither the development nor the expression of responsiveness. Rather, the defect in TI-2 reactivity appears to be carried by the B-cells of the mutant animals.

The more detailed investigation presented here of the unresponsiveness of young adult CBA/N spleen cells to stimulation by Fc fragments supports the suggestion that the defect lies in the splenocytes themselves. Alterations in such variables of the proliferative response as cell density, mitogen concentration, and kinetics of reactivity were ruled out as contributing significantly to the observed unresponsiveness of the young adult defective spleen cells; moreover, we found no evidence for cell-mediated suppression. These data are consistent with a delay in B-cell maturation as the basis for the CBA/N defect, but are also in agreement with the theory that an accessory-cell lesion is responsible. These possibilities are currently under investigation.

Alternative Basis for CBA/N Defect

The B-cell maturation sequence may not be as simple as has been recently suggested, with a single transition from neonatal-type surface-IgD-negative to a mature surface-IgD-bearing lymphocyte (58, 59). For example, a series of maturation steps could occur, unsignaled by such readily recognized markers as surface-immunoglobulin or cell-surface-differentiation antigens. In this scheme, operationally illustrated in Figure 6, the reactivities arise in the sequence shown. As each reactivity is gained, there must be either an alteration in the responding cell, allowing reactivity to be manifested, or a change in an accessory cell. Furthermore, the various reactivities in which young adult CBA/N mice are defective may have different requirements for accessory cells or surface-recognition structures. Whether the sequence of acquisition of responsiveness in both control and CBA/N mice could be explained by sequential changes within the responding B-cells alone depends to a large extent upon what basic activation requirements for B-cells lead to proliferation or antibody production.

Accessory Cells in the CBA/N Defect

Early investigations suggested that TD, but not TI, antigens require accessory cells (macrophages) for immunogenicity (60, 61). However, with improved techniques and attention focused on the depletion of macrophages, TI responses have recently proven to be accessory-cell dependent (62, 63). This quantitative difference in macrophage requirements for TI and TD antigens casts doubts upon the initial results concerning macrophage independence of B-cell mitogenic reactivity. Contradictory reports (64, 65), as well as more recent studies (66) supporting macrophage dependence of nonspecific proliferative responses of B-cells, suggest that macrophage accessory cells may be required for a myriad of B-cell reactions.

Delayed maturation of the accessory cells required for the reactivities lacking in young adult CBA/N mice is an alternate explanation for the defects in responsiveness (67, 68). Because this would appear to necessitate similar accessory-cell requirements for the range of defective reactivities observed in young adult CBA/N mice, delayed accessory-cell maturation is less likely than delayed B-cell maturation; yet a combination of factors may be involved in the appearance of responsiveness. B-cell maturation may result in certain reactivities, although other responses in which B-cells are competent to participate may require collaboration with an accessory-cell population that is not mature enough to take part in the response. Thus, the emergence of certain re-activities could depend upon an accessory cell that matures late or that acquires new antigen-presentation structures or capabilities. Subsets of accessory cells such as macrophages, which differ in the presence of Ia surface antigens *(69, 70)* and other physical characteristics *(71–74)*, and T-cell subsets, which are heterogeneous by a number of criteria *(75–78)*, have been described. T-cell and macrophage functions were originally reported to be normal in mice bearing the CBA/N defect *(8, 55)*.

Although normal phosphorylcholine-specific helper activity has been described in defective mice that cannot elaborate an anti-phosphorylcholine antibody response *(48)*, the idiotype-specific helper function may be abnormal (D. E. Mosier, personal communication). Moreover, Goodman and Weigle *(52)* have demonstrated a defect in T-cell helper activity for lipopolysaccharide-induced nonspecific polyclonal antibody synthesis. Thus, more recent evidence suggests possible areas of accessory-cell malfunction, the correction of which could be involved in the emergence or enhancement of reactivity in aged mutant mice.

Delayed B-Cell Maturation in CBA/N Mice

The mercaptoethanol-induced proliferative response of adult defective spleen cells, which remained negative in aged lymphocytes, and the other responses, which were positive but less than the amounts produced by control nondefective mice, could result from delayed maturation of B-cells or from accessory-cell maturation that did not proceed to completion. However, if in the interest of simplicity we assume only a B-lymphocyte deficiency, the purified-protein-derivative-reactive subset shown in Figure 6 arises just before the maturation defect in young adult CBA/N mice, because the responsiveness of defective mice increases dramatically with age. B-cells responsive to Fc fragments of human immunoglobulin are absent in young adults but appear in aged CBA/N mice. Furthermore, the 2-mercaptoethanol-reactive B-cell subpopulation is shown in Figure 6 as arising at a point in the maturation sequence later than that attained by 12- to 14-month-old (aged) CBA/N mice. All of these B-cell subsets are present in nondefective control CBA/CaJ mice. The extended delay in the appearance of reactivity in the CBA/N mouse strongly suggests that a concomitant delay in B-cell maturation is responsible for the immune defect. The extended time course of B-cell maturation in the CBA/N mouse consequently offers the opportunity for more precise determination of the characteristics of B-cells in various stages of differentiation. Alternatively, this mutant strain presents the possibility of studying the maturation of accessory cells if a developmental lesion in these cells is uncovered. Thus, this model of the CBA/N mouse strain may be used in studies of the requirements for immune reactivity as well as alterations in responsiveness that occur in the context of aging.

This is publication no. 1938 from the Department of Immunopathology, Scripps Clinic and Research Foundation, La Jolla, CA. This work was supported by U.S. Public Health Service grants AI-07007 and AG-00783 and Biomedical Research Support Program grant RRO-5514. John M. Fidler was supported by U.S. Public Health Service grant AI-15226, and Edward L. Morgan is the recipient of Damon Runyon–Walter Winchell Cancer Fund Postdoctoral Fellowship DRG-239-F.

References

1. Walford, R., *The Immunologic Theory of Aging*. Munksgaard, Copenhagen, 1969.
2. Kay, M. M. B., and Makinodan, T., Immunobiology of aging: Evaluation of current status. *Clin. Immunol. Immunopath.* **6**, 394 (1976).
3. Makinodan, T., and Yunis, E., *Immunology and Aging*. Plenum Medical Book Co., New York, NY, 1977.
4. Amsbaugh, D. F., Hansen, C. T., Prescott, B., Stashak, P. W., Barthold, D. R., and Baker, P. J., Genetic control of antibody response to type III pneumococcal polysaccharide in mice. I. Evidence that an X-linked gene plays a decisive role in determining responsiveness. *J. Exp. Med.* **136**, 931 (1972).
5. Scher, I., Frank, M. M., and Steinberg, A. D., The genetics of the immune response to a synthetic double-stranded RNA in a mutant CBA mouse strain. *J. Immunol.* **110**, 1396 (1973).
6. Scher, I., Ahmed, A., Strong, D. M., Steinberg, A. D., and Paul, W. E., X-linked B-lymphocyte immune defect in CBA/HN mice. I. Studies of the function and the composition of spleen cells. *J. Exp. Med.* **141**, 788 (1975).
7. Finkelman, F. D., Smith, A. H., Scher, I., and Paul, W. E., Abnormal ratio of membrane immunoglobulin classes in mice with an X-linked B-lymphocyte defect. *J. Exp. Med.* **142**, 1316 (1975).
8. Scher, I., Steinberg, A. D., Berning, A. K., and Paul, W. E., X-linked B-lymphocyte immune defect in CBA/N mice. II. Studies of the

mechanism underlying the immune defect. *J. Exp. Med.* **142,** 637 (1975).

9. Mosier, D. E., Zitron, I. N., Mond, J. J., Ahmed, A., Scher, I., and Paul, W. E., Surface immunoglobulin D as a functional receptor for a subclass of B lymphocytes. *Immunol. Rev.* **37,** 89 (1977).
10. Mosier, D. E., Scher, I., and Paul, W. E., *In vitro* responses of CBA/N mice: Spleen cells of mice with an X-linked defect that precludes immune responses to several thymus-independent antigens can respond to TNP-lipopolysaccharide. *J. Immunol.* **117,** 1363 (1976).
11. Paul, W. E., Subbarao, B., Mond, J. J., Sieckmann, D. G., Zitron, I., Ahmed, A., Mosier, D. E., and Scher, I., B lymphocyte development and activation: Analysis with a mutant mouse strain. In *Cells of Immunoglobulin Synthesis,* B. Pernis and H. J. Vogel, Eds., Academic Press, Inc., New York, NY, 1979, p. 383.
12. Gershon, R. K., and Kondo, K., Deficient production of a thymus-dependent high affinity antibody subset in mice (CBA/N) with an X-linked B lymphocyte defect. *J. Immunol.* **117,** 701 (1976).
13. Goodman, M. G., Fidler, J. M., and Weigle, W. O., Nonspecific activation of murine lymphocytes. IV. Proliferation of a distinct, late-maturing lymphocyte subpopulation induced by 2-mercaptoethanol. *J. Immunol.* **121,** 1905 (1978).
14. Sieckmann, D. G., Scher, I., Asofsky, R., Mosier, D. E., and Paul, W. E., Activation of mouse lymphocytes by anti-immunoglobulin. II. A thymus-independent response by a mature subset of B lymphocytes. *J. Exp. Med.* **148,** 1628 (1978).
15. Kincade, P. W., Defective colony formation by B lymphocytes from CBA/N and C3H/HeJ mice. *J. Exp. Med.* **145,** 249 (1977).
16. Perlmutter, R. M., Nahm, M., Stein, K. E., Slack, J., Zitron, I., Paul, W. E., and Davie, J. M., Immunoglobulin subclass-specific immunodeficiency in mice with an X-linked B-lymphocyte defect. *J. Exp. Med.* **149,** 993 (1979).
17. Scher, I., Sharrow, S. O., and Paul, W. E., X-linked B cell immune defect in CBA/N mice. III. Abnormal development of B lymphocyte populations defined by their density of surface immunoglobulin. *J. Exp. Med.* **144,** 507 (1975).
18. Ahmed, A., and Scher, I., Studies on non-H-2-linked lymphocyte-activating determinants. II. Non-expression of Mls determinants in a mouse strain with an X-linked B lymphocyte immune defect. *J. Immunol.* **117,** 1922 (1976).
19. Scher, I., Ahmed, A., and Sharrow, S. O., Murine B lymphocyte heterogeneity: Distribution of complement receptor-bearing and minor lymphocyte-stimulating B lymphocytes among cells with different densities of total surface Ig and IgM. *J. Immunol.* **119,** 1938 (1977).

20. Huber, B., Gershon, R. K., and Cantor, H., Identification of a B-cell surface structure involved in antigen-dependent triggering: Absence of this structure on B cells from CBA/N mutant mice. *J. Exp. Med.* **145**, 10 (1977).
21. Ahmed, A., Scher, I., Sharrow, S. O., Smith, A. H., Paul, W. E., Sachs, D. H., and Sell, K. W., B-lymphocyte heterogeneity: Development and characterization of allo-antiserum which distinguishes B-lymphocyte differentiation alloantigens. *J. Exp. Med.* **145**, 101 (1977).
22. Subbarao, B., Mosier, D. E., Ahmed, A., Mond, J. J., Scher, I., and Paul, W. E., Role of a non-immunogobulin cell surface determinant in the activation of B lymphocytes by thymus-independent antigens. *J. Exp. Med.* **149**, 495 (1979).
23. Gelfand, M. D., Elfenbein, G. J., Frank, M. M., and Paul, W. E., Ontogeny of B lymphocytes. II. Relative rates of appearance of lymphocytes bearing surface immunoglobulin and complement receptors. *J. Exp. Med.* **139**, 1125 (1974).
24. Melcher, U., Vitetta, E. S., McWilliams, M., Lamm, M. E., Phillips-Quagliata, J. M., and Uhr, J. W., Cell surface immunoglobulin. X. Identification of an IgD-like molecule on the surface of murine spleen cells. *J. Exp. Med.* **140**, 1427 (1974).
25. Sidman, C. I., and Unanue, E. R., Development of B lymphocytes. I. Cell populations and a critical event during ontogeny. *J. Immunol.* **114**, 1730 (1975).
26. Scher, I., Sharrow, S. O., Wistar, R., Jr., Asofsky, A., and Paul, W. E., B-lymphocyte heterogeneity: Ontogenetic development and organ distribution of B-lymphocyte populations defined by the density of surface immunoglobulin. *J. Exp. Med.* **144**, 494 (1976).
27. Lawton, A. R., Kearney, J. F., and Cooper, M. D., Control of expression of C region genes during development of B cells. *Prog. Immunol.* **3**, 171 (1977).
28. Mosier, D. E., Mond, J. J., and Goldings, E. A., The ontogeny of thymic-independent antibody responses *in vitro* in normal mice and mice with an X-linked B cell defect. *J. Immunol.* **119**, 1874 (1977).
29. Gronowicz, E., Coutinho, A., and Möller, G., Differentiation of B cells: Sequential appearance of responsiveness to polyclonal activators. *Scand. J. Immunol.* **3**, 413 (1974).
30. Shortman, K., Williams, N., and Adams, P., The separation of different cell classes from lymphoid organs. V. Simple procedures for the removal of cell debris, damaged cells, and erythroid cells from lymphoid cell suspensions. *J. Immunol. Methods* **1**, 273 (1972).
31. Fidler, J. M., The induction of hapten-specific immunological tolerance and immunity in B lymphocytes. IV. Induction of TNP-specific tolerance *in vitro* using serum from mice rendered specifically unre-

sponsive by injection of trinitrobenzenesulfonic acid. *J. Immunol.* **121,** 1558 (1978).

32. Williams, N., Kraft, N., and Shortman, K., The separation of different cell classes from lymphoid organs. VI. The effect of osmolarity of gradient media on the density distribution of cells. *Immunology* **22,** 885 (1972).

33. Fidler, J. M., Morgan, E. L., and Weigle, W. O., B lymphocyte differentiation in the CBA/N mouse: A delay in maturation rather than a total arrest. *J. Immunol.* **124,** 13 (1980).

34. Berman, M. A., and Weigle, W. O., B lymphocyte activation by the Fc region of IgG. *J. Exp. Med.* **146,** 241 (1977).

35. Berman, M. A., Spiegelberg, H. L., and Weigle, W. O., Lymphocyte stimulation with Fc fragments. I. Class, subclass, and domain of active fragments. *J. Immunol.* **122,** 89 (1979).

36. Morgan, E. L., Fidler, J. M., and Weigle, W. O., The inability of CBA/N mice to proliferate in response to Fc fragments from human immunoglobulin is an age-related defect. *Cell. Immunol.* (1980), in press.

37. Porter, R. R., The hydrolysis of rabbit γ-globulin and antibodies with crystalline papain. *Biochem. J.* **73,** 119 (1959).

38. Haas, W., Separation of antigen-specific lymphocytes. II. Enrichment of hapten-specific antibody-forming cell precursors. *J. Exp. Med.* **141,** 1015 (1975).

39. Fidler, J. M., *In vivo* immune response to TNP hapten coupled to thymus-independent carrier lipopolysaccharide. *Cell. Immunol.* **16,** 223 (1975).

40. Fidler, J. M., The induction of hapten-specific immunological tolerance and immunity in B lymphocytes. VI. Differential tolerance susceptibility in adult spleen as a function of B cell maturation level. *J. Exp. Med.* **150,** 491 (1979).

41. Mishell, R. I., and Dutton, R. W., Immunization of dissociated spleen cell cultures from normal mice. *J. Exp. Med.* **126,** 405 (1967).

42. Fidler, J. M., The induction of hapten-specific immunological tolerance and immunity in B lymphocytes. III. *In vitro* evaluation of TNP-specific tolerance and evidence for B cell deletion. *J. Immunol.* **121,** 245 (1978).

43. Cunningham, A. J., and Szenberg, A., Further improvements in the plaque technique for detecting single antibody forming cells. *Immunology* **14,** 599 (1968).

44. Mond, J. J., Stein, K. E., Subbarao, B., and Paul, W. E., Analysis of B cell activation requirements with TNP-conjugated polyacrylamide beads. *J. Immunol.* **123,** 239 (1979).

45. Morrison, D. C., Betz, S. J., and Jacobs, D. M., Isolation and charac-

terization of the fraction of LPS responsible for mitogenesis of C3H/HeJ spleen cells. *J. Exp. Med.* **144**, 840 (1976).

46. Sultzer, B. M., and Goodman, G. W., Endotoxin protein: A B-cell mitogen and polyclonal activator of C3H/HeJ lymphocytes. *J. Exp. Med.* **144**, 821 (1976).

47. Schlegel, R. A., Fidler, J. M., Howard, M., and Shortman, K., Antigen-initiated B-lymphocyte differentiation. VII. Quantification of AFC progenitor levels in adoptive and culture response to NIP-POL antigen. *Immunology* **29**, 1029 (1975).

48. Kaplan, R. B., and Quintáns, J., Phosphorylcholine-specific helper T cells in mice with an X-linked defect of antibody production of the same hapten. *J. Exp. Med.* **149**, 267 (1979).

49. Janeway, C. A., Jr., and Barthold, D. R., An analysis of the defective response of CBA/N mice to T-dependent antigen. *J. Immunol.* **115**, 898 (1975).

50. Quintáns, J., and Kaplan, R. B., Failure of CBA/N mice to respond to thymus-dependent and thymus-independent phosphorylcholine antigen. *Cell. Immunol.* **38**, 294 (1978).

51. Mond, J. J., Lieberman, R., Inman, J. K., Mosier, D. E., and Paul, W. E., Inability of mice with a defect in B-lymphocyte maturation to respond to phosphorylcholine on immunogenic carriers. *J. Exp. Med.* **146**, 1138 (1977).

52. Goodman, M. G., and Weigle, W. O., T cell regulation of polyclonal B cell responsiveness. II. Evidence for a deficit in T cell function in mice with an X-linked B lymphocyte defect. *J. Immunol.* **123**, 2484 (1979).

53. Mosier, D. E., Mond, J. J., and Goldings, E. A., The ontogeny of thymic-independent antibody responses *in vitro* in normal mice and mice with an X-linked B cell defect. *J. Immunol.* **119**, 1874 (1977).

54. Coutinho, A., and Möller, G., Immune activation of B cells: Evidence for one non-specific triggering signal not delivered by the Ig receptors. *Scand. J. Immunol.* **3**, 133 (1974).

55. Mosier, D. E., Johnson, G. M., Paul, W. E., and McMaster, P. R. B., Cellular requirements for the primary *in vitro* antibody response to DNP-Ficoll. *J. Exp. Med.* **139**, 1354 (1974).

56. Klaus, G. G. B., and Humphrey, J. H., The immunological properties of haptens coupled to thymus-independent carrier molecules. I. Characteristics of the immune response to dinitrophenyl-lysine-substituted pneumococcal polysaccharide (SIII) and levan. *Eur. J. Immunol.* **4**, 370 (1974).

57. Cohen, P. L., Scher, I., and Mosier, D. E., *In vitro* studies of the genetically determined unresponsiveness to thymus-independent antigens in CBA/N mice. *J. Immunol.* **116**, 301 (1976).

58. Vitetta, E. S., and Uhr, J. W., Immunoglobulin receptors revisited. *Science* **189**, 964 (1975).
59. Möller, G., Ed., Immunoglobulin D: Structure, synthesis, membrane representation and function. *Immunol. Rev.* **37** (1978).
60. Shortman, K., Diener, E., Russell, P., and Armstrong, W. D., The role of nonlymphoid accessory cells in the immune response to different antigens. *J. Exp. Med.* **131**, 461 (1970).
61. Feldmann, M., Induction of immunity and tolerance in vitro by hapten protein conjugates. II. Carrier independence of the response to dinitrophenylated polymerized flagellin. *Eur. J. Immunol.* **2**, 130 (1972).
62. Lee, K.-C., Shiowaza, C., Shaw, A., and Diener, E., Requirement for accessory cells in the antibody response to T cell-independent antigens in vitro. *Eur. J. Immunol.* **6**, 63 (1976).
63. Cosenza, H., Quintáns, J., and Lefkovits, I., Antibody response to phosphorylcholine *in vitro*. I. Studies on the frequency of precursor cells, average clone size and cellular cooperation. *Eur. J. Immunol.* **5**, 343 (1975).
64. Yoshinaga, M., Yoshinaga, A., and Waksman, B. H., Regulation of lymphocyte responses *in vitro*. I. Regulatory effect of macrophages and thymus-dependent (T) cells on the response of thymus-independent (B) lymphocytes to endotoxin. *J. Exp. Med.* **136**, 956 (1972).
65. Kagnoff, M. F., Billings, P., and Cohn, M., Functional characteristics of Peyer's patch lymphoid cells. II. Lipopolysaccharide is thymus dependent. *J. Exp. Med.* **139**, 407 (1974).
66. Persson, U., Hammarström, L., Möller, E., Möller, G., and Smith, C. I. E., The role of adherent cells in B and T lymphocyte activation. *Immunol. Rev.* **40**, 78 (1978).
67. Argyris, B., Role of macrophages in immunological maturation. *J. Exp. Med.* **128**, 459 (1968).
68. Fidler, J. M., Chiscon, M. O., and Golub, E. S., Functional development of the interacting cells in the immune response. II. Development of immunocompetence to heterologous erythrocytes *in vitro*. *J. Immunol.* **109**, 136 (1972).
69. Niederhuber, J. E., The role of I region gene products in macrophage-T lymphocyte interaction. *Immunol. Rev.* **40**, 28 (1978).
70. Hammerling, G. J., Tissue distribution of Ia antigens and their expression on lymphocyte subpopulations. *Transplant. Rev.* **30**, 64 (1976).
71. Montfort, I., and Tamayo, R. P., Two antigenically different types of macrophages. *Proc. Soc. Exp. Biol. Med.* **138**, 204 (1971).
72. Walker, W. S., Functional heterogeneity of macrophages. In *Immunobiology of the Macrophage*, D. S. Nelson, Ed., Academic Press, New York, NY, 1975, p 91.

73. Gorczynski, R. M., Control of the immune response: Role of macrophages in regulation of antibody- and cell-mediated immune responses. *Scand. J. Immunol.* **5,** 1031 (1977).
74. Gorczynski, R. M., Role of macrophage-derived factors in generation of cytotoxic and antibody response. *Scand. J. Immunol.* **6,** 665 (1977).
75. Raff, M. C., and Cantor, H., Subpopulations of thymus cells and thymus-derived lymphocytes. *Progr. Immunol.* **1,** 83 (1971).
76. Shortman, K. D., vonBoehmer, H., Lipp, J., and Hopper, K., Subpopulations of T-lymphocytes. *Transplant. Rev.* **25,** 163 (1975).
77. Cantor, H., and Boyse, E. A., Regulation of the immune response by T-cell subclasses. *Contemp. Top. Immunobiol.* **8,** 47 (1977).
78. Tada, T., Takemori, T., Okumura, K., Nonaka, M., and Takuhisa, T., Two distinct types of helper T cells involved in the secondary antibody response: Independent and synergistic effects of Ia$^-$ and Ia$^+$ helper T cells *J. Exp. Med.* **147,** 446 (1978).

Discussion—Session IV

DR. HABIG: Dr. Hayflick, when you described the recombination or, I think you called it, reconstitution of the nucleus into a cell that had been previously denucleated, I did not picture a process by which this is done. Is it a batch process or does it require a special container?

DR. HAYFLICK: There is an existing technology for doing this, developed eight to 10 years ago. Whole cells are fused to each other with fusion factor from SV-40 or, more recently, with polyethylene glycol. It is possible to fuse isolated nuclei and isolated cytoplasts because the nucleus is essentially a mini-cell. It is surrounded by a thin film of cytoplasm and a membrane, so one can obtain fusion between the nucleus and the cytoplast. This can be done either in mass culture or with single cytoplasts and nuclei.

DR. NATELSON: Apparently cultures of HeLa cells go on dividing indefinitely. One process that has been suggested as a limiting factor in culturing is that something accumulates in the cell or some defect occurs. As you pointed out, there are decreases in various enzyme activities in the normal cell, which eventually make mitosis impossible. Why does that not take place in the HeLa cell? How do these cells differ?

DR. HAYFLICK: You have put your finger on an extremely important phenomenon, which is not restricted to HeLa cells alone but is applicable to all continuously proliferating cell cultures and transplantable tumors. It is probably analogous to the continuity of the germplasm, which we can also regard as an immortal genealogical tree. There is yet another classification of cells that exhibits the same phenomenon, cells that give rise to certain plants. A new technology has developed that involves isolation of very tiny bits of leaves or meristem so that one can make literally tens of thousands of plants from a single leaf. You may know it more commonly as propagation of seedless plants such as banana trees or Williams pears. I am told by Dr. Strehler that aspens may propagate in this clonal manner. I wish I could answer your question, as it is extremely important for those theoreticians who are concerned with the tinker-toy aspects of how aging may occur at the molecular level. Any theory must include a subordinate theorem that explains why these cells can escape the inevitability of aging. I can offer no explanation.

DR. NATELSON: What measurements are actually taken on the HeLa cell? If you select a particular enzyme whose activity decreases in normal cells, does it remain constant in HeLa cells?

DR. HAYFLICK: Yes. Perhaps Dr. Hart can address that, because he looks at repair in continuously propagating cell populations.

DR. HART: The correlation between life span and repair capabilities holds for primary cell cultures. It does not appear to hold, based on a preliminary search of the literature, for permanent cell lines, regardless. For example, V-79, which is derived from the Chinese hamster, has the same capabilities to repair 7-bromodimethylbenzanthracene damage as the human HeLa cell does. The same is true for the transformed mouse lines. There is a difference that seems to exist in transformed cell lines. One possibility, based on very preliminary data from our laboratory, is that while we see a decrease in superhelicity of DNA as a function of age in the mammalian cell, the transformed cell lines do not exhibit this increase.

DR. STREHLER: Dr. Hayflick, the number of doublings obtained from reconstituted cells are relatively limited when you put an old nucleus into a young cytoplast. What is the maximum?

DR. HAYFLICK: I believe that the nuclei we used were rather far along on the scheme, so we do not yet have information on younger nuclei in comparison with older ones. It is something that must be done. That experiment plus other even more important ones can be done with this system. It would be interesting to observe what would happen with nuclei from malignant cells and cytoplasts from normal cells. A number of permutations and combinations could be tried, and we intend to do the one you suggested.

DR. STREHLER: Dr. Hart, could you explain for those of us who have not heard of it before, what is the origin of superhelicity? Is it the acquisition of more histones, or is it single-strand breaks that permit more random coiling?

DR. HART: As a cell ages, apparently negative superhelicity decreases because of an increase in single-strand breaks.

DR. STREHLER: How is this measured?

DR. HART: By sedimentation, thanks to Dr. Beckman's centrifuge.

DR. STREHLER: This is isolated DNA or chromatin?

DR. HART: You can isolate DNA and still measure superhelicity by either gels or centrifugation. We intend to use centrifugation. It has been fairly well demonstrated in bacteria in the last few months that superhelicity is one of the controlling factors in gene expression. This goes back to the idea that if you increase the superhelicity, the tertiary structure is more tightly wound and leads to differential gene expression.

DR. STREHLER: Dr. Weigle, do any of these B cells that respond by undergoing mitosis when exposed to mitogens go on to produce antibodies? Does one here have a model system in which cells that have been sitting around in a nondividing state for a substantial time might be used to measure the magnitude of response at various ages? For instance, one of the things that interests us is the change in post-mitotic cells—cells that have been sitting around for a long time without dividing. Have these B cells that you described that give this polyclonal response been sitting around in a nondividing state? After they are stimulated to divide by a mitogen, do they form large amounts of RNA, rough endoplasmic reticulum, and produce specific antibodies? If they do, one could measure, in an individual cell or a clone, the speed of the response.

DR. WEIGLE: Yes, they do. I do not know if you are talking about mitogenic response or proliferative response. You can have a proliferative response without a mitogenic response. For example, with the Fc fragment that we use to get a mitogenic response and to obtain a polyclone, if you have only B cells, you get only the mitogenic response. To obtain the polyclonal response, you need T cells. This is not the case with lipopolysaccharide (LPS). With LPS you can obtain both mitogenic and polyclonal responses without T cells, although T cells will amplify this response. Thus the proliferation probably precedes the cells' making a specific antibody. It is specific as far as that cell is concerned, although it has not been instructed with a specific antigen.

DR. DEYOUNG (Wichita, KS): Dr. Weigle, is there any correlation between the level of IgG and human survival in the elderly?

DR. WEIGLE: I do not believe there is. There is some correlation with IgA, which, I believe, increases in aged individuals.

DR. STEENBLOCK (El Toro, CA): Dr. Weigle, do you know of any information that would allow us clinicians to measure the immune system and correlate the state of the immune system with the development of cancer?

DR. WEIGLE: There have been many studies in this area, including those at NIH, where they have tried to immunize people with things like DNP bound to a protein. I do not know of one that has worked out well. You are thinking about something to show a decrease in immune response and predict the person will get cancer?

DR. STEENBLOCK: My question really is, you can measure T cells, B cells, and delayed hypersensitivity: If any of those show a lower response, is there any correlation with the development of cancer?

DR. WEIGLE: No.

DR. HART: There is a point to that. Are you familiar with the experiment by Roy Walford? He took a series of different mouse strains, which had different tendencies toward autoimmune disease and different life spans, and measured the DNA repair capability in their lymphocytes. Interestingly enough, he found that the greater the repair capability of the lymphocytes, the less the tendency toward autoimmune disease and the longer the life span of the rodent species. Although not directly related to cancer, this certainly is interesting relative to aging and predictive systems tieing molecular events to the immune system.

DR. STREHLER: In response to the gentleman's question, there is a paper by, I believe, Teller, in which he measured the production of antibodies to the injection of ascites and the frequency of takes of ascites, as a function of age of a particular strain of mouse. He found that the younger the animal, the higher the titer and the lower the frequency of takes.

DR. MEACHUM (Shreveport, LA): Dr. Hart, could you go back and tell us what that third repair system was? I understood there was excision repair and post-replication repair. Was the third one photoreactivation repair? [Yes] The one observed in paramecium, was it a fourth, non-specific type?

DR. HART: It was excision repair. There is a tremendous difference between mouse and man for spontaneous transformation in risk per cell per unit time. None of the systems for assurance of longevity or information stability in and of themselves can totally explain this tremendous difference of over 100 000-fold. However, if we assume that these systems are interlinked and represent the multiple of one another, you could explain the tremendous difference in risk per cell per unit time for spontaneous transformation. The problem is that each of the four general categories, including repair as one of the general categories, not only has excision repair, post-replication repair, and photoreactivation repair, but also can be further subdivided into many forms of excision repair. Post-replication repair can also be subdivided. If we are ever going to determine the actual impact of the degree of importance of each of these systems, we will need to investigate each. It becomes a huge undertaking, as each of the four major systems has subcategories and sub-subcategories.

Dr. Meachum: Could you tell us if photoreactivated repair systems occur in mammalian tissues? If so, are there other things that could stimulate them or other functions they might have rather than simply repairing damage from ultraviolet radiation? This would seem to be relatively minimal in interior tissues in mammals.

Dr. Hart: In the placental mammals the photoreactivation repair capability is very, very low. Otherwise, the experiment that Joan Smith-Sonneborn did could have been done on human cells in vitro. We tried. There is to our knowledge absolutely nothing besides a very specific wavelength of visible light that will activate this repair system in any species. It is a very, very primitive repair system, probably the most primitive.

Dr. Schneider (Durham, NC): I was interested in the concept of the clock mechanism. You have been able to exclude the photoperiodicity and the culture systems. However, one thing that has not been excluded is the interruption of lunar gravity every 24 h with the rotation of the earth. Have there been experiments designed to study the effects of the acceleration of space travel in an orbital system where you interrupt gravity more frequently?

Dr. Hayflick: Only indirectly, strangely enough. I suppose most people here would have thought that the answer would be that we have no information, but in point of fact, one of my cell populations, WI 38, was put on one of the early Skylabs to measure the effects of zero gravity on population-doubling potential and to measure effects on interdivision time. The cells were photographed in a very sophisticated black box, with phase-contrast, time-lapse cinemicrophotography. The upshot of that million-dollar experiment, and I think that is an underestimate, was that there were no changes in any of the parameters that we looked at. I am not sure that speaks directly to your question, but I think it comes close. However, if the difference between the orbiting cells and the terrestrial controls were but three to five population doublings, we would not have picked up that small a difference.

V

CLINICAL CHEMISTRY PROBLEMS IN HEALTH AND MEDICAL CARE OF THE ELDERLY

Practical applications of clinical chemistry to the understanding of problems in health-care delivery—William H. C. Walker, Moderator

Don't just add years to your life. Rather add life to your years.

HANS SELYE

The Study of Body-Fluid Composition in Aging Humans. I. Requirements in Clinical Chemistry for a Lifetime Health-Monitoring Program

George F. Grannis

Not many years ago the principal activities in the clinical chemistry laboratory were the laborious, time-consuming analysis of blood and urine samples for a few constituents. New analytical concepts have emerged in the last two decades that make possible the cost-effective analysis of body fluids for a wide variety of constituents in a large number of samples. Our ability to acquire large amounts of data, both for populations and individuals, should lead to new approaches to health surveillance and early disease detection.

The principal applications of clinical chemistry include: *(a)* the medical testing of ill individuals for the purpose of establishing diagnoses, for monitoring the progress of disease, and for establishing effective therapeutic regimens; *(b)* the screening of populations to detect individuals who are at risk of having a particular medical problem; and *(c)* the health testing of apparently well individuals to detect or rule out covert disease, or to identify risk factors for specific medical problems. It is this latter application of clinical chemistry—health testing—that is of greatest interest in relation to problems of human aging, and in which the need for new knowledge is greatest. Others at this conference will likely discuss specific changes in body-fluid composition with aging. I shall consider, from a general viewpoint, some characteristics that are relevant to health testing, and areas in clinical chemistry that need development if our technology is to be applied effectively. In my second paper I will present a unifying concept that may help provide direction to this future technological development.

The Natural Life Span

Although it has long been common knowledge that, under favorable conditions, the average human life span is about "three score and ten" years, that even under the best conditions individuals rarely survive longer than 105 years, and moreover that other

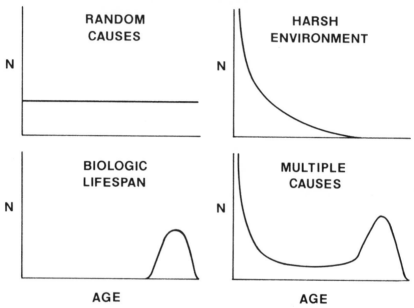

Fig. 1. Four possible types of mortality curves (frequency distribution of deaths as a function of age)

species appear to have unique, biologically constrained life spans, we are uncertain whether the human life span is also fixed, biologically constrained, and species specific. Indeed, only through an examination of the changes in the pattern of human mortality during the past several decades have inherent constraints to human longevity become evident.

Were we the first to observe a human population in its natural setting and record the number of deaths occurring at each year of life, what sort of frequency-distribution curve might we expect?

Figure 1 illustrates four possibilities. If deaths were due to random causes (such as lightning bolts), equal numbers of deaths would occur at all ages. However, if the population were living under conditions that might be described as a "harsh environment," such that survival were quite difficult, then we should expect to find a large number of deaths during the early years of life, with few individuals surviving to the later decades. Another possibility would be a biologically determined life span for the species, in which case there would be a rather symmetrical distribution of deaths about a mean. Finally, if deaths occurred from all of the above causes, and we would observe a composite frequency distribution curve.

The mortality experience of a population can be evaluated by constructing a "current" mortality curve. Such a mortality curve illustrates how a cohort of individuals born in a given year may be expected to survive if the members live out their lives subject to the age-specific mortality rates actually observed in the general population in the given year. The derivation, uses, and limitations of "current" and "cross-sectional" mortality tables are discussed elsewhere *(1)*.

There is little evidence that the apparent natural life span differs greatly amongst the races, or is significantly different for men and women. A review of the changes in mortality curves of various nations shows that all seem to be evolving towards a common endpoint *(2)*. Similarly, the observed difference between the mortality pattern of males and females (which is evident by comparing the curves of Figure 2) is known to be largely due to the premature mortality of men who are cigarette smokers. Mortality curves derived from Hammond's *(4)* study of cigarette smokers and nonsmokers (Figure 3) show clearly that the curve for men smokers is shifted to the left of that of men nonsmokers by about seven years. Of equal interest is the fact that the curve for men nonsmokers is quite similar to that for women. Thus, there appears to be little *inherent* difference between the apparent natural life span of males and females. Thus, a current mortality curve can be considered a crude, but objectively derived, assessment of the current status of a population's overall proficiency in "the arts of survival" in a naturally hostile environment.

Throughout mankind's history most human populations are

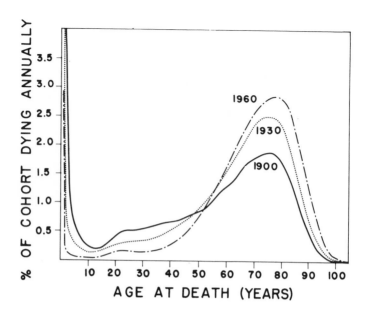

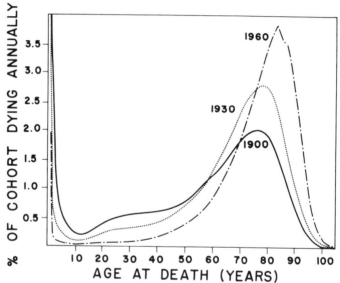

Fig. 2. Historic changes in the current mortality curves of white males *(top)* and white females *(bottom)* living in the United States

Based on life tables from the U.S. Bureau of the Census. Reproduced from the *Journal of Gerontology (3)* by permission.

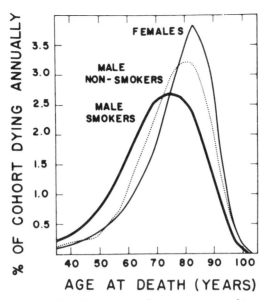

Fig. 3. Mortality curves for cigarette smoking and nonsmoking men and white women in the United States during the 1960's

Reproduced from the *Journal of Gerontology* (3) by permission

believed to have had mortality curves of the "harsh environment" type *(5, 6)*. Even today the populations of some of the underdeveloped nations have this pattern of mortality. However, the many remarkable technical, medical, and sociological advances since 1900 have decreased the death rate during the early decades of life so that more people are living longer. Consequently, the mortality curves of most populations are evolving very much as shown in Figure 2 for the United States *(2)*. However, the human mortality curve has not yet been fully "optimized": many apparently premature deaths still occur, and a reasonable objective is to learn how to detect those individuals who are at risk of premature death and to learn what specific preventive measures might diminish their risk.

The mortality curves also suggest that there is a natural limit to human longevity. The modal value of the frequency curve of adult deaths may be taken as an approximate measure of the

319

apparent natural life span, and as shown in Figure 2, the modal value has been practically constant, being about 80 years in 1900 and about 84 years now. These observations of how the human mortality curve has changed through the years are consistent with the view that the curve is evolving towards a symmetrical distribution of deaths about some limiting natural life span. It is of fundamental importance to learn whether this apparent natural limit may be extended without imposing hardships.

The Stages of Life

William Shakespeare, an astute observer of the human condition, noted that there are seven stages of the human life-course, and eloquently described each (7). These stages of life are indicated at the top of Figure 4 and are clearly demarked by a variety of physiologic, sociologic, and demographic characteristics, which can be quantitatively measured. In Figure 4, the growth curves of boys and girls (8) and the fertility curve (9) are superimposed on the mortality curve of white U.S. females (1). The mortality curve has been subjected to a dissection technique (10) to show that there is probably a major subpopulation (I) in which deaths are symmetrically distributed about the apparent natural life span, and two minor subpopulations (II and III) of individuals who die prematurely. Taken together, these curves serve to identify some of the principal stages of the human life span:

1. *Perinatal:* from conception to birth (pre-natal) and from birth to one year of age (infancy). This stage is clearly demarked by the high rate of mortality.
2. *Prepubertal:* from age 1 to about 12. This stage is demarked in Figure 4 by the growth rate curve, and terminates with the initiation of the adolescent growth spurt. In girls this stage is also terminated at the age of menarche, which is indicated by the lower limit of the fertility curve. The prepubertal stage may be divided into two substages: (a) age 1 to 6, and (b) age 6 to 12.
3. *Adolescence:* about age 12 to 18. This stage encompasses the growth spurt. The rate of growth declines to zero by age 17

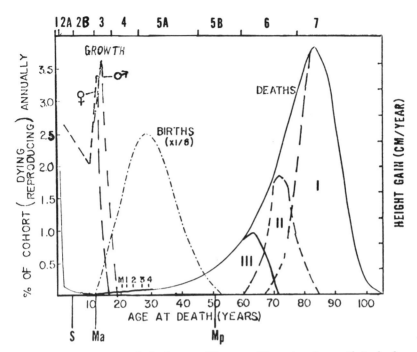

Fig 4. Discrete stages of the human life span: The rate of growth in body stature of boys and girls during the first two decades of life and the fertility curve of white U.S. females is superimposed on the 1960 mortality curve of white U.S. females

The mortality curve has been dissected to show the major subpopulation (I) of individuals who now attain the apparent natural life span and two minor subpopulations (II and III) of individuals who apparently die prematurely. *S* indicates the average age of entry into school; *Ma* and *Mp* are the average ages of menarche and menopause, respectively; *M, 1, 2, 3,* and *4* are the average ages of marriage of white women and the births of successive children. The seven stages of the life span described in the text are indicated on the scale above the graph. Sources: *1, 8, 9*

for women and by age 19 for men, signalling their transition from adolescence to physiological adulthood.

4. *Young adult:* age 18 to 25. This stage is conveniently demarked by the average age at which the procreation rate is adequate to sustain the population.

5. *Middle age(s):* age 25 to 60. This stage of life encompasses the decline in the fertility curve and the early rise in mortality rates. This stage may be divided into two substages: early middle age (25 to 45), which encompasses the peak and decline

of the fertility curve, and late middle age (45 to 60), which encompasses the menopausal years for women, and the years during which the early mortality of subpopulation III (Figure 4) occurs.
6. *Elderly:* age 60 to 75. This stage is clearly demarked as the years during which the early mortality of subpopulation II occurs.
7. *Old age:* over age 75. This stage is demarked by subpopulation I and is characterized by the high mortality rates that prevail as the natural limits of the human life span are approached.

The Concept of a Lifetime Health-Monitoring Program

Breslow and Somers *(11)*, in proposing a "lifetime health-monitoring program," divided the human life span into discrete stages that correspond approximately to the stages listed above, and noted that the medical and health care needs of individuals differ greatly according to their stage in life. They outlined some general health goals and professional services that should be available for each stage; and for two stages, infancy and late middle age, they listed specific screening procedures that should be implemented. Their recommendations for the latter stage, reproduced below, make modest use of clinical laboratory services, particularly the clinical chemistry services, probably because their program was based on existing clinical and epidemiologic information; moreover, the services offered were considered to be the minimum necessary for cost-effective preventive health care in a national health insurance program.

Health goals:
1. To prolong the period of maximum physical energy and optimum mental and social activity, including menopausal adjustment.
2. To detect as early as possible any of the major chronic diseases, including hypertension, heart disease, diabetes, and cancer, as well as vision, hearing, and dental impairments.

Professional services:
1. Four professional visits with the healthy person, once every five years—at about ages 40, 45, 50, and 55—with complete physical examination and medical history, tests for specific chronic conditions, and appropriate immunizations. Also useful would be counseling regarding changing nutritional needs; physical activities; occupational, sexual, marital, and parental problems; and the use of cigarettes, alcohol, and drugs.
2. For those over 50, annual tests for hypertension, obesity, and certain cancers.
3. Annual dental prophylaxis.

Suspected or possible condition

Screening procedures

At 2- to 3-yr intervals

Malnutrition, including obesity	Weight and height measurements; evaluation of history of nutrition and activity*
Hypertension and associated conditions	Blood pressure*
Cervical cancer	Papanicolaou smear
Intestinal cancer	Stool for blood*
Breast cancer	Professional breast examination, with mammography for those > 50
Complications from smoking	Evaluation of smoking history
Endometrial cancer (postmenopausal women)	Evaluation of history of postmenopausal bleeding*

At 5-yr intervals

Coronary-artery disease	Cholesterol, triglycerides, electrocardiography
Alcoholism	Evaluation of drinking history
Anemia	Hematocrit
Diabetes	Blood sugar test (fasting and 1-h p.c. suggested)
Vision defect	Refraction and intraocular tension
Hearing defect	Audiogram

High-risk groups, add to 5-yr intervals

Tuberculosis	PPD
Syphilis	VDRL

* Once/yr after age 50.

I suggest that the concept of a lifetime health-monitoring program, with services designed for specific stages of life, is excellent, but that more use could be made of clinical laboratory services. The science of laboratory medicine is currently in a phase of rapid development, and when fully developed, can contribute much to our knowledge of life-course changes and to the early detection or prevention of disease. To this end let us consider some basic characteristics of clinical laboratory data and how knowledge of these characteristics may contribute to more incisive utilization of such data as are useful.

Homeostasis, Basal Values, and Response to Stress

Most physiological systems are structured to function homeostatically, i.e., to maintain a relatively constant internal environment *(12, 13)*. The concept of homeostasis and its implications are discussed further in the next paper (this volume). Suffice it to note here that the components of blood are important intermediates in the transport and dynamic interchange of materials among tissues, and are subject to various homeostatic control mechanisms that *normally* serve to maintain analyte concentrations within relatively narrow limits. Because blood constituents are components of homeostatic systems, these systems may be evaluated by *(a)* observing basal values under standard resting conditions and *(b)* observing how values change in response to applied stress.

Basal Values in Health and Disease

In Figure 5*A* the normalized frequency distribution of serum calcium values observed for a population of healthy young adults is compared with that observed for a hospitalized population at time of admission. Also shown are the magnitude of analytical error of the measurements and the magnitude of individual variability observed when normal individuals were sampled repeatedly. In Figure 5*B*, the frequency distribution curve of the patient population in 5*A* has been dissected to reveal three overlapping subpopulations. Use of the dissection technique *(10)* produces an estimate of the maximum size of the subpopulation having values within the normal range, and the minimum size of the subpopulations having lower than normal or higher than normal values.

The above dissection technique allows one to estimate the size and frequency distributions of the three major subpopulations (with low, normal, or high analytical values); but because the curves overlap, it is not always possible to classify a specific subject as a member of a particular subpopulation. However, it is possible to calculate the probability that a particular analytical value represents a member of a particular subpopulation *(10)*. These probabilities may be displayed graphically as shown in Figure 5*C* for serum calcium.

Figure 5 illustrates several basic features that are common to all quantitative clinical laboratory analyses:

- *Analytical error.* All measurements are subject to error, and the magnitude of error influences the interpretation of clinical

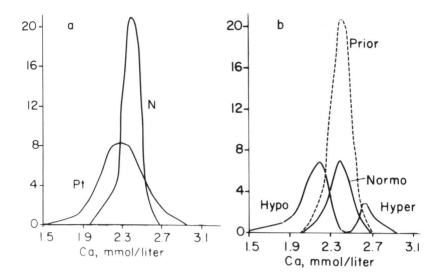

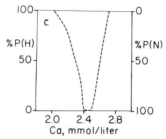

Fig. 5.(a) Comparison of frequency distribution of serum calcium values in normal healthy young adults (N) and in hospital patients (Pt); (b) The frequency distribution curve for hospital patients (from a) dissected into three subpopulations of hypo-, normo-, and hypercalcemic individuals; that is, individuals whose analytical values are below, within, or above the normal range of values; (c) The probability that a given analytical value represents a member of the normo- [%P(N)] or hypo- and hypercalcemic [%P(H)] population

Adapted from Grannis and Lott (10)

assay values. For calcium analyses the analytical error is less than individual variability; i.e., the measurement system varied only slightly less than did the basal values of each subject being measured. Obviously, analytical error should be small; however, the magnitude of acceptable analytical error that does not obscure useful results is a subject of much debate *(14)*.

- *The normal range.* For serum calcium, the values observed in the healthy population are symmetrically distributed over a relatively narrow range because there are homeostatic mechanisms that closely regulate Ca^{2+} concentration in blood *(15)*. Customarily, "normal range" is defined as the range of values encompassing the central 95% of the range of the frequency distribution curve of the normal population. Normal, or reference, ranges for common body-fluid constituents are widely reported in standard textbooks (e.g., *16*), and age- and sex-adjusted ranges observed in a careful population study have recently been reported *(17)*. However, the applicability of such data to other populations is always subject to uncertainty because of methodological differences, differences in the statistical treatment of the data, and other factors *(18)*. A consensus procedure for developing ranges that should be universally acceptable has been described elsewhere *(19)*.

- *The patient population range.* A broader range of values of serum calcium is observed for a population of patients than for the healthy population. Clearly, many of the patients have experienced changes of their basal serum calcium values. It is important to know how many of the patients have changed significantly, and to identify the individuals whose values have either increased or decreased with respect to the normal range.

- *Principal set-point value.* Homeostatic systems are structured to maintain the constancy of key parameters and consequently are characterized by set-point, or steady-state, values. The modal value of the frequency distribution curve of the normal population may be taken as the principal set-point value. The range of individual variability about the principal set-point value for serum calcium is approximately the same as the reference interval for the population, from which we conclude that all members of the healthy population have essentially the same normal set-point values for serum calcium. Principal set-point values have seldom been reported in the literature.

- *Intra-individual variability about the set-point value.* When individuals are sampled repeatedly in the basal state, the analytical values have a certain dispersion in addition to that due to analytical variability. This dispersion is due primarily to variability in the homeostatic mechanisms responsible for maintaining the set-point value. The magnitude of dispersion, or intra-individual variability, is a characteristic of the homeostatic-control mechanisms, and increases from the usual range may be indicative of deterioration of the control mechanisms. Intra-individual variability has been determined for some common serum constituents *(20–28)*, but not for many others.
- *Hypo-, normo-, and hyperanalyte states.* The concentration of an analyte in blood may be described as "low," "normal," or "high" with respect to the reference interval for that analyte; i.e., the value may be indicative of a hypo-, normo-, or hyperanalyte state. It is important to realize that not all analytical values within the normal range of values are "normal" values. For example, as shown in Figure 5B, three subpopulations overlap within the reference interval; for the data illustrated, it can be calculated that although 56% of the patients' values were within the reference interval, no more than 34% could have been members of the normo-calcemic subpopulation, 50% were hypocalcemic, and 16% were hypercalcemic. Obviously, to interpret laboratory data, one must have some idea of the incidence and prevalence of the various abnormal analyte states; at present, however, such information is not available.
- *Probability of dysanalytemia.* Figure 5C illustrates how it is possible to calculate the probability that a subject with a given analyte value is in one of the three major calcemic states. Although such calculations have been reported for several analytes *(10)*, these were presented only as examples; more soundly based data are not yet available.
- *Secondary set-point values.* For many blood constituents (such as fibrinogen; see Figure 7, later), members of the healthy population maintain basal steady-state values that are distinctly lower or higher than the principal set-point value. These sec-

327

ondary set-point values usually occur near the modal values of the patient subpopulations with high or low normal values. Knowledge of secondary set-point values is of value in identifying potential risk factors (see below), but those values are not reported in the literature.

Response to Perturbational Stresses

Homeostatic systems are structured to assure the maintenance of a constant basal state, and much can be learned about the functional integrity of a system by subjecting it to some standard change and observing how it responds to and recovers from the change. The glucose tolerance test is a common example of such a test, and many such stimulation–response types of tests have been developed to diagnose specific diseases. The use of such tests in health monitoring is relatively unexplored. For example, in Figure 6, a graph of serum albumin values vs serum calcium values, both serum albumin and calcium are normally maintained within certain limits, and the bivariate reference interval is indicated. A portion of serum calcium is bound to albumin, and decreases in albumin are associated with decreases in serum calcium. The data are a representative sampling from a hospital population to illustrate the range of values commonly observed in such a population. Also shown are (a) the average shift observed in pregnancy, and (b) the changes observed in one apparently normal individual in changing from the upright and supine positions. Other apparently normal individuals show small proportionate changes in calcium and albumin values, but the changes seldom exceed the bivariate reference interval. It is quite clear then, that the normal individual whose changes are depicted responded differently than other normal individuals. The significance of this observation is of course not known, and in fact may have no practical value. The point is, however, that among the apparently healthy population there are individuals who have normal basal values but who respond to minor stress differently than do the majority and to a degree comparable with that in ill individuals or in those subject to major physiological stress such as pregnancy. Detecting such individuals is not difficult, and learning the long-term health significance of such unusual system behavior could be important.

For any stress or stimulation–response test one must (a) develop

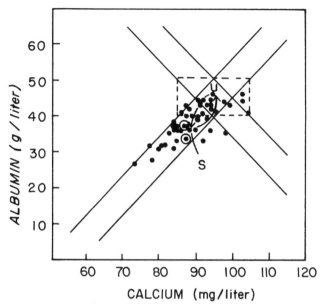

Fig. 6. Simultaneous serum albumin and calcium values in representative hospital patients (●)

The bivariate reference range for healthy young adults is indicated, as is the shift observed during pregnancy (○). *Arrows* indicate the changes observed in one apparently healthy subject when sampled in the upright *(U)* and supine positions *(S)*. Other healthy subjects did not deviate from the reference range when posture was changed. Adapted from data in references *29–31*

the most appropriate (cost-effective) testing conditions; *(b)* establish the direction, range, and deviation of the line representing the "normal" response; *(c)* establish the usual time course for recovery to basal values; and *(d)* learn the long-term health significance of aberrant responses.

The Concepts of Optimum Health and Risk of Disease

Growth and development are orderly, regulated processes that proceed according to a time schedule characteristic of the species and primarily under genetic control *(32–34)*. To a large extent, senescence—the aging processes that occur subsequent to the attainment of adulthood—is also a consequence of genetic programming, or the absence thereof *(6)*. Although individuals may differ in various aspects of their growth, development, and senescence, these processes do occur with sufficient uniformity that one can reasonably suppose that humans are genetically programmed to attain their optimum state of physiological well-being (i.e., health) at about age 20. By age 30 measurable deterioration in various physiological parameters has occurred (35). Certainly most ill individuals were, at one time in their lives, "apparently healthy young adults." This particular stage in life—young adulthood—may therefore be chosen as an ideal physiological reference point towards which younger individuals should be expected to progress, and from which older individuals will regress.

Population studies indicate that interindividual variability (of serum constituents) is minimum during the third decade, with greater dispersion occurring thereafter (36, 37). Presumably, the increased dispersion is due to individuals who are regressing from their optimum state of health; it is tempting to postulate that those who regress earliest, or deviate furthest, are most likely to become ill and are, perhaps, members of subpopulation III or II (Figure 4).

Indeed, implicit in the concept of risk factors in the etiology of disease is the belief that not all "apparently healthy young adults" will be equally susceptible to specific diseases as they grow older. Although some biochemical risk factors have been identified (e.g., increased cholesterol, triglycerides, or fasting glucose values), undoubtedly many more could be identified by critical investigation of unusual basal values, or unusual responses to standardized stress tests.

To illustrate how potential risk factors may be identified from clinical laboratory data, let us consider plasma fibrinogen. The coagulation system is a complex system of pro- and anticoagulant factors, some of which occur with fibrinogen in plasma and serve to modulate fibrinogen utilization when the system is activated by influx of tissue activators. In a simple study, an apparently healthy population was sampled for fibrinogen determination; at the same time about 100 consecutive values were determined from a group of patients (38). The patients were subsequently placed in various diagnostic categories by review of their medical records. From the healthy population, three subjects were selected whose initial fibrinogen values were in the low, mid-, and high normal

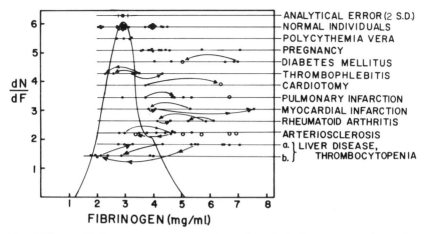

Fig. 7. Plasma fibrinogen assays: comparison of analytical error, normal population distribution curve, physiological variability of healthy individuals, and physiopathological shifts and fluctuations in categorized patients

The ordinate dN/dF was used to plot an apparent distribution curve of the plasma fibrinogen concentrations of a healthy population. The values were derived graphically, as has been described *(38)*. *Open circles* indicate patients who died in less than five weeks after analysis. *Arrows* show how individual values change

range. These subjects were sampled repeatedly over the course of a year to determine individual variability. The results of the study (Figure 7) support the following observations:

- Unlike calcium, for which a rather narrow range of values is normally observed (Figure 5), fibrinogen values are more broadly distributed. Individual members of the normal population who have low, average, or high values within the reference interval apparently maintain these steady-state values within a narrow range.
- The form of the frequency distribution curve of the healthy population obviously depends on the size of the subpopulations of individuals having particular set-point values.
- The usual set-point value may shift when the physiological state is altered, as in pregnancy. This shift is uniform and modest in most pregnant subjects, but may be large in some.
- Various shifts and fluctuations are observed in pathologic conditions, and these changes occur in characteristic patterns. For example, in rheumatoid arthritis the steady-state value

appears to have shifted upwards, and periodic modest deviations from this increased value are seen. Other patterns are seen in other conditions; for example, in some forms of liver disease, rather large fluctuations occur as the coagulation system becomes activated and then returns to a quiescent state.

Given this brief overview of fibrinogen values in health and disease, and noting that increased values are more commonly seen in disease than are decreased values and that the values are less stable in disease than in health, one might ask: If fibrinogen were an indicator of the presence of disease, or a risk factor for future disease, then which members of the present healthy population are the most likely candidates to develop disease?

I believe the most likely candidates are those with "high-normal" values. The "bump" on the upper tail of the normal distribution curve is indicative of a substantial subpopulation of such individuals (estimated at 15% of the healthy population). These individuals maintain values that are distinctly different from the majority of healthy subjects and are more like values seen in chronic disease conditions such as diabetes, arthritis, and arteriosclerosis; moreover, individual variability appears greater than in other normal subjects. As a matter of fact, individuals with latent occlusive vascular disease are known to have "high-normal" fibrinogen values (39, 40). It follows, therefore, that individuals having persistent "high-normal" fibrinogen values carry a certain risk for occlusive vascular disease.[1] If so, the "high-normal" subpopulation really should be excluded from the estimation of the normal or reference range.

Thus, I suggest that a study of the distribution of analytical values in health and disease, and of the characteristic changes that occur in disease, should greatly facilitate the identification of those hypo- and hyperanalyte subpopulations of apparently healthy subjects who differ from the majority of truly healthy subjects, and who are presumably at greatest risk for early devel-

---

[1] The data for the case of myocardial infarction in Figure 7 were acquired in 1964 when the "high-normal" subject was 38 years old and in apparent good health. Subsequently, this man had three confirmed myocardial infarctions at the ages of 44, 48, and 53. Additional assays of fibrinogen during the past 15 years all indicated values within the range illustrated for this individual. Thus, in this case, the chronically increased plasma fibrinogen set-point value apparently was predictive of risk for episodic vascular occlusion.

opment of overt disease. Once identified, these subpopulations could be followed prospectively to determine whether their unusual values were in fact predictors of future disease, disability, or premature death.

Clinical Chemistry Requirements for the Development of a Lifetime Health-Monitoring Program

Currently, "health-monitoring" in clinical chemistry usually consists of acquiring a limited "biochemical profile" of a dozen or so common analytes in serum, and a few qualitative tests of urine (41). Little attention is paid to the relationships between serum and urine constituents, nor are further chemistry tests performed unless indicated by the results of the initial battery of tests or by clinical findings. The usual result is that individuals are pronounced "in good health—for your age" and sent on their way for another year. This cursory type of health evaluation seems rather primitive, and not surprisingly, its efficacy is sometimes questioned. The procedure is designed primarily to detect clearly emergent major medical problems, not to assess the individual's health at a particular stage in the life-course. There is much room for development of effective health-monitoring techniques.

In the preceding sections I have reviewed some basic concepts that seem relevant to the effective use of clinical laboratory science for long-term health monitoring. With these concepts in mind, let us consider just what areas of clinical chemistry are in need of further development if an effective lifetime monitoring program is to evolve.

1. *Long-term accuracy and precision of measurements.* Any quantitative measurement that is to be made repeatedly over a long period of time must be adequately reproducible. Clinical laboratories have participated in quality control and interlaboratory survey programs for many years, and there is excellent documentation of steady improvement in the quality of measurements (42, 43). This improvement is probably related to the abandonment of less-reliable methods, the development of improved methods, the development of more sophisticated and reliable instrumentation, and an improved analytical expertise of the analysts.

A "national measurement system," recently implemented in

clinical chemistry, calls for the development of reference methods and materials involving a wide range of analytes *(44)*, and standards for the acceptable limits of analytical variability are being developed *(14)*. Thus, we are apparently well on our way towards adequate accuracy and precision of measurements.

2. *Batteries of tests appropriate for particular stages of life.* The health-service needs of individuals vary from stage to stage of the life span and among life circumstances, as do the risks for specific diseases *(45)*. To my knowledge, there has never been a listing of the specific laboratory services that should be generally available to individuals in each stage of life. Each newborn enters the world with certain health potentials and liabilities; it is important to the individual and to society that those qualities be assessed and, further, that the potentials be maximized and the liabilities minimized. Yet only recently has neonatal hypothyroidism, for example, been recognized as a significant, correctable problem *(46)*. Undoubtedly, as laboratory data are scrutinized more closely, other treatable conditions will be recognized.

Similarly, pregnancy is a common condition among women and is accompanied by profound physiologic alterations with long-term significance for both mother and child (both maternal and neonatal morbidity and mortality are still major medical problems). Values for specific analytes usually show a large dispersion *(36, 47)* among pregnant women, indicating a wide variation amongst individuals in this physiologic state, and the reference intervals used clinically are correspondingly wide. Yet there is surely an "optimum" course for pregnancy, which could be rather exactly defined by appropriate laboratory testing and by more incisive analysis of laboratory data; as a consequence, the detection of high-risk pregnancies might be easier and their clinical management improved.

It is far beyond the scope of this presentation to present detailed suggestions for specific tests for each of the seven stages of life; suffice it to note that this is an area that is in need of much development.

3. *Efficient batteries of tests.* Once such batteries have been identified, cost-effective testing strategies must be devised. Obviously, it is impractical to repeatedly perform all possible tests on each subject. Rather, tests should be scheduled in a way that is appropriate to the individual, depending on life stage, life circumstances,

22. Cotlove, E., Harris, E. K., and Williams, G. Z., Biological and analytical components of variation in long-term studies of serum constituents in normal subjects. III. Physiological and medical implications. *Clin. Chem.* **16**, 1028–1032 (1970).

23. Young, D. S., Harris, E. K., and Cotlove, E., Biological and analytical components of variation in long-term studies of serum constituents in normal subjects. IV. Results of a study designed to eliminate long-term analytic deviations. *Clin. Chem.* **17**, 403–410 (1971).

24. Statland, B. E., Winkel, P., and Bokelund, H., Factors contributing to intra-individual variation of serum constituents. 1. Within-day variation of serum constituents in healthy subjects. *Clin. Chem.* **19**, 1374–1379 (1973).

25. Statland, B. E., Winkel, P., and Bokelund, H., Factors contributing to intra-individual variation of serum constituents. 2. Effects of exercise and diet on variations of serum constituents in healthy subjects. *Clin. Chem.* **19**, 1380–1383 (1973).

26. Bokelund, H., Winkel, P., and Statland, B. E., Factors contributing to intra-individual variation of serum constituents. 3. Use of randomized duplicate serum specimens to evaluate sources of analytical error. *Clin. Chem.* **20**, 1507–1512 (1974).

27. Statland, B. E., Bokelund, H., and Winkel, P., Factors contributing to intra-individual variation of serum constituents. 4. Effects of posture and tourniquet application on variation of serum constituents in healthy subjects. *Clin. Chem.* **20**, 1513–1519 (1974).

28. Winkel, P., Statland, B. E., and Bokelund, H., Factors contributing to intra-individual variation of serum constituents. 5. Short-term day-to-day and within-hour variation of serum constituents in healthy subjects. *Clin. Chem.* **20**, 1520–1527 (1974).

29. Grannis, G. F., and Lott, J. A., An interlaboratory comparison of analyses of clinical specimens. *Am. J. Clin. Pathol.* **70**, 567–576 (1978).

30. Humphrey, K. R., Gruemer, H.-D., and Lott, J. A., Impact of posture on the "reference range" for serum proteins and calcium. *Clin. Chem.* **23**, 1343–1346 (1977).

31. Renoe, B. W., McDonald, J. M., and Ladenson, J. H., Influence of posture on free calcium and related variables. *Clin. Chem.* **25**, 1766–1769 (1979).

32. Needham, A. E., *The Growth Process in Animals.* D. Van Nostrand Co., Inc., Princeton, NJ, 1964, chap. 24.

33. Timiras, P. S., In *Developmental Physiology and Aging* (see ref. *8*), chap. 20 and 21.

34. Katchadourian, H., *The Biology of Adolescence.* W. H. Freeman and Co., San Francisco, CA, 1977.

337

35. Shock, N. W., Systems integration. In *Handbook of the Biology of Aging*, C. E. Finch and L. Hayflick, Eds., Van Nostrand Reinhold Co., New York, NY, 1977, chap. 25.

36. O'Kell, R. T., and Elliott, J. R., Development of normal values for use in multitest biochemical screening of sera. *Clin. Chem.* **16**, 161–165 (1970).

37. Gillibrand, D., Grewal, D., and Blattler, D. P., Chemistry reference values as a function of age and sex including pediatric and geriatric subjects. Pp 366–389, this volume.

38. Grannis, G. F., Plasma fibrinogen: Determination, normal values, physiopathologic shifts, and fluctuations. *Clin. Chem.* **16**, 486–494 (1970).

39. McDonald, L., and Edgill, M., Coagulability of the blood in ischaemic heart disease. *Lancet* **ii**, 457 (1957).

40. McDonald, L., Blood coagulation changes in thrombosis. In *Biological Aspects of Occlusive Vascular Disease*, D. G. Chalmers and G. A. Greshann, Eds., Cambridge University Press, New York, NY, 1964, p 191.

41. Collen, M. F., Cost effectiveness of multiphase health testing. In *Clinician and Chemist*, D. S. Young, D. Uddin, H. Nipper, and J. Hicks, Eds., American Association for Clinical Chemistry, Washington, DC, 1979, pp 121–130.

42. Gilbert, R. K., The accuracy of clinical laboratories studied by comparison with definitive methods. *Am. J. Clin. Pathol.* **70**, 450–470 (1978).

43. Grannis, G. F., and Statland, B. E., Monitoring the quality of laboratory measurements. In *Clinical Diagnosis and Laboratory Management by Laboratory Methods*, J. B. Henry, Ed., W. B. Saunders Co., Philadelphia, PA, 1979, pp 2049–2068.

44. Boutwell, J. H., Ed., *A National Understanding for the Development of Reference Materials and Methods for Clinical Chemistry*. American Association for Clinical Chemistry, Washington, DC, 1978.

45. Upton, A. C., Pathobiology. In *Handbook of the Biology of Aging* (see ref. *35*), chap. 21.

46. Hayles, A. B., and Cloutier, M. D., Clinical hypothyroidism in the young—a second look. *Med. Clin. North Am.* **56**, 871–884 (1972).

47. Dickey, R. P., Grannis, G. F., and Hanson, F. W., The estrogen/creatinine ratio and the estrogen index for screening normal and high risk pregnancy. *Am. J. Obstet. Gynecol.* **113**, 880–886 (1972).

48. Riggs, D. S., *Mathematical Approach to Physiological Problems*. Williams and Wilkins, Baltimore, MD, 1963.

49. Martin, H. F., Gudzinowicz, B. J., and Fanger, H., *Normal Values in Clinical Chemistry*. Marcel Dekker, Inc., New York, NY, 1975.

50. Grams, R. R., Johnson, E. A., and Benson, E. S., Laboratory data

analysis system: IV. Multivariate diagnosis. *Am. J. Clin. Pathol.* **58,** 201–207 (1972).

51. Ladenson, J. H., Lewis, J. W., and Boyd, J. C., Initial studies of test selection and pattern recognition in the differential diagnosis of hypercalcemia. In *Logic and Economics of Clinical Laboratory Use* (see ref. *19*), pp 187–196.

The Study of Body-Fluid Composition in Aging Humans. II. The Biogyron: Concept and Examples in Clinical Chemistry

George F. Grannis

In dealing with complex problems, it is sometimes useful to review basic concepts, make simplifying assumptions and inferences, and develop general hypotheses that permit quantitative description of the situation. By provoking thought and opening new avenues of scientific inquiry, this strategy can sometimes facilitate further investigations *(1)*. I shall describe such a unifying hypothesis—the concept of the biogyron (Greek: *bios* + *gyrus* + *—on:* a structure generated by the functional gyrations of homeostatic biological systems viewed through time)—and present some examples of biogyronic systems.

Basic Concepts and Simplifying Assumptions

Genetic Messages

Genetic material contains many "messages," some easily demonstrated and others only inferred. For example, at the molecular level the genetic control of protein synthesis and structure is abundantly documented. Similarly, for organisms, the processes of prenatal differentiation and morphogenesis and postnatal growth and development are known to involve timed, sequential events that are subject to genetic control *(2, 3)*. Programmed cellular death is an essential feature of morphogenesis *(4)* and, because all somatic cells are believed to carry a full complement of genetic information *(5)*, one may infer that all somatic cells carry a specific program for cellular death, although the program must normally be suppressed in most cell types. The whole-body phenomena of bilateral symmetry, "handedness," and instinctive behavior are other evidence of powerful genetic messages transmitted from the molecular level to the organism level, messages whose integrity must be maintained for many years.

Homeostasis is such a universal phenomenon among life forms and is so essential for long-term survival that it, too, must surely be specified genetically. Physiological systems are probably structured to behave homeostatically because the genetic material is itself structured to produce cohesive, integrated physiological systems. Perhaps there is a basic, inescapable genetic "message," inherent in the genetic structure, to specify that the normal organism that ultimately develops from the union of two germ cells will possess completely integrated physiological systems structured to function homeostatically. The various genetic diseases (6) that result from incomplete physiologic systems and the consequent homeostatic failure of these systems attest to the existence and importance of this basic message.

Simple Input–Output Systems, and Homeostatic Systems

The left half of Figure 1 illustrates a simple input–output system: a reservoir in which the height of the fluid in the container is determined by the relative rates of input and output. A constant, or steady-state, volume of fluid may be contained in the reservoir, but this occurrence would be purely fortuitous, because neither input nor output is controlled. The right side of Figure 1 illustrates the same system, but with added components that assure homeostatic behavior. The input and output pipes are equipped with regulators; a sensor responds to the fluid height in the reservoir and, through a control device, causes adjustments of the regulators to maintain the fluid at a constant height, within certain limits fixed by the sensitivity of the sensor and the responsiveness of the control and regulatory devices. The simple input–output system is now designed, or structured, to behave homeostatically, i.e., to maintain a constant volume of fluid in the reservoir, even with a dynamically changing flux of material through the system.

The principal body fluids analyzed by clinical chemists—blood and urine—may be viewed as components of homeostatically regulated systems in which blood plasma respresents a fluid reservoir and urine represents the system's output. However, in addition

341

INPUT–OUTPUT SYSTEMS

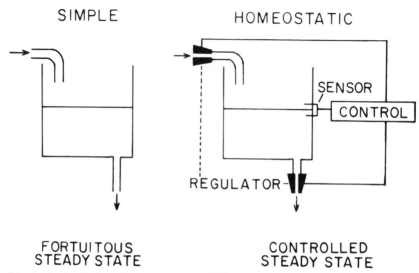

Fig. 1. A simple input–output system *(left)*, a reservoir with input and output pipes, in which the occurrence of a steady-state volume of fluid in the reservoir is purely fortuitous; *(right)* a homeostatic system in which sensory, control, and regulatory mechanisms assure a constant volume of fluid

to the regulation of fluid volumes, the many individual components of these fluids are also subject to various ancillary regulatory controls, which normally maintain the amounts, concentrations, or proportions of these components at relatively constant values.

Mathematical Statements of Homeostasis

There are two basic statements of biochemical homeostasis, graphically illustrated in Figure 2. The left diagram illustrates the classical statement that the changes in concentration of some component, d(A), over some time interval, dt, tend to equal zero. That is, the concentration of A is maintained at a constant set-point value, within certain limits of variability; when excursions beyond these limits occur, compensatory adjustments return the concentration of A to the original set-point value. When the analyte concentration, [A], is graphed as a function of time, the mean basal value and limits define a univariate normal zone of function. The blood glucose concentration and the changes that occur after

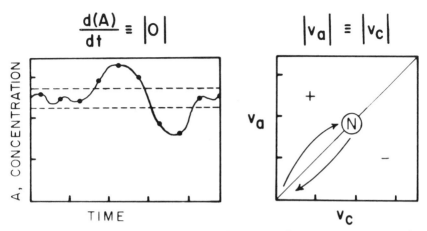

Fig. 2. Classical statement of homeostasis *(left)* and an alternative statement *(right)*

glucose ingestion are a common example, but the equation is generally applicable to all blood constituents.

An alternative statement of homeostatic behavior is given in the right half of Figure 2, by the equation:

$$|v_a| \equiv |v_c| \qquad (1)$$

This equation states that, although anabolic and catabolic rates (v_a and v_c) may differ from one another momentarily, they will, over a period of time, be maintained within certain basal limits, and they tend to equal one another. When v_a and v_c are graphed, as on the right of Figure 2, the basal mean values and limits define a bivariate normal zone of function, N, which is situated on the line of equivalence of v_a and v_c. The usual balance between calorie intake and expenditure is a common example of equation 1. Intake (v_a) and expenditure (v_c) may have different average values for different individuals (i.e., different normal zones, N), but these values should fall along the line of equivalence to v_a and v_c. Values above the line ($v_a > v_c$) indicate weight gain; values below the line ($v_c > v_a$) indicate weight loss.

Biochemical Correlates of Metabolic Rates

Consider the simple reaction sequence:

$$A \xrightarrow{\text{enzyme 1}} B \xrightarrow{\text{enzyme 2}} C$$

in which substrate A is converted by enzyme 1 to intermediate B, which is further converted by enzyme 2 to product C. In a simple closed system, the rate of formation of B, or rate of input, v_i, is given by $v_i = E_1[A]$ and the rate of utilization of B, or rate of output, v_o, is given by $v_o = E_2[B]$ in which E_1 and E_2 are the first-order rate constants of the enzyme activities and

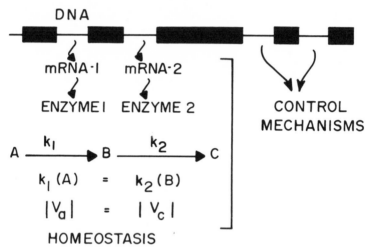

Fig. 3. Conceptualization of the direct relationship between genetic information and the homeostatic behavior of physiologic systems: the genetic material specifies the components of physiological systems and the various control mechanisms that assure that the systems function homeostatically

[A] and [B] are concentrations of substrates. At some time a transient steady state will occur, in which $v_i = v_o$ and $E_1[A] = E_2[B]$.

It is clear from these last two equations the relationship of the rates of input and output are functions of the activities of enzymes 1 and 2, and of the concentrations of A and B. All are *biochemical correlates* of the process rates. Thus, rather than graphing rates (which may be difficult to determine), as illustrated on the right side of Figure 2, we may graph their biochemical correlates (which may be easier to measure) and expect to see comparable relationships. Figure 3 illustrates these basic concepts: that the genetic material specifies the components of the physiologic system, as well as a variety of control mechanisms, and that the integrated, controlled systems function in a manner that is implicit in equation 1. Because of these basic relationships, we may know that when various related system components are graphed, we should be able to define a normal zone of function, presumably situated on some line of physiologic equivalence, and that unusual deviations from normal should be indicative of system dysfunction.

Physiological States

In general, a physiological system may exist in five functional states: the normal state (N), the compensated hypofunctional state, the compensated hyperfunctional state, the uncompensated hypofunctional state, and the uncompensated hyperfunctional state. These five states are illustrated in Figure 4, in which some biochemical correlate of input y, is graphed against some biochemical correlate of output x. Both x and y are presumed to oscillate within limits, as illustrated in Figure 2 *(left)*, and the coordinated oscillatory changes in these parameters result in gyratory fluctuations of the point (x, y) about the normal zone (Figure 2, *right*). These fluctuations, observed in defined "normal" conditions, define the normal zone of function.

A decrease or increase in y should ordinarily be compensated by a subsequent decrease or increase in x. Consequently, a *sustained* decrease (or increase) in y will shift the zone of system function down (or up) the line of equivalence and the system will then exist in the compensated hypo- (or hyper-) functional states (designated 2 and 3 in Figure 4). If compensation does not occur, perhaps because of dysfunction of the system, then a sustained decrease (or increase) in y will shift the zone of function to the uncompensated states 4 and 5 (Figure 4).

Thus, Figure 4 illustrates how, when appropriate parameters are graphed vs one another, the distribution of data can be related to specific states of system function.

Changes in the Normal State

Mean values of some physiological parameters change with age; indeed, physiological age has been estimated by multivariate analysis of such parameters (7, 8). For example, Figure 5 shows the

345

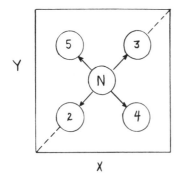

Fig. 4. Five principal states of function of physiological systems

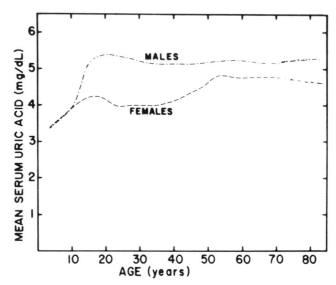

Fig. 5. Mean serum urate values as a function of age

Source: Grannis and Lott (9)

mean values for serum urate concentration in men and women as a function of age. The changes are clearly related to some stages of the human life-course (described in Figure 4 of the preceding chapter in this book). Serum urate concentration is a reflection of the relative rates of input and output of urate in blood. Changes in these mean values, associated with growth and menopause, indicate that the relative rates of input and output have also changed. Thus, the normal or usual state may change during

346

the life-course. One major problem in the interpretation of laboratory data is to ascertain whether such "usual" changes are also
"normal."

The Biogyron

The parameters clinical chemists measure are, to a large extent,
components of homeostatic input–output systems. The funda-

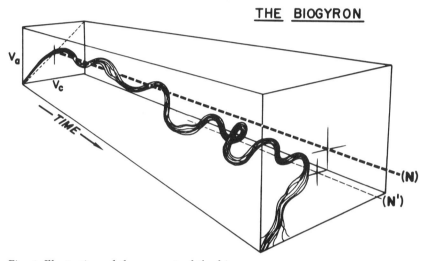

THE BIOGYRON

Fig. 6. Illustration of the concept of the biogyron

A graph of biochemical correlates of anabolic and catabolic processes (v_a and v_c, respectively) defines a zone representing the state of function of the system. When multiple
parameters are graphed, and the data followed through time, the data generate a unique
structure, the biogyron (see text)

mental and bivariate nature of homeostasis (equation 1 and Figure
3) assures that these parameters can be conceptualized in the format of Figure 2 *(right);* data graphed in this format may define
major states of physiological function and indicate significant deviations from normal (Figure 4).

If one observed in this unique perspective the states of function
of several systems of an individual over the course of his or her
lifetime, what sort of changes might occur? I have attempted to
illustrate in Figure 6 how, when the state of system function is
dimensioned through time, the normal zone sweeps out a structure
I have called the biogyron. The form the biogyron assumes de-

347

pends on the nature and adequacy of the specific control mechanisms that are necessary for homeostatic behavior, on the external and internal stresses to which the systems are subjected, and on the physiologic and pathologic changes that may occur. Because young adulthood seems to be the period of maximum physiological well-being, the optimum (most stable) structure probably occurs at this time. As the life-course unfolds, the normal state of function may shift (N'), with progressive degeneration of the structure as the systems increasingly go awry. The point is, a definite multicomponent structure, representing physiological normalcy, can be conceptualized in quantitative terms. Studies of this structure should help our understanding of various life phenomena, including senescence.

Examples of Biogyronic Systems

Metabolically related components in blood. The principal processes involved in bilirubin metabolism are summarized by the equations at the top of Figure 7. Heme, derived from hemoglobin degradation, is converted to bilirubin, which is normally conjugated with glucuronide in the liver and excreted in the bile or urine. Bilirubin and conjugated bilirubin are the principal metabolic intermediates in this system, and both are present in the blood and commonly used to evaluate the state of system function.

In Figure 7 the concentration of bilirubin (indirect) is plotted vs the concentration of conjugated bilirubin (direct). Some standard state, S, exists, the result of the balance between the processes of hemoglobin degradation, glucuronidation, and biliary (or, to a lesser extent, urinary) clearance. Usually, hemoglobin degradation proceeds at a low rate; conjugation and clearance are efficient; and, consequently, the normal state, N, is at the lower left corner of the chart. In abnormal situations, such as increased input, diminished conjugation, or decreased clearance, we should expect to see characteristic deviations from the normal state.

Figure 8 illustrates such deviations. The condition of the patient, a newborn suffering severe hemolysis, was monitored by frequent determinations of direct and indirect bilirubin. The patient was treated by exchange transfusion on days 1 and 4 (X-1, X-2). During the first four days of life the concentrations of direct and indirect bilirubin steadily increased, and the ratio of indirect to direct was generally constant at about 2.0. By a few hours after the

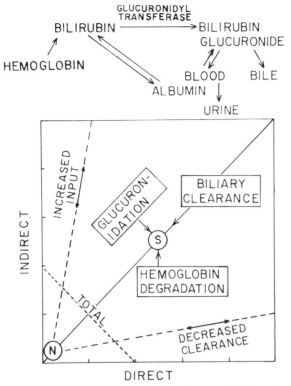

Fig. 7. Conceptualization of bilirubin metabolism in
a gyronic perspective

(Top) In the course of hemoglobin catabolism two intermediates (bilirubin and conjugated bilirubin) are present in blood. *(Bottom)* When the concentrations of these intermediates are graphed (indirect = bilirubin, direct = conjugated bilirubin), the bivariate zone of system function, S, is determined by the relative rates of hemoglobin degradation (input), glucuronidation (conversion), and clearance (output). N indicates the normal zone of function, in which both intermediates are present at low concentrations. Various pathological perturbations of the rate processes should cause characteristic deviations from the normal zone

second transfusion, the ratio changed to 0.5; this value was maintained until the patient's discharge. The glucuronidation system is often not fully functional in the newborn, and this deficiency is particularly hazardous when the infant is subjected to hemolytic stress such that bilirubin concentration exceeds the binding capacity of serum albumin, and kernicterus develops. In the above example the glucuronidation system apparently became active on

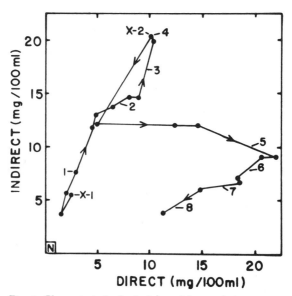

Fig. 8. Characteristic deviations of direct and indirect bilirubin values in neonatal hyperbilirubinemia

Numbers indicate days of hospitalization; X-1 and X-2 indicate exchange transfusions

the fourth day, and the altered state of function was maintained even in the face of continuing hemolysis, as evidenced by the large post-transfusion increase in total bilirubin.

I selected this case to show that there is a normal basal state, and that two distinct states of system function became apparent under stress: one in which glucuronidation is not fully effective, with the data closely following the line of slope 2.0; and another in which glucuronidation is fully effective, with the data following the line of slope 0.5. These two states of function, as well as transitions between the states, are regularly observed in routine clinical laboratory data. Observing such changes in individuals is useful in understanding the adequacy of their systems.

Physiologically related components—the blood coagulation system. The blood coagulation system is composed of several pro- and anticoagulant factors; under physiological conditions the concentrations of these factors are regulated to maintain a normal state of blood coagulability *(10–12)*. The fibrinolytic system is also composed of pro- and antifibrinolytic factors, which may be regulated to maintain a normal state of fibrinolytic capability; presumably, there is a balance between the coagulation and fibrinolytic systems (13, 14). The data presented in Figure 7 of the preceding chapter illustrate that the central component of these systems, fibrinogen, is closely modulated in health and undergoes various characteristic deviations from normal in disease.

The concept of coagulation balance is simply that the coagulability of blood is related to the ratio of procoagulant and anticoagulant activities. If a balance exists, measurements of these activities in normal subjects should fall within some normal zone, N, situated along a line of equivalence. Deviations above or below the line represent hyper- and hypocoagulable states, respectively— increased susceptibility to thrombosis or hemorrhage.

In the reactions leading to fibrin formation, the rate of fibrin formation, v_f, in plasma samples subjected to a controlled thromboplastic stimulus is described by the equation:

$$v_f = k_2 PF/t_0 k_1 \qquad (2)$$

in which t_0 is the time required to generate thromboplastic activity, k_2 is the rate constant of thromboplastic activity, P and F are prothrombin and fibrinogen concentrations, respectively, and k_1 is the rate constant of antithrombin activity (15–20).

Figure 9 shows representative results obtained when the coagulation balance in dogs was perturbed either by injecting fibrinogen to increase coagulability, or heparin[1] to decrease coagulability. Under the conditions of the experiments, k_2 and t_0 were constant and directly proportional to platelet concentration. When the normal balance was challenged by decreasing (Figure 9A) or increasing (Figure 9B) the ratio of antithrombin to fibrinogen (k_1/F), the balance was initially restored by a decrease or increase, respectively, in platelet concentration, after which the concentration returned towards the initial state along the line of equivalence of pro- and anticoagulant activities.

Many enzymes and peptide hormones (such as the digestive enzymes, kallikrein and the complement systems, pro-insulin, etc.), like the components of the coagulation system, are synthesized as inactive precursors and then converted to physiologically active intermediates whose existence is transient because of inacti-

---

[1] Heparin in this low dosage increases antithrombin activity, with no measurable effect on thromboplastin generation (18).

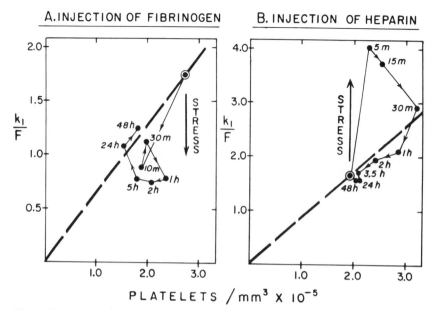

A. INJECTION OF FIBRINOGEN   B. INJECTION OF HEPARIN

Fig. 9. Response in dogs to a change in the ratio of procoagulant to anticoagulant activities, based on measurements of antithrombin, fibrinogen, and platelets

⊙, the initial normal state; a hypothetical line of equivalence is drawn through this point to the origin. The responses to injection of fibrinogen (A) and to heparin (B) show how the balance was rapidly restored, and then progressed along the line of equivalence towards the initial state. k_1/F, ratio of antithrombin to fibrinogen

vating or clearance mechanisms. Just as a balance is maintained for blood coagulability, so a balance undoubtedly exists among the components of these other, similarly structured systems.

Evaluation of function of specific cell types. One common way of evaluating a system is to subject it to some standard perturbation and to observe the response of the system. The glucose tolerance test is a common example of such a test. The response is, of course, modulated by hormones, and in the case of glucose, insulin and glucagon are the *primary* hormones responsible for regulation of blood glucose concentration. Figure 10 illustrates a conceptualization of possible relationships between blood glucose concentration and the activities of these two hormones. The equations at the top of Figure 10 state that the input of blood glucose, ν_i, is some function of tissue glycogen stores and glucagon activity, and that the output of blood glucose, ν_o, is some function of blood glucose concentration and insulin activity. Blood glucose concentration,

$$V_i = V_o$$

$$GLYCOGEN \times GLUCAGON = GLUCOSE \times INSULIN$$

$$GLUCOSE = GLYCOGEN \times \frac{GLUCAGON}{INSULIN}$$

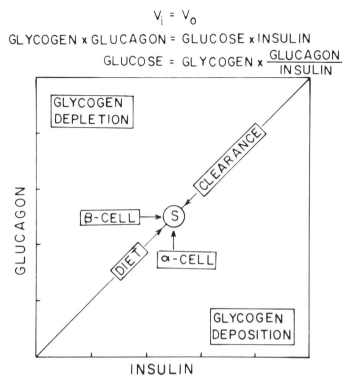

Fig. 10. Conceptualization of pancreatic α- and β-cell function in glucose metabolism, in a gyronic format

then, is related to glycogen availability and the ratio of glucagon activity to insulin activity.

From this relationship, we can plot glucagon activity vs insulin activity (Figure 10), and expect to find, under defined standard conditions, a standard state existing along a line of proportionality of glucagon to insulin. The standard state is maintained by a balance of factors such as diet; the insulin- and glucagon-releasing activities of the α and β cells, respectively, of the pancreatic islets; and the rates of clearance of the hormones from the blood. Extended deviations from this relationship should favor states of glycogen accumulation or depletion, as indicated in the illustration. With blood constituents that are subject to control (i.e., glucose), it is the deviation from normalcy that indicates abnormality. However, with the primary controllers themselves (i.e., glucagon

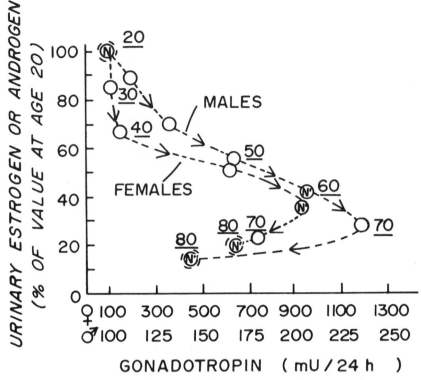

Fig. 11. Changes in the urinary output of gonadotropins and androgens or estrogens in men and women at various ages

N, N′, N″, sequential "normal" states; numbers by points indicate subjects' ages. Adapted from data in Figures 27–1 and 27–2 of ref. *21*

and insulin), the *failure* to deviate from normalcy under stress is indicative of abnormality.

Assessment of hormone production. Physiologic systems are regulated, in part, by hormones produced by specific cell types; no doubt, some of the changes associated with aging will be traced to changes in these cell populations. The interplay between the trophic hormones of the anterior pituitary and the hormones of their target glands (thyroid, adrenal cortex, gonads) should be particularly interesting. Figure 11 shows reported changes in the excretion of gonadotropins and gonadal hormones in men and women as a function of age. Normally, decreases in concentrations of gonadal hormones in blood cause release of pituitary gonadotropin, which stimulates an increase in the gonadal hormones. The latter increase then signals a decrease in the release of pituitary hormone, which results in a decrease of the gonadal hormones. By means of this negative feedback control, the system is structured to assure that in the normal state, N, both gonadotropins and gonadal hormones will be maintained within specified concentration limits.

Figure 11 shows that the urinary output of gonadal hormones, after age 20, steadily decreases in both men and women. In both sexes, the output of gonadotropins increases until about age 70, after which the gonadotropins also decrease; this is how the "normal" or usual state changes (to N', N", etc.) throughout the lifecourse. Thus, although the feedback mechanism may remain intact during aging, the overall state of function of the system changes dramatically. The curves these data describe closely parallel the human mortality curves (see the preceding chapter), and it should be informative to learn how the functional states of other similarly structured endocrine-control systems change with age.

Conclusions

The phenomenon of human aging is one of the more challenging of the unsolved biomedical problems. The problem is important not only because of the implications of increased longevity to human societies, but also because aging changes are involved in, and may be prerequisite for, the development and progression of diseases of the elderly. Thus it is important to understand how physiologic systems change with age, how their functional capabilities and limitations change, and how the changes relate to health, disease, and disease management.

I have developed the concept of the biogyron as a unifying hypothesis to bring together diverse observations into a common perspective. The concept is derived from a fundamental statement of homeostasis (equation 1), and is an extension of well-accepted concepts in physiology (Figure 3). There are numerous examples in the literature of data that can be presented in the format of Figure 2 *(right)* and interpreted in the perspective of Figures 4 and 6. The examples selected (Figures 7–11) illustrate how the concept can be applied to a variety of system parameters.

Physiologic systems do not function independently of one another, and the biogyron is intended to represent the functional state of these systems *as a whole.* Functional relationships between regulatory parameters (e.g., Figure 11) and parameters regulated (e.g., coagulation and hemolysis) probably change as the organism ages. The concept of the biogyron should facilitate the study of these complex functional and temporal relationships. I imagine that as the human life-course progresses, the biogyron rhythmically expands, contracts, and undulates as the integrated systems respond to environmental and internal stresses, physiologic signals, and pathologic perturbations. With aging and deterioration of controlled response, shifts of the "normal" zones of function of various systems occur, the systems' abilities to respond appropriately diminish, and the responses become increasingly bizarre; the biogyron undergoes progressive bifurcations and disintegration as the natural limit to the life span is approached.

The mathematics necessary for the description of gyronic structures is well advanced *(22).* Investigations of the characterization, optimization, and stabilization of biogyronic systems should facilitate our understanding and mastery of problems of health maintenance, life improvement, and life-span extension.

References

1. Plass, J. R., Strong inference. In *The Step to Man,* John Wiley and Sons, Inc., New York, NY, 1966, pp 19–36.
2. Needham, A. E., *The Growth Process in Animals.* D. Van Nostrand Co., Inc., New York, NY, 1964.
3. Timiras, P. S., *Developmental Physiology and Aging,* MacMillan Co., New York, NY, 1972, pp 375–405.
4. Saunders, J. W., Jr., Cell death in embryos: Accelerated senescence? In *Topics in the Biology of Aging,* P. L. Krohn, Ed., Interscience/John Wiley and Sons, Inc., New York, NY, 1966, pp 159–162.
5. Borek, E., What every cell knows. In *The Sculpture of Life,* Columbia University Press, New York, NY, 1973, pp 1–31.
6. Stanbury, J. B., Wyngaarden, J. B., and Frederickson, D. S., Eds., *The Metabolic Basis of Inherited Disease.* McGraw-Hill, New York, NY, 1972.
7. Furukawa, T., Inoue, M., Kajiya, F., Inada, H., Tagasugi, S., Fukui, S., Takeda, H., and Abe, H., Assessment of biological age by multiple regression analysis. *J. Gerontol.* **30**, 422–434 (1975).

8. Comfort, A., *The Biology of Senescence,* 3rd ed., Elsevier North-Holland, Inc., New York, NY, 1979, pp 299–318.

9. Grannis, G. F., and Lott, J. A., A collaborative approach for the establishment of reference values for defined categories of patients. In *Logic and Economics of Clinical Laboratory Use,* E. S. Benson and M. Rubin, Eds., Elsevier North-Holland, Inc., New York, NY, 1978, pp 203–214.

10. Astrup, T., The haemostatic balance. *Thromb. Diath. Haemorrh. (Stuttg.)* **2,** 347–357 (1958).

11. Alexander, B., Blood coagulation and thrombotic disease. *Circulation* **25,** 872–890 (1962).

12. Hjort, P. F., and Hasselback, R., A critical review of evidence for a continuous hemostasis in vivo. *Thromb. Diath. Haemorrh. (Stuttg.)* **6,** 580–612 (1961).

13. Jensen, H., Dynamic concept of fibrin formation and lysis in relation to haemorrhage and thrombosis. *Exp. Med. Surg.* **14,** 189–201 (1956).

14. Roos, J., Blood coagulation as a continuous process. *Thromb. Diath. Haemorrh. (Stuttg.)* **1,** 471–481 (1957).

15. Grannis, G. F., Kazal, L. A., and Tocantins, L. M., The spectrophotometric determination of thrombin activity in plasma. *Thromb. Diath. Haemorrh. (Stuttg.)* **13,** 330–342 (1965).

16. Kazal, L. A., Grannis, G. F., and Tocantins, L. M., The reactions of thrombin with fibrinogen and plasma antithrombin. *Thromb. Diath. Haemorrh. (Stuttg.)* **13,** 343–360 (1965).

17. Grannis, G. F., Kazal, L. A., and Tocantins, L. M., The kinetics of thrombin activity in recalcified blood plasma. *Thromb. Diath. Haemorrh. (Stuttg.)* **13,** 361–372 (1965).

18. Grannis, G. F., and Kazal, L. A., Prothrombin and antithrombin: Their opposing functions in blood coagulation. *Thromb. Diath. Haemorrh. (Stuttg.)* **16,** 497–506 (1966).

19. Grannis, G. F., and Kazal, L. A., The fibrinotic index and evidence for a blanced regulation of coagulation activities. *Thromb. Diath. Haemorrh. (Stuttg.)* **14,** 52–64 (1965).

20. Grannis, G. F., and Kazal, L. A., A theoretical experimental approach to blood coagulation. *Trans. N. Y. Acad. Sci.* **27,** 607–612 (1965).

21. Timiras, P. S., Changes in gonadal function. In *Developmental Physiology and Aging* (see ref. *3*), pp 527–541.

22. Gurel, O., and Rossler, O. E., Eds., *Bifurcation Theory and Applications in Scientific Disciplines (Ann. N. Y. Acad. Sci.* **316**), 1979. The following papers are of particular relevance: Gurel, O., Poincaré's bifurcation analysis (pp 39–42); Gurel, O., Necessary and sufficient conditions for cooperative peeling of multiple generating singular points (pp

39–42); Rosen, R., Bifurcations and biological observables (pp 78–187); Hess, B., and Plesser, T., Temporal and spatial order in biochemical systems (pp 203–213); Glass, L., and Mackey, M. C., Pathological conditions resulting from instabilities in physiological control systems (pp 214–235).

Biochemical Diagnosis in the Elderly

H. Malcolm Hodkinson

In the past, elderly patients have often been less extensively investigated than their younger counterparts. Doctors have tended to regard accurate diagnosis as superfluous because of the mistaken view that diagnosis would not lead to useful therapeutic intervention. The development of geriatric medicine shows such views to be unfounded: accurate diagnosis is the basis of effective medical care in old and young alike.

The relative neglect of investigation of the elderly in the past, coupled with the greatly increased availability of admission profiles of automated biochemical tests over the past decade, has lead to a rapid expansion of our knowledge of the biochemistry of the elderly. It has also resulted in an increased recognition of the special problems of biochemical diagnosis in the elderly patient.

Only in the last 10 years or so has biochemical diagnosis in old age been put on a secure foundation by the determination of appropriate reference ranges. Earlier studies of age effects such as that of Roberts (1) stopped short at 65 years because the series was based on studies of blood donors, for whom that is the maximum age.

However, normal ranges for the elderly are now reasonably well established for the commonly used tests, and have been summarized by Caird (2) and Hodkinson (3). In general, the ranges are not very different from those for younger subjects. Even where there are significant changes with age, the magnitude of these may be insufficient to make a practical difference. For example, one of the most powerful effects is the decrease in albumin concentration with age (4); even so, the range for serum albumin in old age is only 2 or 3 g/L lower than in middle age. A practical difference occurs in the case of serum phosphate, however: this decreases progressively with age in men, but increases slightly in elderly women so that the sex difference becomes marked, ranges in old age being 0.65–1.23 mmol/L in men and 0.86–1.32 mmol/L in women (3).

Changes in normal ranges thus provide only a minor difficulty in the interpretation of biochemical tests in the elderly. More serious problems affecting biochemical diagnosis of elderly patients are related to the characteristics of the patients seen by the physician interested in geriatric medicine. These patients typically have multiple diseases and are often taking a number of different drugs. Renal function is often impaired, either from renal disease or because of dehydration. Patients are often severely ill and have considerable constitutional upset. All these characteristics are associated with special difficulties in the interpretation of biochemical test results.

Finally, it is necessary to screen for some treatable diseases in old age that cannot be reliably detected clinically (5). The relatively low prevalences of such diseases creates the need to optimize the diagnostic value of the tests used, and calls for more sophisticated interpretational strategies than the simple use of the concept of normal range.

Consequences of Drug Therapy

The elderly are often grossly overtreated. For example, in one British study 87% of people over 75 years old living at home were found to be on regular medication (6). More strikingly, 34% were on three or more drugs daily! Old people admitted to hospital are often on many different drugs; according to a multi-center British study, 12% of the elderly patients admitted to a department of geriatric medicine suffered from adverse drug effects (7).

Drugs may affect biochemical tests in many ways, by in vivo or in vitro effects, and many such effects are known (8). Particularly common examples of such disturbances in elderly patients are increases of serum thyroxine with L-DOPA treatment, and the decrease of serum phosphate and calcium and increase of thyroxine-binding globulin with stilbestrol therapy (9). Such gross effects are readily recognizable, once we have become aware of them. We probably often fail to recognize less dramatic disturbances, and we are totally ignorant as to the effects of combinations of multiple drugs.

Unrecognized drug effects may well substantially reduce the diagnostic usefulness of laboratory tests in elderly patients. For example, the range is considerably skewed upwards for free-thyroxine index in elderly in-patients, compared with well elderly subjects; this difference is very likely to be due to unrecognized drug effects (10). Moreover, the wider "normal" range decreases the value of the test in diagnosing thyrotoxicosis in elderly hospital patients.

Effects of Multiple Disease

Multiple disease may often complicate the interpretation of a test. For example, the value of alkaline phosphatase (EC 3.1.3.1) as a screening test for osteomalacia is very much diminished in the elderly patient because of the high prevalence of other diseases that also increase its concentration. Thus in 500 patients admitted to a geriatric department, osteomalacia accounted for only 14% of above-normal alkaline phosphatases in women and none of those in men (11). Liver disease, fractures, rheumatoid arthritis, and Paget's disease were all more frequent causes of increases in the enzyme. A high concentration of alkaline phosphatase in serum is thus of relatively little value in the diagnosis of osteomalacia, though determination of a normal value has considerable value in helping to exclude the presence of the disease.

Impairment of Renal Function

Renal impairment is frequent in elderly hospital patients, the 95% range for blood urea at admission being 3.1 to 20.6 mmol/L in one series of studies (3). This impairment has major effects on the concentrations of serum phosphate and urate. The distribution of serum phosphate is skewed severely upwards in elderly patients (3), significantly reducing the value of the test as a screen for osteomalacia. The value of urate in the diagnosis of gout is similarly impaired.

Effects of Severe Illness

Many elderly patients are severely ill, constitutional upset being recognizable in almost 40% of those admitted to my own department, and 19% are clinically dehydrated. Severe illness may considerably affect the biochemical findings, as a general rather than specific effect, and complicate test interpretation.

Dehydration, apart from its effects on renal function, leads to increases in values for the plasma proteins because of hemoconcentration. A spurious increase may be observed, or an abnormally low concentration may be brought back into the normal range and remain unrecognized until full hydration has been restored.

Severe illness may also lead to impaired homeostasis; for example, osmoregulation appears to be generally less efficient in old age *(12)*, and severe illness may quite often lead to marked hyponatremia.

Perhaps the most common disturbances associated with severe illness are those of the plasma proteins. Commonly, albumin and other carrier proteins such as thyroxine-binding globulin and iron-binding protein decrease. These changes appear to be non-specific effects related to the degree of constitutional disturbance produced by the illness. Indeed, decreased concentrations of these proteins have a considerable adverse prognostic significance *(13)*.

Low concentrations of carrier proteins have considerable effects on the measured values of protein-bound substances such as thyroxine, iron, and calcium. Interpretation of such values is likely to be highly unreliable in ill old people unless appropriate corrections for protein-binding changes are made. The considerable magnitude of these protein disturbances needs to be emphasized. For example, the age changes in albumin (2 to 3 g/L) are dwarfed by the changes due to illness; old people admitted to a geriatric department had a mean albumin concentration 8.3 g/L less than that of well elderly subjects *(3)*.

Screening for Treatable Diseases

Screening for clinically inapparent but treatable diseases in ill elderly patients has considerable attractions. Osteomalacia has an incidence of approximately 3% in elderly women and is often not clinically apparent. Myxedema, with an incidence of a little over 2%, is often atypical in its presentation, and only a minority of cases can be recognized without the help of screening tests *(14)*. Because diseases such as these can be serious if they remain unrecognized, and yet are eminently treatable once diagnosed, there is a sound case for screening elderly patients. Such screening presents considerable difficulty.

Clearly, interpretation depends on accurate knowledge of the normal range appropriate to age and sex. As already indicated, allowances will also need to be made for the confounding effects of drugs, disturbances due to other diseases the patient may have, changes secondary to impaired renal function, and the consequences of illness itself. Many difficulties may arise and will in general lead to a weakening of the discriminatory power of the tests we wish to use. Even when we have surmounted these difficulties, we are left with the severe limitations of interpretation related to the low prevalence of the diseases that are the targets of our screening.

These difficulties can be better understood by reference to a simple model of the test situation. Most of the tests we use do

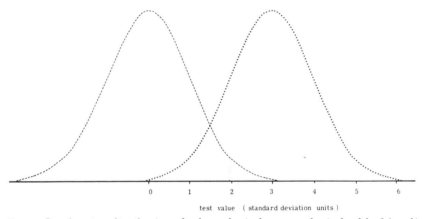

test value (standard deviation units)

Fig. 1. Overlapping distributions for hypothetical test results in health *(left peak)* and disease *(right peak)*

not discriminate particularly well between those with and without disease, and the distribution of test results in those without disease (i.e., the reference range) usually shows considerable overlap with that for subjects who have the disease. This is shown in Figure 1, where the range of values in health is shown to the left and the range in disease to the right. The two populations are shown as the same size, which is equivalent to the situation where, before the test result was known, the individual's chance of having the disease was equal to the chance of not having it. This is the sort of situation we are in when we use a test to help confirm or refute a diagnosis that is clinically strongly suspected. In mathematical language, the model shows a prior probability for disease of 0.5. Once we have the test result, we can assess a new probability for disease, the posterior probability, by looking at the relative heights under the two curves at that test value and dividing the height under the disease curve by the sum of the heights under the two curves. So, for example, a test value of 1.5, which corresponds to the intersection of the two curves, leads to an unchanged posterior probability of 0.5; lower values will give lower posterior probabilities and higher values increased ones. This point of intersection value, the *critical limit* of Murphy and Abbey *(15)*, affords a far more logical basis for interpretation in this situation than the normal limit, which is now essentially arbitrary.

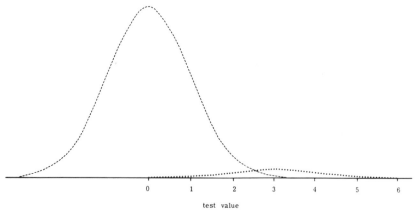

Fig. 2. Overlapping distributions for the hypothetical test when the prevalence of disease is 0.05

In contrast, Figure 2 shows the distributions for the test in a screening situation where prevalence of the disease being tested for is 5%; i.e., the right-hand population now has 5% of the combined area of both. The critical limit is now shifted to a higher value of 2.5, showing that a far more extreme test value is now needed to achieve a posterior probability of the same magnitude as before. In other words, the discriminatory power of the test is greatly reduced when prevalence of disease is low. In this type of situation, I have found it more useful to base clinical decisions on an actual estimate of posterior probability, rather than on a yes/no classification based on the critical limit. The mathematics are quite straightforward *(3)*, and calculations are easily performed on a pocket programmable calculator. The method can easily be extended to cope with the results of multiple tests, if these are combined as a discriminant function *(3)*.

References

1. Roberts, L. B., The normal ranges, with statistical analysis for seventeen blood constituents. *Clin. Chim. Acta* **16**, 69–78 (1967).
2. Caird, F. I., Problems of interpretation of laboratory findings in the old. *Br. Med. J.* **iv**, 348–351 (1973).
3. Hodkinson, H. M., *Biochemical Diagnosis of the Elderly*. Chapman & Hall, London, 1977.
4. Keating, F. R., Jones, J. D., Elveback, L. R., and Randall, R. V., The relation of age and sex to distribution of values in healthy adults of serum calcium, inorganic phosphorus, magnesium, alkaline phosphatase, total protein, albumin, and blood urea. *J. Lab. Clin. Med.* **73**, 825–834 (1969).
5. Hodkinson, H. M., Non-specific presentation of illness. *Br. Med. J.* **iv**, 94–96 (1973).
6. Law, R., and Chalmers, C., Medicines and elderly people: A general practice survey. *Br. Med. J.* **i**, 565–568 (1976).
7. Williamson, J., Principles of drug action and usage. In *Recent Advances in Geriatric Medicine*, B. Isaacs, Ed., Churchill Livingstone, Edinburgh, London & New York, 1978, pp 109–120.
8. Young, D. S., Thomas, D. W., Friedman, R. B., and Pestaner, L. C., Effects of drugs on clinical laboratory tests. *Clin. Chem.* **18**(5), 1041–1303 (1972). Special issue.
9. Hodkinson, H. M., Biochemical side effects of drugs in the elderly. *Gerontol. Clin.* **16**, 175–178 (1974).
10. Baruch, A. L. H., Davis, C., and Hodkinson, H. M., Causes of high free-thyroxine index values in sick euthyroid elderly patients. *Age Ageing* **5**, 224–227 (1976).
11. Hodkinson, H. M., and MacPherson, C. K., Alkaline phosphatase in a geriatric inpatient population. *Age Ageing* **2**, 28–33 (1973).
12. Mukherjee, A. P., Coni, N. K., and Davison, W., Osmoreceptor function among the elderly. *Gerontol. Clin.* **15**, 227–233 (1973).
13. Hodkinson, H. M., Diagnostic and prognostic aspects of routine laboratory screening of the geriatric inpatient. D.M. thesis, University of Oxford, 1975.
14. Bahemuka, M., and Hodkinson, H. M., Screening for hypothyroidism in the elderly inpatient. *Br. Med. J.* **ii**, 601–603 (1975).
15. Murphy, E. A., and Abbey, H., The normal range—a common misuse. *J. Chron. Dis.* **20**, 79–85 (1967).

Chemistry Reference Values as a Function of Age and Sex, Including Pediatric and Geriatric Subjects

Dale Gillibrand, Darshan Grewal, and D. Paul Blattler

Preliminary studies of chemistry results plotted as a function of age and sex reveal a remarkable variation of results. These conclusions have been formalized by a systematic study of 800 men and 800 women uniformly distributed over the ages of 11 to 90 years in five-year intervals. We have used nonparametric percentile estimates to establish population ranges as a function of age in conjunction with a curve-fitting technique. Results from 21- to 40-year-olds are often different from those obtained from children and older people, and are believed to represent a more nearly optimum physiological state.

The phrase "normal range" means different things to different people. "Normal" is not readily defined; it is rarely equivalent to ideal or perfect, and is not necessarily represented by a single average (1). Frequently, stated normal ranges have been taken directly from reports on older, established methods (2). Normal ranges at one laboratory may differ from normal ranges at other laboratories and may also vary according to population, age, sex, race, menstrual status, previous diet, exercise, posture, kind and precision of the method, human bias, and many other less easily discerned factors. As an alternative to the normal range, several investigators have adopted the concept of the "reference range." We support this approach. The neutral term "reference values" is preferable on semantic and scientific grounds, and its use in clinical chemistry is rapidly gaining acceptance (3). Though "reference values" for a number of chemical constituents in sera of healthy adults have been well documented, comparatively few studies have been made to establish these values in children and older people *(4–17)*. An investigation undertaken to study the influence of age and sex on such "reference values" has given us interesting results, which we present here.

The process of developing our age-related reference ranges has led us to the concept of an Abnormality Index. In general, most investigators have considered three states of health: serious illness, borderline illness, and good health. But there is obviously a continuum of states between optimum health and serious illness, and it is this continuum that we are trying to measure.

Our Abnormality Index is our first attempt to quantify the relative health of individuals as monitored by a standard panel of chemistry assays. These assays have been developed, historically, because they reveal problems in the organs of the body. Our health index will not reflect all causes of problems—for example, hematology factors are not included, but could be included in future indexes.

The 1737 subjects include a few children under 11 and a few old people over 90. They were selected from over 60 000 SMAC panels performed from November through March. The advantages of the SMAC panel are the use of standard methodology and the highly precise data that the SMAC generates. Subjects were selected according to the following criteria: *(a)* all samples originated in doctors' offices (no hospital-based patients were included in the study); *(b)* if more than four of the results were outside our published normal range, we rejected the sample. The population studied lived in the western part of the United States, including Chicago, Denver, San Francisco, Salt Lake City, the Pacific Northwest, the Southwest, and southern California. All reagents used were bought directly from Technicon Instruments Corporation, Tarrytown, NY. Methods used in this study were essentially the standard methods recommended by Technicon for the SMAC. The glucose tests were performed with Technicon single-channel continuous-flow analyzers. The SMACs (Models 333 and 509) were calibrated with assayed SMAC Reference I and SMAC II purchased directly from Technicon.

Quality-assurance material, normal and abnormal, was from Ortho, Raritan, NJ. Quality assurance was monitored by a computer-controlled system. We continually checked accuracy with assayed control material from Hyland Laboratories (Costa Mesa,

CA), Q-PAK Chemistry Control serum I and II. Day-to-day precision was monitored by daily inspection of the mean of our patient population and distribution via our automated histogram Quality Control Program.

Statistical Methods for the Reference Range

Several papers have examined the relative merit of various techniques of population range estimation *(2, 18–25)*. The most consistently reliable appears to be the nonparametric percentile estimate described by Reed et al. *(18)*. This procedure, however, has an annoying requirement for a large number of results. We have attempted to overcome this disadvantage by modifying the procedure for our particular application. Each five-year interval contains 50 results, far below the recommended minimum necessary for nonparametric estimates of the 2.5 and 97.5 percentiles *(18)*. Because of this, the central 95% limits for each age interval will have a large amount of inherent uncertainty, which in turn makes identification of age regressions difficult. We have, instead, used the 10th and 90th percentiles (along with the 50th percentile) in the regression analysis. The regressions curve for the 10th (or 90th) percentile is then shifted by a constant so that exactly 2.5% (or 97.5%) of the results over all age intervals fall below or above the regression curve. This method relies on the assumption that the regression of the 2.5 percentile is closely approximated by the regression of the 10th percentile (and similarily for the 97.5 and 90th percentiles).

The two obvious advantages of using this method are: *(a)* the regression curve is much more representative of the actual change with age because of the increased accuracy of the percentile estimates, and *(b)* all results (800 when all age intervals are combined) are used in establishing the final 2.5 and 97.5% limits. This method also reduces the sensitivity of the nonparametric percentile estimate to outliers and therefore lessens the importance of inclusions or exclusions of unusual results.

The curves fitted through the 10th, 50th, and 90th percentile estimates are polynomials of degree less than or equal to four. A stepwise multiple linear-regression analysis was used in which age raised to the powers 1 through 4 was the independent variable *(26)*. Only those intervals having 50 results were included (i.e., the 16 five-year age intervals from 11 to 90: 11–15, 16–20, . . . , 86–90). All coefficients in the regression equations as well as the regressions themselves are statistically significant at $p \leq 0.05$.

In general, these polynomials seem to fit the data adequately so long as the change in the range of results is not drastic. A fourth-degree polynomial was unsatisfactory in representing the regression over all ages for the values of alkaline phosphatase (EC 3.1.3.1) and lactate dehydrogenase (EC 1.1.1.27) because of the abrupt shift in results from the 11- to 20-year age groups. The curves for these two tests were instead calculated for ages 21–90. All the curves are somewhat less reliable at the extreme ages and conversely more reliable in the middle age groups [26]. Also, the curves should not be extrapolated to construct limits for age intervals not included in the regression analysis.

Subjects having four or more abnormal results were eliminated. The probability of this occurring in a healthy patient is very small. For individual tests, outliers were deleted when the distance from the outlier to the next closest result exceeded one-third of the entire range of results [18].

Statistical Methods for the Multivariate Abnormality Index

Data from ages 21–40 are used as a reference with which all ages can be compared through the following process: Data from each test for ages 21–40 (n = 200) are transformed to gaussian form. Transformations used are log (data + constant) and (data + constant)^p, where p is some appropriate power. Transformed data for each test are then put in standard units with a mean of 0 and a standard deviation (SD) of 1 by the formula

$$x_i = (y_i - \bar{y})/\text{SD}$$

The transformed gaussian assay result is y_1, and $\bar{y}$ is the mean value of the population of y_i. The value x_i is in standard units commonly referred to as a z score. The ordered 16-tuples (x_1, and x_2 . . . x_{16}) corresponding to the 16 test results, expressed in standard units, have a joint probability function of

$$f(x_1 x_2 \ . \ . \ . \ x_{16}) = (2\pi)^{-8} |M|^{-1/2} e^{-1/2Q}$$

where M is the covariance matrix and

$$Q = (x_1, x_2, \ . \ . \ . \ x_{16}) \, M^{-1} \, (x_1, x_2, \ . \ . \ . \ x_{16})$$

369

Q represents a vector–matrix–vector multiplication, and the result of this is a single number. M is a 16 x 16 matrix of the correlation coefficients of each test vs every test. The inverse matrix M^{-1} is used in the calculations. Multiplying the matrix M by M^{-1} yields the identity matrix. For computational simplicity, the value of Q can be examined for each subject because the function will vary as Q varies. Because Q values will have a chi-square distribution with 16 degrees of freedom, the percentile value can be easily determined. The Q value has now become an "Abnormality Index."

Reference Values for 19 Analytes

Alkaline Phosphatase (EC 3.1.3.1)

Our studies (Figure 1) confirm that children of both sexes have higher values than adults. Teenage girls appear to reach adult values several years sooner than teenage boys. The data also suggest, especially in women, that results tend to increase with age. Thus, elderly women may have high results that, although not unusual for their age, are probably not optimum for good health; on the other hand, women who live past 90 years tend to have lower alkaline phosphatase values.

Aspartate Aminotransferase, AST (EC 2.6.1.1)

Young children tend to have aspartate aminotransferase values higher than adults (Figure 2). Men also tend to have higher values than women. There is no change of the results with ages between 10 and 90.

Alanine Aminotransferase, ALT (EC 2.6.1.2)

Women tend to have the same range of alanine aminotransferase values over their whole life span (Figure 3). There are a few "outliers" during middle age, but only very few after age 65. Men have higher values than women, and their 2.5 and 50 percentile lines have a maximum around age 60. The 97.5 percentile line is unusually high, and is not parallel to the 2.5 or 50% lines; the maximum is around age 35. Because this enzyme is unusually sensitive to liver damage, we suggest that this pattern of outliers in men may be due to excessive use of alcohol. This hypothesis

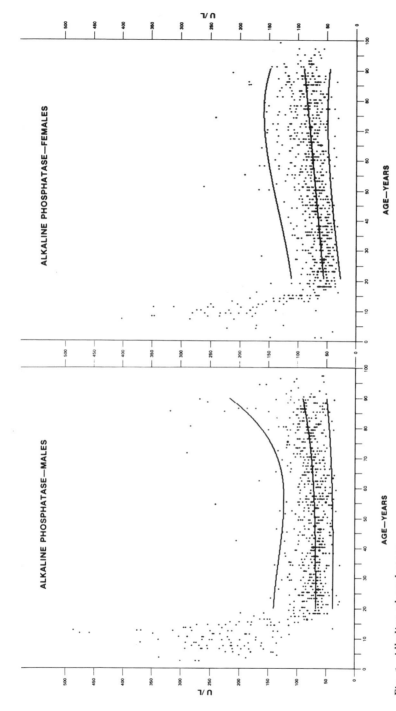

Fig. 1. Alkaline phosphatase

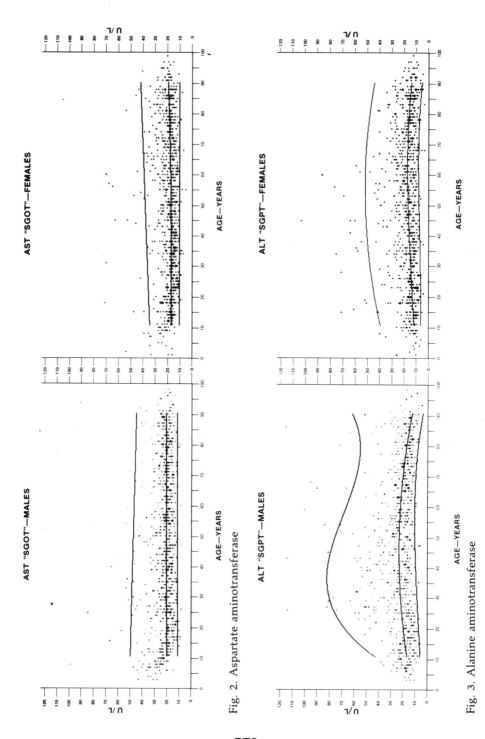

AST "SGOT"—FEMALES

AST "SGOT"—MALES

AGE—YEARS

AGE—YEARS

Fig. 2. Aspartate aminotransferase

ALT "SGPT"—FEMALES

ALT "SGPT"—MALES

AGE—YEARS

AGE—YEARS

Fig. 3. Alanine aminotransferase

is certainly testable, and if correct, the alanine aminotransferase test could constitute one component of a multifactorial test for alcoholism. It is also possible that men are exposed to a variety of hepatotoxic agents so that their livers are damaged to a greater extent than those of age-matched women.

Lactate Dehydrogenase, LDH (EC 1.1.1.27)

Young children have higher values than adults (Figure 4). There is also a tendency for lactate dehydrogenase results to increase with age.

Bilirubin

Bilirubin results (Figure 5) are the same for both sexes and remain constant throughout the life span.

Glucose

Several surprising observations can be made from our glucose data (Figure 6). The normal range is often quoted as 0.70 to 1.05 or 1.10 g/L. For young adults, our results are lower than this, and thus a "normal" result of 1.10 is really abnormal. Most of our subjects, incidentally, were nonfasting.

All of our assays were performed on plasma from NaF-treated blood. We believe our assay to be accurate as well as precise, and have no explanation to offer for our results except the following: our data show clearly that glucose results increase with age and also become more variable with age; thus a "normal range" based on a population of heterogeneous ages will be too high and wide for young adults. Among men, we have outliers (obviously diabetics) scattered over the whole adult age range. Among women, the incidence of diabetes seems to increase in women over 40. We therefore suggest that the range obtained for young adults is probably also desirable for older people.

The 97.5 percentile line deserves comment. In no sense can this line be regarded as the upper limit of the normal range. As is clear, our sample population includes diabetics plus people with a tendency towards diabetes; moreover, our statistical approach is sensitive to the presence of many outliers. The many high glucose results are not sufficiently high to be classified statistically as outliers but are sufficiently numerous to influence the 97.5 percentile line. We wished to present our data with the least

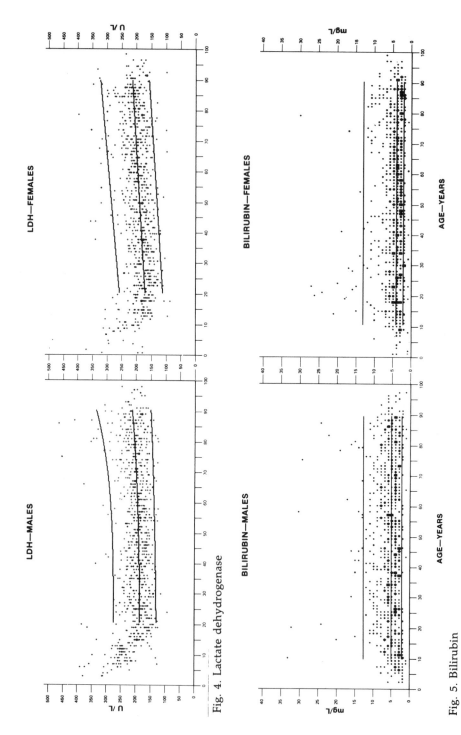

LDH—FEMALES

LDH—MALES

Fig. 4. Lactate dehydrogenase

BILIRUBIN—FEMALES

BILIRUBIN—MALES

AGE—YEARS

AGE—YEARS

Fig. 5. Bilirubin

374

amount of subjective editing possible, and with a common format. Thus, we left the high glucose results in.

Triglycerides

Triglycerides are increased in nonfasting subjects, and our population was primarily nonfasting; still, we can draw several conclusions about this analyte. Men have higher concentrations than women (Figure 7). Very high results may occur in men of all ages, whereas in women, very high results tend to occur after age 40. In women, the results increase with age; in men, the results have a maximum value around age 60. Finally, as for many other tests, very old people tend to have values similar to young adults.

Cholesterol

Our data (Figure 8) show that cholesterol increases with age in both men and women; then, after reaching a maximum value, it decreases. There are several surprising facts. In men, maximum cholesterol values occur at approximately age 55; in women, at age 70. From approximately age 50 on, women have higher cholesterol values than men. Very old people of both sexes tend to have lower cholesterol values, which is possibly related to survivorship. Very old people also tend to lose weight with age, and cholesterol fluctuates with body weight.

Total Protein

There is a slight decrease in total protein with age (Figure 9). Results for men and women are very similar. However, the lower limit in men is less than in women.

Albumin

Albumin decreases with age in both sexes (Figure 10), which is in agreement with previous studies (10–15). However, we find that albumin decreases more sharply in men. In women, albumin is relatively constant until age 40 and then gradually decreases. The albumin/globulin ratio also decreases with advancing age.

Globulin

Globulin increases with age in men (Figure 11). In women, globulin is fairly constant, with only a slight increase with age. Very old people, over 90 years old, tend to have values clustered around the same median as for young people.

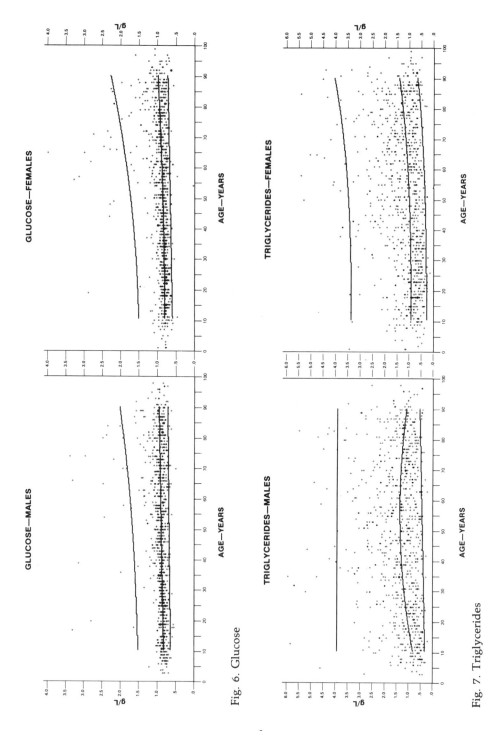

Fig. 6. Glucose

Fig. 7. Triglycerides

376

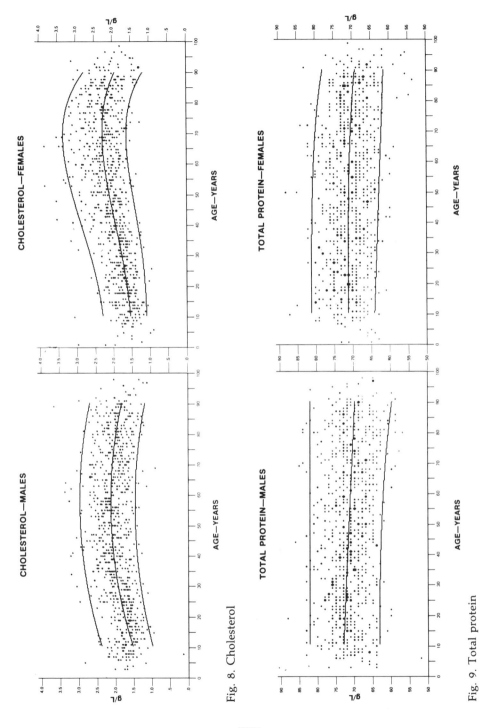

Fig. 8. Cholesterol

Fig. 9. Total protein

377

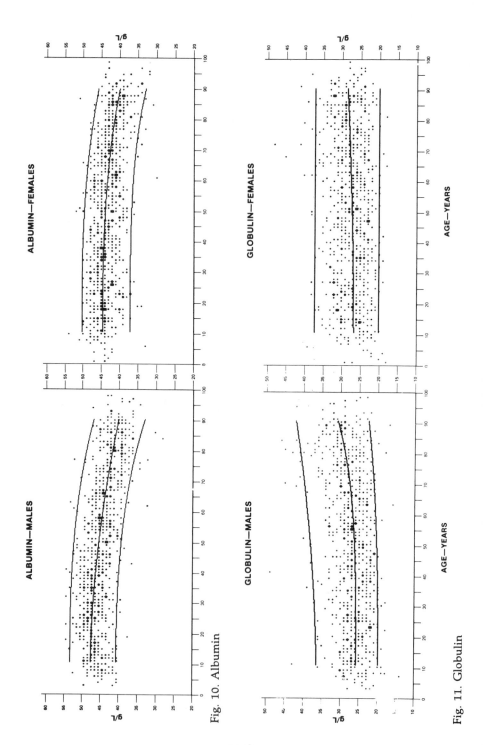

Fig. 10. Albumin

Fig. 11. Globulin

378

Calcium

In young adult men, calcium is definitely higher than in women (Figure 12). Our data suggest that calcium concentrations decrease in men, but remain constant in women. Other studies have reported that calcium decreases in women only *(13)* or in men only *(10)*, or shows no age regression *(6)*.

Approximately one-half of the calcium is bound to albumin as non-ionized calcium. Thus our finding may be due to the fact that men show a marked decrease in albumin with age, while in women the decrease in albumin is relatively minor. This observation is supported by our correlation studies, which show a definite relationship between albumin and calcium ($r = 0.34$).

There is no obvious change in calcium during puberty in spite of the rapid bone growth; however, there is a faint suggestion that prepubertal children have slighter higher calcium values than adults.

Phosphorus, Inorganic

Phosphorus values exhibit a marked drop in both sexes during early childhood, puberty, and up to age 25 *(1, 5, 6)*. Adult values are relatively constant, with similar limits for both men and women (Figure 13).

Traditionally, there is supposed to be an inverse relationship between calcium and phosphorus. Although this is probably true for ionized calcium and phosphate, we do not observe this for total calcium and phosphorus.

Potassium

Our data indicate that potassium concentration is kept constant, independent of age, in both sexes (Figure 14). Men may have slightly higher values than women.

Sodium

Our results (Figure 15) are essentially independent of age or sex. The upper limit for men may be higher than for women, but the median is the same.

Chloride

We found a higher upper limit for chloride in men than in

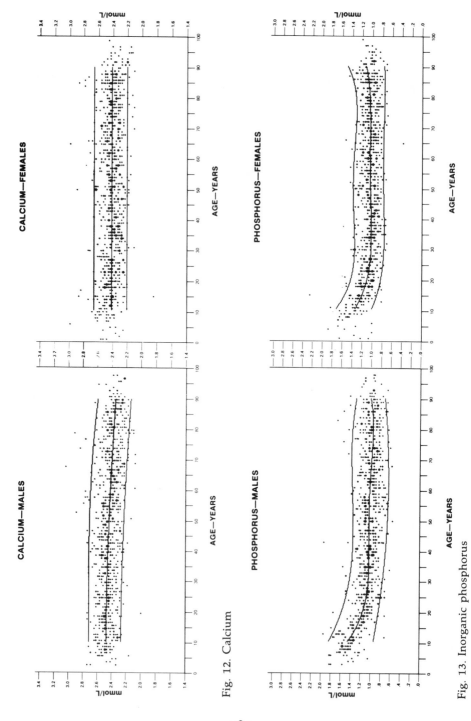

Fig. 12. Calcium

Fig. 13. Inorganic phosphorus

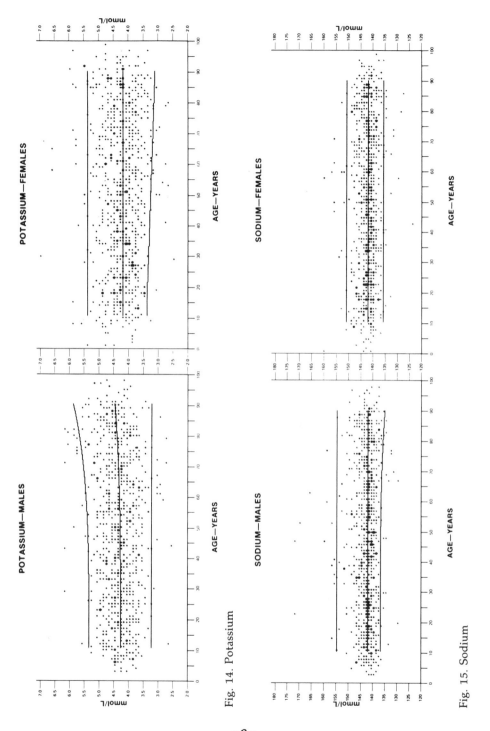

Fig. 14. Potassium

Fig. 15. Sodium

381

women (Figure 16). There is no significant relationship to age in men, but in women the median and lower limit decrease with age.

Urate

Some investigations (13) have found a slight increase with age for men, but not in women. In contrast, our data show that urate in women also increases with age (Figure 17). Men have higher concentrations of urate and their results increase with age.

Creatinine

Creatinine values are much higher in men than in women, and increase with age in both sexes (Figure 18). In both sexes, the 50 percentile line increases slightly with age, whereas the 97.5 line increases rapidly after age 40. These facts may indicate deterioration of kidney function with age.

Urea Nitrogen in Serum

Previous studies (2, 10, 13) have shown higher values in men than in women. One study (13) reported that only in women did urea values increase with age. Our studies show that urea concentration increases with age in both sexes, and that men have higher values (Figure 19).

Multivariate Abnormality Index

We developed this index to meet a practical problem and to deal with a statistical difficulty. It is possible, and common, for a patient to have all "normal" chemistry results and yet be highly abnormal, statistically and physiologically. For example, having a high "normal" calcium and a low "normal" protein is statistically unlikely and is also suggestive of hyperparathyroidism. The anion-gap calculation is a statistically primitive approach toward dealing with a three-dimensional problem involving Na^+, Cl^-, and HCO_3^-.

To demonstrate the practicality of our statistical system, we calculated a 16-dimensional index, using total protein, albumin, bilirubin, aspartate aminotransferase, alanine aminotransferase, alkaline phosphatase, lactate dehydrogenase, serum urea nitrogen, creatinine, urate, calcium, phosphorus, cholesterol, Na^+, K^+, and

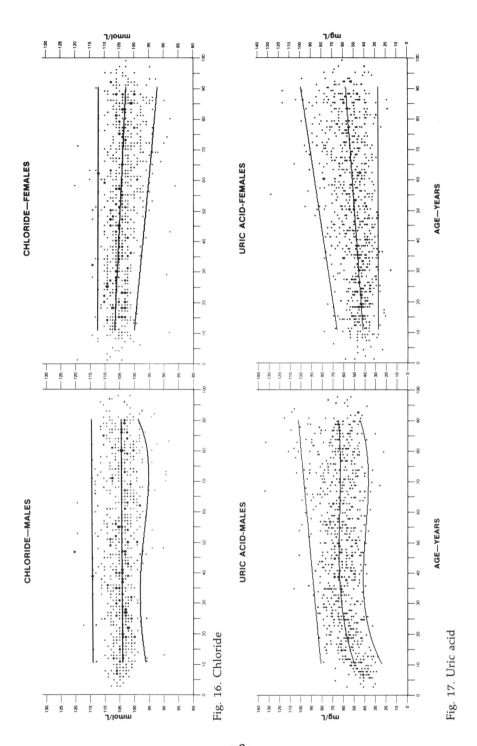

CHLORIDE—MALES

CHLORIDE—FEMALES

Fig. 16. Chloride

URIC ACID—MALES

URIC ACID—FEMALES

AGE—YEARS

AGE—YEARS

Fig. 17. Uric acid

383

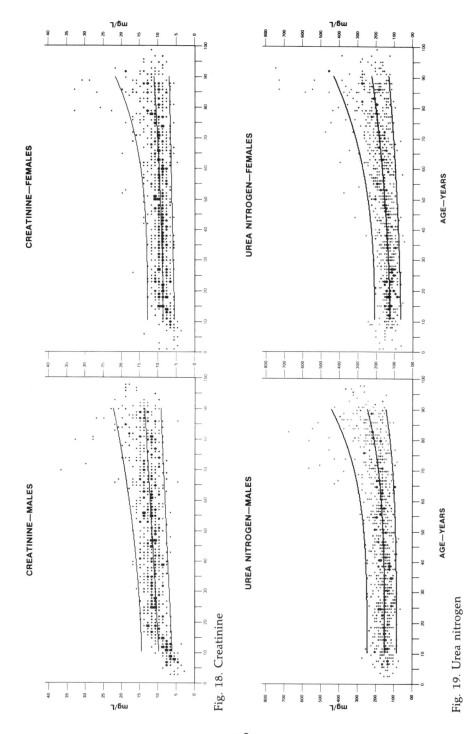

Fig. 18. Creatinine

Fig. 19. Urea nitrogen

384

Cl⁻. We excluded glucose and triglycerides because our subjects were nonfasting; total CO_2 was omitted because of the age of the samples.

For each test we measured the distance from the mean to the data point, and squared this result. Then, all 16 terms were added together. Our assumption is that the population mean test value is the one most representative of good health. This hypothesis is probably valid for metabolites such as Na^+, but is less valid for cholesterol, where the population mean is probably too high to represent optimum health.

A few simple examples will illustrate how Abnormality Index scores vary. A person for whom every result is identical to the mean will have a score of 0. No such score was observed, but there were low scores of 3 or 4. By our hypothesis, this should indicate excellent health. A person who has every result 1SD from the mean will have a score of 16. Another individual with every result 2SD above or below the mean will have a score of 64. The average Abnormality Index score for our 16-dimensional index is 16. The range and mean of this Abnormality Index are relatively constant for men and women from age 21 to 40 (Figure 20). Above age 40, the mean increases, the range of results increases, and many more outliers are observed. Some Index scores were as high as 330, in spite of the fact that no subject had more than three "above-normal" results. A few individuals in their eighth decade of life had scores below 16; their absence of organ defects, as measured by our assays, and quantified by our index, makes them excellent candidates for even greater longevity.

A few comments on the statistical methodology are necessary. For example, a patient with liver disease may have a low albumin and consequently a low total calcium because the non-ionic calcium bound to albumin is low. The statistical method includes correlation coefficients between calcium and albumin so that when we calculate the abnormality due to calcium, we subtract the contribution due to albumin. Each subject has 16 results, which form a vector $(x_1, x_2 \ldots x_{16})$. This vector is multiplied by a matrix M^{-1}, and the resulting vector is multiplied by the original vector. The result of this vector–matrix–vector multiplication is that correlations between assays are considered. For 16 assays with no correlation with each other, the resulting calculation would be $(x_1^2 + x_2^2 + \cdots x_{16}^2)$. We used this approximation in calculating

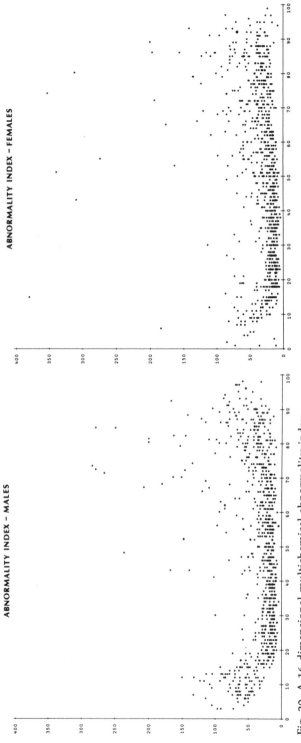

Fig. 20. A 16-dimensional multichemical abnormality index

the previous examples, where the standard deviations were 0, 1, and 2.

The population and samples used in this study deserve comment in that our data are presented as a function of two variables, age and sex. A hypothetical, perfect study would include many other factors such as posture, fasting status, season, altitude, race, medication, and health status, among others. Such a "perfect" study would require hundreds of thousands of patients' results at enormous expense, and the product would be too cumbersome for practical benefit. Our population is representative of people seen by physicians in non-acute care situations, and our study is intended to examine the influence of age and sex on chemistry assays. Our results for young adults 21 to 40 years old are compatible with commonly accepted "normal" ranges (27). Our population includes people from sea-level elevation in southern California and from more than 5000 feet above sea level in Denver. Most samples were collected in January and February, 1979, but some samples from November and December, 1978, and March, 1979, are included.

We believe that our reference ranges are a useful guide for physicians who wish to evaluate results for young or old patients. Furthermore, the statistical methodology, the uniform data density as a function of age, and the graphical presentation of results represent a new refinement in reference range studies.

The Abnormality Index is our first attempt to measure the continuum of health states between optimum health and acute illness. In spite of recognized and acknowledged limitations to our model, the index varies with age in the way that one would predict. It also demonstrates how extra information can be extracted from existing data. Moreover, we contend that the Abnormality Index will help the physician recognize disease states in an earlier and more treatable form. Finally, we predict that a major thrust of clinical laboratory medicine will be improved pattern recognition and information extraction from existing data.

This work began as the result of the superb leadership of Dayle Bailey, Laboratory Operations Manager of Laboratory Procedures. The quality-control program she developed led directly to this work. Furthermore, the pioneering work of Dr. Henry Stevens in the area of biochemical determinants of health helped lay the conceptual foundations of this work.

References

1. Tolls, R. E., Werner, M., Hultin, J. V., and Mellecker, J., Sex and age dependence of seven serum constituents in a large ambulatory population. In *Advances in Automated Analysis, Technicon International Congress*, **3**. C. E. Barton et al., Eds., Mediad, Inc., White Plains, NY, 1970, p 9.

2. Reed, A. H., Cannon, D. C., Winkelman, J. W., Bhasin, Y. P., Henry, R. J., and Pileggi, V. J., Estimation of normal ranges from a controlled sample survey. 1. Sex and age related influence on the SMA 12/60 screening group of tests. *Clin. Chem.* **18**, 57–66 (1972).

3. Sunderman, F. W., Jr., Current concepts of "normal values," "reference values," and "discrimination values" in clinical chemistry. *Clin. Chem.* **21**, 1873–1877 (1975).

4. Meites, S., Ed., *Pediatric Clinical Chemistry*. American Association for Clinical Chemistry, Washington, DC, 1977, p 259.

5. Greenberg, B. G., Winters, R. W., and Graham, J. B., The normal range of serum inorganic phosphorus and its utility as a discriminant in the diagnosis of congenital hypophosphatemia. *J. Clin. Endocrinol.* **20**, 364–379 (1960).

6. Round, J. M., Plasma calcium, magnesium, phosphorus, and alkaline phosphatase levels in normal British school children. *Br. Med. J.* **iii**, 137–140 (1970).

7. Ward, A. M., and Hirst, A. D., The automated ultramicro-estimation of total serum protein and protein fractions, with the changes due to renal tract disease in children with spina bifida. *Am. J. Clin. Pathol.* **51**, 751–759 (1969).

8. Wilding, P., Rollason, J. G., and Robinson, D., Patterns of change for various biochemical constituents detected in well population screening. *Clin. Chim. Acta* **41**, 375–387 (1972).

9. Cherican, A. G., and Gelgerhill, T., Percentile estimates of reference values for fourteen chemical constituents in sera of children and adolescents. *Am. Soc. Clin. Pathol.* **69**, 24–31 (1978).

10. Keating, F. R., Jones, J. D., Elvebeck, L. R., and Randell, R. V., The relation of age and sex to distribution of values in healthy adults of serum calcium, inorganic phosphorus, magnesium, alkaline phosphatase, total protein, albumin, and blood urea. *J. Lab. Clin. Med.* **73**, 825–834 (1969).

11. O'Kell, R. T., and Elliot, J. R., Development of normal values for use in multitest biochemical screening of sera. *Clin. Chem.* **16**, 161–165 (1970).

12. Werner, M., Tolls, R. E., Hultin, J. V., and Mellecker, J., Influence

of sex and age on the normal range of eleven serum constituents. *J. Clin. Chem. Clin. Biochem.* **8**, 105–115 (1970).

13. Roberts, L. B., The normal ranges with statistical analysis, for seventeen blood constituents. *Clin. Chim. Acta* **16**, 69–78 (1967).
14. Best, W. R., Mason, C. C., Barron, S. S., and Sheperd, H. G., Automated twelve-channel serum screening. *Med. Clin. North Am.* **53**, 175–188 (1969).
15. Files, J. B., Van Peenen, J., and Lindberg, A. B., Use of "normal range" in multiphasic testing. *J. Am. Med. Assoc.* **205**, 684–688 (1968).
16. Johnson, J. R. K., and Riechman, G. C., Normal serum calcium levels by atomic absorption spectroscopy. *Clin. Chem.* **14**, 1218–1227 (1968).
17. Yendt, E. R., and Gagne, R. J. A., Detection of primary hyperparathyroidism, with special reference to its occurrence in hypercalciuric females with "normal" or borderline serum calcium. *Can. Med. Assoc. J.* **98**, 331–339 (1968).
18. Reed, A. H., Henry, R. J., and Mason, W. B., Influence of statistical method used on the resulting normal range. *Clin. Chem.* **17**, 275–284 (1971).
19. Harris, E. K., and De Mets, D. L., Estimation of normal ranges and cumulative proportions by transforming observed distributions to guassian form. *Clin. Chem.* **18**, 605–612 (1972).
20. Reed, A. H., and Wu, G. T., Evaluation of a transformation method for estimation of normal range. *Clin. Chem.* **20**, 576–581 (1974).
21. Massod, M. F., Nonparametric percentile estimate of clinical normal range. *Am. J. Med. Technol.* **43**, 243–252 (1977).
22. Glick, J. H., Statistics of patient test values: Application to indirect normal range and to quality control. *Clin. Chem.* **18**, 1504–1513 (1972).
23. Amador, E., and Hsi, B. P., Indirect methods for estimating the normal range. *Am. J. Clin. Pathol.* **52**, 538–546 (1969).
24. Elvebeck, L. R., and Taylor, W., Statistical methods of estimating percentiles. *Ann. N. Y. Acad. Sci.* **161**, 538–548 (1969).
25. Elvebeck, L. R., Guiller, C. L., and Keating, F. R., Health, normality and the ghost of Guass. *J. Am. Med. Assoc.* **211**, 69–75 (1970).
26. Draper, N. R., and Smith, H., *Applied Regression Analysis,* John Wiley and Sons, New York, NY, 1966.
27. Munan, L., Kelly, A., Petitclerc, C., and Billon, B., *Atlas of Blood Data,* Epidemiological Laboratory and the Laboratory of Clinical Biochemistry, Faculty of Medicine, University of Sherbooke, Quebec, 1978.

Human Performance as a Function of Optimum Metabolite Concentrations in Serum

Henry A. Stevens and D. Paul Blattler

We wish to raise the question of whether there is any performance significance in the distribution of blood metabolites in humans. The vast majority of human blood metabolites have a unimodal form of distribution. We propose a working hypothesis that not only is human performance, both mental and physical, influenced by many of these serum metabolites, but also optimum performance may require optimum serum metabolite concentrations. We suspect that this requirement has led to the evolution of these unimodal distributions, and that the population mean represents the optimum concentration for performance. Thus, normal ranges of metabolites are maintained because they reflect the concentrations consonant with optimum performance. This concept is the physiological equivalent of the Laffer Curve in economics (1).

Many biochemical factors influence performance. The availability of serum for investigation makes it a convenient starting point in the systematic scanning for these biochemical factors. We shall briefly refer to research in which there has been both direct measurement of performance as a function of serum metabolite concentrations and epidemological assessments of several population groups. The results of this research support the consideration of a general hypothesis that specific concentrations for optimum performance probably exist for a number of serum metabolites.

Our hypothesis is a corollary of the known relationship between disease states and abnormal concentrations of metabolites. Many diseases, for example, diabetes, are accompanied by impaired performance and abnormal metabolite (glucose) concentrations. Normal performance generally requires normal amounts of the metabolite.

This "optimum amount hypothesis" grew from some of our earlier work on serum urate as a central nervous system stimulant. In this work we re-interpreted Orowan's hypothesis *(2)* on intelligence and uric acid. Orowan noticed the close chemical rela-

HYPOTHESIZED OPTIMAL ZONE

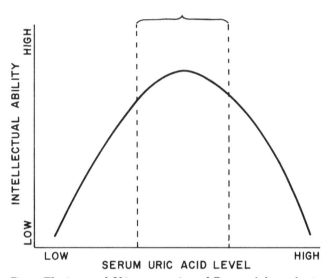

Fig. 1. The inverted-U interpretation of Orowan's hypothesis *(4)*

This figure follows the shape of the Laffer Curve if government tax income is substituted on the *y*-axis and taxation rate on the *x*-axis

tionship between uric acid and caffeine and also recognized that humans are the only primate with highly increased concentrations of urate in serum (normal range for men, 30–70 mg/L). He postulated that part of our evolutionary success was due to the mental stimulation afforded by endogenous uric acid.

We have hypothesized that a strictly linear (i.e., the more stimulation the better) interpretation is incorrect *(3)*, and that an inverted-U or optimum amount model (see Figure 1) could accommodate the existing literature to a greater extent than the linear interpretation. In our own research (4), men with a serum urate concentration of 50 mg/L scored higher on standardized learning tests than subjects whose urate concentrations deviated from this value in either direction. Furthermore, various groups selected on the basis of increasing intellectual ability clustered tighter around this 50 mg/L optimum as the groups' general level of intelligence increased. Thus, the inverted-U model proved to be a useful concept and may offer a plausible explanation as to why man did not evolve towards utilization of even higher concentrations of serum urate.

The critical point in our study of men was that the value of urate that was optimum for performance coincides with the population's mean concentration of serum urate. These results led us to postulate that men had evolved to this mean concentration because of its selective advantage. Men with higher or lower concentrations of urate suffer some selective disadvantage. Men with lower concentrations are presumably hindered by lack of mental stimulation, and those with higher concentrations are hindered by hyperstimulation and uric acid toxicity. Our study was limited to men but the logic applies to women as well.

Certain principles of pharmacokinetics are probably involved in the selection of optimum metabolite values and normal ranges. For example, it is known that stimulants such as amphetamine may help increase intellectual concentration up to some point, but that further increases in amphetamine are not advantageous and may lead to emotional depression and, in extreme cases, toxicity (5). Thus the inverted-U relationship is well recognized in pharmacology and drug dosage requirements, and represents a compromise between opposing factors.

This principle appears to apply for serum urate concentrations, and may very well apply for other blood metabolites as well (i.e., calcium, glucose, lipids, etc.). Experimenters will need insight, however, to decide which performance parameter to measure against a given metabolite. However, knowledge of the consequences of metabolic diseases is such that informed guesses and experiments may be devised.

In summary, we suggest that there is an important corollary to the current concept of normal ranges for concentrations of serum metabolites. If metabolite values outside the normal concentration range are pathognomonic for a disease state, then values inside the normal range, and particularly near the population mode, must represent optimum values. Our purpose in presenting this hypothesis is to provide a rather simplistic and testable theoretical perspective for the examination of multicomponent biochemical systems that may be related to human performance. Specific performance tests and epidemiological studies can be used to evaluate this concept, as was done for uric acid.

References

1. Laffer, A., The Third World on the Laffer Curve. *The Way the World Works,* J. Wanniske, Ed., Basic Books, New York, NY, 1978, pp 238–279.
2. Orowan, E., The origin of man. *Nature* **175,** 683–684 (1955).
3. Stevens, H. A., and Cropley, A. J., Uric acid and behaviour: A new look at Orowan's hypothesis. *Psychol. Rep.* **30,** 967–970 (1972).
4. Stevens, H. A., Cropley, A. J., and Blattler, D. P., Intellect and serum uric acid: An optimal concentration of serum urate for human learning? *J. Soc. Biol.* **22,** 229–234 (1975).
5. Sprague, R. L., and Sleater, E. K., Methylphenidate in hyperkinetic children: Differences in dose effects on learning and social behavior. *Science* **198,** 1274–1276 (1977).

Therapeutic Drug Monitoring in the Elderly

A. Douglas Bender

Papers presented at this conference clearly document the decline in biological function and capacity that occurs with age. Decreases in cardiac output, renal function, respiratory capacity, metabolic rate, lean body mass, total body water, and other changes directly and indirectly influence drug disposition. On the basis of these observations, and the fact that the elderly are more vulnerable to disease and tend to take more drugs than do younger patients, it is not surprising that the incidence of adverse drug reactions increases with age.

In describing the pharmacokinetic and pharmacodynamic basis for the increased sensitivity exhibited by the elderly to drugs, I will focus on two principles that explain most of the clinical observations on this topic. The first deals with changes in drug concentrations in blood; these changes in the elderly are consequent to alterations in biological systems that involve the transport and disposition of drugs. The second deals with changes in the sensitivity of receptor sites, organ systems, and tissues to the action of a drug at a given or fixed concentration.

Incidence of Adverse Drug Reactions

Seidl et al. *(1)* and Hurwitz *(2)* report a marked increase with age in the incidence of adverse drug reactions in a large series of patients both in the United States and England. In the study conducted by Seidl et al. the incidence of adverse reactions was 11.9% in patients 60 years and younger, and 17.5% in patients over the age of 60. Hurwitz reported an incidence of adverse reactions of 6.3% in patients under the age of 60 and 15.4% in patients 60 years and older. In a study by Caranasos et al. *(3)*

the incidence of drug-induced illness requiring hospitalization increased from 2.5% for patients under the age of 60 to 3.8% in patients 60 years and older.

Similar data have been reported concerning the incidence of adverse reactions to specific drugs. For example, Pemberton (4) has shown that the incidence of serious reactions to phenylbutazone increases with age. In a group of patients 21 to 30 years old, the incidence of adverse reactions was 23%, increasing to 60% in patients over 60 years old. Studies by Greenblatt and Allen (5) and Greenblatt et al. (6) show that the incidence of adverse reactions to two benzodiazepines, nitrazepam and flurazepam, is a function of dose and age. At high doses the incidence of depression with nitrazepam and adverse reactions with flurazepam are significantly higher in older patients. At low doses, efficacy is not compromised and the incidence of adverse reactions is no different between young and older patients. These data suggest that lower doses of drugs may be used in the elderly to reduce the incidence of adverse reactions. This observation is supported by a number of pharmacokinetic studies, which I will describe later.

Most changes in drug reactivity with age are quantitative; that is, the same side effects occur in older people as in younger people, but the frequency of their occurrence is higher in older patient populations. In some situations, the response of older patients to a drug is qualitatively different from that in young patients. Very erratic responses and frequently bizarre behavioral changes are seen in older patients after administration of a barbiturate, unlike the more consistent sedative effect observed in young individuals (7). Further, Ayd (8) has observed that if extrapyramidal symptoms occur with phenothiazine therapy, they vary in type according to the age of the patient; in the young patient, there is a greater likelihood that dyskinesia may be observed, while parkinsonism is more frequently noted in older patients.

Decisions regarding drug selection and dose for an elderly patient are not influenced solely by a consideration of biological consequences of aging, but also by the effects of disease and concomitant therapy on drug action and disposition; for example, liver disease affects the binding and metabolism of drugs (9, 10), and one drug can significantly alter the metabolism and disposition of another drug (11–13). The focus of my review is drug disposition in the elderly. However, because multiple pathology and concomitant drug treatment are more common in elderly patients, these important factors are also incorporated.

Preclinical Studies

For many years, knowledge about the effects of age on drug activity in adults was based on studies in animals (7, 14). Chen and his colleagues at Eli Lilly noted that increased age in experimental animals was associated with an increased sensitivity to the effects of morphine (15), picrotoxin and secobarbital (16), ouabain (17), and alcohol (18). Interestingly, increased age was not always associated with an increased toxicity; for example, the lethal dose of methadone was unrelated to age (15). Dearing et al. (19) found that digitalis-induced myocardial lesions in cats occurred more frequently with increasing age, and MacNider (20) observed in dogs that the toxic effects of ether and chloroform were more marked in older animals. Verzar and Farner noted that the pharmacological response to various drugs was modified by age (21–23). They observed that older animals were more susceptible to agents that exert a depressant action on the central nervous system, and that the pharmacological actions of compounds that stimulate the central nervous system were decreased with age. The different actions of amphetamine are interesting in this regard: in old animals, the appetite-depressant action was more marked and the stimulant properties were less evident than in young animals. In a series of biochemical studies reported by Kato and his associates (24, 25), increasing age in the rat was associated with a decrease in microsomal enzyme activity. Meprobamate, carisoprodol, pentobarbital, and hexobarbital were more slowly metabolized in the older animal; consequently, amounts of these drugs in plasma and tissue increased. These observations in animals are valuable in explaining some of the changes in drug action that occur in humans, particularly in dealing with increased sensitivity and decreased metabolism with age.

Pharmacokinetics

The starting point for pharmacokinetic analysis is the curve for the time course of a drug's concentration in blood or plasma,

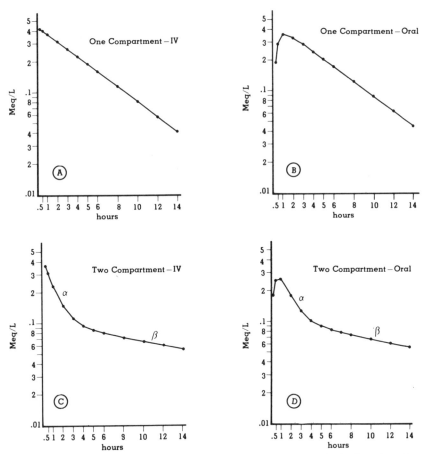

Fig. 1. Plasma concentration curves for oral and intravenous (iv) administration fitted to one-compartment and two-compartment models

Data represent actual values from a study of the kinetics of lithium carbonate and are the basis for the calculations of pharmacokinetic parameters in Fig. 2

the net expression of several functions that reflect absorption, binding and distribution, transfer, metabolism, and excretion of drugs. Figure 1 shows the plasma concentration–time curves for lithium carbonate after oral and intravenous administration. The pattern of the curve for drug concentration in plasma is often described mathematically by assuming a one-compartment or a two-compartment model. The compartmental relationships for both models are shown in Figure 2. The kinetics of lithium carbon-

ONE-COMPARTMENT MODEL

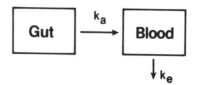

TWO-COMPARTMENT MODEL

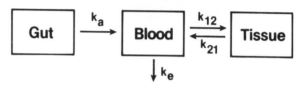

Where k_a = absorption rate constant, k_e = elimination rate constant, k_{12}, k_{21} = rate constants from blood to tissue and vice versa.

Fig. 2. Pharmacokinetic parameters as defined by one-compartment and two-compartment models

Blood plasma concentration curves are shown in Fig. 1

ate best fit a two-compartment model (Figures 1C and 1D). For a two-compartment model there are two slopes for the curve representing the decay of the plasma concentration. These are the α and β phases noted in Figure 1C and 1D, and represent fast and slow disposition rate constants. The data for the one-compartment model for lithium carbonate (Figures 1A and 1B) were obtained by using the relevant parameter values from the two-compartment example but eliminating the second compartment from the calculations. The result is a single decay curve for the plasma concentration. I am not going to give a detailed derivation of the formulas used to calculate the plasma concentration curve (10, 11, 26, 27), but will provide simplified definitions of various pharmacokinetic parameters so that you can better appreciate the changes in these functions that have been reported to occur with age (28–32).

Elimination rate constant (k_e) in a one-compartment model (Figures 1A and 1B) is derived from the decay slope of the curve for drug concentration in blood and is expressed as reciprocal time units, i.e., the fractional decrease in plasma concentration per unit of time. In a two-compartment model, k_e is a function of the two slopes (α and β) of the plasma concentration curve and the k_{21} rate constant of transfer from the peripheral to the central compartment. The k_e is a composite of several rate constants, including those that reflect renal excretion, extrarenal excretion, and metabolism. For drugs excreted primarily by the kidney, k_e is a direct reflection of the level of kidney function; for drugs that are eliminated by metabolic degradation, k_e is a reflection of the metabolic rate.

Absorption rate constant (k_a) can be estimated from the blood data by using the equations that describe the serum concentration of a drug after oral administration. However, before k_a can be calculated, other pharmacokinetic parameters, including k_e, must first be estimated.

Elimination half-life ($t_{1/2}$) is the time required for a drug concentration in blood to decrease by 50%. In the case of a one-compartment model the elimination half-life is calculated from the formula:

$$t_{1/2} = 0.693/k_e$$

In the case of a two-compartment model the following formula is used:

$$t_{1/2} = 0.693/\beta$$

where β is not equal to k_e but is a function of k_e, k_{21}, and k_{12}.

Apparent volume of distribution (V_d) represents the hypothetical volume required to accommodate a drug in the same concentration that is present in the circulation. V_d is most easily calculated from the data obtained after intravenous administration, and in this situation is simply the dose of drug divided by the γ-intercept of the plasma concentration curve extrapolated to time zero. In the case of oral administration, the derivation of the volume of distribution is less straightforward and involves the estimation of various rate constants. An additional problem in this situation is that the amount of drug absorbed is not known.

Total body clearance of a drug expresses the efficiency with which the drug is eliminated and is a composite of all processes of elimination. Total body clearance is the product of k_e and V_d, and may also be estimated by dividing the dose absorbed by the area under the blood concentration–time curve.

Absorption

Effect of age. A number of factors influence the rate of absorption of drugs after oral administration (33, 34) and some of these factors are modified with age in such a way as to suggest that drug absorption in the elderly may be incomplete or delayed. These changes include:

—A decrease in basal and maximum acid output, which may affect the ionization and solubility of some drugs.
—A decrease in splanchnic and gastric blood flow.
—A decrease in the number of absorbing cells.
—A decreased rate of gastric emptying.
—A decrease in the viability of transport mechanisms in the gut.

The absorption of some dietary constituents such as galactose, 3-methyl glucose, calcium, and iron, which require active transport mechanisms, is decreased in the elderly (33). As noted by Stevenson et al. (34), most drugs do not require active transport mechanisms, but are absorbed by passive diffusion; studies so far indicate that drug absorption is not consistently decreased in older individuals. Most of the studies in the literature show that the rate and extent of drug absorption is unchanged with age (Table 1). Two studies contradict this conclusion. Kampmann et al. (42) have reported that the absorption constant for propylthiouracil is decreased by 70% in older subjects, and Shader et al. (43) have shown a similar decrease in the absorption rate constant for chlordiazepoxide. But for the moment we can reasonably assume that for well-absorbed drugs, age is not particularly relevant to the issue of increased drug sensitivity in the elderly.

Influence of disease and concomitant drug therapy. Disease is not an important factor in controlling or influencing the rate of absorption of drugs. Although chronic liver disease may lead to malabsorption of fat, there is little evidence that liver disease per se influences drug absorption. Preliminary work suggests that antipyrine absorption may be delayed in patients with portal hypertension (9). Because most drugs are absorbed mainly from the small intestine, absorption may be delayed because of prolonged

Table 1. **Drug Absorption in the Elderly**

Drug	Effect in old age (reference)
Mecillinam	k_a unchanged (35)
Indomethacin	Absorption probably not changed (36)
Tetracycline	k_a unchanged (37)
Paracetamol	Rate and extent of absorption unchanged (38)
Sulfamethiazole	Rate and extent of absorption unchanged (38)
Acetylsalicylic acid	k_a unchanged (39)
	k_a unchanged (40)
	k_a slightly decreased (41)
Practolol	k_a unchanged (39)
Quinine	k_a unchanged (40)
Propylthiouracil	k_a decreased by 70% (42)
Chlordiazepoxide	k_a decreased by 72% (43)
Propicillin	k_a unchanged (44)

k_a, absorption rate constant.

gastric-emptying time after surgery. The absorption of antipyrine has been reported to be delayed two days after cholecystectomy (45). For poorly soluble drugs such as digoxin, delayed intestinal motility could work to increase the rate of absorption (45).

The bioavailability of drugs may be altered by the presence of other materials in the gastrointestinal tract. For example, ferrous sulfate impairs the absorption of tetracycline and oxytetracycline, and the absorption of tetracycline can also be reduced by the presence of sodium bicarbonate (12).

Drug Binding

Effect of age. Drugs are distributed according to their physico-chemical properties, and it is the amount of free drug in the circulation that determines the pharmacological response. One important element in the distribution of a drug is the degree to which it is reversibly bound to plasma proteins, particularly to serum albumin. For drugs that are highly protein-bound, a small change in the degree of binding will cause a significant increase in the amount of free drug available in the circulation and, therefore, available to the receptor site. If, for example, a drug is 90% bound, a 10% decrease in binding nearly doubles the concentration of free drug.

Changes in drug binding can result from a decrease in the amount of serum albumin present, a change in the spatial confor-

401

mation of the protein molecule (resulting in fewer binding sites), or competition for binding sites by a second drug or by a substance of endogenous origin. In the elderly, the factors apparently of greatest importance are a decrease in serum albumin concentration and the competition for fewer binding sites by drugs given concomitantly.

Greenblatt (46), to assess the relationship of serum albumin concentration to age, studied more than 11 000 subjects and found

Table 2. Effect of Age on Plasma Protein Binding

Drug	Effect in old age (reference)
Phenobarbituric acid	Unchanged (47)
Benzylpenicillin	Unchanged (47)
Phenytoin	Unchanged (47)
	Maximum binding decreased (48)
Tolbutamide	Decreased (49)
Diazepam	Unchanged (50)
Carbenoxalone	Decreased (51)
Salicylate	Unchanged (52)
Phenylbutazone	Decreased (52)
Sulfadiazine	Unchanged (52)
Warfarin	Unchanged (53)
	Maximum binding decreased (54)
Quinidine	Unchanged (55)
Pethidine	Decreased (56, 57)
Chlormethiazole	Decreased (58)

that the serum albumin concentration decreased progressively with each decade of age, from 3.97 kg/L in subjects less than 40 years of age to 3.68 kg/L in patients 80 years old and older. Patients with dysproteinemia, renal insufficiency, hepatic dysfunction, and malnutrition were excluded from the study. Greenblatt noted that the decreased concentration of serum albumin in the elderly could be a factor in age-dependent changes in the actions of protein-bound drugs. The results of studies concerning the role of age in drug binding are noted in Table 2.

For the most part, these data suggest that age has neither a dramatic nor a consistent effect on plasma binding. Furthermore, age per se is apparently not associated with a defect in drug-binding protein, or with the presence of an endogenous material that competes for drug-binding sites (47), or with a change in the affinity of a drug for protein-binding sites *(48, 54)*. These data, however, need to be examined more closely, in that there appears to be a quantitative relationship between the concentration of serum albumin in individual patients and the extent to which drugs are bound. There also appear to be differences related to the various methods used in the studies conducted. Evidence for decreased drug binding in older patients includes the following:

- Decreases in plasma binding of some drugs have been reported *(49, 52)*, associated with a decrease in plasma albumin. For the most part, the plasma albumin concentrations noted were lower than those in studies that showed little variation in plasma binding with age.
- Low serum albumin concentrations correlate with a decrease in maximum protein binding, in situations where the concentration of drug is increased to a point of binding-site saturation *(48, 54)*.
- Samples from subjects with extremely low serum albumin concentrations are associated with low plasma-binding values *(47)*.
- Multiple-drug therapy is associated with decreased plasma binding, most likely as a result of competition for binding sites *(52)*.

The results of the study by Wallace et al. *(52)* are particularly important to the study of changes in plasma binding with age. The occurrence together of low albumin concentration and the presence of a second drug decrease the plasma binding of salicylate and sulfadiazine; moreover, the degree to which binding was decreased correlated with the number of drugs administered. A brief summary of these data is given in Table 3.

Table 3. **Effect of Age on Competitive Drug Binding**				
	Young subjects		*Old subjects*	
Taking additional drugs	No	Yes	No	Yes
Plasma albumin, g/L	42	39	36	36
% salicylate unbound	27	28	27	42
% sulfadiazine unbound	49	50	51	67

Source: Wallace et al. *(52)*

Influence of disease and concomitant drug therapy. Liver disease, kidney disease, and surgical procedures can influence the binding of certain drugs. In liver disease, for example, serum albumin concentrations are decreased, which is perhaps the most important factor in decreased drug binding *(9)*. Qualitative changes in the albumin molecule or competition for binding sites by such endogenous substances as bilirubin or bile represent other potential mechanisms for changes in protein binding. The degree of plasma-protein binding of phenytoin decreases after surgery, probably because of a decrease in the albumin concentration in the plasma *(45)*. Competitive inhibition by endogenous substances such as free fatty acids may also play a part in certain patients. Decreased plasma-protein binding has been reported for phenytoin and digitoxin in patients with impaired renal function *(10)*.

Increased binding to plasma protein has been reported for quinidine in post-operative patients *(45)*, and the binding of sulfadiazine, phenylbutazone, and phenytoin is increased after dialysis *(10)*.

Drug interactions may also influence the binding of drugs to plasma proteins or to receptor sites. Drug binding to proteins is usually nonspecific, with many drugs bound to the same binding site on the molecule. A drug with a higher affinity for binding will displace one with a lower affinity, thus altering the amount of free drug available in the circulation, and presumably, at its site of action.

There are several important examples of competitive displacement. Phenylbutazone will displace warfarin and, as a result, significantly increase the activity of the anticoagulant. Because phenylbutazone and the salicylates will also displace tolbutamide, the elderly diabetic may exhibit a more pronounced hypoglycemic effect than in a younger patient *(12)*.

Drug Distribution

In addition to the decrease in the concentration of serum albumin and the potential that this may represent for less binding of some drugs, other age-related changes can also influence drug distribution. These factors, recently reviewed by Mitchard *(57)*, include a decrease in body weight, an increase in the proportion of adipose tissue to functional tissue (sometimes called lean body mass), a decrease in total body water, and diminished cardiac output, renal blood flow, and splanchnic blood flow. Membrane permeability may also be increased with age *(28, 57)*. The net result of these changes is that *(a)* the action of drugs that accumulate in fatty tissue will be prolonged, and *(b)* plasma will contain higher concentrations of drugs that are distributed primarily in body water; for example, peak concentrations of ethanol in blood are higher in older subjects *(59)*.

In terms of changes in the apparent volume of distribution

Table 4. Changes in Volume of Distribution Reported with Increasing Age

| | Changes | | |
Drug	Blood concentration	Volume of distribution	Reference
Ethanol	Increased	Decreased	59
Digoxin	Increased	Decreased	60, 61
Propicillin	Increased	Decreased	44
Diazepam		Increased	50
Chlormethiazole	Increased	Increased	62, 58
Amobarbital	Increased	Unchanged	63
Acetaminophen		Unchanged	64
Acetylsalicylic acid	Decreased	Increased	41
Quinine	Increased	Unchanged	55
Sulfamethiazole	Increased	Unchanged	38
Practolol	Increased	Decreased	65

that occur with age (Table 4), apparently the volume of distribution will increase and amounts in blood will decrease for lipid-soluble drugs, whereas with polar drugs the volume of distribution will decrease and the amounts of drugs in blood will increase *(57)*. As noted earlier, the volume of distribution is a mathematical concept used to estimate the volume of water into which the drug is distributed at a concentration equal to that of the plasma.

Concentrations of Drugs in Blood and Rates of Elimination

Effect of age. With increasing age, the magnitude and time course of the curve for a drug's concentration in blood is influenced most consistently and significantly by changes in the rates of metabolism and elimination. For the most part, the maximum concentration of a drug in blood is increased and the elimination half-life ($t_{1/2}$) of the drug is extended. There are exceptions, however. An extended elimination half-life may be associated simultaneously with an increase in the volume of distribution, therefore minimizing changes in the amount of drug in plasma, as in the case of acetylsalicylic acid (42). With chlordiazepoxide, the elimination half-life is increased and the clearance is decreased; however, the peak concentrations in plasma are lower with increased age (44). In the case of a single dose, this is due to a delay in the rate of absorption.

A decrease in renal function with age has been observed by many investigators (66), and is reflected in lower values for renal

Table 5. Effect of Increasing Age on the Kinetics of Drugs Eliminated by the Kidney

Drug	Concentration in blood	$T_{1/2}$	Clearance	Reference
		Effect		
Benzylpenicillin	Increased			67
Procaine penicillin	Increased			67
Dehydrostreptomycin	Increased	Increased 61%		68
Tetracycline	Increased			68
Digoxin	Increased	Increased 43%	Decreased 36%	60
Sulfamethiazole	Increased threefold at 6 h	Increased 72%	Decreased 46%	38
Kanamycin		Increased 163%		69
Penicillin		Increased 126%		66

plasma flow, glomerular filtration rate, and tubular secretory capacity. Endogenous creatinine clearance (used to estimate renal blood flow) is reduced with age. Serum creatinine concentrations, however, do not change significantly with age (66), and are therefore of limited value in estimating the degree of renal function in the elderly. The effect of age on the kinetics of drugs excreted primarily by the kidney is shown in Table 5. The increase in drug concentrations in plasma is consistently associated with a decrease in clearance and an extended elimination half-life.

Many drugs are extensively metabolized before excretion. As noted earlier, studies in the rat clearly show that old age is associated with a decrease in activity of microsomal drug-metabolizing enzymes (24, 25) and a consequent increase in a concentration

Table 6. Effect of Age on Kinetics of Extensively Metabolized Drugs

Drug	Route of metabolism	Effect of increasing age (reference)
Amobarbital	Hydroxylation	$T_{1/2}$ increased 280% (63)
Propranolol	Hydroxylation	Concentration in plasma increased fourfold after 2 h (65)
Acetaminophen	Glucuronide and sulfate conjugation	$T_{1/2}$ increased 24%; clearance decreased 25% (64)
Antipyrine	Hydroxylation	$T_{1/2}$ increased (26); clearance decreased (70); V_d decreased (71)
Imipramine	Demethylation	Steady-state drug concentration in blood increased; $T_{1/2}$ unchanged (72)
Acetylsalicylic acid	Glycine conjugation	$T_{1/2}$ increased 56%; clearance unchanged; V_d increased; concentration in plasma unchanged (42)
Phenylbutazone	Hydroxylation	$T_{1/2}$ unchanged (39)
Quinidine	Hydroxylation	$T_{1/2}$ increased 36%; clearance decreased 35% (55)
Diazepam	Demethylation	$T_{1/2}$ increased 350%; V_d increased (50)
Nitrazepam	Reduction	$T_{1/2}$ unchanged; clearance unchanged; concentration in plasma unchanged in normal subjects (73) $T_{1/2}$ increased 38%; concentration in blood decreased; V_d increased 100% in bed-ridden patients (74)
Chlordiazepoxide	Demethylation	$T_{1/2}$ increased 80%; clearance decreased 42%; peak concentrations in plasma lower; V_d increased (44, 75)

of drug in the plasma and tissues. The results of studies in humans are shown in Table 6.

For many drugs, the concentration in plasma increases with age, the clearance decreases, and the elimination half-life increases. This is not a uniform observation, however, because a prolonged half-life of a drug in plasma in the elderly may be offset by an increase in the apparent volume of distribution. For example, with diazepam (50) the half-life in plasma increases significantly with age, but is accompanied by a significant increase in volume of distribution; therefore, the concentrations in plasma are not substantially altered with age.

Another exception is acetylsalicylic acid (42). Although the plasma half-life is increased, the fact that the volume of distribution is also increased means that the clearance and plasma values are unchanged. In the case of nitrazepam (73), age is not a factor with regard to the kinetics of the drug in normal elderly subjects; in geriatric bed-ridden patients, however, the concentration in blood is less, the elimination half-life is prolonged, and the volume of distribution is doubled *(74)*.

Dosage implications. Based on the results of pharmacokinetic studies, changes in drug dosage have been suggested. With digoxin, the decrease in clearance *(60, 61)* was associated with a blood concentration of drug almost twice as great in the elderly as in younger subjects *(60)*. Because there is a correlation between the plasma concentration of digoxin and evidence of digitalis toxicity, it has been suggested that the dosage of digitalis be decreased for elderly patients *(60)*. For propranolol the peak concentration in blood in elderly subjects was nearly fourfold that observed in a group of younger subjects. On the basis of these data, Castleden et al. *(65)* suggested that the dosage of propranolol given to elderly patients be substantially decreased.

High concentrations of imipramine and amitryptyline have been observed in plasma of older depressed patients *(72, 76)*. In imipramine-treated patients this increase was associated with a decreased rate of drug elimination *(68)*. Nies et al. *(72)* concluded that the dosage of tricyclic antidepressants should be decreased by one-third to one-half of the usually recommended amount.

The pharmacokinetics of quinidine has been studied by Ochs et al. *(55)*, who concluded that decreased clearance and prolongation of the elimination half-life could predispose the elderly to toxicity unless the dosage was appropriately adjusted. In the case of chlordiazepoxide, Shader et al. *(43)* have expressed concern regarding decreased clearance in elderly patients, despite the observation in a single-dose study that concentrations of the drug in blood were lower in older subjects; their concern was that the decreased clearance could result in a greater accumulation of chlordiazepoxide in the elderly during chronic therapy. Indeed, Roberts et al. *(75)* have cautioned against the use of chlordiazepoxide in the elderly. Further, Reidenberg et al. *(77)* reported that a lower dose of diazepam would produce the same degree of sedation in elderly patients as that in younger patients treated with higher doses.

Hewick and Newbury *(78)* surveyed daily lithium carbonate dosage as a function of age and found that the daily dose given to patients 80 years old was about 47% of that given to patients 20 years old. The corresponding decrease in the concentration of lithium in plasma was 23%.

Influence of disease and concomitant drug therapy. In patients with cirrhosis or acute viral hepatitis, the elimination half-life of diazepam, chlordiazepoxide, and pethidine is lengthened, as is the duration of action of the barbiturates, which depend on the rate of hepatic metabolism. These changes are the result of a decrease in plasma clearance; for diazepam, they are due also to an increase in the volume of distribution. In patients with acute hepatitis, clearance of pethidine is decreased and the half-life is increased, but the values return to normal upon recovery from the disease *(9)*.

Renal disease and impaired renal function influence the pharmacokinetic profile of a drug. A decrease in renal function, such as a lessening of renal blood flow, glomerular filtration, and tubular excretion, results in high concentrations of drugs that are primarily eliminated by the kidney. Thus the dosage of some drugs should be adjusted in patients with decreased renal function, on the basis of endogenous creatinine clearance. For example, in patients with renal disease, lower doses of such drugs as digoxin, cephalexin, penicillin-G, sulfadiazine, and tetracycline should be used *(10)*.

Other diseases can influence the elimination half-life of a drug. Persistent hypercapnia results in a shortened elimination half-life for tolbutamide. This change may be related in part to microsomal enzyme induction caused by the prolonged stress of difficulty in breathing. Lower than normal serum concentrations of digoxin are also known to occur in patients with chronic obstructive lung disease *(10)*. Abnormalities of thyroid function may also influence the metabolism of drugs. The plasma half-lives of antipyrine and digoxin were shortened in hyperthyroid patients; in hypothyroid patients, the half-life of antipyrine was prolonged. Correction of thyroid function was found to produce more normal values *(10, 79)*. In patients with cystic fibrosis, renal clearance of dicloxacillin has been reported to be two- to threefold greater than in normal patients *(10)*.

Drug interactions may also alter the metabolism of drugs *(11)*. For example, phenobarbital and other barbiturates stimulate the metabolism of a number of drugs, including phenylbutazone, bishydroxycoumarin, and tolbutamide; tolbutamide and glutethimide will also stimulate the metabolism of hexobarbital and other barbiturates. Other drugs may serve to inhibit the metabolism of a second drug: oxyphenylbutazone inhibits the metabolism of bishydroxycoumarin, and the latter inhibits the metabolism of phenytoin *(11).*

A special case of drug interaction occurs with those drugs that are excreted renally via an active transport system. Drugs of this type when given concurrently compete for similar transport systems and, therefore, the presence of one drug may interfere with the elimination of another. Probenecid, a well-known example, is often given with penicillin to delay excretion and maintain high blood concentrations of the antibiotic. As noted in Table 5, the elimination half-life of penicillin is increased in older subjects *(66).* After probenecid administration, the penicillin half-life is increased in both young and old subjects, with the increase being greater in the younger subjects *(64).* Probenecid and salicylates can also inhibit the excretion of indomethacin *(12).* Therefore, it is important in considering drug regimens in the elderly to take into account the effect that one drug may have on the duration and magnitude of the activity of a second drug by influencing its rate of metabolism and elimination.

Pharmacodynamics and Age

Changes in drug activity with age are not limited to those that simply reflect an increase in plasma concentration and a prolonged elimination half-life. Other age-related changes, such as a decrease in the number of receptor sites and a less flexible set of integrated homeostatic systems, are responsible for a modification in drug activity and sensitivity with age *(7, 28, 31).* For example, the pharmacokinetics of nitrazepam are unaffected by age, yet the incidence of depression is higher *(5)* and deficits in performance greater *(73)* in old subjects, suggesting an increase in the sensitivity of the central nervous system.

The elderly are also more sensitive to the depressant effects of diazepam *(77).* Many drugs, including the phenothiazines and tricyclic antidepressants, produce postural hypotension secondary to their primary therapeutic action. In young patients, this response is limited by homeostatic adjustments of the cardiovascular systems; however, in the older patient these adjustments are less responsive and, therefore, orthostatic hypotension is more pronounced.

The catecholamines provide another example of changes in drug sensitivity with age. As noted earlier, the stimulant properties of amphetamine are less apparent in older animals, but the appetite-suppressant effects are more pronounced *(21–23)*. Isolated strips of aortic tissue from old rats are less responsive to norepinephrine than tissue from young animals *(80)*, which is attributed to mechanical limitations associated with atherosclerotic changes. The cardiovascular actions of isoproterenol are also diminished with age *(81, 82)*; however, in this situation the decreased response is attributed to a decreased number of beta-receptors. Interestingly, thyroxine reverses the age-related decrease in the response of rat aortic tissue to isoproterenol *(82)*.

Guidelines for Drug Use in the Elderly

In conclusion, I present some general guidelines for the effective use of drugs in the elderly:

- Higher blood concentrations of most drugs can be anticipated in elderly patients because of decreased renal function and decreased rates of drug metabolism. Occasionally, the concentrations in blood should be monitored.
- Various diseases, particularly renal and liver diseases, can contribute to higher blood concentrations of some drugs. Therefore, an accurate diagnosis is a prerequisite to prescribing.
- Lower doses should seriously be considered for elderly patients, at least initially to establish tolerance. The prescribing information should be consulted as a guide.
- The potential for drug interactions should be assessed before drugs are prescribed concomitantly, and the number of drugs administered should be minimized wherever possible.

I thank Dr. Wilfred J. Westlake for his contribution to the discussion of the mathematical relationships involved in the derivation of the pharmacokinetic calculations and for providing the data for Figures 1 and 2.

References

1. Seidl, L. G., Thornton, G. F., Smith, J. W., and Cluff, L. E., Studies on the epidemiology of adverse drug reactions. III. Reactions in patients on a general medical service. *Bull. Johns Hopkins Hosp.* **119**, 299 (1966).

2. Hurwitz, N., Predisposing factors in adverse reactions to drugs. *Br. Med. J.* i, 536 (1969).
3. Caranasos, G. J., Stewart, R. B., and Cluff, L. E., Drug-induced illness leading to hospitalization. *J. Am. Med. Assoc.* **228,** 713 (1974).
4. Pemberton, M., Use of phenylbutazone in rheumatoid arthritis. *Br. Med. J.* i, 490 (1954).
5. Greenblatt, D. J., and Allen, M. D., Toxicity of nitrazepam in the elderly: A report from the Boston collaborative drug surveillance program. *Br. J. Clin. Pharmacol.* **5,** 407 (1978).
6. Greenblatt, D. J., Allen, M. J., and Shader, R. I., Toxicity of high-dose flurazepam in the elderly. *Clin. Pharmacol. Ther.* **21,** 355 (1977).
7. Bender, A. D., Pharmacodynamic aspects of aging: A survey of the effect of increasing age on drug activity in adults. *J. Am. Geriatr. Soc.* **12,** 114 (1964).
8. Ayd, F. J., Jr., Tranquilizers and the ambulatory geriatric patient. *J. Am. Geriatr. Soc.* **8,** 909 (1960).
9. Roberts, R. K., Desmond, P. V., and Schenker, S., Drug prescribing in hepatobiliary disease. *Drugs* **17,** 198 (1979).
10. Wagner, J. G., *Fundamentals of Clinical Pharmacokinetics.* Drug Intelligence Publications, Inc., Hamilton, IL, 1975, pp 382–388.
11. Ritschel, W. A., *Handbook of Basic Pharmacokinetics.* Drug Intelligence Publications, Inc., Hamilton, IL, 1976.
12. Cadwallader, D. E., *Biopharmaceutics and Drug Interactions,* 2nd ed., Rocom Press, Montclair, NJ, 1974.
13. Richey, D. P., and Bender, A. D., Effects of human aging on drug absorption and metabolism. In *Physiology and Pathology of Human Aging,* R. Goldman and M. Rockstein, Eds., Academic Press, New York, NY, 1975, pp 59–63.
14. Bender, A. D. Drug sensitivity in the elderly. In *Drugs and the Elderly: Perspectives in Geriatric Clinical Pharmacology,* J. Crooks and I. H. Stevenson, Eds., Macmillan Press, London, 1979, pp 147–153.
15. Henderson, R. G., and Chen, K. K., Effect of age upon toxicity of methadone. *Proc. Soc. Exper. Biol. Med.* **68,** 350 (1948).
16. Chen, K. K., and Robbins, E. B., Age of animals and drug action. *J. Am. Pharmacol. Assoc.* **33,** 80 (1944).
17. Chen, K. K., and Robbins, E. B., Influence of age of rabbits on the toxicity of ouabain. *J. Am. Pharmacol. Assoc.* **33,** 61 (1944).
18. Chen, K. K., and Robbins, E. B., Influence of age of mice on the toxicity of alcohol. *J. Am. Pharmacol. Assoc.* **33,** 62 (1944).
19. Dearing, W. H., Barnes, A. R., and Essex, H. E., Experiments with calculated therapeutic and toxic doses of digitalis. I. Effects on the myocardial cellular structure. *Am. Heart J.* **25,** 648 (1943).

412

20. MacNider, W. deB., The factor of age in determining the toxicity of certain poisons. *J. Gerontol.* **1**, 189 (1946).

21. Verzar, F., The age of the individual as one of the parameters of pharmacological action. *Acta Physiol. Acad. Sci. Hung.* **19**, 313 (1961).

22. Verzar, F., and Farner, D., Untersuchungen über die Wirkung von Pharmaka auf Tiere verschiedenen Alters. *Gerontologia* **4**, 143 (1960).

23. Farner, D., and Verzar, F., The age parameter of pharmacological activity. *Experientia* **17**, 421 (1961).

24. Kato, R., Chiesara, E., and Frontino, G., Induced increase of meprobamate metabolism in rats pretreated with phenobarbital or phenaglycodol in relation to age. *Experientia* **17**, 502 (1961).

25. Kato, R., and Tanaka, A., Metabolism of drugs in old rats. *Jpn. J. Pharmacol.* **18**, 389 (1968).

26. Ritschel, W. A., Pharmacokinetic approach to drug dosing in the aged. *J. Am. Geriatr. Soc.* **24**, 344 (1976).

27. Creasey, W. A., *Drug Disposition in Humans: The Basis for Clinical Pharmacology*, Oxford University Press, New York, NY, 1979.

28. Bender, A. D., Pharmacodynamic principles of drug therapy in the aged. *J. Am. Geriatr. Soc.* **12**, 296 (1974).

29. Crooks, J., O'Malley, K., and Stevenson, I. H., Pharmacokinetics in the elderly. *Clin. Pharmacokinet.* **1**, 280 (1976).

30. Lamy, P. P., Therapeutics and the elderly. *Addict Dis.* **3**, 311 (1978).

31. Richey, D. P., and Bender, A. D., Pharmacokinetic consequences of aging. *Ann. Rev. Pharmacol. Toxicol.* **17**, 49 (1977).

32. Triggs, E. J., and Nation, R. L., Pharmacokinetics in the aged: A review. *J. Pharmacokinet. Biopharm.* **3**, 387 (1975).

33. Bender, A. D., The effect of age on intestinal absorption. Implications for drug absorption in the elderly. *J. Am. Geriatr. Soc.* **13**, 1331 (1968).

34. Stevenson, I. H., Salem, S. A. M., and Shepherd, A. M. M., Studies on drug absorption and metabolism in the elderly. In *Drugs and the Elderly* (see ref. *14*), pp 51–63.

35. Ball, A. P., Viswan, A. K., Mitchard, M., and Wise, R., Plasma concentrations and excretion of mecillinam after oral administration of pivmecillinam in elderly patients. *J. Antimicrob. Chemother.* **4**, 241 (1978).

36. Traeger, A., Kunze, M., Stein, G., and Ancherman, G., Zur Pharmacokinetic von Indomethacin bei alten Menschen. *Z. Alterforsch.* **27**, 151 (1973).

37. Kramer, P. A., Chapron, D. J., Benson, J., and Mercik, S. A., Tetracycline absorption in elderly patients with achlorhydria. *Clin. Pharmacol. Ther.* **23**, 467 (1978).

38. Triggs, E. J., Nation, R. L., Long, A., and Ashley, J. J., Pharmacokinetics in the elderly. *Eur. J. Clin. Pharmacol.* **8**, 55 (1975).

39. Castleden, C. M., Volans, C. N., and Raymond, K., The effect of aging on drug absorption from the gut. *Age Ageing* **6,** 138 (1977).
40. Salem, S. A. M., and Stevenson, I. H., Absorption kinetics of aspirin and quinine in elderly subjects. *Br. J. Clin. Pharmacol.* **4,** 397 (1977).
41. Cuny, G., Royer, R. J., Mur, J. M., Serot, J. M., Faure, G., Netter, P., Maillard, A., and Penin, F., Pharmacokinetics of salicylates in elderly. *Gerontologia* **25,** 49 (1979).
42. Kampmann, J. P., Mortensen, H. B., Bach, B., Waldorff, S., Kristensen, M. B., and Hansen, J. M., Kinetics of propylthiouracil in the elderly. *Acta Med. Scand.* **624** *(Suppl.),* 93 (1979).
43. Shader, R. I., Greenblatt, D. J., Harmatz, J. R., Franke, K., and Koch-Weser, J., Absorption and disposition of chlordiazepoxide in young and elderly male volunteers. *J. Clin. Pharmacol.* **17,** 709 (1977).
44. Simon, C., Malerczyk, V., Muller, U., and Muller, G., Zur Pharmacokinetic von Propicillin bei geriatrischen Patienten im Vergleich zu jungeren Erwachsenen. *Dtsche. Med. Wochenschr.* **97,** 1999 (1972).
45. Elfstrom, J., Drug pharmacokinetics in the postoperative period. *Clin. Pharmacokinet.* **4,** 16 (1979).
46. Greenblatt, D. J., Reduced serum albumin concentration in the elderly: A report from the Boston collaborative drug surveillance program. *J. Am. Geriatr. Soc.* **27,** 20 (1979).
47. Bender, A. D., Post, A., Meier, J. P., Higson, J. E., and Reichard, G., Plasma protein binding of drugs as a function of age in adult human subjects. *J. Pharm. Sci.* **64,** 1711 (1975).
48. Hayes, M. J., Langman, M. J. S., and Short, A. H., Changes in drug metabolism with increasing age: 2. Phenytoin clearance and plasma proteins. *Br. J. Clin. Pharmacol.* **2,** 73 (1975).
49. Miller, A. K., Adir, J., and Vestal, R. E., Tolbutamide binding to plasma proteins of young and old human subjects. *J. Pharm. Sci.* **67,** 1192 (1978).
50. Klotz, U., Avant, G. R., Hoyumpa, S., Schenker, S., and Wilkinson, G. R., The effects of age and liver disease on the disposition and elimination of diazepam in adult man. *J. Clin. Invest.* **55,** 347 (1975).
51. O'Malley, K., Judge, T. G., and Crooks, J., Geriatric clinical pharmacology and therapeutics. In *Drug Treatment Principles and Practice of Clinical Pharmacology & Therapeutics,* G. S. Avery, Ed., Adis Press, Sydney, Australia, 1976, pp 123–142.
52. Wallace, S., Whiting, B., and Runcie, J., Factors affecting drug binding in plasma of elderly patients. *Br. J. Clin. Pharmacol.* **3,** 327 (1976).
53. Shepherd, A. M. M., Hewick, D. S., Moreland, T. A., and Stevenson, I. H., Age as a determinant of sensitivity to warfarin. *Br. J. Clin. Pharmacol.* **4,** 315 (1977).
54. Hayes, M. J., Langman, M. J. S., and Short, A. H., Changes in drug

metabolism with increasing age. 1. Warfarin binding and plasma proteins. *Br. J. Clin. Pharmacol.* **2**, 69 (1975).

55. Ochs, H. R., Greenblatt, D. J., Woo, E., and Smith, T. W., Reduced quinidine clearance in elderly persons. *Am. J. Cardiol.* **42**, 481 (1978).
56. Mather, L. E., Tucher, G. T., Pflug, A. E., Lindop, M. J., and Wilkerson, C., Meperidine kinetics in man: Intravenous injection in surgical patients and volunteers. *Clin. Pharmacol. Ther.* **17**, 21 (1975).
57. Mitchard, M., Drug distribution in the elderly. In *Drugs and the Elderly* (see ref. *14*), pp 65–76.
58. Nation, R. L., Vine, J., Triggs, E. J., and Learoyd, B., Plasma level of chlormethiazole and two metabolites after oral administration to young and aged human subjects. *Eur. J. Clin. Pharmacol.* **12**, 137 (1977).
59. Vestal, R. E., McGuire, E. A., Tobin, J. D., Andres, R., Norris, A. H., and Mezey, E., Aging and ethanol metabolism. *Clin. Pharmacol. Ther.* **21**, 343 (1977).
60. Ewy, G. A., Kapadia, G. G., Yao, L., Lullin, M., and Marcus, F. I., Digoxin metabolism in the elderly. *Circulation* **39**, 449 (1969).
61. Cusack, B., Kelly, J., O'Malley, K., Noel, J., Lavau, J., and Hargan, J., Digoxin in the elderly: Pharmacokinetic consequences in old age. *Clin. Pharmacol. Ther.* **25**, 772 (1979).
62. Nation, R. L., Learoyd, B., Barber, J., and Triggs, E. J., The pharmacokinetics of chlormethiazole following intravenous administration in the elderly. *Eur. J. Clin. Pharmacol.* **10**, 407 (1976).
63. Ritschel, W. A., Age-dependent disposition of amobarbital: Analog computer evaluation. *J. Am. Geriatr. Soc.* **26**, 540 (1978).
64. Briant, R. H., Dorrington, R. E., Cleal, J., and Williams, F. M., The rate of acetaminophen metabolism in the elderly and the young. *J. Am. Geriatr. Soc.* **24**, 359 (1976).
65. Castleden, C. M., Kaye, C. M., and Parsons, R. L., The effect of age on plasma levels of propranolol and practolol in man. *Br. J. Clin. Pharmacol.* **2**, 303 (1975).
66. Kampmann, J. P., and Mølholm Hansen, J. E., Renal excretion of drugs. In *Drugs and the Elderly* (see ref. *14*), pp 77–87.
67. Leikola, E., and Vartia, K. O., On penicillin levels in young and geriatric subjects. *J. Gerontol.* **12**, 48 (1957).
68. Vartia, K. O., and Leikola, E., Serum levels of antibiotics in young and old subjects following administration of dihydrostreptomycin and tetracycline. *J. Gerontol.* **15**, 392 (1960).
69. Kristensen, M., Hansen, J. M., Kampmann, J., Lumholtz, B., and Siersbaek-Nielsen, K., Drug elimination and renal function. *J. Clin. Pharmacol.* **14**, 307 (1974).
70. Vestal, R. E., Norris, A. H., Tobin, J. D., Cohen, B. H., Shock, N.,

and Andres, R., Antipyrine metabolism in man: Influence of age, alcohol, caffeine, and smoking. *Clin. Pharmacol. Ther.* **18,** 425 (1975).

71. Liddell, D. E., Williams, F. M., and Briant, R. H., Phenazone (antipyrine) metabolism and distribution in young and elderly adults. *Clin. Exper. Pharmacol. Physiol.* **2,** 481 (1975).

72. Nies, A., Robinson, D. S., Friedman, M. J., Green, R., Cooper, T. B., Ravaris, C. L., and Ives, J. O., Relationship between age and tricyclic antidepressant plasma levels. *Am. J. Psychiat.* **134,** 790 (1977).

73. Castleden, C. M., and George, C. F., Increased sensitivity to benzodiazepines in the elderly. In *Drugs and the Elderly* (see ref. *14*), pp 169–178.

74. Kangas, L., Iisalo, E., Kanto, J., Lehtinen, V., Pynnonen, S., Ruikka, I., Salminen, J., Sillanpaa, M., and Syvalahti, E., Human pharmacokinetics of nitrazepam: Effect of age and diseases. *Eur. J. Clin. Pharmacol.* **15,** 163 (1979).

75. Roberts, R. K., Wilkinson, G. R., Branch, R. A., and Schenker, S., Effect of age and parenchymal liver disease on the disposition and elimination of chlordiazepoxide (Librium). *Gastroenterology* **75,** 479 (1978).

76. Carr, A. C., and Hobson, R. P., High serum concentrations of antidepressants in elderly patients. *Br. Med. J.* **ii,** 1151 (1977).

77. Reidenberg, M. M., Levy, M., Warner, A., Coutinho, C. B., Schwartz, M. A., Yu, G., and Cheripko, J., Relationship between diazepam dose, plasma level, age and central nervous system depression. *Clin. Pharmacol. Ther.* **23,** 371 (1978).

78. Hewick, D. S., and Newbury, P. A., Age: Its influence on lithium dosage and plasma levels. *Proc. Br. Pharmacol. Soc.* **3,** 354 (1976).

79. Bonelli, J., Haydl, H., Hruby, K., and Kaik, G., The pharmacokinetics of digoxin in patients with manifest hyperthyroidism and after normalization of thyroid function. *Int. J. Clin. Pharmacol.* **16,** 302 (1978).

80. Tuttle, R. S., Age-related changes in the sensitivity of rat aortic strips to norepinephrine and associated chemical and structural alterations. *Gerontologia* **21,** 510 (1966).

81. Lakatta, E. G., Alterations in the cardiovascular system that occur in advanced age. *Fed. Proc.* **38,** 163 (1979).

82. Parker, R. J., Berkowitz, B. A., Lee, C-H., and Denckla, W. D., Vascular relaxation, aging and thyroid hormones. *Mech. Ageing Dev.* **8,** 397 (1978).

Nutritional Deficiency in Aging due to Protein–Calorie Semi-Starvation

David R. Weir

Semi-starvation is a general term implying the suboptimal dietary intake of calories over a prolonged period of time. For this presentation it is defined as the suboptimal intake of protein and calories for a prolonged time without reference to essential nutrients other than protein.

What is meant by good nutrition for the elderly? It may be defined as nutrition that preserves the finest qualities of youth, or that sustains a physical and mental state of health that cannot be improved by providing or withholding food. More specific definitions for the aging population are difficult to make. Unlike the pediatric population, the aged do not have nutritional problems capable of unique solution. There is too much variation among the elderly, the result of insults of disease during the person's lifetime, variations in body structure and metabolism, and differences in physical activity.

To have a somewhat homogeneous study group, subjects were selected according to the following criteria:

1. Those with malignant disease, liver disease, significant infection, increased concentrations of serum urea nitrogen, hemorrhage, blood dyscrasia, significant endocrine disease, and malabsorption were excluded.
2. Persons with intact gastrointestinal systems and who had no great difficulty in chewing or swallowing were included, such as patients with fractured hip, amputation, moderate emphysema, compensated heart disease, and hemiplegia without mental impairment.

The great majority of the study group were elderly persons, but

417

some were middle aged—certainly, the semi-starvation that has been described can occur at any age.

Rejection of Food

There are two primary causes for protein–calorie semi-starvation. The first is unavailability of food, which is relatively uncommon in our affluent society. The second, and more clinically important in our society, is the rejection of food when it is available. This is an extraordinary phenomenon in the elderly and too often is not clinically recognized.

The reasons for this rejection of food may be obscure. Older persons living alone simply may not bother to obtain and cook the food they should eat even though they have the money to do so. Their low-calorie diet may consist largely of snack foods and sweets, which are also low in essential nutrients; often, they selectively reject protein.

From the criteria described above, a group was selected in which the individuals were significantly underweight. In the hospital their daily consumption of a diet containing 1800 calories and 85 g of protein was ascertained by the weigh-back method. A few ate all the food offered, but most rejected about half of the calories and consumed only 10 to 30 g of the protein daily.

For some older persons, the reasons for this rejection of food seem to be psychiatric in origin. Loss of status can be very important. Retired persons are often considered no longer productive; too often the elderly lose their influence in the constellation of family and friends, who become fewer as the years pass; and plain loneliness sets in. Crippling disability may make them dependent upon others. They have lost their power and the dominant position they once enjoyed in society. The rejection of food may become a weapon whereby they consciously or subconsciously express their resentment of this loss of status; in severe form, it can be viewed as a passive suicidal intention.

Clinical Findings

The determination of past dietary intake by history-taking may be accurate, particularly if informants who live with the patient are available. On the other hand, the history may be inaccurate and it may be necessary to determine current intake by a diary-recording method or by direct observation under controlled conditions *(1, 2)*. Included in the history should be information about changes in behavior, mental state, weight, physical activity and endurance, and interpersonal relationships. Many of our patients showed apathy and indifference, loss of interest in former activities and hobbies, mental confusion, forgetfulness, sometimes incontinence, and even full-blown "senility." The overall performances of the individuals were suboptimal.

In assessing nutritional status, body weight is the most useful single observation. Within the group studied, those considered to be suboptimally nourished had weights below the ideal *(1–3)*, and body fat, as determined by physical examination *(1)*, was subnormal. Often, physical examination showed various changes in the skin and mucous membranes such as dryness, roughening, and pigmentation of the skin; glossitis; and fissuring at the corners of the mouth.

Laboratory Findings

Besides body weight, estimations of hemoglobin, hematocrit, and serum protein fractions are the most useful observations in determining the presence of protein–calorie undernutrition due to semi-starvation. A study of patients conforming to the criteria mentioned earlier was designed to discover differences between those who were anemic and those who were not *(3)*. For the anemic group the study showed a modest decrease of weight, hemoglobin, and hematocrit; a significant decrease of serum albumin; and a significant increase in total globulin and α_1- and γ-globulin. The serum iron values were also decreased (see Tables 1 and 2). The estimation of blood and plasma volume (Table 3) showed an increase in plasma volume and percent of blood volume in anemic patients. Quantitative calculation of the components of the blood confirmed the previous observations but did not add much useful information. The concentrations of vitamin B_{12}, folic acid, pyridoxine, and thiamine (Table 4) were not below normal, indicating that the anemia and symptoms and signs of malnutrition were not due to deficiency of one of these factors. At the end of the study, we concluded that the anemia and other findings in the anemic group were due to protein–calorie semi-starvation.

Therapy

The semi-starvation caused by food rejection can be extremely difficult to treat. Even when the proper food is presented under

Table 1. Mean Hemoglobin, Hematocrit, and Percent Ideal Weight of Patients

	Anemic patients (11)	Nonanemic patients (12)
Hemoglobin, g/L	89	143
Hematocrit, %	30	43
Percent of ideal weight	83	97

Table 2. Mean Serum Iron and Protein Concentration in Elderly Patients

	Anemic	Nonanemic	p
Serum iron, μg/L	583	960	< 0.001
Total iron-bonding capacity, μg/L	2027	2668	< 0.05
Percent saturation, %	27.2	39.7	< 0.05
Total protein, g/L	61	67	< 0.05
Albumin, g/L	24.6	38.2	< 0.001
Globulin, g/L	36.5	28.9	< 0.02
Alpha$_1$-globulin, %	5.4	4.4	< 0.01
Gamma-globulin, %	29.7	17.3	< 0.001

Table 3. Quantitative Values of Blood Components in Elderly Patients

	Anemic	Nonanemic
Blood vol, L	3.18	3.93
Plasma vol, L	2.23	2.19
% of blood vol	70	56
Erythrocyte vol, mL	970	1746
% of blood vol	30.7	43.6
mL/kg wt	19.5	28.3
Serum protein		
Total g	140.6	149.4
g/kg wt	2.7	2.5
Serum albumin		
Total g	58.0	88.5
g/kg wt	1.2	1.45
Serum globulin		
Total g	80.5	59.8
g/kg wt	1.6	0.98

Table 4. Concentration (μg/L) of Vitamins in the Blood of
Elderly Patients

	Anemic	Nonanemic	Normal range
Serum B_{12}	0.76	0.65	0.25– 0.91
Serum folic acid[a]	6.8	4.3	3.2 – 13.7
Serum pyridoxine	46.9	44.0	29.6 –112.4
Thiamine			
Whole blood	22.4	20.5	14.9 – 43.8
Serum	18.6	14.8	2.5 – 15.2
Erythrocyte	32.3	27.9	19.3 – 85.9

[a] Difference between values in anemic and nonanemic patients significant at $p < 0.001$; differences for other vitamins not significant at $p = 0.05$.

ideal conditions, patients may still refuse to eat. All the skills of the physician, the nutritionist, the nurse, or other care-giver must be brought to bear (1). The best approach is to provide smaller serving portions and more frequent feedings, cater to the patients' likes and dislikes, and encourage them to eat everything offered. When the therapy is effective, a miraculous change may occur, which I will illustrate by a case report previously cited (1).

J. B., an 80-year-old black man, was admitted to the Metabolic Ward with the diagnoses of arteriosclerotic heart disease, mild diabetes, and chronic brain syndrome. Medications consisted of digoxin, orinase, and colace. He was allowed wine. No iron or vitamin supplements were given. With constant attention from the nutritionist, the patient consumed over a 90-day period a daily diet averaging 1900 calories, 75.6 g of protein, and the recommended allowances of all other essential nutrients. The changes in the laboratory findings are shown in Table 5. He gained weight and his hemoglobin, hematocrit, and serum albumin values were restored to normal. The serum globulin decreased, and all the bone marrow iron was used up. Even more striking were the observations of the head nurse on the ward, who wrote:

Three months ago the patient was wearing a pro-kit because of incontinence of urine, was often incontinent of feces, required restraints both at night and in the wheelchair, could not walk because of unsteadiness, and was almost completely dependent in the activities of daily living. By contrast he is now bright in conversation, doubly continent, unrestrained, dresses himself, shaves himself, gets in and out of the bath

Table 5. **Realimentation of Patient J. B.**

	On admission	After three months of treatment
Weight, kg	48.4	53.6
Hematocrit, %	34.5	44.0
Erythrocyte vol, L	1.26	1.71
Serum albumin, g/L	26	42.9
Serum globulin, g/L	39	35.1
Total circulating albumin, g	66.0	79.0
Total circulating globulin, g	85.0	79.0
Bone marrow iron	+++	0

tub, brushes his own teeth, reads the paper, goes to the Highland Workshop, ambulates independently in the ward, feeds himself, and has a much improved appetite.

What she did not write down was that he also showed sexual interest in the nurses.

With this note it is difficult to deny that J. B. escaped from the state of "senility" into the state of a human being, again participating in society in a satisfactory manner. The chronic brain syndrome had disappeared.

Implications of Protein–Calorie Undernutrition

The clinical syndrome of protein–calorie undernutrition in the elderly due to semi-starvation is common, yet receives far less recognition than it should. There are reasons for this: the patients are not emaciated, and the anemia and changes in serum proteins may be slight and attributed by the physician to the normal aging process. There is no good evidence, however, that the normal aging process has such an effect. The elderly, sedentary person does require fewer calories for the maintenance of function and body weight, but anything below 1800 calories, particularly with selective protein rejection, may become critically adverse.

The mental symptoms, including advanced "senility," are too often attributed to degenerative brain disease or multiple "little strokes." The fact that chronic brain syndrome can be due to undernutrition is too seldom recognized by physicians, nutritionists, and other health workers. The fact that the syndrome can be reversed by proper alimentation is hardly mentioned in the literature. In the foreword to *The Biology of Human Starvation (4)*, Sir Jack Drummond described the variety of mental symptoms that occur in whole populations subjected to famine. He made particular reference to the Dutch, who had been starved during World War II. As soon as they were provided with 1800 calories or more daily after the war, the mental symptoms disappeared without a trace. In June 1979 I heard a talk by a British gerontologist on the subject of mental problems of the elderly, in which he made no mention of the etiologic significance of undernutrition. When questioned about this, the speaker stated that this wasn't a factor in England because old people there are provided with plenty of milk and eggs. The phenomenon of food rejection had not entered his mind. The fact that semi-starvation can occur in an individual living in an affluent society and result in mental symptoms seems to elude the average clinician.

As has been pointed out, the establishment of the diagnosis of protein–calorie undernutrition is not difficult. If physical and mental suboptimal performance is accompanied by weight loss, modest anemia, low serum albumin, and high serum globulin, the presumptive diagnosis should be undernutrition. More elaborate laboratory testing provides little additional useful information. The association of low serum albumin concentration with protein deprivation has often been observed in animals and man *(3, 5)*. Albumin of less than 35 g/L should be considered abnormal and possibly due to deprivation. As discussed previously *(3)* the association of a high concentration of serum globulins with serum albumin of less than 30 g/L and modest anemia in protein–calorie semi-starvation has rarely been described.

A successful therapeutic trial will confirm the diagnosis: for several months, provide a daily dietary intake of about 1800 calories or more, with the recommended daily allowances of all essential nutrients, including protein. Too often the therapeutic trial is unsuccessful because the individual continues to refuse to eat. However, the trial must be carried out; if it is successful, there can be an almost miraculous result, as in the case of J. B.

It is also extremely important to keep in mind that improving the nutritional status of the disabled person can be a most important part of his overall rehabilitation. Frequently, it is the only important therapeutic measure that can be carried out.

In the elderly population of our affluent society, nutritional deficiency due to the inadequate intake of calories and protein is common. This is more often related to the rejection of food than to its unavailability. The deficiency syndrome is manifested by weight loss, suboptimal physical and mental performance, modest anemia, a low concentration of serum albumin, and a high concentration of serum globulin. If proper realimentation can be carried out over a period of months, the syndrome will largely disappear. Too often the trial is not carried out because the etiology of the syndrome is not recognized.

References

1. Weir, D. R., Houser, H. B., Davis, M., and Schenk, E., Recognition and management of nutrition problems of the elderly. In *Clinical Aspects of Aging,* William Reichel, Ed., Williams and Wilkins Co., Baltimore, MD, 1978, pp 183–198.
2. Weir, D. R., and Houser, H. B., Problems in the evaluation of nutritional status in chronic illness. *Am. J. Clin. Nutr.* **12,** 278–286 (1963).
3. Weir, D. R., Dimitrov, N. V., Houser, H. B., Suhrland, L. G., and Myint, T., Serum proteins and blood vitamins in anemia of the chronically ill. *J. Chron. Dis.* **22,** 407–419 (1969).
4. Keys, A., Brojek, J., Henshel, A., Michelson, O., and Taylor, H. L., *The Biology of Human Starvation,* University of Minnesota Press, Minneapolis, MN, 1950.
5. Brock, J. F., Dietary protein deficiency: Its influence on body structure and function. *Ann. Int. Med.* **65,** 877–897 (1966).

Discussion—Session V

DR. WALKER: Are the changes that have been described this morning the result of reaching an age like 90, or are some a result of being born in the 1880's and being exposed to different environments during life, perhaps being exposed to influenza epidemics?

DR. WEIR: It is a good question, but I do not think we have enough data to come to a conclusion. The variability of the population is so great that you cannot assign an individual or even a group of individuals an etiologic factor that has brought on the disability they may have or that is the reason for their suboptimum performance.

DR. BLATTLER: The hypothesis I have, and it is strictly an hypothesis, is that people who are very fit in the older ages were probably very fit as younger persons. If you have an appropriate abnormality index, the people who will score very high on that index as young people will not make it to advanced age, and conversely, people who do make it to old age probably scored very low when younger.

DR. MEACHUM (Shreveport, LA): What correction factors did you, Dr. Blattler, apply in "gaussianizing" your data? Were they derived empirically or were they already available?

DR. BLATTER: For our work, we have 32 sets of data. We empirically transform the data to a gaussian form. Another laboratory that uses different methods might have to use a slightly different transformation, and if a laboratory is not careful to maintain a consistant quality control over a long time, the transformation might change.

DR. MEACHUM: Is it not something that could be determined just once? Would it have to be done for each study?

DR. BLATTLER: The broad trend of the transformation function is going to be the same. For alkaline phosphatase it will be the log type in my laboratory or your laboratory, but some of the

425

fine details are probably going to vary from method to method.

PROF. HODKINSON: I have used much simpler transformations, only log transformations. These effectively normalize most skewed distributions, and we do not feel the need for more sophisticated ones such as $x + 10$ or log graphs as used by Dr. Blattler. There is consistency between different studies, with simple logarithmic transformation normalizing most people's data for glucose, urea, creatine, and all enzymes. This argues for using simple transformations rather than more complicated ones.

DR. MEACHUM: How do you think the question of gaussian vs nongaussian, parametric vs nonparametric statistics, or other approaches to statistical studies is going to be solved?

PROF. HODKINSON: If you use nonparametric methods just to determine range, the methods are good but you are wasting data. Nonparametric methods are about half as efficient as gaussian methods if the distribution is gaussian. If you want to make the most of your data and they are gaussian, which has been shown to be true for most biological data, you obtain the best values for effort expended by using gaussian statistics. As soon as you do anything more sophisticated than wanting to determine range, nonparametric methods fail you, because the extention of nonparametric methods to multivariate cases has hardly been developed. There have been some attempts, but the methods are incredibly cumbersome and they break down as soon as you have more than two or three variables. If you want to look at multivariate situations with more variables, you must use gaussian statistics; there is nothing else.

DR. BLATTLER: I agree.

DR. GRANNIS: I would like to take exception to that. In our experience many of the laboratory parameters are not gaussian, and, when you think about it, they should not be, under ordinary conditions of measurement. Considering the flux of materials into and out of the bloodstream and the various perturbations that go on normally, many sets of nongaussian data could be expected. For example, if we measure protein and sodium in an individual in a rested state, we will have certain values and most likely a gaussian distribution. If that individual drinks some water, the protein values will change but the sodium values will not, because they are rapidly compensated for. The sodium values will retain a gaussian distribution, but the protein values will have a skewness. This is an exaggerated case, but under ordinary conditions we would expect these perturbations of different constituents in the blood to be affected in different ways, and for many of the constitutents the data would be skewed upward or downward.

I would like to comment further on gaussian statistics. Because the biological data are not gaussian distributed, I do not believe we can use gaussian statistics. I do not quite know what needs to be done, but I learned in growing up that there are many ways to skin a cat. It is very challenging to say that there is no other approach, for we could devise an approach if it were necessary.

DR. BLATTLER: Some of the parameters of some of the tests we looked at are approximately gaussian—certainly symmetrically distributed. We are interested in multifactorial analysis, and it does no harm to carry out the transformation. I hope that Dr. Hodkinson is right that a simple transformation is adequate. The statisticians I work with want to polish things perhaps more than necessary. In data on sodium, where you have a Laffer-curve type of phenomenon, very high values or very low values are discriminated against because of incompatibility with health. In this case you do have a symmetrical distribution. With urea nitrogen in blood, which is basically a waste product, the skewness is to the high side, because as the urea accumulates, the body cannot handle it. In trying to obtain maximum information from data, multifactorial analysis is very difficult if you do not use the transformations to obtain it in the gaussian form.

PROF. HODKINSON: May I come back to the graphs, because, I think, we must take one of two viewpoints. We can be philosophical and argue from first principles, but it does not get us very far. Perturbations are multiple, and with multiple perturbations, the distribution will tend towards the normal. Binomial, chi-squared, and other distributions will tend towards normal if the numbers are large. That is philosophy; but what matters is practicality. In practice, if you look at your data carefully and take out those perturbations due to sex and age, you have homogeneous data. They are normally distributed or log normal, as shown by Flynn and coworkers (Flynn, F. V., Piper, K. A. J., Garcia-Webb, P., McPherson, K., and Healy, M. J. R., *Clin. Chim. Acta* **52**: 163–171, 1974). Let us not argue about it from first principles, but let us do experiments and look at the data.

DR. GRANNIS: There is another way of looking at the data. We know that by looking at individual variability, there are people who are characteristically low normal, average normal, or high normal for certain constituents. They have characteristic individual set-point values. What does this mean so far as population distribution is concerned? Total distribution for the population clearly depends on the numbers of these people with different characteristic set-point values. There is no reason these values should have a gaussian distribution.

DR. BLATTLER: We are discussing something I find very fascinating: biochemical individuality and the concept of optimum values. If we were to go to the Air Force Academy and look at a very elite population of young men, elite mentally and physically, we would find a much narrower distribution of results. Those are the people we should be compared with. If you go to less and less fit populations, you will see a wider and wider distribution of data.

DR. McEwen (Palo Alto, CA): I understand that in over-medication with digitalis some of the symptoms are hallucinations and loss of appetite. Dr. Weir and Dr. Bender, would you care to estimate the frequency with which this is encountered in the elderly?

DR. WEIR: I could not give you figures on it. I can say that it is not at all uncommon, and is due to many factors. One is the type of data Dr. Bender has shown us on binding capacity, but also it is often due to human error. Many of these older people are confused and forget they have taken their digitalis. They can become toxic because they have taken perhaps 20 pills instead of 15 over a period of time. From a clinician's point of view, you cannot, when beginning therapy, prescribe a dosage of digitalis and say, "Take this daily for the next two months and come back and see me." You can easily be in trouble, unless the effects of the dose are in some way monitored, as by regularly having the patient take his own pulse if he is fibrillating. It is human error and metabolic variation, and it is bad medical practice to give patients potent drugs and require that they take it for a prolonged period without monitoring.

DR. BENDER: I do not have the figures, but from what is published on digitalis toxicity, adverse effects are more common than one would think. People tend to think that prescribing a certain dose will result in the same response for each patient. I feel, however, that there is a trend toward concern for individual variability and differences in drug responses and a recognition of the need to alter therapeutic programs accordingly.

PROF. HODKINSON: The frequency is very high and it is also quite common to see digitalis intoxication occur in people who have been safely on digitoxin therapy for a long time. This is because when they fall ill, they very often show deterioration of renal function. Digitalis is almost entirely excreted by the kidney and when persons become ill, their normally safe dose becomes toxic. It is incredibly common in hospital practice.

DR. CARAWAY (Flint, MI): Prof. Hodkinson, in your slide showing the difference in the albumin concentration in your hospitalized patients vs controls, the difference was about 10 g/L. Were both these populations either erect or supine? We know that by going from the erect to the supine position we can lower the serum albumin by 4 to 5 g/L.

PROF. HODKINSON: Blood was usually drawn while the patients were sitting. There were very few taken lying down. They were also taken at the same time of the day and were estimated in the same laboratory.

DR. BECKMAN (Irvine, CA): I am reminded, by the controversy developing here as to whether or not the transformations are properly used, that some 50 years ago I did some work on statistical theory. I sympathize with the desire to simplify the mathematical difficulties, but I should like to point out that the aim should be to try to find the proper function of a parameter that will follow a gaussian distribution, and not arbitrarily assume that a given function will follow a gaussian curve.

For example, suppose you wished to find the distribution of the number of apples that could be lined up on a shelf. You would expect a gaussian distribution based on the diameter of the apples. If you wished to study the distribution of a pesticide on apples, however, the surface area rather than the diameter is a significant factor, and a normal distribution would be expected for the square of the diameter rather than the diameter itself. The amount of juice obtainable from apples would involve their volumes, so a normal distribution curve would be more likely to result from plotting the cube rather than first power of apple diameters.

429

As another example, in biochemistry we may study aspects of chemical reactions that involve linear functions of concentration. Normal distributions based on concentrations probably would result. In dealing with electrochemistry, however, you will come up against the Nernst equation, which states that electrical potentials are linear functions of the logarithmic values of ionic concentrations, so a gaussian distribution should not be expected in a plot of electrical potentials vs ionic concentrations, but probably would occur in a plot of potentials vs the logarithms of ionic concentrations.

Thus the aim should be to try to find, from the nature of the scientific phenomenon involved, what function of a parameter will logically follow the normal gaussian distribution.

DR. GRANNIS: I would like to point out that for a number of years people have been trying to dissect populations and find subpopulations. In the process, assumptions are often made about means and standard deviations, assumptions about some type of gaussian distribution. We published a paper [see reference *10* in Dr. Grannis' first paper, this volume] in which we were able to dissect the patient population and the laboratory data without resorting to gaussian statistics. It was a matter of simple subtraction.

DR. BLATTLER: One sin commited in the laboratory is the reporting of different electrolytes in different units. For example, calcium is often presented in mg/dL and frequently omitted from equations in attempting to balance the charges. Albumin bears considerable charge but is often neglected. Thus if you try to understand the electrostatics in serum, there are a number of charged particles you do not consider. It would be a relatively simple thing, as Dr. Bender suggested, if we would express all components in the same units. We would see relationships we now miss.

DR. WALKER: I would like to reiterate a comment Dr. Goldman made yesterday. We do not expect creatinine to be normally distributed, because it is a ratio of lean-body mass and the number of glomeruli, both of which have normal distributions.

DR. SHARPE (Kensington, MD): Dr. Bender, from a pragmatic standpoint, after sitting through these past three days enthralled, I am now asking, how can we accept the credibility of clinical investigation in developing new drugs for the elderly, in view of the variability of homeostatic changes and acceptance of clinical values? How do we go about, especially in the elderly, accepting credibility of research or of clinical investigation reports? I would like to see the clinical group develop some parameters that could be applied.

DR. BENDER: I would like to separate the concern for credibility in clinical trials into two parts: efficacy and safety. With regard to efficacy, I believe that considerable progress has been made in judging the therapeutic utility of drugs in both young and older patient populations. Improvements in methodologies to evaluate the effectiveness of the new and potent drugs now being introduced have not only led to advances in treatment but also have provided new information regarding the progress and course of the disease. For example, SmithKline has developed and introduced a new drug, "Tagamet," a specific H_2-receptor antagonist. In gathering data to demonstrate the therapeutic utility of this agent, we had to develop improved methods for evaluating the effectiveness of therapeutic agents in the treatment of ulcer disease. In the course of these studies, new information regarding the rate, extent, and time course of ulcer healing, as well as the incidence of recurrence, was gathered. Much of the credibility in evaluating efficacy comes from the fact that clinical trials are established on a multi-investigator or multi-center basis, and, to be accepted, positive results must therefore be confirmed in other laboratories.

With regard to adverse drug reactions, a considerable amount of credibility has been brought to the system by improvements in the way that adverse drug reactions are reported. Physicians, clinical investigators, the drug's sponsors, and the Food and Drug Administration are concerned about and alert to trends in the incidence of adverse drug reactions, whether these occur in the course of a new drug's development or during its use after FDA approval.

Epilogue

As I noted in the prologue, a purpose of this symposium and this volume is to review our present knowledge of the chemistry of aging. It thus becomes important to decide what new information would be valuable for understanding and improving the health of the elderly. Throughout the volume, there are many suggestions for further research. One of the best sources of suggestions is in the discussions at the end of each section, the questioners often asking for unknown information. I will summarize here some of the possible avenues of research that have drawn my attention.

Many theories have been proposed to explain the aging process. Many factors enter into the final results, but the importance of each and its relations to other factors are not adequately understood. An excellent place to start when seeking a project with which to research the problems of aging is to digest Dr. Strehler's summary of the theories of aging and to correlate it with one's own experiences and expertise to generate new ideas to test. Dr. Strehler predicts that in the 1980s highly talented individuals involved in aging research will rapidly increase the fundamental molecular/cellular knowledge for a fuller understanding of the aging process.

Dr. Shock shows that changes in composition or response to challenge may correlate positively or negatively with age. These include several renal function tests, cardiac output, and glucose tolerance. He points out that further work needs to be done on these and other tests. Some of these have been evaluated by Dr. Blattler, but many more data are needed to better characterize the regression of analytes on age. It may be necessary to apply the statistical analyses to more homogeneous populations, rather than the population in general, because variables other than sex and age must be considered. Dr. Shock also points out the difficulties in arriving at an aging factor. A multivariate analysis, as suggested by Dr. Blattler (Gillebrand et al.), may be required, but we need to determine the best combination of variables.

Dr. Strehler suggests the need for additional research to elucidate the neuroendocrine failure during aging, pointing out that it is a weak link in human physiology. He further identifies the lack of knowledge of the causes of changes in enzymic activity with age, and suggests possibilities that might be investigated. Answers to questions such as those he suggests could lead to a fuller understanding of the aging process and answer speculations as to the cause(s) of aging.

Dr. Timiras et al. also stress the need for greater knowledge of the neuroendocrine interrelationships. Current investigations are "opening the way to experimental designs suitable for exploration of eventual neuroendocrine causes of the aging process." The design should lead to better understanding and to an improvement of the quality of life, if not longevity. Because aging may be the consequence of synaptic deficits in specific brain areas, animal models are needed; additional study is needed to learn how the deficits may be modified by drugs. Dr. Nelson et al. suggest that the changes in endocrine and neural factors can best be sought in the early stages of aging. Their paper follows this theme and could act as a guideline for others. Dr. Adelman, continuing this approach, suggests the kinds of questions that those doing research on aging should ask. Dr. Weigle (Fidler et al.) identifies the immune system as a potential source for research involving surveillance against the emergence of the diseases of aging.

Dr. Meites asks a number of questions that arise from observing the differences in organ functions and the endocrines in aging rats and humans. A broader base of knowledge of the advantages of specific properties and conditions to the welfare of each species is needed to understand the aging process.

Elderly persons have frequently been diagnosed as diabetics when their plasma glucose is above the reference range for young healthy persons. Dr. Levine questions this practice, noting that, on the average, the glucose concentration increases at the rate of 5 mg/L per decade after the age of 50. The reason for the increase in the average concentration of glucose in plasma with age awaits further research efforts. Further, Dr. Liss notes that

433

the brain of the elderly is often starved of oxygen and glucose, causing a vascular dementia. Because glucose is the main substrate for energy in the brain, its requirement by the brain could stimulate an increase in the plasma glucose concentration, permitting greater amounts to cross the blood–brain barrier so that the brain might function normally. Some researchers have found that the glucose concentration in the brain may parallel that in blood (Nakanishi, M., Uemura, E., Harai, S., Takabatake, S., Nakada, I., and Sekimoto, H., On cerebral energy metabolism in experimental cerebral hemorrhage. *Acta Neurol. Scand.* **60** (Suppl. 72):332–333, 1979). Another possible explanation may be found in the altered glucagon/insulin ratios noted by Dr. Adelman as animals age. Dr. Levine asks several questions concerning glucose metabolism in the elderly; these questions also need answering by future research.

Dr. Thurlbeck points out the need for more conclusive studies on the role of elastin in the aging lung. Although the elastin content increases with age, our lack of knowledge about its function and localization leaves room for further investigation.

Dr. Goldman describes several unknown factors of the aging process as they affect renal function. Although important changes occur at the capillary or arteriolar level, the role of the vascular system as the site of primary and secondary changes needs to be solved.

In discussing the risk factor in cardiovascular disease, Dr. Hazzard describes the unsatisfactory nature of the several tests that have been postulated but that apply poorly to the individual. We know that effective prevention of atherosclerosis must start when a person is young, but much still must be learned concerning the factors to be considered. The role of the present addiction to exercise in the delay of cardiac and other diseases offers grounds for research into the management of total health care.

A major problem of the elderly is the loss of bone mineral with age, especially in white, postmenopausal women. Dr. Gordan shows that low doses of estrogen can prevent or diminish the loss in postmenopausal osteoporosis. Less is known for other types of bone loss. Studies of the problem must include the effects of the administration of hormones, calcium, vitamin D, calcitonin, and fluoride; each of these is known to enter into the maintenance of mineral metabolism, but the expressed value of each factor is dependent on the type of research that has been done.

Dr. Meites earlier questioned the advisibility of administering estrogen to postmenopausal women or androgens to elderly men, but feels that there are great possibilities in utilizing the neuroendocrine approach to problems of the aging reproductive system. In discussion Dr. Gordan quoted evidence to show that, with the small doses of estrogen he advises, the chances of producing cancer are negligible compared with the benefits received. The problem will remain until future research workers resolve it.

At several times during the symposium, the value of exercise for optimum health was broached. Dr. Shock did not feel that exercise contributes to the variances noted in several analytes, but stated that a thorough study would be needed to define the quantitative effects. If disuse is a cause of osteoporosis, can exercise prevent this disorder?

It was a major revelation when Dr. Hayflick's work showed that fibroblast cultures could undergo only a limited number of divisions related to the age of the organism from which the cells were derived. How do the cells differ from those that seemingly have immortality, such as HeLa cells and cells that clone? Can conditions be found that will explain the differences? What would be the consequences of such knowledge? The paper by Dr. Goldstein et al. shows that the difference is not in the mechanisms of protein synthesis. Could it be in the DNA synthesis and repair, as suggested by the paper of Drs. Hart and Stephens? Is there really a sex difference in mortality, as reflected in mortality tables? Could it be demonstrated by the culturing methods used by Dr. Hayflick? The identification of such a factor could be important.

Drs. Pearson and Manni suggest that the discovery of the etiology of breast cancer would offer the best solution for solving the problems. This is difficult because of the primary and secondary roles of steroids, pituitary hormones, and hormone receptors in the development of the cancers. That the best therapy required five drugs also suggests the complexity of the problems that need to be solved.

In the discussions, Drs. Adelman and Thurlbeck pointed out the need for greater knowledge of altered enzymes in older individuals and suggested that this is an open field for the biochemist to pursue. How do the changes in the enzymes reflect the protein synthesis and degradation, and the production of necessary components of the body such as surfactants?

Important to clinical chemists are the research challenges dealing with analytical results and their interpretation. Dr. Grannis discusses the parameters necessary for meaningful values. We need more information on intra- and interindividual variability of many analytes. What are the optimum concentrations of the analytes, and how can knowledge of the values be used in estimating risk factors for the whole or for a subpopulation? What battery of tests can best identify risk factors, and is this identification cost effective? Much more research is needed to understand how the physiological system changes with age and how the changes relate to health. Dr. Grannis suggests plasma fibrinogen concentration as an indicator of survival. This requires verification and a search for other indicators. Correlations of other analytes with clinical observations over long intervals are needed to establish possible helpful patterns.

Dr. Liss more specifically calls for the identification of the risk factor in persons who will develop Alzheimer's dementia. The interrelationships of the morphological changes representing neurofibrillary tangles and neurogenic plaques need elucidation—is one a prerequisite of the other? Although aluminum has been implicated in dementia and may produce neurofibrillary tangles in certain areas of the brain, its effects are not understood. Considering the large amounts of aluminum consumed by the public, why are dementias from it not more common? According to Dr. Liss, research with a high priority is the determination of the type of changes governing susceptibility to and increases of the risk factor.

Should there be a battery of tests for each stage of life, as suggested by Dr. Grannis? If so, what should they be? A thorough compilation of existing data could be helpful, but a prospective study designed for this purpose would be most valuable, and probably could best be done through the cooperation of a number of investigators in different locations.

Dr. Blattler and his co-workers postulate that optimum analyte concentrations are important to the health of individuals, and that these optimum values lie near the population modes. They suggest that this principle applies to urate, but it needs testing for all analytes. They also propose an "Abnormality Index" to distinguish between states of health. The index they calculated is based on 16 analytes and needs to be extended to others. Of great importance would be the ability to obtain diagnostic information from existing data.

In the papers by Drs. Grannis, Hodkinson, and Blattler, and in the final discussion, the statistical analyses of results are featured in important roles. Complete agreement was not reached, except that all agreed that more complete analyses of the data are needed. As Dr. Beckman suggested in the discussion, one must first understand the nature of the phenomenon before the values are analyzed statistically. Statisticians disagree as to the degree of exactness that should be applied. Laboratorians and clinicians, with the help of statisticians, are needed to design the studies of the many parameters involved and to correlate the results with health and disease.

It is important to understand the effects of drugs in the aged, as Dr. Bender indicates. Drug binding is often low in older persons because of hypoalbuminemia, resulting in higher concentrations of free (unbound) drugs upon which pharmacological responses depend. At present little is known about free-drug concentrations, and very few laboratories even attempt to estimate them. Laboratories need to establish methods for estimating free-drug concentrations in vivo. It is doubtful whether this can now be done reliably for any *one* drug, which leaves the field wide open for research on methods of analysis and of reporting the results. The therapeutic drug monitoring programs do not now relate to free-drug concentrations. The monitoring for free drugs in vivo will require much research effort before it is meaningful.

The possibile research problems discussed in this volume and in this chapter are multiple. Problems of different degrees of difficulty can be selected—from those that improve methods, to those that accumulate data for correlation with clinical findings, to those that test new postulates by procedures that are yet to be designed. All will lead to an improvement in the health of the elderly. There is plenty of room for new talent to be involved in research on aging. Those wishing source material can consult the library of the National Council on the Aging, 1828 L St., N.W., Washington, DC 20016. The library has over 5000 volumes on various aspects of aging and may be used by any who can visit it.

As indicated in the prologue, there is an impetus for increased research into the problems of the aged, the age group where health care is least cost-effective. I hope that this volume will be helpful in finding solutions to the problems involved, and that this epilogue may be the prologue for others to initiate their research into the problems of aging.

—A.A.D.

As a well-spent day brings happy sleep, so life, well used, brings happy death. Time abides long enough for those who make use of it.

LEONARDO DA VINCI

Index

440

441

Drugs
    adverse reaction, 394–396, 431
    concentration in blood, 396–400, 405–
        411
    distribution, 397, 399, 404–405
    dosage changes for elderly, 408
    effect of disease, 395, 400–401, 404, 409
    effect on clinical data, 360–361
    free, in serum, 401, 437
    interactions, 409–410
    monitoring, 394–411, 430–431
    pharmacodynamics, 410–411
    pharmacokinetics, 396–410
    rate of elimination, 398–399, 405–406,
        409–410

Elastin, 36
    kidney, 150
    lung, 114, 117, 123, 126, 434
Electroencephalograms, 192
Electrophilic agents, 264, 268
Emphysema, 117, 128, 143–144
Endocrine aging, 28, 355, 433
Enzymes, 344
    adaptability, 132
    alteration in aging, 141, 232–237, 433,
        435–436
    degenerative, 265
    induction, 133
    loss of specific activity with age, 33–34
    lytic, 37
    monoamine oxidase, 92, 232
    neurotransmitter metabolizers and
        synthesizers, 91–92
    scavenging potential, 268
Epithelial cells, proliferation, 238–240
Epiphysitis, osteoporosis-like, 176
Epoxide hydrolase, 268
Erythrocytes, in anemia, 420–422
Estradiol, 66–67, 71, 85
Estrogen, 82–86, 99
    administration to postmenopausal
        women, 94, 175, 177–181, 435
    breast cancer, 208–211
    changes in excretion with age, 354
    deficiency and bone loss, 170, 175, 177–
        181, 218, 434–435
    in men, 88
    in pregnancy, 66–68
Estrogen, anti-, 209–210, 213
Estrogen receptors, 210–211, 213, 216
Estrone, 85
Estrous
    constant, 86–87, 99, 103, 144
    cycle, 54–56, 68–71, 74–76, 82, 91, 94,
        98, 99
    effect of androgens, 75–76

Estrous *(Continued)*
    hypothalmic-pituitary regulation, 70–
        71, 74–76, 82–94, 99, 144
    irregularities in, 68–71
    prevention by estradiol or testosterone,
        75
    steroids, 72–73
Ethanol, concentration in elderly, 396, 405
Ether, 396
Exercise
    effect on clinical measurements, 97
    effect on osteoporosis, 218, 435

Fatty acids, interference with drug binding,
    404
Fc fragments, 282–284, 288–290, 292, 294–
    297, 309
Fertility, *see* Reproduction
Fibrinogen, risk-factor index, 327, 330–
    332, 436
Fibrinolytic system, 235, 350–352
Fibroblast cultures, 227–229, 231, 235, 240,
    248–257
    donor age, 248–257, 272, 435
    protein synthesis in, 248–257
    relation to life span, 266–268, 271
    SV-40 transformed, 249, 251, 252, 255,
        271
5-Fluorouracil, 211–213
Flurazepam sensitivity of elderly, 395
Folic acid, in anemia, 419, 421
Follicle-stimulating hormone (FSH;
    follitropin), 83–86, 88–90, 92, 93, 99,
        103
Follicular atresia, 30, 91–92, 103
Fracture, *see* Bone
Framingham study, risk factors, 137
Functional age, 17–18

Gastrointestinal tract, as endocrine organ,
    143
Gene expression, 37–38, 272–273
Gene repression, 39
Geriatrics, gerontology, 46, 162, 164, 359–
    361, 407
Germ cells, immortal, 243
Glaucoma, 173
Gliosis, astrocytic, 187
Globulin, serum
    changes with age, 20, 21
    in anemia, 419–424
    reference values, 375, 378
Glomerular filtration rate, 108, 153
Glucagon, 134, 135, 142, 143, 352–353, 434
Glucocorticoid receptors, 211
Glucokinase synthesis, 133–134, 136

443

Life span *(Continued)*
DNA repair capabilities and, 308
effect of calorie restriction, 57
effect of L-dopa, 101
effect of tryptophan deficiency, 57, 59, 102
error frequency related to, 251–256
fibroblasts, 248–249, 252–257
genetic instability, 241
IgA and IgG, 310
modifying, 47
mortality curves, 97–98, 316–319, 435
number of cell divisions, 239
species differences, 237, 243, 259–273
stages, 320–322
Lipid-associated polypeptide (LAP), 287–288, 294, 296
Lipids, 110–111, 232, 392
Lipofuscin, brain, 35, 37, 46, 48, 97, 183–185
Lipopolysaccharide, mitogenic response, 279–288, 293–294, 296, 299
Lipoproteins, 110–111
Lithium, 397–398, 408
Liver disease, effect on drug metabolism, 395, 400, 404, 409, 411
Longevity
assurance mechanisms, 259–274
calorie intake, 57, 111
cholesterol and lipoproteins, 111
relation to reproductive activity, 99
see also Life span
Low-density lipoprotein, 110–111
and atherogenesis, 164–165
Lung
changes with aging, 114–127
disease and drugs, 409
K cells, 143
surfactant, 142
Luteinizing hormone (LH; lutropin), 54–56, 82–93, 103
effect of photoperiod, 55
estrous cycle, 71, 73
receptors, 103
surge, 73, 74
Luteinizing-hormone-releasing hormone (LHRH; luliberin), 82, 85, 87, 88, 90, 93, 103
Lutropin, *see* Luteinizing hormone
Lymphocytes
B-cells, 278–300, 309–310
T-cells, 28, 239, 265, 280, 293, 297, 299, 309–310
Lysosomes, 37, 232

Mammary tissue, transplanted, 238–239
Mastectomy, 212, 213

Mecillinam absorption, 401
Membrane permeability, increase with age, 405; *see also* Basement membrane
Menopause, 83–85, 91–94, 435
and bone loss, 28, 169–181, 434
evolutionary function, 30
relation to breast cancer, 208–209, 212–213
serum calcium and phosphate, 175
Menstrual cycle, 82, 83
2-Mercaptoethanol, mitogenic response, 280–282, 286, 293, 294, 296, 299
Mestranol, 177–178
Metabolic rate, biochemical correlates, 343–344
Metabolite concentrations, optimum, 390–393, 436–437
Methadone, 396
Methionine, 233, 252–253
Methotrexate, 211–213
3-Methylcholanthrene, 268
α-Methyl-*p*-tyrosine, 54
Mitogenic response in immune-defective mice, 277–300
Mitosis, 29, 37
Monoamine oxidase, 92, 232
Monoamines, 47–56, 59
Morphine, 396
Mortality curves, 316–319, 355
predicted future shape, 97–98
sex differences, 98, 168, 318, 435
Mutagens, 31, 267–268, 271
ultraviolet light, 32, 269–271
Mutations, 31, 280–300
Myeloma and idiopathic osteoporosis, 175
Myxedema, 362

National Council on the Aging, 437
National Institute on Aging, xiii, xiv
Neoplasia, decreased resistance to, 28
Nerve conduction velocity, decrease with age, 8, 108
Neural failure or malfunction, 26, 28, 36
Neuroendocrine aging, 28, 433, 435
Neurofibrillary tangles and plaques, 46, 217
aluminum, 197–199, 436
Alzheimer's disease, 195–201, 203–204, 436
content of, 203
Neurotransmitters, 46–47, 53, 56, 60, 91
Nicotine, 237
Nissl substance, 46
Nitrazepam, 395, 407, 410
Nitrogen mustard, 211
Nitrogen, urea, 382, 384, 427
4-Nitroquinoline-1-oxide, 271

Procaine penicillin, elimination, 406
Progeria, 249, 251–255
Progesterone
  in pregnancy, 66–68
  receptor assay, 216
  secretion, 82–83, 86
Progestogen, 177, 179
Prolactin, 83, 89–90
  receptors, 211
Propicillin, 401, 405
Propranolol, 407–408
Propylthiouracil, 400–401
Prostate
  tumors, 89–90
  uremia, 221
Protein-caloric undernutrition, 417–424
Proteins
  changes with age, 34, 232–234, 362
  drug binding, 401–404
  polymerization, 140
  serum, 419–420, 426
    effect of dehydration, 362
    reference values, 375, 377
  synthesis, 39, 248–257, 265, 266, 435, 436
Protozoa, clone, 29
Purified protein derivative, mitogen
  response, 279–282, 284–285, 295–296,
  299
Puromycin inhibition of leucine
  incorporation, 250
Pyridoxine, in anemia, 419, 421

Quality control, 333–334
Quinidine, 402, 404, 407, 408
Quinine absorption, 401, 405

Radiation
  breast cancer, 212
  cell damage from, 269–271
  stress effects, 265
  tolerance, increase with age, 233
Rats, correlation with humans, 82–94, 142
Receptor, drug, 410
Receptor, hormone, 39, 47, 73–74
  breast cancer, 210–211, 213, 216, 435
Reference values, 359, 366–387; see also
  specific analytes
Renal, see Kidney
Reproduction
  animal models, 46–60, 64–76, 83, 85–87,
    90–94, 98–101, 435
  cycle, 54–57
  decline, 72–74, 82–91
  early changes, 64–65
  function, 82–91
  serotonin and, 57

Risk factors, 137, 330
  atherogenesis, 164
  cardiovascular disease, 332, 434
  dementia, 200, 202
  distribution of, 137
  monitoring for, 315
  population studies, 164–165, 330
  screening for, 137, 322–333
RNA, 30, 31, 38, 39
  changes with age, 97, 232, 234, 236–237
  messenger, poly(U), protein synthesis,
    248–252, 254–255
  relation to lipofuscin, 97
  ribosomal, 31–32
  transfer, 38, 249, 256

Salicylate, 402, 403, 410; see also
  Acetylsalicylate
Screening for disease, 322–323, 362–364
Semi-starvation in the elderly, 417–424
  causes, 418
  clinical and laboratory findings, 418–419
  therapy for, 419–424
Senility, 183, 185, 419, 422; see also
  Dementia
Senescence, 39
  definition, 329
  DNA damage, 32
  reproductive, 91, 93
Serotonin, 47–59, 87, 92, 93, 102
Set-point values, 326–328, 331, 428
Singh index of bone mass, 222
Skin cell transplants, 238, 240
Smoking
  and emphysema, 117, 128
  effects of, 233, 323
  effect on heart disease, 165, 166
  effect on mortality curves, 317, 319
  effect on physiological age, 18
Sodium, serum, 362, 426, 427
  reference values, 379, 381
Somatomedin, 139–140
Somatostatin, 135, 140, 143
Somatotropin metabolism, 139
Spermatogenesis, testosterone decrease
  with age, 83, 88, 90, 92
Statistical methods, 363–365, 368–370, 382,
  385, 387, 425–430, 436–437
Steady state, 326–327, 331, 341–342, 344
Steroids, 28, 208–211
Stilbesterol therapy, 360
Structural damage in cells, 33–34
Stress
  cellular, 264–266
  physiological response to, 323, 328–329
Sugar, blood, 107–110; see also Glucose
Sulfadiazine, 402–404, 409

447

Sulfamethiazole, 401, 405, 406
Sulfation factor, *see* Somatomedin
Superhelicity, DNA, 263–264, 273, 308–309
Superoxide dismutase, 236, 268
  and Down's syndrome, 200, 217
Surfactant synthesis, 142, 436
Syphilis screening, 323

Tamoxifen, 209–211, 213
T-cells, 28, 239, 265, 280, 293, 297, 299, 309–310
Testes, changes with age, 88–93, 99–100
Testosterone, 56, 88, 100
  in aging men, 88–90, 92–93
  in rats, 90, 92–93, 100–101
  role of female presence, 100
Tetracycline, 401, 406, 409
Thiamine in anemia, 419, 421
Thymus, 28
  -dependent antigens, 279, 298
  -independent antigens, 278–279, 285–287, 293–298
  regulation of cell proliferation, 240–241
Thyroid, 354–355, 409
Thyrotropin, 59, 134–135, 140
Thyroxine, 59, 360–362, 411
Thyroxine-binding globulin, 360, 362
TNP-Ficoll, antibody response, 284–287, 293–294, 296–297
TNP-lipopolysaccharide (TNP-LPS), 279, 285–288, 294–296
Tolbutamide, 402, 404, 409

Tomography, computerized, 191–194
Translation inhibitors, 37–38
Transplanted cells, survival of, 237–240
Tricyclic antidepressants, dosage, 408, 410
Triglycerides, serum, 110–111, 330
  reference values, 375–376
Trueta shunt, 221
Tryptophan deficiency, effect on reproduction, 56–59, 102
Tuberculosis screening, 323
Tumors, *see* Cancer
Tyrosine aminotransferase, 133, 232

Ulcers, 431
Ultraviolet damage of fibroblasts, 235
Urate, serum, 137, 346, 361, 437
  effect on intelligence, 391–393
  reference values, 382–383

Vasectomy, 164
Vasoactive amines from lung tumors, 143
Vasopressin, kidney response, 158
Vincristine, 211
Virus, 36, 200, 202–203, 237
Visual acuity and age, 16, 20, 21
Vital capacity, change with age, 16, 20, 21, 108, 122
Vitamin B_{12} in anemia, 419, 421
Vitamin D and osteoporosis, 218–219, 434

Warfarin binding, 402, 404
Werner syndrome, 249, 251–255